R63850

14.99

D0299984

THE COMPANION GUIDE TO
THE LAKE DISTRICT

WITHDRAWN

* 000133481 *

THE COMPANION GUIDES

It is the aim of these guides to provide a Companion
in the person of the author, who knows intimately
the places and people of whom he writes, and is able to
communicate this knowledge and affection to his readers.
It is hoped that the text and pictures will aid them
in their preparations and in their travels, and will
help them remember on their return.

BURGUNDY
THE COUNTRY ROUND PARIS
DEVON · EAST ANGLIA
EDINBURGH AND THE BORDER COUNTRY
FLORENCE · GASCONY AND THE DORDOGNE
LONDON · MADRID AND CENTRAL SPAIN
MAINLAND GREECE · NEW YORK · SICILY
SOUTH OF FRANCE · TURKEY · VENICE
JUGOSLAVIA

In preparation
ROME

THE COMPANION GUIDE TO

THE LAKE DISTRICT

Frank Welsh

COMPANION GUIDES

Copyright © 1989, 1997 by Frank Welsh

All Rights Reserved. Except as permitted under current legislation
no part of this work may be photocopied, stored in a retrieval system,
published, performed in public, adapted, broadcast,
transmitted, recorded or reproduced in any form or by any means,
without the prior permission of the copyright owner

First published 1989

Revised and updated edition, 1997
Companion Guides, Woodbridge

ISBN 1 900639 23 8

Companion Guides is an imprint of Boydell & Brewer Ltd
PO Box 9, Woodbridge, Suffolk IP12 3DF, UK
and of Boydell & Brewer Inc.
PO Box 41026, Rochester, NY 14604-4126, USA

A catalogue record for this book is available
from the British Library

Library of Congress Cataloging-in-Publication Data
Welsh, Frank.
The companion guide to the Lake District / Frank Welsh. – Rev.
and updated ed.
p.   cm. -- (The Companion guides)
Includes bibliographical references and index.
ISBN 1-900639-23-8 (pbk. : alk. paper)
1. Lake District (England) – Guidebooks.   I. Title.   II. Series.
DA670.L1W43   1997
914.27'804859–dc21   96–29907

Printed in Great Britain by
St Edmundsbury Press Ltd, Bury St Edmunds, Suffolk

Contents

Acknowledgements

In preparing this revised edition I would like to thank many helpful people in tourist agencies, hotels, bed and breakfast establishments, and a wide variety of enterprises. In particular I must thank George Bott for many corrections and suggestions, and among many others:

Michael Mitchell	Reverend Alan Gibson
Paul Bell	George Booth
Derek Woodruff	Sue Palmer
Robert McCosh	Rosemary Adams
Tom Murray	Michael Moon
Eric Holland	Janet Williamson
Sandie Johnson	Joan Slade
Peter Frost-Pennington	Agnes Ashwood
Emma Chaplin	Christian Barnes
Edward King	Carolyn Johnson
Alasdair Galbraith	Dickon Knight
Reverend Griffith Jones	

With so much advice and information any errors which remain are, indisputably and regretfully, all my own.

Maps and plans

Illustrations

Unless otherwise credited all photographs are by the author

Introduction

The Lake District must be the most written-over area of the United Kingdom. Guide-book writers have been industriously cataloguing its virtues for the last couple of centuries since Father Thomas West published his *Guide to the Lakes* in 1778, and many of them have done so extremely well; Wordsworth, Harriet Martineau, W. G. Collingwood and Norman Nicholson are hard acts to follow. Add to these the names of those who have, without producing a formal guide, written perceptively about the region – Thomas Gray, Keats, Scott, Coleridge, Ruskin, Mrs. Humphry Ward, Beatrix Potter, Arthur Ransome, and more recently Melvyn Bragg – and the Wordsworths, William and Dorothy, who stamped the idea of the Lakes on the English-speaking consciousness. Then every inch of the territory has painstakingly been over by the uniquely industrious Alfred Wainwright; and Hunter Davies has given two entertainingly useful pocket reports.

One excuse for adding to the list might be that the Central Lake District has become too popular for comfort – quite intolerable on summer weekends – and that the peripheral areas, Furness, the coast and Skiddaw, can do with a little attention. Another is that the lakes and mountains are only one part of the whole; the animals, archaeology, people, history, industries and buildings combine to make the Lake District – what Norman Nicholson calls Greater Lakeland – a fascinating unity.

Since within this small area there is to be found such a diversity of scenery it is hardly surprising that guide books tend to start with an explanation of the geology. Rocks are after all the bones on which scenery is formed.

But as most geological explanations bristle with scarcely comprehensible words – 'granophyres, Upper Ordovician, pyromorphite, Palaeozoic' – it is equally unsurprising that most readers skip them (although 'basement beds' and 'cleavages' may stir a flicker of interest).

This is a mistake. Knowing, at least roughly, which bit of the area is made of what adds greatly to the pleasure of any visit. Not only the scenery, but the buildings, and even the history and customs of the region, depend upon its rocks. And since geology is in itself a rewarding study, there is no better place than here to start it, for the Lake District is a geologist's paradise.

The layout is easy enough. The central massif is formed of three belts stretching right across it, from east to west, of which the northernmost is the sedimentary Skiddaw slate, which forms rounded whale-like hills, such as Skiddaw itself. Next comes the Borrowdale volcanic series, a group of fire-formed rocks which give rise to jagged crags. All the most dramatic of the peaks – Scafell, Helvellyn, the Langdales – lie in this district.

A thin line of limestone, from Furness to Shap, separates this from the third, southernmost belt, of mixed Silurian shales and slate, spiky jagged rocks sloping south and forming lower, but picturesque hills.

Lapped round the whole is a limestone bed, which contains coal over towards the coast, and circling this in turn is a belt of technicolour sandstone. Where the harder limestone forces itself to the surface 'scars' or escarpments appear – Whitbarrow and Scout Scar near Kendal are particularly good examples. Limestone also appears, picturesquely weathered in the north of the area, near Caldbeck and Greystoke, and forms the whole of the Pennines, completely surrounding the Lake District itself. Stuck into this general scheme are bits of other rocks of which the most prominent are the granites of Eskdale/Ennerdale and Shap.

Acting on the whole, and comparatively recently, in geological terms, glaciation has scooped out the rounded valleys in which the lakes sit, and left a host of striking features, which can be dealt with as they crop up. These can be almost as striking on the ground as on the map. Even moving at 60 mph along the A590 from Levens to the west the contrast between the precipitous architectural pale grey sides of Whitbarrow (limestone) and the spiky gorse-tufted rocks of Newton Fell (Silurian) is eye-catching.

Then the appearance of towns and villages is dictated by the stones available. Sandstone is easy to work, and its use makes such towns as Penrith distinctively red; it is also permeable, and therefore often rendered to keep out the rain. Limestone renews itself in the rain, and gives a sparkle to pearl-grey towns like Kendal and Ulverston. Slate is a terrible building material: other stone has to be used in door and window frames; and building square chimneys is impossible. Hence the dramatic aspect of such houses as Coniston

Introduction

Old Hall, with its power-house chimneys, and the heavy, crude arches of Grasmere church.

Over most of the central area these rocks are highly visible, sticking up out of the ground, with little surface cover. It should not be thought, however, that this is all a natural state of things. Far from being the unspoilt wilderness of romantic fantasy, the Lake District has been subject to 8000 years of active interference. The Furness area shows the best surviving example of a large and compact medieval agro-industrial complex: efficiently managed by the Furness monks, not an inch of virgin woodland remains. Coniston Old Man, the view of which Ruskin pronounced the best in Europe, is honeycombed and scarred with a thousand years of mining works. Even on the tops of the Langdale Pikes the mess made by Stone Age men chipping out axes is clearly to be seen.

More recently – since about AD 900 or so – sheep, cropping under the trees, have prevented natural regeneration of the forests. As a result, and very quickly, wooded slopes have become bare fellside. The much-criticized Forestry Commission, in its replanting schemes, is doing nothing more than starting to repair the damage.

But if the Lake District, apart from the summits of the highest fells, which even sheep avoid, is no untouched wilderness, it does offer a remarkable display of antiquity. The lack of cultivation has resulted in the preservation of archaeological evidence. From the Stone Age axe factories, through Roman roads, fortifications and mines, and monastic deer fences, examples are abundant. It is no accident that the Cumberland and Westmorland Archaeological Society is one of the country's most distinguished, since they have so much material lying to hand.

This continuity is paralleled in the people. Cumbrians stay put; a great number, even the majority, of substantial houses – there are no real 'great houses' in the district – are still lived in by the descendants of those who owned them in the twelfth century. Very probably the same thing could be said of the less well documented smaller holdings. Then the Western Lakes peninsula remains to a great extent purely Norse. It was colonized by second-stage Viking settlers who had already lived in Ireland, and brought with them their language and culture which remained more unaffected by the later Norman penetration than any other part of the country, leaving families that can go back a millennium: the language, customs, cast of mind and sense of humour are still identifiably non-Saxon and non-Norman.

These two characteristics – diversity and continuity – can be seen

xiii

in all aspects of Cumbrian life. Climate, and the resultant vegetation, is as varied as could be imagined. To move from the sheltered warm lowlands of Duddon Sands to the top of Scafell, a distance of about sixteen miles, is to move from one of the mildest English climates to Iceland. The idea of the Lake District being uniformly cold and wet could not be more mistaken! Palms grow – hardy ones, and with much petting, but palms nevertheless – at Grange-over-Sands; the Sizergh figs ripen reliably.

The truth of the matter is that average weather varies amazingly within the area. The coast is really quite dry, averaging thirty inches of rain a year, with consistently mild temperatures; even Keswick has only fifty-one inches a year. But only a few miles off, Seathwaite Farm is the wettest inhabited place in England, with 130 inches a year and Esk Hause even wetter at 170 inches. Temperature can change even more quickly; the dales may be basking in warm sunshine when the north slopes, a few hundred feet up, are icy. In the Pennines farming and habitation go up to 1500 feet; we made hay on our Stainmore land up to 1100 feet; but in the Central Lakes the tundra has set in by that level. Watendlath, the highest farm, is at 850 feet. Grange-over-Sands, on sea level, by contrast has a climate which it compares proudly with that of Torquay, and has quite a reputation as a wintering place.

What is true about the Lake District as a whole, and no mere slander, is that it does rain quite often. The corollary of this, however, is that it doesn't do so for long. But since the principal attractions of the region are out of doors, visitors do usually get wet at some time.

One of the purposes of this book is to describe what can be seen when one is so footsore, or the weather is so discouraging, that long walks are not welcomed. Serious walkers are amply catered for by Alfred Wainwright's unique set of pictorial guides, to which reference is abundantly made. There is no substitute for Wainwright plus the 1:25 000 Ordnance Survey map, which covers the whole of the National Park area in four sheets. But since no visit to the Lakes would be complete without essaying at least one or two high fell walks, if at all possible, some observations on the subject follow.

There is a great deal of nonsense talked about fell walking, which it may be as well to dispel. In one recent year, twenty-seven people perished in incidents to which mountain rescue teams were called; this figure does not of course include road traffic accidents or any other misadventures. Of these, twelve were victims of heart attacks, which ought to be a warning against the unduly aged or unfit embarking on expeditions for which they are not constitutionally prepared. It is better to limber-up on such gentle slopes as Orrest Head or Finsthwaite, before moving on to, say, Catbells, and thence to more rugged walks. Of the remaining deaths, five were non-mountain accidents – pilots crashing into hills and industrial injuries. Only ten fatalities were the result of true fell-walking or climbing accidents, and in six of these instances the victims were properly equipped. In all four of twenty-seven deaths might have been partly due to unsuitable clothing and equipment. One does not need to venture up to the tops, in anything like reasonable weather, equipped for the Matterhorn, any more than summer sailing in the Solent requires Decca navigators and radio direction-finding equipment.

To avoid any doubts I have tried to make it clear when anything remotely perilous is suggested. Helvellyn is climbed by thousands of children every year, going the exciting way via Striding Edge and Swirral Edge, but no one could suggest it is free of dangers; people slide off Helvellyn in the best of conditions. This sort of walk, which involves something of a scramble, calls for solidly seated trousers and respectable boots, and should not be attempted by the inexperienced at all. Accidents usually happen because feet slip, quite often on grassy slopes, and non-slip footwear is essential. Fell huntsmen wear great leather boots with massively studded soles; these will not slip, but cannot be recommended to the beginner (besides which, heavy boots can create great damage to paths; huntsmen do not usually follow paths, and are careful where they put their feet). The best footwear is a light boot, with a good ridged sole that will not create embarrassment when pubs, churches or museums are being visited. On no account should leather soles without studs be used: these are impossible on wet grass.

For the rest it should be remembered that it gets colder the further up you go and that the Lake District weather makes Zola's Nana appear a model of predictability. A small rucksack which contains extra layers of clothing, iron rations, cameras, maps, sketching things, volumes of verse, is useful. What is essential is an impermeable outer layer of clothing long enough to enable you to sit on it; and it should not be something plastic that keeps the rain out at the cost of creating a turkish bath of your own sweat within. My own preferred garment is a sort of Australian sheep-drover's long proofed-cotton coat.

Breeches are much nicer to wear than trousers, the bottoms of which, unless tucked into gaiters (which only renders them inferior breeches), tend to get unpleasantly wet. Shorts should be used with discretion and never, no matter how flattering to the wearer, when attempting anything rugged.

I find it adds to the pleasure as well as to the safety of walking to carry a compass. Orienteering is a pleasant sport, and it is plain daft not to know where one is at any moment. If you are caught in a mist then rely on your compass rather than your instinct, and proceed with care. If not, then at least you will be able to identify the tops correctly, and feel smug when others get them wrong.

Spending large sums of money on the 'right' gear helps local industries, but this is really only necessary for serious fell walking in poor conditions. Sensible people will not go far wrong if they follow my guidelines, which have the merit of flexibility and economy, and idiots will come to grief anyway.

One of the attractive features of the region is that it is quite impossible to forecast how long anything may take. There are rules of thumb for walks – two and a half miles per hour, extra hours at the rate of one per one thousand foot of ascent, say – but none of these cater for sketching, eating, botanizing, philosophizing, bird watching, fishing, swimming, sailing, taking photographs, or going to sleep. Hours may be spent rooting out a bloomery site or deciphering monuments.

The arrangement of the book is therefore in geographical sections, each of which could be the object of an expedition lasting between, say, a day and a week. Planning a Lake District holiday is one of the best parts of it, snug at home with maps and a collection of guides. Selection of the time of year is a major constraint; if mid summer is dictated the Central Lakes should be altogether avoided as they become far too crowded. The coasts, which are sunnier and drier, or the Eden Valley are then to be preferred. April, May and June are the sunniest months, and often the most pleasant, but the 'back end' – the autumn – although wetter, is very beautiful. There are worse places, too, in the winter, than the Morecambe Bay coast.

On the other hand there are many attractions to a Lake District summer, not least of which are the sports. Grasmere's, which take place the third Thursday after the first Monday in August, are deservedly the most famous; Ambleside sports are a little earlier. The Lowther horse trials are also in early August. Most of the local shows, including the Kendal gathering, take place that month.

As for time, serious walkers could spend years in the steps of Wainwright, but an average holiday of, say, three weeks would best be passed by choosing two or three centres and exploring them thoroughly.

The area covered in the first two chapters, centred on Penrith, has some extremely good hotels, but is not well provided with the middling range. Bed-and-breakfasts, self-catering accommodation and country pubs with bedrooms are the best bet here. A week could easily be spent tackling the best walks on fine days, fishing, visiting churches, sights and pubs on less good ones, and pottering around in boats in any weather.

The southern part – Kendal, Cartmel, Furness – would also afford a balanced week, with plenty of interest at all seasons and a reasonable selection of accommodation. It is when one gets to the Central Lakes that the difficulties begin, for here is the place for outdoor occupations, where continued poor weather or sheer pressure of numbers can make for disappointing holidays. Ambleside, Grasmere and Keswick are the best centres, and offer some diversions for evenings and rainy days. The rural, and very beautiful, villages of Borrowdale, Wasdale, the Langdales, and the smaller lakes, are for those who can rely upon their own resources to pass the time. Out of season, with appropriate equipment for tackling the fells and a selection of good books, there is nothing to compare with a small dales hotel.

Choosing accommodation presents problems, since standards of hotel keeping are patchy, and, although the English Tourist Board is improving the accuracy of its classifications, these remain complex and sometimes dubiously correct. The *Good Hotel Guide* is reliable, but tends to focus on expensive establishments and Egon Ronay is not critical enough of the food provided. Small hotels and inns are usually at least reasonable value; it is the larger ones, run by chains, that need watching. A test I have found useful is to see if they provide suitably large bath towels and whether two people can share a breakfast table in comfort; it is meanness in such matters that is an infallible mark of a poor hotel. Bed-and-breakfasts are often excellent, but families with children need a base during the day. The often abused time-share complexes do give this, and the best of them offer a number of welcome diversions.

Unfortunately the west coast, which would make a good holiday base, with urban amenities, the seaside, and easy access to the splendid coastal valleys, is badly off for hotels. Apart from the pleasant pubs of Wasdale and Loweswater, there is no nucleus of accommodation, which is a pity, for this area has something to offer everyone.

In writing this guide a perpetual problem has been deciding what exactly are the confines of the region. The answer to this has depended on a combination of inclination, idleness and principle. You could say that the Lake District is that bit which has lakes; but any rational appreciation of the region that excludes Furness is impossible. Nor does the National Park, for the same reasons, meet the test. Nor, since it includes too much, is the area once known as the Lake Counties: Cumberland, Westmorland and Furness. (Northerners, deeply conservative as they are, deplore the action of the *soi-disant* Conservative government of Edward Heath in mucking about with the counties. We knew where Cumberland and Westmorland were; Furness had – and has – an individuality of its own; no apology is therefore made for retaining these ancient names whenever it makes things clearer.)

Inclination would lead me to include the Eden Valley and its tributaries, a largely unknown garden of delights, and Carlisle, a distinguished, gritty town. In the end, some arbitrary boundaries suggest themselves: Furness in the south, the A6 in the east, which includes Kendal, an absolutely essential town (but with a little exception for the environs of Penrith), the sea in the west, and in the north everything as far as Wigton. This last is the most difficult boundary to define; Skiddaw and Blencathra must be included, although the latter is nowhere near a lake, but this massif also comprehends Caldbeck; and where would the Lake District be without John Peel's home? And Caldbeck is a satellite of Wigton (and besides, Wigton is too good to be missed out, as tourists tend to do). Carlisle and the Eden Valley except for the villages around Penrith are, with great reluctance, excluded.

This definition has the merit that it corresponds reasonably precisely with what might be described as 'Wordsworth Country' (excepting the Caldbeck fells and Back o'Skiddaw country, for which John Peel, who is post-Wordsworth, can be argued). And Wordsworth is significant.

More than any other writer except Thomas Hardy, Wordsworth has a sense of the place. There are differences, however: Hardy's Wessex is an essential part of his novels, indeed their major character. Prose and landscape interact; knowing Wessex adds much to the pleasure of reading the books, and anyone who has done so inevitably sees the countryside to some extent through Hardy's own personal Claude-glass. But his poetry – although Hardy is the preeminent Wordsworth successor – is less intimately bound up with topography. It speaks, as Wordsworth's, to 'the natural heart', but the twining of imagery and psychology is looser.

From thousands of examples, take two. 'Trailing clouds of glory', and the dawn-lit streamers from the peak of Great Gable; the last parting with his brother John on Grisedale Hause:

> Here did we stop; and here looked round
> While each into himself descends,

– and each brother, going from opposite sides, one home to Grasmere, the other to his death in the sea.

This seems, at least to me, to be the essence of poetry. It would take pages of halting prose to convey the sense of that passage from being together in love, and the resumption of separate identities and fate given by 'While each into himself descends'.

Wordsworth works in almost an opposite fashion to Hardy. Knowing the Lake District is not vital to understanding Wordsworth, although to do so adds much to the interest and makes for a much livelier appreciation of the region. Not only William's poetry, but his letters, and even more the letters and journals of his sister Dorothy, for it is she who, more often than Wordsworth, strikes the true flash of insight. So the Wordsworths, like cheerfulness, do tend to creep in.

And the Lakes – apart from the mountainous core – have been part of the Border history. Scottish invasions have generally preferred the western to the eastern route, and some of these, in the thirteenth and fourteenth centuries, were devastating. As a result the region bristles with fortified dwellings, literally hundreds of them, from the smallest bastle to castles like Cockermouth or Brougham.

Finally, while this book is directed mainly towards those who will get about in cars and on foot, it would not do to neglect the very beautiful railway line that runs around much of the shoreline of the Cumbrian peninsula. Going from south to north, trains leave Lancaster more or less hourly and go via Carnforth, Arnside, Grange and Ulverston to Barrow, the journey taking about an hour. A change at Barrow puts one on the coast line to Carlisle, twenty-four stops and three and a half hours away, right along the coast as far as Maryport before turning to go across country to Carlisle. Many of these stops are on request only: it gives a fine impression of nineteenth-century lordliness to wave a train down at a station, or to request the guard please to stop at Corkickle (yes, it exists!). Almost throughout the views are superb, and for much of the time the line runs along the very edge of the sea.

In the end, whatever aspect of the Lake District strikes the imagination – the grandeur of the high fells, the beauty of the waters under restless skies, literary associations or the evidences of a rich history – it is likely to be the people themselves who will provoke the liveliest recollections, Courteous, amused, tolerant, single-minded in their enthusiasms, the country is fortunate to have them as custodians of this invaluable part of the natural heritage.

Note to the Second Edition

One generous critic described the first edition as unimprovably good. That was too kind, and I have taken the opportunity to correct a number of errors (although doubtless letting others survive). It is surprising how much can change in eight years, and gratifying to see how many new enterprises have begun. Bearing in mind, however, that they may not always continue, it is well worthwhile to make use of the admirable and efficient network of Tourist Offices.

1

Penrith and Environs

Penrith: the Gateway to the Lakes

It is worth taking pains to choose the right approach to the Lake District, especially if it is to be for the first time. Wordsworth, the mentor of all guidebook authors, discusses the subject at some length in his *Guide to the Lakes* and recommends the best method of arriving at individual views, as well as the region as a whole.

Some of his caveats – 'roads so bad that no one can be advised to take them in a carriage' – no longer stand. The M6 provides a fast route to the borders of the National Park, and the only decision to be made is whether to start from Kendal to Windermere, or from Penrith to Ullswater. Ideally the choice, as Charles Lamb on his visit to Coleridge decided, is not difficult; Windermere, with Ambleside and Bowness, has suffered so much from the pressures of mass tourism, while Ullswater has remained almost unspoiled, as to make Penrith a much better starting point. If you had only a limited time – a day or so – there would be no question: see Ullswater and Helvellyn properly, and put all the rest aside for later.

The immediate neighbourhood of Penrith is particularly good for wet-weather visits, being rich in accessible sights – castles, churches and ancient monuments – and in villages with cheerful pubs, as well as the amenities of a modest country town.

While it is near enough to the lakes – Haweswater and Ullswater are both about five miles away – **Penrith** is the commercial centre of the Pennine Vale of Eden rather than a Lake District town. Its skyline is dominated by the Pennine summits of Cross Fell and Murton Pike as well as the Cumbrian mountain of Blencathra. Being considerably drier than the Lake District, the quality of light in the Eden Valley is perceptibly different: there is a brighter, less subtle feeling, fewer of the rapidly changing cloud effects. The Eden Valley's rich red earth, forming the most valuable pasture in the country, is very unlike the sparse rocky soils to be found further west, and supports a more prosperous farming community. The same red earth is the cause of Penrith's striking colour; it is a dark red sandstone town, varied with occasional colour washes.

The town is to be seen at its best on Tuesdays, market day, when it is given over to livestock. As much as any Basuto or Masai an Eden farmer's prestige and wealth is measured by his cattle. Not merely number, but quality and variety. Conversation in the Agricultural Hotel will centre on the merits of different breeds and crosses, for Cumbrian farmers are nothing if not fashion-conscious on this subject. Charolais, Limousin, Blond d'Aquitaine, Simmental and Chianna have each their champions, and very large sums are paid for fine specimens which are then crossed with the local dairy cow, now the ubiquitous Friesian. Some remain faithful to native breeds, at any rate for beef – belted Galloways, that stand out well in the hillsides by reason of their bold markings, and Herefords. A Jersey may be kept for family milk and some Highland cattle as decorative pets; Shorthorn, fifty years ago the most popular dairy breed, are enjoying a revival, somewhat in the spirit of vintage car replicas, and there are increasing numbers of Ayrshires. Sheep farmers do not have quite as much fun, and for the most part have to content themselves with the established breeds – blackfaced Swaledales, Teeswaters (looking like fashionable wet-ringleted blondes), Border Leicesters, and shaggy Rough Fells, in this part of the world – although recently one or two exotics, such as Jacobs, Rouge de l'Ouest and Bleu-de-Maine, have found supporters.

The Agricultural Hotel used to be a good place to catch the flavour of cattle auctions before they moved the markets further off to the other side of the M6. It has a portrait of Hugh Lonsdale, the 'Yellow Earl', who is still regarded with affectionate respect half a century on, in pride of place. Marston's beers – the Pedigree is good – are served, as are substantial luncheons. On Tuesdays, like all the other pubs, it is open all day. Parking in the centre is impossible on market days and difficult at any time, but it is no hardship to use one of the only slightly off-centre parks, especially since walking round Penrith is always a pleasure.

Penrith has been a market town since the Middle Ages, its centre, like that of Bruges, composed of a series of market places, the gaps between them being filled up with shops. After the Castle Mart comes Great Dockray, with an overflow by Princes Street, the Corn Market, the Market Place, which has no market, the Market Hall, which has, and Sandgate. Each is served by its own pubs. Great Dockray has the oldest, the Gloucester Arms, once Dockray Hall, where Richard III lived when in Penrith as Warden of the North, and the Two Lions, once the town house of the Lowthers. The Gloucester

2

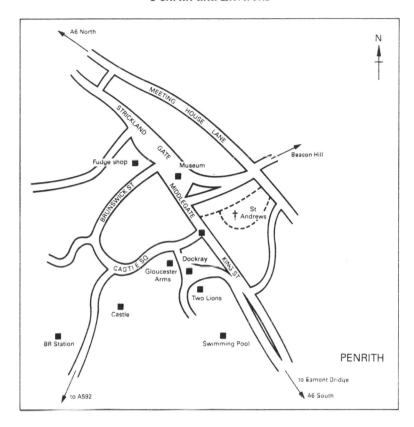

Arms looks more impressive from the market place, but if King Richard stayed here, it was certainly not in the present house, which is of the same period as the Two Lions; indeed the plaster work was probably done by the same craftsmen. The main bar is the original hall, and has some pleasant woodwork and panelling.

Many of the Two Lions' original features have survived intact: the kitchen, with its huge fireplace, is an outhouse (the owners, Whitbread Breweries, should do something about restoring this) and the old dining room and hall are bars, the former with its original plaster ceiling, emblazoned with armorial bearings of Lowthers, Dudleys, Threlkelds, Radcliffes, and other distinguished families. Stepping outside to the bowling green – an agreeable rarity – the character of the house become clearer; from the front, tucked away behind another pub, one would never suspect the existence of any such thing. Charles Edward Stuart, the Young Pretender, preferred the

3

George, in Market Street, when he paid a short visit in 1745; the choice of name indicates where the sympathies of the Penrithians lay. It is a fine early Georgian building, and serves as a more expensive rendezvous for market-goers than the Market Hotel. Arthur Young, the much-travelled agricultural reformer, stayed there in 1768 and found it 'Exceeding good, reasonable, and very civil' – all still tolerably true.

Unlike the inner Lakeland towns which concentrate on walking and climbing gear, and an infinity of horrid objects made of slate and horn, Penrith shops stock the real things: working shirts, stiff as board, trousers that reach the armpits, woollen vests and the staple foods of the Eden Valley – meat and cakes. The meat is the best that can be found anywhere: Robsons of Angel Lane used to be pre-eminent for beef and Cumberland sausages, although Ewbanks of Appleby probably had the edge on them for mutton, but since Mr Robson's retirement Cranstons of King Street are judged the best. Even the less distinguished Penrith butchers produce very good things, for the pick of the marts does not always go off to London, where they don't understand these things, but is eaten where it lived.

Fudge is the other product for which Penrith is famous. The sober little toffee shop in Brunswick Road, near the car park off Middlegate, chastely decorated with painted china, produces a delectable sweetmeat which is sent to all corners of the world. They make chocolate fudges, and toffees, but the original straightforward article is the best; it will not keep for too long (it rarely gets the chance) and needs to be eaten fresh.

And cakes. Farmers' families like a little cake with elevenses, after lunch, for the pre-milking tea, with the cheese at supper, and on its own at bedtime. The cakes that are bought have to be as good as those made at home, and they are. Birkett's the bakers in Penrith, with branches all over, are the best.

Until the 1970s cakes and pastries were not much eaten at breakfast, but a change took place when the gas pipeline from the North Sea was laid through Cumberland. For some shameful and inexplicable reason (I have taxed successive governments with this) no British firm was, or is, able to produce the pipe required, and a French company was employed as contractor. The French workers based in the town welcomed most items of local cuisine but complained at the absence of croissants. Within days the Penrith bakers had mastered the art of croissant-making, and continue to produce excellent examples – and in wholemeal flour for the health enthusiast.

The A6, which used to go in a single lane straight through the centre, now bypasses Penrith, which makes it easier to wander through the town. It is the agreeable aspect of all, rather than the excellence of any individual building, that impresses. St Andrew's church and churchyard, just off the Market Square, almost equal to some cathedral closes, form the architectural core. The church itself is striking enough. Rebuilt in 1722 by an unknown architect but very Hawksmoorish in style, and of majestic scale, it would look entirely at home in the City of London were it not for the blood-red sandstone of its construction and the massive thirteenth-century tower, built like a castle keep adjoining the west end. Judging from the money lavished on the rebuilding of the church the retention of the tower must have been a military precaution; even at that date the Scots were not trusted, and rightly enough in view of what happened twenty-three years later. Penrith's attachment to the Hanoverians is commemorated by two candelabra donated by the Duke of Portland, but it should be recalled that in spite of Scottish raids the dedication of the church to St Andrew has been retained; Penrith was, of course, like all Westmorland north of Kendal, originally part of the Kingdom of Strathclyde.

Inside the colour scheme seems immediately outrageous – dark grey, two shades of light grey, pale blue, turquoise, dark pink, maroon, and gilt, with oak woodwork – but it is said to be authentic, and certainly cannot go unremarked. In the face of this chromatic invention the wall paintings in the sanctuary seem subdued: they are competent eighteenth-century work by a local artist, Jacob Thornton.

A few fragments of medieval glass stand out in the otherwise perfect early-Georgian church, including two portraits, one of which is said to be of Richard III: this cannot be so since it is both too early and too bearded, but it might be of Richard II. He is gesticulating wildly, in an agitated fashion, at a lady in another panel: possibly later, this is clearly a portrait, perhaps of Cicely Neville. Outside the north door is a piece of ancient whimsy, known as the Giant's Grave, and reputed to be the tomb of one Sir Ewan Caesario, but in fact four sides of hogbacked Saxon coffins, between two contemporary crosses. These are from about AD 1000, arranged to resemble an enormous sepulchre, the same period as the Gosforth Cross (see chapter 13), but of cruder workmanship, and badly eroded by the smoke of centuries. Another, slightly less badly damaged, stands round to the north, and is known as the Giant's Thumb. Grevel

Lindop points out the unlikely, but accurate, connection between the Giant's Grave and James Joyce's Finnegan.

A real historic personage may be concealed under the unlikely name of Sir Ewan Caesario; Owain or Ewan or Huen latinized as Eugenius was a common name among the kings of Strathclyde in the tenth and eleventh centuries – it was a King Owain who signed the treaty of Earmont in 927. More entertainingly, Arthurians speculate on the Carle of Carlisle, the giant baron of Tarn Wadling, who features in the *Marriage of Sir Gawain*. Tarn Wadling lies, or did until it was drained, only a few miles away.

A monument to Robert Virtue, in the shape of a handsome pinnacled Gothic screen, is the other prominent feature of the churchyard. The inscriptions in English and in Latin are by now almost indecipherable, and should in all decency be recut. Virtue was John Stephenson's superintendent in the construction of the Lancaster and Carlisle railway, and died in 1846 while the work was being done.

Examples of architecture from every century since the fifteenth are to be found around the churchyard; the tower in its different stages, a pele tower attached to Hutton Hall, the old Grammar School of 1563, the Mitre Hotel of 1669, the Mansion House, a splendid building of 1750, and the Parish Rooms of 1894, not so splendid.

The remains of the castle are further off, opposite the railway station. One advantage possessed by Penrith is that it is on the main line between Glasgow and Euston, called at by a reasonable number of 'express' trains, but if one is planning to come by train, and has enough time, the splendid views presented by the Settle–Carlisle route should not be missed – seventy miles of spectacular scenery, naturally now threatened by railway accountants; take it while it still exists!

Penrith was never much of a castle, and has suffered a good deal, most recently by having its earthworks absorbed by the railway builders. The most dedicated students of fortifications would do better a mile away, at Brougham, but supporters of Richard III come on pilgrimage to Penrith castle, since that much maligned king had his headquarters here.

Robinson's school, in Middlegate, an unaltered seventeenth-century building, houses the tourist office and a small museum. The tourist office will arrange accommodation, which can otherwise present difficulties, for apart from the George, Penrith, in spite of one or two small restaurants, is generally not well served either by hotels or eating places. It could have been otherwise, for the Hussar, another

6

historic coaching inn, was recently destroyed in order to be converted into a supermarket. The stupidity of that particular bit of official vandalism was quickly demonstrated when, to general embarrassment, the new supermarket decided to close its doors to be replaced by a more convenient one on the site of the old cattle market. Penrith should be the last place for a supermarket, since shopping is a major pastime, and one brought to near perfection: gossip is exchanged with regulars, and newcomers are cordially welcomed; service is usually affable and patient. Shopkeepers have withstood the invasion of the multiples, and most of the names have been local for generations. Grahams, the Market Place grocers, is described on the 1880 façade as 'Jas and Jn Graham, Agricultural Seed Cake and Manure merchants, established 1793, Italian Warehousemen, tea and provision merchants'.

The Quaker meeting house in Meeting House Lane, behind the bus station, is larger and more complex than usual, with two galleries formed from the original stables, and some severely elegant eighteenth-century woodwork. For more fleshly pleasures the swimming pool, with its own car park, is found at the eastern entrance to the town.

To the north the town is sheltered by the wooded hill of Penrith Beacon, a square signal tower topped by a pyramid commemorating the 1715 invasion and continuing in use at least until 1805, when its fire warned Walter Scott, who was staying in the vicinity, of the Napoleonic invasion threat. It was here that the five-year-old Wordsworth, who as a child stayed with his unsympathetic grandparents, living over what is now Arnison's drapery shop, had one of those experiences which haunted him for the rest of his life. He had lost the servant who had been leading his pony (one should remember that Wordsworth, for all his later plain living at Grasmere, was brought up in some affluence) and came across a clearing where the gallows had stood. Although it had by then disappeared, the spot was clearly marked by a stone. Young William fled in terror, until he came across a girl carrying a pitcher.

> . . . and to this hour
> The characters are fresh and visible:
> A casual glance had shown them, and I fled.
> Faltering and faint, and ignorant of the road:
> Then, reascending the bare common, saw
> A naked pool that lay beneath the hills,
> The beacon on the summit, and, more near,

7

A girl, who bore a pitcher on her head,
And seemed with difficult steps to force her way
Against the blowing wind. It was, in truth,
An ordinary sight; but I should need
Colours and words that are unknown to man,
To paint the visionary dreariness
Which, while I looked all round for my lost guide,
Invested moorland waste, and naked pool.
The beacon crowning the lone eminence,
The female and her garments vexed and tossed
By the strong wind.

The beacon in winter is still an uncanny spot.

Just south of the modest eminence on which the town stands runs the River Eamont, draining Ullswater to join the Eden some five miles further on and forming the boundary between Cumberland and Westmorland. The A6 crosses the river at **Eamont Bridge** over a fine sixteenth-century bridge originally built with money raised from the sale of indulgences, now happily free of most of the twentieth-century traffic that prefers the alternative M6.

An inscription on one house, the first after the county boundary, reads: '*Omne solum forti patria est.* HP 1671'. This is Ovid, in exile by the Black Sea, comforting himself with the thought that a brave spirit may make of any place a homeland. The sentiment is explained by its position, but gains in appositeness since just south of here, on **Clifton Moor,** the last battle to take place on English soil (not Welsh, since the French landed at Fishguard in 1796) was fought on 18 December 1745, during the retreat of Prince Charles Edward's army before its final defeat at Culloden. The Prince had insisted that no supplies be left behind, and Lord George Murray, in command of the rearguard, had carried out his orders to the letter, commandeering all the available carts. When one of them was lost he persuaded his men to carry the cannon balls themselves. 'I gave them 6d a piece for it doing it by whatever means. I got above 200 carried.'

All this had the effect of delaying this movement and allowing the Duke of Cumberland's cavalry to catch up. Murray halted his forces just south of Clifton village among the dykes and hedges, while the government troops drew up on the open moor. Although ordered to fall back on Penrith, Lord George, the most competent soldier in that miserably led army, elected to hold his ground with one thousand men of the rearguard. Cumberland sent five hundred dismounted dragoons, of the 3rd, 10th and 11th regiments, against them. A brisk

8

engagement took place, with a dozen or so killed on both sides, before the dragoons retired, and allowed Murray to go without further molestation.

It was not much of a battle, but the government troops sustained proportionately heavier casualties than at Culloden; fourteen dead from five hundred engaged, while at Culloden only fifty died from an army of fourteen thousand. The Jacobite dead were at any rate luckier than the four hundred of their companions whom the Prince, against all advice, insisted on leaving to garrison Carlisle; when, inevitably, they surrendered, some score of the most unlucky were hanged and disembowelled on Capon Hill.

The dragoons were buried in the churchyard, the Jacobites under the Rebel Tree, opposite Town End Farm, but there is no memorial to the battle, as there most certainly should be. The Hall has a handsome restored pele, and there are two nice bits of fifteenth-century glass in the Norman church, one of which is said to be a portrait of Eleanor Engayne of the Hall.

To the immediate east of Penrith, **Brougham Castle** stands in a bend of the River Eamont. It is altogether a much finer ruin than that of Penrith, and of much greater antiquity, overlapping the site of a Roman fort. These forts, and the subsequent castles, form a line stretching up to the Eden Valley from Brougham, through Appleby and Brough, up to Bowes on Stainmore. Relics of the Roman occupation are preserved in a small museum on the site.

Collections of Roman tombstones may not sound the most entertaining of exhibitions, but those shown at Brougham deserve a second glance. They come from the civilian settlement around the fort and are those of prosperous Britons, not Roman citizens, but having adopted Roman customs and – at least for formal occasions – the Latin language. A nameless boy, in a cloak, is remembered by Annamoris his father and Ressona his mother; Vidaris mourns his son Crescentius who died at the age of eighteen; Lunaris his '*conjugi carissimae Pliuna*'; all the single British names stand out oddly in good cursives that might be expected to record the deaths of Romans with three duly ordered Latin names. And the altars are not to any Roman deity, but to Belatucadrus, the Fair Shining One – or the Beautiful Killer. If anyone still thinks in terms of ancient Britons covered in woad these evidences of Romanization should come as a salutary reminder that the Romans were here for four hundred years.

The castle itself is as good a ruin as you could wish for, set on a raised platform – the original Roman earthwork – at the confluence

9

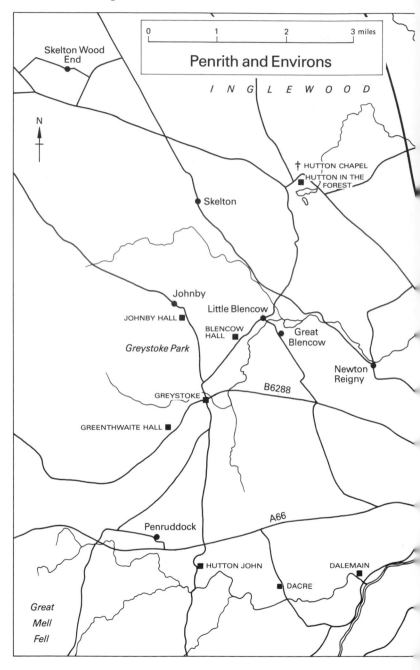

0   1   2   3 miles

Penrith and Environs

I N G L E W O O D

Skelton Wood End

N

† HUTTON CHAPEL
HUTTON IN THE FOREST

Skelton

Johnby

Little Blencow

JOHNBY HALL

BLENCOW HALL

Great Blencow

Greystoke Park

Newton Reigny

GREYSTOKE

B6288

GREENTHWAITE HALL

A66

Penruddock

HUTTON JOHN

DALEMAIN

DACRE

Great Mell Fell

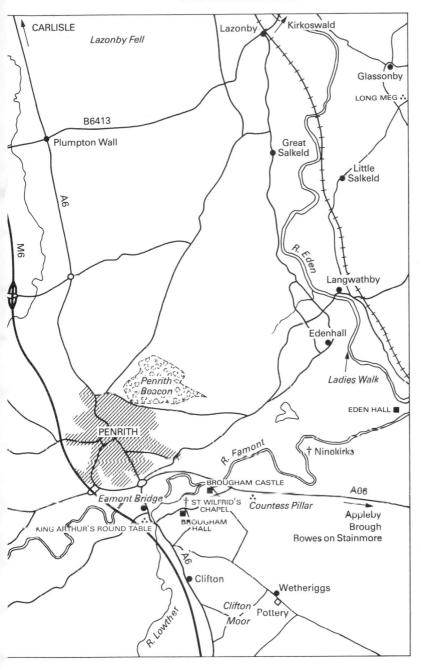

of the Eamont and Eden, with a fine bridge and an oldish mill. Even allowing for the changes in a century and a half, Turner must have allowed himself considerable artistic licence when he painted his 1825 view.

From a technical standpoint the castle is interesting in that the twelfth-century keep has been reinforced by a thirteenth-century gatehouse; a more usual development would have been to have a separately fortified gatehouse at some distance away, with the keep retained as an ultimate place of refuge. All this is Clifford work, for Brougham was a Clifford castle for centuries. The 'Shepherd Lord' or the 'Good Lord Clifford' was famous in his day and for long thereafter; as a boy during the Wars of the Roses he had been hidden away, given to a shepherd to bring up until times should be more settled. After the Battle of Bosworth he appeared, illiterate and in rags, to claim his title, which he did successfully, living to fight at Flodden, and to study astronomy and alchemy. The story is recorded in one of Wordsworth's worst poems, the 'Song at the Feast of Brougham Castle'. It is in rhymed tetrameter couplets, not his happiest form:

> Alas when evil men are strong,
> No life is good, no pleasure long,
> The Boy must part from Mosedale's groves,
> And leave Blencathra's rugged coves.

The Shepherd Lord also appears in 'The White Doe of Rylstone', which is rather better.

The last of the Cliffords, the redoubtable Lady Anne, who ran Westmorland for half a century, has left her mark there, as on so many places in the county. Lady Anne Clifford was one of the most remarkable women in a period rich in redoubtable females. She was the only daughter of George, Earl of Cumberland (see p. 41) and married successively the Earls of Dorset and of Pembroke: since the latter was also Earl of Montgomery she was a countess three times over as well as commanding the great Clifford estates in her own right. In her long life she contrived to outface all the Stuarts and even Cromwell himself; one gets a taste of her quality in the comment that John Donne made of her: 'She knew well how to discourse of all things, from pre-destination to slea-silk.' Her main passion was for building, and she restored her castles at Skipton, Brougham, Brough, Pendragon, Appleby and Bardon, living in turn in each, keeping the domestics and builders up to the mark; in addition she rebuilt or restored the Brougham churches and those of Appleby, and built the still existing Appleby almshouses. Brougham was however her favourite spot, and the keep-gatehouse complex was altered to accommodate her, although not much trace of this is now visible (to see how the countess lived you should go to Appleby where parts of her castle are open to the public). A more intact creation of Lady Anne's is **St Wilfred's chapel** a little way off, back towards Eamont Bridge. A church certainly stood on the site long before Lady Anne's, and the chancel contains the tombs of Edward and Cuthbert de Brougham, thirteenth-century custodians of Appleby Castle. The dedication to St. Wilfred may reflect a Dark-Age foundation, for that saint was known for taking a band of masons with him on his journeyings. (Wilfred was a much travelled man and lived, while Archbishop of York, in a princely style.) Seventh-century England (Wilfred lived between 634 and 709, being therefore an older contemporary of Bede) before the Danish invasions and after the Synod of Whitby, at which Wilfred was a prominent figure, was very much part of the Roman system. Wilfred, a Northumbrian, was educated in Rome and Lyons, and in his squabbles with the kings of Northumbria appealed, at least once successfully, to Rome. Remains of his churches survive at Hexham and Ripon, and probably at Wing in Buckinghamshire.

The chapel's plain exterior conceals a collection of eclectic and decorative furnishings, the result of some extensive nineteenth-century looting. These include a splendid French screen and stalls of the late fifteenth century, parts of a Flemish triptych on the reredos, and a good deal of panelling. The whole is lit only by candles, and presents a most convincing picture of a gentleman's chapel.

Sir John Betjeman, in his books on English parish churches, is ecstatic, and devotes more space to it than any other northern country church.

> Here is rich cathedral opulence. The church is as full as it can be of beautifully carved oak, an elaborate parclose organ casing, pillars tall pews, screen with rich round posts and beautiful cornice. The reredos is of oak gilt and includes a magnificent fifteenth-century altar-piece with superb carvings 'in the round'. This is a triptych with a central representation of the Crucifixion and a group below it. It is set under a deep canopy and the sculptured scenes are bordered by medieval wood work of the finest craftsmanship. Some has been attributed to Dürer. Companion to this continental carving is a lock on which is a representation of Christ rising from the tomb whilst the guardians sleep. It has a magnificent lock and

hinges. On the walls of the chapel are wonderfully carved scenes. The pulpit is enriched with medieval carving, the roof of oak is divided into panels each with richly emblazoned shield or crest. The E and W windows are stained. The stalls are superb. There is nothing in Westmorland, or indeed anywhere, to compare with this plain and simple building that might have been compelled by some extraordinary sumptuary law to hide its opulence within.

A foot bridge over the road leads to **Brougham Hall**. Originally, when owned by a Mr. Bird, it was less pretentiously known as 'Bird's Nest'. The house was bought in 1727 by John Brougham, a descendant of the ancient family, whose grandson Henry became the famous Whig politician, Lord Brougham and Vaux. He was a friend of Grey, a founder of the *Edinburgh Review* and one of the great figures of the Reform campaign, but Greville accurately described him as a 'very remarkable instance of the inefficacy of most splendid talents, unless they are accompanied with other qualifications . . . which must serve the same purpose that ballast does to a ship'. Dr Johnson described the same deficiency more tersely as 'lacking bottom'. Except to amateurs of nineteenth-century politics and history Brougham is now a footnote; apart from the carriage named after him, his greatest claim to recognition lies in his establishing the Côte d'Azur as a holiday resort, where he passed his last thirty winters, an understandable preference in one brought up to the rigours of the Westmorland climate.

It was Brougham who collected the furnishings of St Wilfred's chapel, and rebuilt the Hall between 1829 and 1840 to render it 'one of the handsomest and most pleasing residences in the North'. Until recently ruinous, apart from the intact curtain wall, Brougham Hall is being restored as a craft centre, housing, among others John Harrison, a metalworker in the great tradition of the Keswick School of Industrial Arts, and Rena Newsom, an internationally renowned *chocolatière*, who also produces a wide range of smoked foods. Since the Wetheriggs Country Pottery is only a couple of miles off, a diversion through Brougham is well worthwhile. Housed in the original eighteenth-century building, Wetheriggs boasts a steam-powered blunger ('an apparatus for blunging'! Oxford English Dictionary, perhaps tongue in cheek) and makes handsome traditional slip ware.

Back on the A66, raised on a mound on the side of the road, is the Countess Pillar, erected by Lady Anne to mark the spot where she saw her mother for the last time (and Appleby church has a splendid monument to that lady). The pillar is an exuberant creation, octagonal, some fourteen feet tall, with sundials and Lady Anne's twin heraldic bearings, all well restored. An inscription records both the daughter's farewell, and a commemorative bequest of £4 to the poor to be paid on an adjoining stone table every year: the money is, naturally in these conservative parts, still handed over at the correct place.

A little further off on the opposite side of the road (there is space to park a car by the entrance) a footpath leads a mile across the fields above the river to yet another of Lady Anne's memorials. **St Ninian's Chapel, or Nine Kirks**, was rebuilt by her in 1660, and, untouched by the antiquarian fervour of Lord Brougham, still possesses its almost complete furnishing of the period – font, screen, pews, communion rails, cupboards and even poor box. It represents one of the latest and best examples of the survival of the Gothic tradition in the north, a generation after St Paul's, Covent Garden, and only a couple of years before Wren's chapel at Pembroke College, Cambridge. One intrusion, probably earlier, is a screen in the south-east doorway, which features two lively figures: a drummer and a dancing girl, barefooted, with a flounced skirt, beads, and a ruff – perhaps a gypsy, although she is reading.

The dedication is rare – there are only two others in England – but Ninian is an important Scottish figure. Bede describes him as having been educated at Rome and based at Whithorn on the north bank of the Solway in the fifth century, before the legions left, in a still Romanized Britain: recent archaeological evidence has confirmed this, down to the fact that the masonry of the early church at Whithorn was painted white, giving rise to the place's name (*Candida Casa* in Latin).

Villages near Penrith

It has to be admitted that the Eden Valley is not part of the Lake District, however widely the net is cast, but while visiting Penrith it would be a pity not to take a little tour round the nearest villages in the interesting and exceptionally pretty area.

Two miles from Nine Kirks, flowing north-west, the Eden curves round the site of **Eden Hall**, once the seat of the Musgraves, and the home of the famous Luck of Edenhall. The region is rich in Lucks, objects which are meant to be the custodians of a family's fortunes. Muncaster, Burrell Green and Hareseugh all have ancient vessels of glass, brass or treen associated with the family, while Levens has a white fawn which serves a similar purpose (see pages 64–5). Dalemain edged into the act with a nice eighteenth-century glass, too late to be taken seriously, but the others all go back to the Middle Ages and the Arthurian legend.

That of Eden Hall is at once the most famous and the most accessible. Its fame is due to Longfellow's poem, a translation from the German of his contemporary Johann Uhland:

> Of Edenhall the youthful Lord,
> Bids sound the festal trumpet's call
> And rises at the banquet-board
> And cries 'mid the drunken revellers all,
> 'Now bring me the luck of Edenhall.'

> The butler hears the word with pain,
> The house's oldest seneschal,
> Takes slow from its silken cloth again,
> The drinking cup of crystal tall,
> They call it the Luck of Edenhall.

The cup came near disaster at least once, when the debauched young Philip, Duke of Wharton, the only non-royal personage to be made a Duke in his teens (by George I, and again, when he changed sides, by the Young Pretender, thus establishing two records) threw it in the air and failed to catch it. An agile butler saved the day, and the Duke commemorated the party in a mock ballad, which begins:

> *True and Lamentable Ballad called*

> THE EARL'S DEFEAT
> (*to the tune of Chevy-Chase*)

> God prosper long from being broke
> The Luck of Eden Hall;
> A doleful drinking-bout I sing,
> There lately did befall

> To chase the spleen with cup and can
> Duke Philip took his way;
> Babes yet unborn shall never see
> The like of such a day . . .

and ends

> Thus did the dire contention end,
> And each man of the slain
> Were quickly carried off to bed,
> Their senses to regain

God Bless the King, the Duchess fat,
And keep the land in peace,
And grant that drunkenness henceforth
'Mong noblemen may cease

And likewise bless our royal Prince,
The nation's other hope,
And give us grace for to defy
The devil, and the Pope . . .

After many adventures the Luck is now safely housed in the Victoria and Albert Museum, together with its magnificent leather case, of fifteenth-century workmanship. The legend has been proven wrong, since the cup survives while the Musgraves have long left Eden Hall, which was demolished in 1934. All that remains is a collection of gate pillars, lodges and a range of stables with a handsome clock tower, now a house, and, more prosaically, the estate gas house.

Ladies' Walk, a part of the estate, is a riverside promenade that dates from the early seventeenth century and is still in use; with its stone benches and retaining walls, distant views of the fells, celandines and campions closer at hand, it remains as Sandford in his account of 1670 described it: 'A fair, fine and beautiful place . . . with walks as fine as Chelsea fields'.

Edenhall village has a pleasant hotel, formerly a boarding house for estate workers, which serves good rich Westmorland food, and will arrange fishing. The Norman church of St Cuthbert, externally much disguised by a squat fifteenth-century tower, contains some medieval glass and an interesting brass, of William Stapliton who died in 1458 *'Quondum Dominus de Edenhall'*. He wears a handsome Milanese sallet, and is accompanied by a modestly diminutive wife. These attractions have to be taken on trust, since the brass itself is concealed under a fitted carpet; one would think that at least a reproduction, which could easily be obtained, should be on show. The early fourteenth-century glass includes representations of King Ceolwyn and St Cuthbert, and a quantity of Musgrave and allied family armorials. Much of the original glass has gone, replaced by glass brought from the Hall chapel, which had in turn come there from Hylton Castle. Cuthbert is one of the best documented of early medieval saints, for the thorough Bede was a younger contemporary of his, and wrote his definitive Life within twelve years of Cuthbert's death. Nor is there any mystery about his remains: the body, which remained well preserved at least until the sixteenth century, eight

17

hundred years after his death, lies under the high altar of Durham, and his vestments, cerecloths and jewels are preserved in the Cathedral library. A reluctant prior and bishop, he preferred a retired life on the Farne Islands, and is generally shown with otters and eider ducks, known throughout the north-east as 'Cuddy ducks' in his honour.

Like most churches hereabouts Edenhall is some little distance from its village. This reflects the practice of building churches on the sites of ancient temples or, as here, a spring, now known as St Cuthbert's Well, but also, and doubtless for as long, as Fairy's Well. It has been suggested, without much evidence, that a village was once sited around the church, and moved after a plague, but where this happened elsewhere, as at Maulds Meaburn, traces are evident. There certainly was a terrible outbreak in the sixteenth century, commemorated by the trough next to the Plague Cross. Those unfortunates stricken by disease camped out on the fell and left money for provisions in the trough, which was filled with vinegar. They were buried where they died, and their shelters burned over them.

Langwathby, on the opposite side of the river to Ladies' Walk, groups itself around an extensive green. St Peter's is a modest version of Penrith church, rebuilt about the same time but incorporating earlier work in the north aisle, where the Early English capitals have been oddly squeezed into the reconstruction. Some pieces of seventeenth-century armour are relics of the parish levies' equipment, once kept in the church in readiness for service against the old enemy from the north. **Little Salkeld** has a working water mill, restored by an enthusiast who abandoned his career in the City to learn the business of milling from scratch. His mill is open for inspection, sells its own flour, and runs educational courses in the miller's craft.

Five miles to the north a remarkable stone circle, **Long Meg and her daughters**, sits on a hill overlooking the Eden. Long Meg is a megalith, 18 feet high and 15 feet round; the daughters are a circle of 59 rather small stones, 360 feet in diameter, making it one of the largest stone circles in the country, nearly as big as Avebury. The whole was enclosed by a rampart, only part of which is now visible. Wordsworth was much struck by Long Meg and wrote: 'Every body has heard of it, and so had I from very early childhood . . . Next to Stonehenge, it is beyond dispute the most noble relick of the kind that this or probably any other country contains.' This is pitching it a trifle strong, as Wordsworth later admitted, but the strangely angled figure of Meg is unforgettable.

The original purpose of this site, as of others similar, is unknown; an astronomical explanation is unlikely, but the entrance-like feature just by Long Meg suggests a processional order, while the carvings on Meg herself are connected with funerary sites. These are quite visible whorls, one of which has associated arched cups, a type of design common in late Neolithic and early Bronze Age remains. One lady at least is quite clear as to Meg's history. Iris Campbell, a paranormal 'psychometricist', wrote: 'It dates from a period approximately 15000 BC. The period covered by the Ministry was for 1000 years during which time an excess of magic of various kinds caused eventually its break up and down fall.' It must be pleasant to be so sure, but most other authorities make Long Meg about twelve thousand years later. It still may be that there is more about Meg than meets the eye. Quite literally so, since Joe Ferguson of Blackburn claims to have photographed extraordinary designs on the stones, and on many others throughout Britain. Meg, he insists, is actually Portuguese; you can tell this from her headgear.

There may be something in the magic, though, for when an eighteenth-century farmer tried removing the stones he was punished by the worst storm in any man's memory, and wisely desisted. Like other similar sites – Castlerigg near Keswick, and the newly discovered Crickley Hill circle near Cheltenham – the Long Meg stones can be seen from a great distance, and command wide prospects.

Wordsworth's sonnet on Long Meg reflects something of an aura of the place:

> A weight of awe, not easy to be borne,
> Fell suddenly upon my spirit cast
> From the dread bosom of the unknown past,
> When first I saw that family forlorn.

The loneliness of the place, its views of the bleak hills, and its freedom from fences and car parks, make Long Meg much more atmospheric than Avebury, a larger monument, but one that has lost a sense of isolation. Strange collections of objects are sometimes found under Long Meg, left by unknown persons: they are allowed to stay there, for no one seems inclined to disturb them.

Little Meg, a smaller circle, is half a mile away, and once enclosed a barrow. Two of the stones bear 'cup and ring' and spiral carvings similar to those on Long Meg.

Glassonby has a church confusingly known as Addingham church, although Addingham itself was inundated and destroyed at the beginning of the eighteenth century. It is an oddly domesticated building, again some distance from the village, and with the remains of an uncommonly large ninth-century cross in the churchyard. William Nicholson was vicar here before he became Bishop of Carlisle. His sometimes waspish accounts of the pastoral visitations he made to his diocese in the early 1700s are an entertaining source of information on church life of that period.

Returning, the next bridge to Penrith is at **Kirkoswald**. Oswald, with Cuthbert and Wilfred, completes the trio of major Northumbrian saints. His was a more active role; he was King of the Northumbrians when the Britons under Cadwaller were finally defeated, at the Battle of Hevenfeld, near Hexham, after which the realm of Northumbria was left in peace for some time, although Oswald himself was killed in battle with the heathen King Penda of Mercia in 642. Once more the choice of site is on pagan ground, literally so since the sacred spring is actually under the west end of the church. Kirkoswald was conventual for a short period in the sixteenth century and the local great house is still known as the College. The Fetherstonhaughs live there, as they have since the Reformation. Ancient families tend to stay put in this area – Vanes, Lowthers, Hudlestones, Hasells, Howards, Stricklands and Hornyolds still live on their forebears' lands, and the names on the village shops are to be found on the most ancient tombstones in the churchyards.

The church has a number of monuments, including a nice alabaster plaque of Thomas and Margaret Bertram, kneeling on either side of a prie-dieu, a memorial to the unfortunate Sir Timothy Fetherstonhaugh, beheaded in 1651 for his efforts on behalf of Charles I. A ridiculous campanile stands a couple of hundred yards off, upon the hill.

Kirkoswald has an attractive, steep main street, rendered even more pleasant by the presence of three pubs, all serving good beer in a friendly fashion. Before the plague of 1598, when two-thirds of the population died, it was a prosperous market town, with a fine castle: 'One of the fairest that ever was looked on. The hall I have seen, 100 yards long, and the great portraiture of King Brute . . . and of all his successors, Kings of England portraited to the waist, their visages, hats, feathers, garbs and habits' (Sandford, 1610).

This was a hold of the Dacres, one of the most renowned border families, whose power reached its apogee in the time of Thomas, Lord Dacre from 1485 to 1525, who built the moat which is now the most prominent part of the castle. Thomas led the reserve cavalry at Flodden:

> Lord Dacre with his horsemen light
> Shall be in rearguard of the fight,
> And succour them that need it most.

Their charge, to the cry of 'A Dacre, A Dacre, a red bull, a red bull', was the culminatory episode of that fight and it was Lord Dacre who found the body of the Scottish king on the field. Border history has been rewritten from the Scottish point of view, and it comes as something of a shock to those of us brought up on Scott to find Flodden and Culloden remembered as much-needed lessons given to ancient enemies. The Butcher's Arms in Crosby Ravensworth is named not after the trade but to commemorate the Duke of Cumberland, a local hero.

But Flodden was really the end of the Scottish threat, as the contemporary English ballad (understandably, there were no Scottish ones) made clear:

> Then presently the Scots did flie,
> Their cannons they left behind;
> Their ensignes gay were won all away,
> Our souldiers did beate them blinde.

> To tell you plaine, twelve thousand were slaine
> That to the fight did stand,
> And many prisoners tooke that day,
> The best in all Scotland.

> That day made many a fatherlesse child,
> And many a widow poore,
> And many a Scottish gay lady
> Sate weeping in her bower.

> Jack with a feather was lapt all in leather,
> His boastings were all in vaine;
> He had such a chance, with a new morrice-dance,
> He never went home againe.

'Jack with a feather' was of course the dead King James IV, sewn up in a leathern shroud.

Lazonby, on the other side of the river, is not exciting; it was more so in Henry VIII's time, when it was the home of one Jack-a-Musgrave, who 'was so metled a man, as the country people would say, that if they had a spirited boy he would just be a Jack-a-Musgrave' (Camden's *Britannia*). 'Metle' is a quality much prized in Cumbria. Today, the most popular man hereabouts is George Bowman of Penrith, friend and rival of Royalty, and an unparalleled sportsman. If this gives the impression of landed wealth it is erroneous. George certainly comes from an old farming family, but his father was a prizefighter and George and his brother Robert's early careers were as bouncers, dealers and scrap-metal merchants.

George always liked horses, and an accident encouraged him to take up driving rather than riding. Within a few years he became one of the best whips in Europe. His annual tussle with the Duke of Edinburgh in the four-in-hand class at Lowther is a major sporting event, even if the outcome is predictable. George always wins. He can often be seen driving a training rig through Penrith, the undisputed if unofficial first citizen, a man of great 'metle'.

There is a large piece of cross-shaft in the churchyard, but any carving has been eroded, and the most entertaining thing in Lazonby is now the village school, an eclectic mid-Victorian essay in Venetian Dutch.

Great Salkeld has a fortified fourteenth-century church of St Cuthbert, built with an eye to defence against the Scots after the disastrous thirteenth-century invasion. The nave barely projects beyond the great protective tower; the contemporary door separating it from the rest of the church is a remarkable piece of smith's work, which still opens and closes smoothly and effortlessly. Within, the tower is prepared for a siege; the first floor has a fireplace, for the better comfort of the besieged, and the basement a dungeon, for the accommodation of the captured Scots. This is very much Border country, and every lowland village as far south as Carnforth has its fortified church or pele. Even the farmhouses themselves were often fortified; the bastle house was a first-storey refuge, approached only by a defensible external staircase, the animals housed underneath. These have often been converted to a simple barn, but a recognizable bastle house remains at White Cross Farm, near Glassonby.

Aeneas Sylvius Piccolomini, the fifteenth-century humanist who became Pope Pius II, travelled through the Borders on his way back from an embassy to Scotland, and describes how at night the men and beasts took to the pele tower, leaving the women and children to cope with the Scots, who would harm them only in an acceptable fashion. Aeneas Sylvius, on winning through to Newcastle, sighed with relief, realizing himself once more back in civilization.

The south door of St Cuthbert's is entered through an exotic Romanesque arch, much more like those of Gascony than of the north of England, with dragons, birds, beasts and human heads in luxuriant abandon.

The deplorable Edward Law, who became Lord Ellenborough, was born in the Rectory. An able but viciously brutal lawyer, he is remembered for the Ellenborough Act passed during the post-Waterloo repression which introduced ten new capital charges in an already savage calendar, declaring that 'laws could not be too severe', and pressing his cases in a broad Cumbrian that 'hardly omitted one epithet of coarse invective than the English language could supply him with'.

At the junction of the B413 and the A6 is **Plumpton Wall** church, a good modern (1907) building by Sir Robert Lorimer, with sharply battered walls and a pele-like tower, a successful interpretation of the local idiom. The interior furnishings, and the window by the influential and long-lived Henry Holiday, are of a uniformly high standard. It was here in 1920, on the road by the church, that Percy Toplis, the 'Monocled Mutineer', confidence trickster and murderer, was killed in an exchange of fire with Inspector Ritchie and Sergeant Bertram.

Armathwaite should not be missed, since Steve Wilson's woollen mill is there, open all year round. You can see classic tweeds and radiant original fabrics being woven – and buy both cloth and imaginative garments, which may then be admired in one of the village's two good pub/hotels.

Moving west from Great Salkeld, **Hutton-in-the-Forest** is on the other side of the motorway. The forest is Inglewood, which in the Middle Ages stretched from Cross Fell to the sea, and the name of which the owner of Hutton, William Fletcher-Vane, MP for Westmorland for twenty years, chose as his title. Hutton is open to the public and is not to be missed. It was bought in 1605 by a forebear of Lord Inglewood's, one Richard Fletcher, a Cockermouth merchant, whose family quickly started modernizing the old pele and transforming it into the extensive and heterogeneous house it now is. Richard was knighted by James I in recognition of the courteous welcome Richard's grandfather had given to the King's mother, Mary Queen of Scots, on her way through Cockermouth.

In all parts of England, one comes across the work of Anthony Salvin, who is responsible for the larger part of Hutton, and more should be known about him. He came of an old Durham family, not as sometimes thought a Huguenot, and was a pupil of Nash. Like Viollet-le-Duc in France, he made himself expert in medieval fortifications; a good deal of Windsor, Alnwick, the Tower of London and the magnificent, marvellous Peckforton Castle in Cheshire are due to Salvin.

The original pele is almost unrecognizable from the outside, having been heavily restored, but internally, with its massive walls and stone vaults, is unmistakable. It contrasts oddly, but not disagreeably, with the delectable five-bay seventeenth-century baroque wing adjoining, sandwiched in between the pele and a larger Victorian corner tower. Not much remains from the seventeenth century apart from the façade. Only the staircase is of the right period, and that may not originally have belonged to the house. But Salvin made a good, typically restrained job of the interior and of the large south and east wings; the interior decoration is something of a showpiece, since it was done by William Morris, a friend of the family. He used his own wallpapers, simple designs in pastel colours, not nearly as ornate as his later work.

Apart from the pele, the oldest part of the house is the long gallery that adjoins it, forming half a courtyard, and dating from the 1630s. It looks very convincingly of that period, with arcaded cloisters and a two-storey bay, very much like an Oxbridge college, but was substantially rebuilt in the nineteenth century, making it difficult to see exactly what was the original intention and detailing.

The Vanes are better known than the Fletchers; the Marquesses of Londonderry are Vanes, and Sir Henry Vane was a prominent Parliamentarian. Although not universally popular (Cromwell's lieutenant, Lambert, described him as an 'unworthy coveteous earthworm' and Cromwell himself prayed 'God preserve me from Sir Henry Vane'), Vane was an energetic and able statesman, so able indeed that Charles II thought him 'too dangerous a man to let live, if we can honestly put him out of the way'. Honestly or not Vane was executed in 1662, the only non-regicide to so perish.

The Fletchers took the opposite side in the Civil War, having become baronets, like so many prosperous Jacobeans. Sir George, who built the baroque wing, was the county member for nearly forty years in the reigns of Charles II, James II and William and Mary.

Hutton makes a pleasant family house, reflecting in its uncoordinated mixture of styles the succession of tastes as a bourgeois family worked its way up the social scale and adopted new fashions. The gardens evolved in a similar way, from formal seventeenth to a romantic nineteenth century, and traces of all periods, including some unintentionally comic eighteenth-century statues, are evident.

Salvin also worked at Hutton church, which is half a mile from anywhere, in a field, an ancient foundation – there is a tenth-century cross fragment embedded in the masonry – but now eighteenth-century altered by Salvin. The original communion rails (original meaning of course seventeenth-century, since there were no medieval rails) survive, and a couple of attractive Fletcher memorials.

Salvin almost reconstructed the next house, **Greystoke**, which has been a Howard house since the sixteenth century, when the male Dacre line failed and the Duke of Norfolk took over the guardianship of the Dacre daughters. It sits on the edge of an extensive park, the magnificence of which overwhelms what is now mainly, after two disastrous fires, a hospitable and pleasant Victorian house, designed by Salvin between 1839 and 1879. The medieval pele, and some Georgian interiors, have survived. Greystoke is only open to the public for occasional functions, when it is well worth seeing.

The eleventh Duke of Norfolk, Charles, who succeeded in 1786 at the age of forty, is certainly the most entertaining of his family and the only Protestant member in modern times. He was a gross, drunken, lively Whig, a friend of Fox, who went around in shabby clothes and had an eye for the girls, but was also a man of taste and energy. Arundel today is largely his work, and the beautiful library is exactly as he designed it. But Greystoke, where he had been brought up, was his favourite house, and he consistently arranged matters there so as to annoy those Tory upstarts, the Lowthers. He enlarged Greystoke park to 5000 acres, to make it the biggest in the land (Lowther was a thousand or so acres smaller), and gave it the present wall, but his most noticeable works are the castellated farmhouse follies to which he gave American Revolutionary heroes' names – Fort Putnam, Bunker Hill, Jefferson – which was built with a tower and spire in order to irritate the tenant, a farmer who believed churches to be unnecessary, the word of God being best heard in the open.

Edgar Rice Burroughs ensured another sort of immortality for the name of Greystoke by choosing Lord Greystoke as the rightful title for his hero, Tarzan of the Apes. The real John, Lord Greystoke, can be found in the church in shining white alabaster, although a little battered, alongside some charming small palimpsest brasses, all of the second quarter of the sixteenth century; unlike those carpeted at Edenhall, these are available for rubbing. A smaller effigy is that of William, fourteenth Lord Greystoke, who founded the college in 1358: the comparison between the fourteenth- and fifteenth-century armour is instructive, showing the development during that last age of practical body armour. William also has a brass which describes him as: '*Le bon Baron de Graystok plys vaillieant, noble et courteyous chevalier de sa paiis en son temp.*'

The church, St Andrew's, was collegiate, so has some fine choir stalls, with misericords, one with a very Eeyoreish donkey and another with three men grooming a horse. Most of what can be seen in the church is early seventeenth-century, which illustrates vividly the conservatism of building in these parts since it looks most convincingly medieval. The stained glass is medieval in fact, although reassembled in 1848, and depicts the story of St Andrew. A boundary between Celtic and Northumbrian Christianity is indicated by the dedication of the church; to the east of Penrith the Northumbrians, to the west Saints Andrew, Ninian, Kentigern and Patrick.

Since the Eden Valley has always been the invasion route from the north, and a prosperous place, the Greystoke area is the best spot to inspect large peles. Johnby Hall, Greenthwaite Hall, Blencow Hall, are all fine fortifications, easily seen from the road, to which substantial sixteenth-century houses have been added and all within a mile of Greystoke. Blencow, with its twin peles, is striking, and has an enigmatic inscription: *Quorsum* (whither) *Vivere* (to live) *Mori* (to die) *Mori Vitae* (of life), the name Henricus Blencow, and the date 1590.

Hutton John, a little further off, on the south of the A66, is withdrawn and secluded within its own walls, the residence of the ancient recusant family of Hudlestone, formerly Lords of Millom. The agricultural college at **Newton Reigny** has informative open days and a pleasant church, originally twelfth-century, but much restored. When the roof was rebuilt in the sixteenth century the workmen carved in a beam:

The Naymes of the Carpynteis that have builded the Roofe An Domi 1583, Videlicit John Atkinson & Henry Bymont.

The twelfth-century arcades and piscinas – three of them – have also survived and there is a good modern window of St Nicholas of Smyrna. Opposite the church is a good example of the typical Cumbrian longhouse, with barn, byre and living quarters under a single elongated roof.

This is a famous area for racing stables, a northern Newmarket, but without a racecourse: the best known are those of Gordon

26

Richardson at Greystoke and Jonjo O'Neill at Skelton Wood End. Something of the climate can be learned from this for horses do not prosper in unduly damp places, and the precipitation here is in fact much less than that just a few miles west.

2

Ullswater and Haweswater

Although Windermere comes in for much more attention, Ullswater is the finest of the lakes, with Helvellyn, the most famous of the mountains, towering over it, and preserved from the worst of the horrors that two centuries of popular tourism have inflicted on Windermere.

Like the first approach to the Lakes, the route to Ullswater is worth choosing carefully, since it should be, if the weather is at all kind, a striking experience. Two possibilities present themselves; one may follow the Eamont up to its source at Pooley Bridge, or take the main road towards Keswick, turning off left to descend through **Matterdale**. The first allows the prospect to unfold in a sedate manner, while the latter gives a sudden and dramatic view from the heights of Matterdale Common, before descending to the middle of the lake. This is the route preferred by Wordsworth: 'It is better to go . . . through Matterdale and descend upon Gowbarrow Park; you are thus brought upon a magnificent view of the two higher reaches of the lake.'

Even better might be to take the east side of Gowbarrow and meet the lake near Watermillock. The first stages of the descent discover only the placid lower reaches of the lake, bordered by neat round hills, until a turn in the road reveals a breathtaking prospect. Steep gloomy crags are pressed in by peaks of the Helvellyn range, and crowd out the view. Nothing prepares you for the sudden transition from a quiet domesticated countryside to the awesome conjunction of the hills. On paper these may sound inconsiderable eminences; Helvellyn is but 2500 feet above the surface of the lake, but the impression confounds statistics.

Turning left on the lake shore, **Pooley Bridge** is not worth lingering in, unless you need ice-cream, hamburgers or film, and although the Crown Hotel has nice gardens reaching down to the river there are too many noisy campers to make it pleasurable for any but the most sociably inclined. Legs can be stretched in a stroll up Dunmallard Hill, which bears traces of a small hill fort, and the tourist board office is in the car park near the steamer pier. That is all one needs to know about Pooley Bridge; it is a warning of what to expect in other Lakeland centres.

The steamers are however important, not only enabling the lower reaches of the lake by Barton Park, which are not exciting, to be quickly passed, but being themselves vessels of some interest. The older, *The Lady of the Lake*, was launched in 1877, while *Raven* celebrated her centenary in 1989. Both, alas, have been changed from steam to diesel. They sail three times a day to Glenridding during the season, stopping at **Howtown**, and that is what one should do. The first real Lakeland walks can then be samples of the very best.

Disembarking at Howtown there is a choice of sedate lake shore promenade or a more energetic climb. It is better to do the lakeside walk from Howtown to Glenridding, rather than the opposite direction, since the views are much better, becoming increasingly dramatic as the head of the lake is approached. Rounding Silver Point, Glencoyndale and Glenridding open up, with the fells rising precipitously, culminating in the harsh profile of Catstye Cam.

The other walk is perhaps the best known in the Lakes; it follows the expedition made by William and Dorothy Wordsworth on 9 November 1805, a date which reminds one that the Lakes are not only for summer visits, and described in the *Guide to the Lakes*. The valley has changed less perhaps than any other corner of the county, remaining as William described it and as it was for centuries before.

Starting from the Howtown landing you can either go straight up the road to Hause Farm (Hause is Cumbrian Norse for pass, and met with frequently), or, if authenticity is required, walk on along the lakeside to Sandwick, which is where the Wordsworths disembarked:

> Quitted the boat in the bay of Sandwyke, and pursued our way towards Martindale along a pleasant path – at first through a coppice, bordering the lake, then through green fields – and came to the village (if village it may be called, for the houses are few, and separated from each other), a sequestered spot, shut out from the view of the lake.

At Hause Farm both routes join, passing the **Martindale** chapel which has escaped vandals, conservationists and electric light, and retained the entire aspect, down to the furnishings, of its building in 1633. Even the great yew remains, as it has done for 600 years; the bows of the Martindale archers who fought at Flodden were made from its wood. The only mildly intrusive note is a monument to one William Dawes of Finsbury Square, a world removed from

29

Martindale. George Woodley, the perpetual curate of the parish, is buried under the yew, and described as 'an Author, a Poet, and a Christian', which is as much as anyone might reasonably ask.

Above the church the road continues to the Dale Head Farm, which used to double as a hunting lodge for the Hasells of Dalemain. This may also be reached, if absolutely required, by car, but at Dale Head you walk up about 800 feet over Beda Fell Knott and down towards Patterdale. Wordsworth described:

> a room built by Mr Hasell for the accommodation of his friends at the annual chase of red deer in his forests at the head of these dales. The room is fitted up in the sportsman's style, with a cupboard for bottles and glasses, with strong chairs, and a diningtable; and ornamented with horns of the stags caught at these hunts for a succession of years – the length of the last race each had run being recorded under his spreading antlers.
>
> A few old trees remain, relics of the forest, a little stream hastens, though with serpentine windings, through the uncultivated hollow, where many cattle were pasturing.
>
> While we paused to rest upon the hill-side, though well contented with the quiet everyday sounds – the lowing of cattle, bleating of sheep, and the very gentle murmuring of the valley stream, we could not but think what a grand effect the music of the bugle-horn would have among these mountains. It is still heard once every year, at the chase I have spoken of; a day of festivity for the inhabitants of this district except the poor deer, the most ancient of them all. Our ascent even to the top was very easy; when it was accomplished we had exceedingly fine views, some of the lofty Fells being resplendent with sunshine, and others partly shrouded by clouds. Ullswater, bordered by blacksteeps, was of dazzling brightness: the plain beyond Penrith smooth and bright, or rather gleamy, as the sea or sea sands. Looked down into Boardale, which, like Styebarrow, has been named from the wild swine that formerly abounded here; but it has now no sylvan covert, being smooth and bare, a long, narrow, deep, cradle-shaped glen, lying so sheltered that one would be pleased to see it planted by human hands, there being a sufficiency of soil; and the trees would be sheltered almost like shrubs in a greenhouse.

The red deer of Martindale are no longer hunted with hounds, but stalked, a much less picturesque operation; it is, in fact, the only deer forest in England. On the descent you pass the ruined chapel in the Hause (a different hause by now) and Wordsworth Cottage (by Broadhow on the Ordnance Survey map). Wordsworth bought a little estate here in 1806 – nineteen acres and the cottage, intending to build a home, but was annoyed that a friendly conspiracy between Lord Lonsdale and Thomas Wilkinson of Yanwath had led to the property being bought for more than Wordsworth thought it worth (he was, after all, the son of a land agent!). Even though Lord Lonsdale had settled the difference, for which Wordsworth was properly grateful, he was cross, and stayed put at Grasmere. Today there could be no question but that Broadhow should be preferred, the tranquillity of Grasmere having been destroyed by the new road.

The deer, sensible beasts, will keep out of the way, but the sheep are the now ubiquitous Herdwicks, whose fleeces are used for carpet manufacturing. They are the only sheep that will thrive on this thin soil, where not even Rough Fells are content, and have a proudly independent attitude. That perceptive observer Karel Capek was much struck by them: 'They graze on silken lawns, and remind one of the souls of the blessed in heaven. Nobody watches them, and they spend their time in feeding, sleeping, and divine pondering.' Buzzards are frequently seen, and, if one is lucky, one of the pairs of golden eagles that nest on the crags.

A possible reward would be tea, or even dinner, in the **Sharrow Bay Hotel**. Lakeland is not only supreme for scenery but for more fleshly enjoyments, and the Sharrow Bay has long been foremost among these for memorable meals, its only rival being the **Miller Howe** in Ambleside. The hotel is a modest country house in a superb position and the décor is almost as striking as the food: I have counted fifteen pots of flowers in one small sitting room. Flowers sometimes find their way on to the plates, but in spite of what may be regarded as eccentricities the food is superb, as is the service, and as are the wines. Naturally enough, bookings need to be made weeks or even months in advance.

Neither **Glenridding** nor **Patterdale** can compete with this, though there are some decent pubs, which offer perhaps more suitable refreshment after an extended walk, and one or two houses provide excellent coffee and cakes. The Ullswater Hotel, which may in other respects be an admirable hostelry, has deserved a special commination for erecting vile and prominent plastic structures intended for the amusement of children. What can be done, quite magnificently, is shown by the play-sculptures in Grizedale (see p. 248): it is a great pity that hotels and roadside eateries and amusement parks do not do likewise, in an imaginative act of patronage.

31

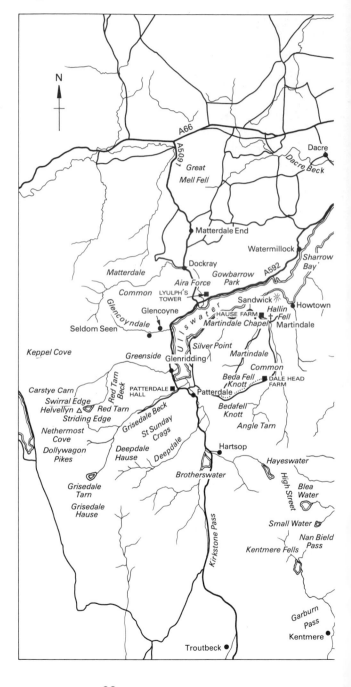

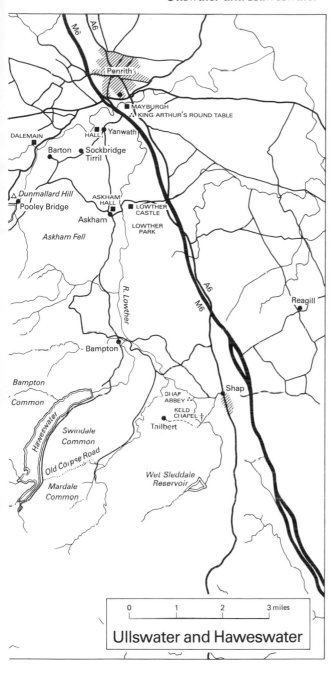

Ullswater and Haweswater

33

Patterdale church is good nineteenth-century work by Salvin – once more – and enjoys an unsurpassed situation, looking straight up Glenridding to the Helvellyn heights. There are some pleasant embroidered panels and tapestry kneelers inside.

Salvin also worked on Patterdale Hall, the house of the Mounseys, who were known as 'Kings of Patterdale'. The title, unofficial but unquestioned, came from the prowess of one Mounsey in fighting off a Scottish raid.

Moving south from Patterdale along the A592 towards the Kirkstone Pass, a turning to the left leads to Hartsop, one of the most picturesque spots in Lakeland, with handsomely restored cottages demonstrating all the features of the vernacular architecture of the district. Styles change remarkably quickly and distinctly; round chimneys, external galleries, not to be seen north and east of Ullswater, become common as one penetrates into Cumberland. A car park at the end of the village enables a walk of just over a mile to be taken to Hayeswater, one of the most secluded of the smaller lakes. From there the High Street range can be tackled, and the walk over into Haweswater.

Brotherswater, shallow and reedy, is not an enticing lake, but fishermen speak highly of its trout, and Dorothy Wordsworth wrote moving of an April day there in 1802:

> There was the gentle flowing of the stream, the glittering lively lake, green fields without a living creature to be seen on them, behind us a flat pasture with forty two cattle feeding to our left, the road leading to the hamlet, no smoke there, the sun shone on bare roofs. The people were at work, ploughing, harrowing and sowing – lasses spreading dung, a dog's barking now and then, cocks crowing, birds twittering, the snow in patches on the top of the highest hills, yellow palms, purple and green twigs on the Birches, ashes with their glittering spikes quite bare.

Apart from the work being mechanized, you can see the same scene today, in every particular.

Going from the lake up the Kirkstone Pass, the Roman road on the west side is distinctive, built on continuous substantial embankment rather higher than the motor road, and making a much pleasanter walk up the pass to the inn. When Celia Fiennes went up the pass she 'was walled in on both sides by those inaccessible high rocky barren hills, which hang over one's head in some places and appear very terrible', but she was more interested in her food, potted char 'very

34

fat' and clapbread 'a vast deal of difference in which is housewifely made and what is ill made'.

The Kirkstone Pass inn is not the highest pub in England – the Pennines claim at least two higher – but it will do nicely as a visiting place before going down 'The Struggle' into Ambleside.

Glenridding-Patterdale is not a bad base for family holidays. As well as a number of good walks, pony trekking and rowing boats are available, with the services of a sailing school, but the main centre for this sort of activity is at Watermillock, further down the lake. Fishermen come for the trout, and on the offchance of catching that peculiar fish the schelly, a sort of miniature salmon. They have had famous sheepdog trials – the Patterdale Dog Day – since the 1890s, in August, but unless you know the competitors a short time is enough for most people; like snooker, you see things better on television.

The Glenridding car park is the start for the **Helvellyn** ridge walk. This should not be attempted by novices except when the weather appears as near settled as possible. Striding Edge and Swirral Edge are dangerous and should not be taken lightly: even experienced fell walkers have been killed in bad weather, but it remains one of the finest and most exciting walks of the Lake District. Wordsworth took Humphry Davy and Walter Scott up in August 1805, one month after the body of young Charles Gough was discovered: Gough had fallen off Striding Edge, and his dog had guarded the corpse for three months before it was found, an incident which caught the imagination of the time. Their own expedition ended without incident, although it had begun with some difficulty. No beds were available in Patterdale, and the two poets were obliged to sleep on the floor of the main inn's sitting room. Some ladies insisted on staying up late, and talking excitedly about the journey they were about to make to Scotland in the hope of meeting the famous Walter Scott. Wordsworth and Scott, anxious to get to bed, pretended to be night watchmen, walking outside calling out the half hours, proving the sense of humour Wordsworth undoubtedly possessed, but rarely demonstrated in his writing.

Scott was lame, and Wordsworth recorded that: 'I could not but admire the vigour with which Scott scrambled along that horn of the mountain called "Striding Edge". Our progress was necessarily slow, and was beguiled by Scott's telling many stories and amusing anecdotes, as was his custom.' The direct route is unpleasantly steep, and it is better to go up Glenridding beck to the old mine buildings, under

Glenridding screes. The mineworks are not a pretty sight, not yet having decayed enough to make them as picturesque as those of Coniston. They were worked until the 1950s, quite intensively, with the shafts going down over 150 fathoms, well below the level of the lake bed, and employed over 100 men. Processing the lead, which was done at Elswick, also produced silver, about eight ounces to every ton of lead. The Patterdale church's communion set is made from Glenridding silver. A mile further up the beck takes you to the remains of the Keppel Cove dam, which burst in the 1920s causing considerable destruction in the valley below.

But for Helvellyn you take the left-hand path after the works, up the Red Tarn beck to the tarn itself; idle people have been known to stop there, bathe and picnic, contenting themselves with the view up to the summit rather than the summit itself.

From the tarn it is apparent that the prepossessing top is not Helvellyn but Catstye Cam, a couple of hundred feet lower. The short route is to go right up Swirral Edge, which is the easier ridge, to the summit and down Striding Edge: in good weather this is quite suitable even for prudent children. A more extended version is to go straight up Striding Edge, have a look at the view from the summit, and then take the ridge south to Grizedale Tarn via Nethermost and Dollywagon Pikes. From Grizedale Hause, just above the tarn, a path leads through Deepdale Hause under the quite magnificent St Sunday Crags, back down into Patterdale.

Helvellyn's summit is often a little crowded – it is after all one of the only four Lakeland 'Munros' (hills over 3000 feet), and people like to climb them all, even Skiddaw, leaving, regrettably, many traces of their passing. There are three memorials: one to Gough and his dog, one commemorating the landing of an aeroplane here in 1926, and a cross on Striding Edge itself. The view from the top gives you the whole of the rest of Lakeland and some of the Pennines for good measure, probably the most extensive panorama in the region: Skiddaw, Blencathra to the north, Robinson and Grasmoor to the west, then Great Gable, Scafell, Bowfell and the Langdales, Coniston and Wetherlam to the south, continuing past Fairfield to the High Street Range and Cross Fell, with the lower part of Ullswater shining 2600 feet below. On a good day you can see the Solway Firth and Morecambe Bay, part of Windermere and Bass Lake as well.

The next valley is **Glencoyndale**: the farm is the last to show the characteristics of Lakeland vernacular as seen at Hartsop; quite different from those of the Eden Valley, and reflecting the change from the slate and limestone of lower Ullswater to the volcanic rocks of the valley head. Seldom Seen is a group of cottages concealed round a corner of Glencoyndale, supposed to have got its name from being a place of refuge during Scots raids. The farm is owned by the National Trust, and the Wilsons, who live there, manage over 4000 acres of hill land, and have open days so visitors can see how such an operation is run. Glencoyndale farm is built for shelter against the elements, facing into the hillside, with no windows overlooking the magnificent view of the lake.

Completing the circuit of the lake back to Pooley Bridge the road passes closer to the shore, and there are a few places where parking and swimming, at any rate for the hardy, are possible. These tend to become crowded in the season and it is better to park in one of the larger car parks and walk.

One such, at the junction of the road to Matterdale, complete with café, serves **Aira Force** and **Gowbarrow**. Forces (the word is Norse) are northern waterfalls. High Force in Teesdale is the most spectacular, and not to be confused with the much smaller fall of the same name above Aira. On paper there should be nothing spectacular about Aira; it has a drop of no more than seventy feet and even after rain the body of water is not large. But again reality belies statistics. The picturesque path up the sheltered valley of the beck gives no hint of the proximity of the fall, until the noise begins to make itself heard. A sudden turn in the path brings you on it, the water tumbling from above your head, the falls surmounted by a high and narrow arch.

It was here that Wordsworth saw the famous daffodils and Dorothy recorded:

> When we were in the woods beyond Gowbarrow park we saw a few daffodils close to the water side. We fancied that the lake had floated the seeds ashore and that the little colony had sprung up. But as we went along there were more and yet more and at last under the boughs of the trees, we saw that there was a long belt of them along the shore, about the breadth of a country turnpike road. I never saw daffodils so beautiful they grew among the mossy stones about and about them, some rested their heads upon these stones as on a pillow for weariness and the rest tossed and reeled and danced and seemed as if they verily laughed with the wind that blew upon them over the lake, they looked so gay ever glancing ever changing.

Her account was made at the time, and it is clear that her brother's poem, which was written at least two years later, owes much to it:

37

I wandered lonely as a cloud
That floats on high o'er vales and hills,
When all at once I saw a crowd,
A Host of golden daffodils;
Beside the lake, beneath the trees,
Fluttering and dancing in the breeze.

Continuous as the stars that shine
And twinkle on the milky way
They stretched in never-ending line
Along the margin of a bay:
Ten thousand saw I at a glance,
Tossing their heads in sprightly dance.

But Wordsworth was always conscious of how much he owed to the sensitivity and acuity of his remarkable sister, and never made any bones about acknowledging the debt.

The Gowbarrow daffodils would be less colourful and showy than today's specialized blooms, and can never have been so widespread and reliable indications of a Lakeland spring as bluebells and primroses; but neither of these much more common plants would have stimulated the metaphor in the same way as did Dorothy's daffodils.

The present-day Gowbarrow Park is more restricted in area and begins further down the lake, on the other side of the A5091.

Wordsworth is at his best in his famous poem 'Airey-Force', describing the quiet of the valley before the falls are reached:

not a breath of air
Ruffles the bosom of this leafy glen.
And yet, even now, a little breeze, perchance
Escaped from boisterous winds that rage without
Has entered, by the sturdy oaks unfelt,
But to its gentle touch how sensitive
Is the light ash! that, pendent from the brow
Of yon dim cave, in seeming silence makes
A softy eye – music of slow-waving boughs
Powerful almost as vocal harmony
To stay the wanderer's steps and soothe his thoughts.

The oak and ashes still exist, but have been joined by a later exuberant planting of more exotic and quite unsuitable trees. Monkey-puzzles doubtless have their place, but it is not here. A little way off – the National Trust has the paths clearly marked – is Lyulph's Tower, another picturesque Gothic creation of the eleventh

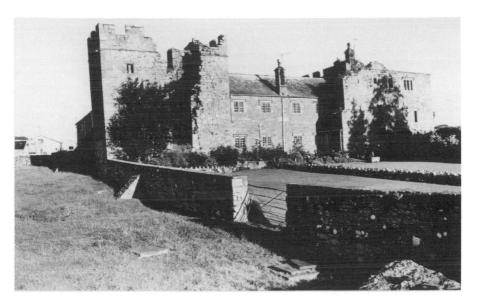

Blencow Hall: a two-towered pele

Dalemain: the eighteenth-century front

Brougham Castle

Lowther Castle: a romantic ruin, given over to rabbits and sheep

Duke of Norfolk, contemporary with his Greystoke farms. Built in 1780 it suited the romantic feeling of the period exactly, and is celebrated by all the Lake poets, including Wordsworth in 'The Somnambulist'.

> List ye who pass by Lyulph's Tower
> At eve, how softly then
> Doth Ara Force,
> That torrent hoarse
> Speak from the woody glen.

It is difficult to believe that both poems were written by the same man. J. K. Stephen was right:

> Two voices are there: one is of the deep . . .
> And one is of an old half-witted sheep . . .
> And, Wordsworth, both are thine . . .

The walk can be prolonged up the beck to High Force – not so exciting as Aira – and the village of **Dockray**, where there is a pleasant small hotel, the Royal, where sailing and pony trekking are arranged. Matterdale church, a little further up the hill, is another modest Lakeland structure much like Martindale, with contemporary benches and altar rail, an eighteenth-century pulpit, and some Kempe glass.

Back along the lakeshore is **Watermillock**, the best centre for sailing lessons. Ullswater is a good place for learning; the novice is not distracted by tides, all hazards are visible, and the weather offers just enough in the way of sudden squalls to make things interesting. The Outward Bound School has a sailing establishment here: more hedonistically the Leeming House Hotel sits in pretty lakeside gardens, and does its commendable best to keep up with the Sharrow Bay on the opposite shore, a task difficult of accomplishment.

Watermillock church is up the hill a mile from the lake: its exterior is, frankly, dull, but the inside is worth attention. Apart from a black-letter brass of 1562 commemorating John and Margaret Castlehow, who lived 'man and wyffe for LX yeres', and were 'buryed both on new yeris day', there are some pleasant windows, including one in the north aisle – probably Morris and Co. – with angels surrounded by a luxuriant selection of flowers.

The great attraction is, however, a superb collection of photographs, taken in 1936, which includes all the parishioners, 114 families, with their favourite dogs and horses. At that time social distinctions were clearly marked in dress, even when everyone was in their Sunday best: very uncomfortable they look, a world away from contemporary casualness.

In the churchyard a sculptured stone of some sort, though whether a coffin lid or cross shaft is unclear, supports a sundial, and from here the view across the lake is superb.

From Pooley Bridge back to Penrith the A592 follows the River Eamont. **Dalemain**, at the junction of the Eamont and Dacre Beck, is one of the few large houses in the area, and like Conishead, Muncaster, Holker, Sizergh and Levens is on the fringe of the Lake District proper. Lakeland villages have the homes of 'statesmen', as the independent yeomen of the area are known, and towns have some relics of prosperous tradesmen, but there is nothing at all in the way of a grand country house. Not that Dalemain is particularly grand. It began, inevitably, as a pele tower, which in the twelfth century belonged to one John de Morville, whose brother Hugh was one of the four knights who murdered Becket. After the assassination Hugh escaped to Dalemain before shutting himself up in his castle at Knaresborough. The medieval scatter of buildings surrounding the pele had become a recognizable house by the sixteenth century, of which the old hall and a magnificent barn survive.

The most striking feature today however is the fine nine-bay front built in the 1740s, of pink Eden Valley sandstone, by Edward Hasell, whose father had been steward to the famous Lady Anne Clifford, and who married the daughter of the unfortunate Sir Timothy Fetherstonhaugh of Kirkoswald; in the best Cumbrian tradition their descendants have lived there ever since.

Since the family still live there, only part of the house is open to the public. It is very much worth a visit. The Chinese Room is a little jewel – charming contemporary Chinese wallpaper, set off by a frivolous rococo chimneypiece. By contrast the entrance hall, with its cantilevered oak staircase and the fielded and raised oak-panelled drawing room are restrainedly elegant, although the Adam pier glasses give a light touch to the latter.

From the front it would be impossible to guess that an Elizabethan house is hiding behind, but it is unmistakable as soon as one steps into the Fretwork Room with its strongly plastered ceiling and small panels. The Old Hall is even older, part of the original hall built with the pele, while the pele itself now serves as a museum for the Westmorland and Cumberland Yeomanry. Hasells, sensible folk that they are, have always preferred to stay on their estates rather than distinguish themselves in national affairs; it would take a good deal to make any wise man leave such a very beautiful surroundings, and the family portraits reflect this. There is, however, a fine portrait of Lady Anne's father, George Clifford, Earl of Cumberland, who commanded one of the largest English ships *Elizabeth Bonaventure* against the Armada, and later devoted himself to attacking Spanish possessions, equipping no fewer than nine expeditions, most of which he commanded himself. The largest of these resulted in the temporary expulsion of the Spaniards from San Juan in Puerto Rico, but they cannot have been entirely successful, since he died in debt.

Dalemain's tea shop and gardens are worth attention for their cakes and old roses respectively. So is the Fell Pony Museum, as an introduction to these amiable creatures. Fells are all said to descend from one stallion, Lingcropper, left behind after the '45 uprising, but something very similar was around long before that, serving as pack ponies. No one, having seen a Fell, is likely to confuse him with a child's riding pony. Although short – not exceeding 14.2 hands – they are powerfully built, capable of carrying a fourteen-stone man all day (I can vouch for that!), alternating trot and walk, or being driven in a suitable cart. With long manes, tails and furry legs, they are capable of surviving the worst winters on the open fells; admirable animals.

But as soon as the country changes, becoming a little less open, so do the ponies. The Eden Valley, and straight over into Durham and the North Riding, is more suitable for Dales ponies: similar to Fells, but bigger, and rather more sedate in temperament.

For one day – 12 June 927 – **Dacre** became known to history, since it was here that King Athelstan of England received the homage of Constantine, King of Alba who was baptized here, and – although the records do not all agree – that of Eugenius/Owain, King of Strathclyde, and Ealdred, Lord of Bamburgh, who all undertook also to suppress heathenism. This state of affairs failed to last, for the two Scottish kings joined ten years later with Olaf of Dublin in an invasion which was crushed by Athelstan at Brunanburh (probably Bromborough, in the Wirral) in one of the decisive battles of English history.

Dacre has preserved its fourteenth-century pele intact, without additions, or much alteration except for the enlargement of windows and doorways. It was described in 1675 as 'Almost at the foot [of the Matterdale mountains] stands Daker alone; and no more houses about it; and I protest looks very sorrowful', but now it seems a pleasantly habitable house. Even before 927 Dacre was flourishing;

Bede mentions a monastery here in 731, and recent excavations by Lancaster University have uncovered some of its foundations, an early cemetery and some artefacts that appear to link the convent with that at Jarrow. Since Dacre churchyard served as burying place to a number of outlying farms, there are, as in many local parishes, old corpse roads, ritual tracks down which the bodies were carried to burial. The Dacre roads met at Town Head, where the body rested before being carried to the church on a sheet.

Dacre is part of the Dalemain estate, and in June both village and churchyard are resplendent in yellow roses.

Exactly what the stone bears in the churchyard are meant to be up to has been the subject of much speculation; the commonest explanation is that it is a three-dimensional action strip showing the animal being attacked by a cat – Pevsner says a lynx – which it finally eats. Bishop Nicolson thought they were heraldic bears, holding a ragged staff. Frankly I don't see it at all, and suspect that the medieval sculptor, who undoubtedly meant them to be four pinnacles on a tower – probably that of Dacre Pele – was just having a bit of sly Cumbrian fun.

Inside the church there are two quite important cross shafts; the older is Anglian, about ninth-century and sophisticated, a grinning animal head in luxuriant foliage pattern. The larger is Viking tenth-century, naïf but lively, offering few difficulties in interpretation; Adam and Eve picking the apple off the tree, a stag attacked by a hound, and an animal figure at the top. This is probably the sacrificial ram, since the two figures beneath it are said to be Abraham and Isaac, with an altar.

Two Hasell monuments, one florid of 1708 and the other discreetly elegant of 1830, by Sir Francis Chantrey, aptly reflect the taste of their time.

The south door is secured by a fine lock, marked AP. It was given by Lady Anne Clifford, who made a habit of presenting locks to her friends. Dalemain too has one, on the front door, made by George Dent of Appleby.

There is a good story connecting Dacre and Lyulph of the Tower, to the effect that one Sir Guy Dacre's wife Eloise ran off with an Italian tutor, who was seized by Guy's friend Lyulph. Sir Guy retrieved his wife, brought her back to Dacre, and took her to a dungeon she had never seen before, where she beheld her lover chained to the wall. Eloise rushed to kiss him, only to have his head fall to the floor. She was kept there with the disintegrating corpse

42

until she went mad and died; they are both believed to haunt the castle.

It is worth retracing one's steps to Pooley bridge and returning to Penrith on the south side of the valley, by the B5320. St Michael's **Barton** is an unusual church for these parts, with a central rather than a west tower. Inside it looks more unusual still, for the original 1150 chancel arch has had to be reinforced by another, lower arch, which gives the crossing a peculiar tunnel-like aspect, which Bishop Nicolson called 'a long and dark passage (under the Tower or Bellfry) crowded with Seats, and very ill floor'd, although 'the body of the Church is . . . put into a very decent Order, at a great and cheerful expense of the whole Parish'.

Barton used to be the centre of a large parish, stretching from Patterdale to Eamont Bridge, which is why on the north side stables and a mounting block were provided. Glebe Farmhouse is the vicarage built by Lancelot Dawes, who was not only vicar but squire, living at the considerably more extensive Barton Hall, which explains the motto he had carved above the door: *'Non mihi sed successoribus* – Not for me, but for those who came after.' It must have been Lancelot's son who erected the memorial to his wife inscribed:

> Under this stone Reader interr'd doth lye
> Beauty and Vertue's true Epitomy.
> At her appearance the noone sun
> Blushed and shrunk in cause quite outdone
> In her concenter'd did all Graces dwell.
> God pluck'd my rose, that he might take a smell.

Sockbridge and **Tirril** are indistinguishable; the pub, the Queen's Head, which has been well known for many years, is in Tirril; Sockbridge Hall, a small fifteenth-century manor house, and Wordsworth House are in Sockbridge. It was here that William's grandfather Richard (who is buried in Barton church) set up house when he came to Westmorland from Yorkshire, and where William's elder brother Richard lived when not in London. But the best house, and the most important Wordsworth connection, are at the next village, **Yanwath**, the last before getting back to Eamont Bridge. Yanwath Hall is down a little road, right up against the railway, and is the best preserved and finest fourteenth-century manor house in the region. It sits right on the Eamont, guarding a ford which may well have been the Roman river crossing leading north from High Street. The pele has a rather later square mullioned bay cutting into the original large hall – forty-two feet long – adjoining the tower. Originally the main entrance was to the north facing the river, and had a fortified gateway. Now a working farm, it is not open to the public, but you can get a good look from footpaths on both sides of the river, and see why it was described in the seventeenth century as having 'a delicate prospect when you are in it, and the grace of a little castle when you depart from it'.

The Wordsworth connection is not with the hall, but with the house on the other side of the railway line. 'The Grotto', home of Thomas Wilkinson the Quaker, whose spade Wordsworth apostrophized in one of his sonnets:

> Spade! with which Wilkinson hath tilled his lands
> And shaped these pleasant walks by Eamont's side.

Wilkinson, a multi-talented man, poet and landscape gardener, built a veritable grotto, as well as a comfortable house. Grottoes are frequently found in these parts, usually sheltered gazebos, whence the contemplative retire. Wilkinson's is more than usually sheltered, being in most part underground.

Back at Eamont Bridge, behind the pub, squeezed in between the B5320 and the motorway (which misses it by inches) is **Mayburgh**, a huge henge monument; although now only one of the stones remains in place, in the centre of the circle (a 'henge' consists of a banked earth circle with a stone circle inside). It is an impressive piece of work, especially since there is no ditch, as at Avebury, the whole being constructed of stones covered with turf, thus requiring an immense volume of stones.

King Arthur's Round Table, on the other side of the road, between it and the A6, is smaller, less noticeable, and has a ditch, an altogether easier method of construction. Needless to say it has no connection with King Arthur, being a couple of millennia earlier.

Moving south, but keeping to the west of the A6, one comes to **Lowther**. There are older families in Cumbria and more distinguished, who have played a greater part in the affairs of the county, and certainly some better-conducted than the Lowthers, but none who have exercised more influence for longer. Their fortunes started with coal, in the seventeenth century, and very nearly ended with coal in the twentieth, but during that period the Lowthers were one of the richest families in England.

The first Earl, known to all, even to the family, as 'Wicked Jimmy', being altogether too highly flavoured for the not unduly sensitive eighteenth century, controlled no fewer than nine Members of Parliament, and his rule was only challenged in Westmorland by the eleventh Duke of Norfolk. Political jobbery on this scale came expensive, and the next Earl continued to ensure Lowther expenditure was in keeping with Lowther income by building that enormous house, Lowther Castle, which aroused the enthusiasm of nineteenth-century admirers to fever pitch:

> . . . the present magnificent and elegant mansion, which combines in itself the majestic effect of a fortification with the splendour of a palace . . . built in the decorated Gothic cathedral style, with pointed mullioned windows, delicate pinnacles, niches, cloisters . . . below which the River Lowther pursues its devious course, 'twixt flowery meads, stately trees, sometimes ending its pellucid waters beneath the umbrageous foliage which skirts its banks, and anon peeping through the matted branches, in the full glow of picturesque beauty.

Lowther was designed by the – very – young Robert Smirke, who was only twenty-five when he was given the commission, and nearly unlimited funds – £60,000. His later work, of which the British Museum is the best known example, is very much in the classic manner, and although Lowther is Gothic in its detailing it – or what is left of it - makes a handsome well-balanced composition. It is ironic that this hugely expensive edifice endured for a mere century and a half, and is now a ruin, its contents scattered, its owners living modestly (and much more conveniently) in Askham Hall, while the less privileged pitch their caravans in the groves where once the Kaiser William II rode and shot a wide selection of carefully released birds and rabbits. His visit is commemorated by one of the park roads, Emperor's Drive.

It was Hughie, the fifth Earl from 1880 to 1944, the most popular sporting figure of his time, who nearly ruined the family. He splashed the Lowther colour, yellow, over the face of Cumbria: yellow liveries, yellow labradors, yellow cars, yellow for the Penrith Conservative party favours (still) and even nationally – the Automobile Association, of which he was first president, adopted his colour. Hughie's sporting fame was settled when he challenged the world heavyweight champion, the Irish American John L. Sullivan, to a fight, and beat him.

But on his death the Lowther coffers, already seriously damaged by the decline in mining royalties, nationalized before the war, were nearly emptied by estate duties. It proved impossible to keep up Lowther Castle, and it was stripped, converting it into the very spectacular ruin it is today. This rapid decline is hardly as surprising as it may sound; the Grosvenors, even richer than the Lowthers, felt that they had to pull down their own home, Eaton Hall, at about the same time.

Since Hughie's day, under the management of James, the seventh Earl, things have got better, and Lowther Industries has become a local force, and a mini-conglomerate, but the park is still open to the public and has tarmac rights of way running through it, and remarkably fine it is. An area of the park has been developed as a 'Leisure and Wildlife' Centre, a magnet for children, which provides trains, boats, rides, a puppet show and a circus. The best approach is to the park proper from **Askham**, an attractive village with two good pubs – the Queen's Head and the Punch Bowl. Below the village the River Lowther runs under a steep cliff past St Peter's church, beautifully situated by the bridge.

The Lonsdales now live in Askham Hall, which is much pleasanter than inhabiting what would today be the decaying, damp and incredibly expensive corridors of Lowther, since Askham is a handsome Elizabethan house built on a substantial pele, and of modest enough dimensions to make life comfortable.

Climbing the hill from the river, Lowther church is in the park on the left, an odd-looking edifice, with a squat Victorian tower sitting on what seems to be a seventeenth-century nave. Once inside all is revealed – a straightforward twelfth-century church which has been adapted to become the Lowther family chapel, inhabited by a motley collection of memorials. The best of these is hidden away, in a most undignified fashion, behind the organ. It is to Sir John Lowther, who became the first Lord Lonsdale and died in 1700; he is represented life size, leaning elegantly back, a faint smile on his face, gazing adoringly at the object held in his hand; his coronet! Sir John's grandfather and great-grandfather have more discreet busts, white against a black marble background; these also are banished behind the organ, but in the north transept, in full view of the congregation, is what must be the funniest brass in England. It is to Henry, Lord Lowther, who died in 1887; he is shown in full Life Guards uniform, waxed moustaches, with his cuirass inlaid in silver metal, looking as

46

if he had just stepped out of the chorus of heavy dragoons in *Patience*.

Bishop Nicolson was greatly taken with the church, and reported that: 'The whole Church here, haveing been lately put into a new form . . . is in the fairest condition of any parish church in the Diocese.'

In the churchyard there is an epitaph to one Thomas Cook, who died at the age of twenty-four in 1695. 'Hast thou, Health, Strength, Art, Industry. Yet dye thou must; for these had I.' But the commanding feature is the mausoleum of William, the second earl, who died in 1844. He is sitting in gloomy isolation, leaves on the floor, surrounded by representations of horses, cows, sheep, and a portion of a naked female torso.

Lowther Park is seen at its best during the three-day August horse-driving trials, especially if you can get yourself qualified as a competitor, when you are able to exercise your animals in the morning along what must be the most beautiful rides in the north.

The park also contains two estate villages, the older built by the Sir John who renovated the church, at about the same time, in the 1680s, the other a century later, designed by James Adam. This last is designed as two courtyards, with houses of varying sizes, but arranged as a composition. It is beautifully simple, open and elegant; if only council estates had been designed as well as that!

The Park stands on an escarpment which terminates in some low cliffs overlooking the river at **Bampton**, famous in the eighteenth century for its grammar school. It was not so much that there was a grammar school in such a modest village, for Westmorland was one of the best provided counties in the matter of schools, but that Bampton stood out even among such schools as Appleby, where the elder Washingtons went (one of the few comprehensives to have once had a saint as a headmaster – although admittedly only a Roman one, St John Boste). Bampton is now famous for the Mardale Shepherds' Meet, held at the end of autumn, when the sheep that have got themselves separated from their flocks are rounded up and claimed by their rightful owners.

These lively occasions mark the onset of winter, and follow a regular pattern, starting with a hunt by the local pack, which is followed by a great deal of drinking, eating tatie pie, singing songs, and telling stories, while the sheep and dogs wait patiently for the business to be over. Fred Hunter, our old gardener, recalled a meet attended, ill-advisedly, by the vicar, who addressed the convivial gathering, saying that he, too, was a shepherd, but a shepherd of men. A voice enquired, 'Oh aye, parson, how was tuppin time this year?' Every area has a meet but that of Mardale is best known. It does not take place in Mardale since Mardale is no longer, having been, like Thirlmere, drowned to make a reservoir. The inundation of Mardale was a sadder business than that of Thirlmere, for Mardale was a real community, with an ancient church and school, while at Thirlmere only a few scattered houses were destroyed. It would be more acceptable if **Haweswater**, Mardale's lake, were treated as a lake rather than a reservoir, but the water authorities have tried to keep people from swimming, sailing and all the other activities proper to a real lake, although things are improving, for fishing and scuba diving are now permitted, and better things may follow. In a hot summer, like that of 1976, the water is drawn off, exposing a rim of unpleasantly sterile earth. That year the ruins of the old village were visible, and became for a time a popular attraction. Today the only trace of the old village is seen in the reservoir tower, which incorporates some windows from the demolished church. The area is protected as a nature reserve, and provided with an observation post from which the golden eagles, now safely installed on the fells, may be seen during their nesting season. Buzzards are often visible, and both peregrine falcons and ravens may be encountered.

A motor road runs along the east side of the lake to the head, where a car park is the starting point of walks over the Kentmere Fells. This convenient arrangement means that some of the finest tops in the Eastern Fells are easily accessible. The best course for a newcomer is to take the old routes through Nan Bield Pass past Small Water down into Kentmere, thence on the Garburn Pass to Troutbeck and its pubs. This long, but not too strenuous, expedition enables a good look to be taken at Ill Bell, Harter Fell, High Street, and the other fells one might wish to climb later.

Not everyone shares my desire to retrace ancient routes, but those who do should attempt High Street, which formed the Roman road from Brougham towards Ambleside, and which makes a peaceful high-level walk without the crowds found further west, but with some excitements and splendid views, including that down to Blea Water. 'Blea' is blue, but there is not much blue about this, the deepest tarn in the region, surrounded by precipitous crags, quite unlike the sylvan setting of Blea Tarn over in the Langdales. The route is well defined over the ridge from Askham Fell south past the summit, after which one has to take a view as to whether the

Ordnance Survey map has got it right, for there is not much to see on the ground as one descends by whatever route to the Garburn Pass.

Shap Abbey is no great monastic ruin, like Furness, but gains immeasurably by the seclusion of its site – no railways, pubs, or even English Heritage exhibitions, interrupt the beauty of the lonely and unfrequented site. The Praemonstratensians or White Canons, the order that founded Shap in the thirteenth century, looked for solitude, and here they found it.

The great fifteenth-century tower, considerably the most dramatic part of the ruin, stands in a small meadow of the river valley, with only a cottage adjacent. You can wander about the stones uninterrupted, but preferably with a good guide to the Abbey (the best is that section in Clare's *Archaeological Sites of the Lake District*, but the official guide is adequate), for what distinguishes Shap is the completeness of the conventual arrangements, at least in plan. With Clare, and some imagination, it is possible to trace not only claustral buildings (the reredorter and cesspit are always popular) but the precinct wall, farm building, mill and field system.

Half a mile further along a path from the Abbey is another pre-Reformation building, on a very different scale. **Keld** chapel is a barn in appearance, built in the fifteenth century as a place of worship for the scattered valley farms. Almost unaltered since, it comes to life and is full of flowers once a year for a service in August. Preserved by the National Trust (the key is available from the cottage opposite), it has no memorials, carved stones, stained glass, or any characteristic that we associate with a medieval church. Its crude simplicity is an indication of how common people actually lived, in a fashion entirely removed from any beauty or grandeur.

Shap village is famous for weather and granite. Exposed on a windy ridge below High Street it does tend to be a chilly, blustery spot, but its reputation was won in pre-motorway days, when the A6 over Shap summit was, almost every winter, blocked, and the village became a refuge for stranded lorry drivers. There is now little through traffic, and in consequence the village has become a very much pleasanter place, although trade in the Greyhound, an old coaching inn, may have fallen off.

St Michael's church was given a very thorough rebuild in 1898, but since this involved stripping off the plaster, leaving the more modern parts in keeping with the twelfth-century arcade, the general effect of the interior is agreeably medieval. Before 1729, the date when Mardale church was licensed to bury its own dead, bodies had to be carried on horseback over the hills to their graves in Shap churchyard. Mardale church has gone, but the old Corpse Road – marked on the map – remains, and is typical of these peculiarly lakeland paths. It makes a pleasant walk, over Mardale Common down into Swindale and up through Tailbert and Keld.

On the opposite side of the main road from the church stands an arcaded Market House of 1690, which is when Shap was given its market, although it had been a trading village of some importance well before then. Shap's fleeces certainly found their way as far as Italy, as an Italian wool merchant's list of 1315 names *Ciappi in Vestre bellanda* as one of his suppliers.

The worst place to see Shap granite is in Shap, for it is much too expensive and hard to work to justify using it for buildings of the domestic sort. But in London, or any large town, the dark rose of polished Shap stone is ubiquitous. Piccadilly Circus has it in the pilasters of the Trocadero; St Paul's in its bollards; any Victorian bank in Manchester is likely to have samples somewhere in the façade. In its natural state it crops up in the valleys as erratics – rocks shifted there by the movement of glaciers. Darker than the Eskdale variety (Norman Nicholson aptly, if unkindly, says it looks like frozen potted meat), it has passed out of favour with architects, which is sad for Shap. The glory has departed and the old granite works are now used for making concrete pipes.

It is easy to miss the sign on the left-hand side of the road south of Shap announcing the Shap Wells Hotel, and there is no trace of an hotel in what seems an entirely empty countryside. But there has been a spa and a substantial hotel there for some years, first built by the good second Earl of Lonsdale, 'for cleanliness, abundance of furniture and contrivances, as well as for the excellence of the beds . . . far superior to most (first rate London hotels)'. They are sensibly renovating the springs (the water tastes quite nasty enough for you to be sure it is doing you good), and there is a splendid monument to Queen Victoria, and sculptures by Thomas Bland of Reagill, a farmer turned sculptor. On the Blands' farm, at Reagill, three miles off, is a whole garden full of Bland's work, crumbled and lichened, oddly impressive in a Westmorland mist.

3

South of Windermere

Although the area around Kendal can offer nothing so spectacular as Ullswater and Helvellyn, the town itself is the most attractive in the region, and the countryside includes both pretty wooded valleys and the southern approaches to the High Street range: as good fell walking as could be wished. Also it must be admitted that whatever the attractions of the northern route most tourists will approach the Lakes from the south, since that is where the centres of population lie, and by road, especially if they are planning an extended stay. But they should not be in too much of a hurry to reach the Central Lakes, for if the unwary motorist, dashing up the M6 from Preston, is seduced by the signs directing him to the Southern Lakes he will find himself swept off past Kendal and on the outskirts of the Windermere–Bowness conglomeration before he knows what has hit him. This fate should certainly be avoided, since the countryside between Lancaster and Kendal is some of the prettiest in the north of England; it would be quite possible to spend several happy days pottering about there without wishing to go further.

John Ruskin foresaw this difficulty when he wrote: 'The lake scenery really begins on the south at Lancaster . . . but the stupid herds of modern tourists let themselves be emptied like coals from a sack, at Windermere and Keswick.' Ruskin nominated the view over the Cumbrian Fells from Lancaster Castle Hill as the best starting point, but in his day the municipality of Lancaster had not permitted two large gas retorts to be stuck immediately in front of Castle Hill. It might now be better to go round to Morecambe, stopping off in the Midland Hotel on the sea front in order to admire the Eric Gill murals, and appreciate the panorama from the promenade there. North and west, across the golden sands only occasionally covered by the sea, the view extends from Black Combe on the edge of Furness over the whole Lakes massif; and from here one has the considerable advantage of not having to look at Morecambe. Having got as far as that it would be a pity not to go a little further along the coast towards Heysham, and admire the twin Saxon chapels of St Peter and St Patrick.

But this is to digress: **Lancaster** is where the lake mountains can first be seen and in spite of the gasworks Lancaster Castle itself should be visited. Viewed from Castle Green below, the great gatehouse looms up; multi-corbelled machicolations jut out threateningly: it would make a fitting illustration for some game of dragons and sorcerers, but it is genuine enough – the gatehouse at least – about 1400, with a statue of John of Gaunt, 'time-honoured Lancaster', and the arms of Henry IV and his Prince of Wales to prove it. Most of the rest of that side of the castle has been restored, and is in current use for the Assizes and for holding prisoners.

The priory church of St Mary is tucked away around the corner, a decent late-medieval building with an eighteenth-century tower. Inside, the choir stalls are remarkable, crowned with flamboyantly carved pinnacles of oriental intricacy. Their backs accommodate modern naïf needlework panels, which relate oddly to the sophistication of the canopy, but better to the earthy misericords – one on the south side depicts an angel apparently performing an act which ought to be impossible for sexless creatures. Elsewhere in the church is a collection of elegant eighteenth-century memorials, including one by Roubillac.

If one stands in the porch, eyes averted from the gas works, the castle presents a very different aspect from that of the grim gatehouse wall. Built to the designs of J. M. Gandy, a pupil of Wyatt and of Soane, it is dominated by an immense bay in finely detailed, almost frivolous, Strawberry-Hill Gothic. The interior, which contains the Shire Hall, is all Gandy; offenders hauled before Lancaster courts have at least the consolation of an elegant setting for their trial.

The houses on Castle Hill are all good, and there are some nice eighteenth-century buildings in the city centre; in spite of its medieval origins Lancaster is essentially a Georgian town – even its two great medieval relics, castle and church, have been to some extent 'refined'. There is not much refined about Lancaster market, which is as bustling and jolly as perhaps the northernmost limit of that pigs'-trotters tripe-and-chip-butty-comfortable Lancashire working-class tradition which still flourishes in places like Bolton and Wigan.

But Lancaster, it has to be admitted, lies within the scope of this book only by reason of it being the starting point of that track across the sands of Morecambe Bay which was the route favoured by Lakesbound travellers before the railway came. Not only was this route more direct than the alternative – which was to follow the toll road almost as far as Kendal before being able to cross the River

Kent at Levens Bridge and then to make south once more down the right bank of the estuary – but the sands route offered much easier going. Seven miles of level sand, interrupted only by the splashes through the rivers, came as a welcome change from hammer, hammer down the hard high road. Not only walkers, but carts and carriages went north from Lancaster between the tides. It must have been particularly pleasant for the riders; no land gallop affords the opportunity to extend an animal like the sands of the north-west, and it is no coincidence that the finest horse of modern times, the heroic Red Rum, was trained a few miles off on Southport Beach.

The crossing was not without its dangers. In 1325 sixteen people were drowned in a single tide, as a result of which the Abbot of Furness petitioned King Edward to make provision for a guide. The office was duly filled, and still exists: the Carters, appointed by the Duchy of Lancaster, rewarded by a salary of £15 a year, are responsible for ensuring the safe passage of travellers across the sands. You may still call upon them for assistance, but not unfortunately at the Lancaster end. Hest Bank, a not particularly attractive spot, where the right of way across the sands starts, has no map, or any offers of help, only a warning of the dangers of the crossing. Things must have been easier in the 1780s when a regular coach service operated thrice weekly, 'conducted by a sober and careful driver', between the Sun Inn, Lancaster, and the King's Arms, Ulverston.

Given today's choice, between the A6 and the motorway, the old road is far better; the M6 has some good views, but a motorway is no place for admiring the scenery. Indeed it can be positively dangerous, for the first sight of the hills, coming out of the Lancaster turnoff and up the slope, is breathtaking. Farleton Knot, on the right, gives a first taste of the pastel limestone colours, and the distant outline of the fells is washed in on the skyline. By contrast the A6 is tame, since immediately north of Lancaster the sea walls cut off most of the view, although Bolton-le-Sands is a pretty village.

Carnforth is a famous place for steam engines, and the centre for these veterans' repair and maintenance. Enthusiasts turn up all the year round to admire such visitors as the Flying Scotsman or Lord Nelson, and regular trips are made in the summer.

Kyril Bonfiglioli, that unjustly neglected thriller writer, who points out that it was on Carnforth station that *Brief Encounter* was made, described Carnforth as one of the ugliest of towns with the nicest people, and was not far wrong. There is a good bookshop in Carnforth which is worth visiting.

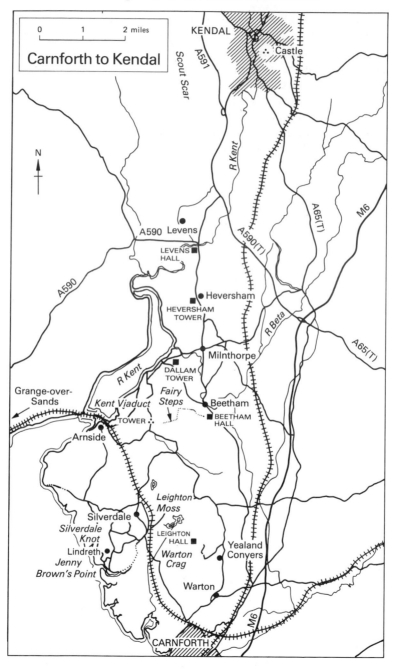

0   1   2 miles

Carnforth to Kendal

KENDAL

Castle

Scout Scar

A591

R Kent

A590

N

A590 Levens

LEVENS HALL

A590(T)

A65(T)

M6

Heversham

HEVERSHAM TOWER

R Beta

A65(T)

Milnthorpe

DALLAM TOWER

Fairy Steps

Grange-over-Sands

R Kent

Kent Viaduct

Beetham

BEETHAM HALL

TOWER

Arnside

Leighton Moss

Silverdale

LEIGHTON HALL

Yealand Conyers

Silverdale Knot

Lindreth

Jenny Brown's Point

Warton Crag

Warton

M6

CARNFORTH

Picturesque scenery starts with the limestone country north of Carnforth. Its approach is heralded by the appearance of cottage walls crested with upright stone slabs weathered to grotesque shapes. Not much of the original limestone pavement survives in place on the fells after the depredations made by gardeners who find the weathered stone irresistible. It is undeniably attractive; some of the bigger pieces could be exhibited as abstract sculptures and win prizes at the Tate Gallery. The gardens of our Westmorland house were landscaped in the 1840s, when the use of rugged chunks of limestone became popular. There was an ice-house concealed under a cascade, and on an island a dragon, eight feet long, on whose jagged back children gave themselves an uncomfortable ride and which could be seen to lap the water when the beck was in spate.

As explained on page xii there is little limestone in the Central Lakes, apart from a narrow band of Coniston stone that runs diagonally across, but a wide curve of limestone encircles the whole area, from Silverdale through Kendal and Shap to Caldbeck, Cockermouth and Egremont, providing some very pretty scenery. The colours – green turf, white stone, a whole range of yellows from the cadmium of gorse to the Indian yellow of the autumn birches and the gamboge of bracken – are much sprightlier than the more subdued, even sullen, tones of the Lake District fells.

In greater masses – the scarp of Whitbarrow, the gorge of High Cup Nick, near Appleby, or further off, at Goresdale Scar as painted by James Ward – limestone country can be dramatic enough, but here, in the Silverdale peninsula, on a smaller scale, it is downright light-hearted. The peninsula in fact consists of three hills, Warton Crag, Silverdale and Arnside Knot, separated by Silverdale Moss and Leighton Moss. Only the northernmost of these, Arnside, is within the strict boundaries of this guide, but the countryside of the three is indistinguishable. The steep-sided hills are covered in deciduous woods, pretty at all times of the year. A large hill fort sits on the top of Warton Crag and Warton itself is an attractive village with a good church and an ancient rectory. At Yealand Conyers, Leighton Hall is now open to the public. The Gillows, an ancient Lancastrian recusant family, rebuilt a modest eighteenth-century house, itself incorporating a ruinous pele tower, in the Gothic fashion. Robert Gillow was one of the first English joiners to use mahogany, and Leighton houses many beautiful examples of his firm's work, which epitomises the restrained tradition of English furniture making. Set in a dramatic amphitheatre of smooth green turf, the pale grey limestone of Leighton is memorable.

Leighton is still Lancashire, and the first village that can truthfully be claimed as ours is Beetham, just across what is now the Cumbrian border. In the 1973 local reorganization, Cumberland and Westmorland were amalgamated to form the new county of Cumbria. The Furness district, which used to belong to Lancashire, and the Trough of Bowland, previously part of Yorkshire, were also pulled into the new county. This aroused considerable local resentment; Appleby, which was the county town of Westmorland for many centuries, insisted on rechristening itself Appleby-in-Westmorland, Cumbria, but it has to be admitted that the new arrangement does, at least in this case, make sense and that the name of Cumbria has the merit of antiquity.

The first objects of remark inside the new county boundary are the ruins of **Beetham Hall**, just to the left of the A6. In its time the Hall was quite an extensive fortification, as the architectural details – the presence of a chapel and a hall, together with the curtain wall – indicate. Such refinements make it a small castle rather than a large pele, and Leland, who described it in the sixteenth century, refers to there being 'much Gothic work about . . .' Although some window tracery of about 1380 remains, bits of the castle are now so mixed with those of the farm that it is not easy to distinguish between them. Beetham and the neighbouring peles are the results of the Scottish raids during Edward II's reign, which swept round by sea and devastated the coasts of Cumbria. Previous fighting had been on the Borders themselves, which at their nearest here are some sixty miles to the north, and the ferocity of these unprecedented incursions stimulated feverish fortification. But after Edward III restored order many peles became abandoned or domesticated, expanded into permanent dwellings. Most great Lakeland houses – Dallam, Hutton Forest, Levens, Sizergh, Muncaster, Dalemain – have a pele as their core.

The Beethams who built the house picked the losing side at Bosworth, and their land, like so much more in the region, was given by Henry VII to the Stanleys. For rather more than a couple of centuries now the Wilsons of Dallam Tower have been the largest landowners in the neighbourhood; by local standards they are just settling in nicely.

The A6 sweeps past Beetham, missing the church by a hair's breadth. There is a convenient car park opposite, belonging to the

Wheatsheaf pub, which provides acceptable meals and beer so that the obligatory visit is no hardship. Some hardship might be encountered if any but the most slim-legged of visitors attempt to enter by the sheep style that leads into the churchyard.

Norman Nicholson, not always enthusiastic about churches, quite rightly thought Beetham something special:

> It has a sort of prettiness which at first seems to belong to a shilling calendar, with a setting which might be copied for an antimacassar – road nearby, inn, big trees with the river behind, and a trellis-avenue up to the front porch, full of the red curly-hair of rambler roses. But you realize that the church has a deeper beauty which is not spoilt by this prettiness, just as a beautiful woman is not spoilt by ribbons and trinkets. The stone is so old that it has worn smooth, and the tower looks as if it had come off a wedding-cake, with a little sugary spike at each corner. Yet inside the air is grave and rich, like organ music.

It was here in 1900 that Dame Clara Butt was married to Robert Kennerly Rumford, and attended by Ivor Novello as a page boy.

Dame Clara was outstanding in many ways: six foot two in her socks, massive of figure and with a unique contralto voice. She was trained initially by a bass singer, and, as records of *Land of Hope and Glory* – which she inspired – prove, had a voice of incomparable range and volume which was, as one critic remarked, 'more remarkable for its broad effect rather than its artistic finesse'. Mr Rumford was also a singer, and much of their happily married life was spent touring together.

A less gay event is commemorated by a plaque inside the church to the memory of one Jonathan Bottomley, 'a clothier of Halifax, who unhappily perished on these sands in 1787' – a reminder that we are only a couple of miles from the sea, although at Beetham, protected by the limestone hills, there is no hint of its proximity. The fate of Mr Bottomley suggests that commercial travellers were, then as now, always in danger of meeting an untimely end in their efforts to do a spot of business. St. Michael's was formerly St Lioba's, a more interesting and rarer dedication. Lioba, who was said to be 'beautiful as the angels', wrote poetry, and became Abbess of Bischofsheim. She was a Devon girl, cousin to St Boniface, the first English missionary martyr, and is buried next to him in the Abbey of Fulda. She now has a shrine, up the hill towards Slackhead, but surely Lioba deserves a church of her own.

There is some old glass inside, and there was more until it was smashed by Fairfax's troopers during the interregnum, egged on by a local schoolmaster, one Richard Sill. The best that survives is in the west window of the tower, not easy to see, but perfect fifteenth-century work, of astonishingly fresh colour and vigour. The modern glass in the east window is soppy, a long way after Holman Hunt, but the pretty Hutton window in the south-west corner of the nave shows what pre-Raphaelite work can be like when it behaves itself.

Pevsner believes the church tower to be late twelfth-century, but with all appropriate diffidence I would place the lower stages at least a hundred years earlier. Both the masonry of the exterior, with its typical Anglo-Saxon long-and-short work, and one interior column, argue a pre-Conquest origin. But it is unwise to be dogmatic in the north about dates; fashions often took a long time to penetrate as far as this, and it is easy to be some way adrift. Even as late as the beginning of the twentieth century the news of Queen Victoria's death apparently took three years to reach Beetham since the church school bears the inscription 'VR 1904'. Beetham is in Domesday Book and near the boundary of the first Norman settlement which ended with the Barony of Kendal. Westmorland and Cumberland, north of Kendal, were at the time of the Conquest nominally part of the Scottish kingdom of Strathclyde and too sparsely inhabited to attract the attention of the first Norman wave. It was only in William Rufus's day that most of Cumbria became English.

A pleasant woodland path (signposted to Fairy Steps) leads through good samples of limestone pavement to Hazelslack Tower, another pele. The fact that so many fortifications – Arnside, Hazelslack, Leighton, Beetham, Dallam, Heversham – lie within a mile or so of each other indicates the seriousness with which the threat of raids was received, and suggests the devastation that the early fourteenth-century incursions had caused.

The oldest part of Beetham Parsonage Farm was originally a wing of the priest's house, which was known as the College of St Mary. Some interesting farm buildings have been preserved, including a practicable dovecot and a horse walk, where horses were used to power a huge capstan drive to a threshing mill. Beetham parish used to stretch across the other side of the Kent, the channel of which was much narrower, and the owners of Parsonage Farm had the right to collect peats from the marshes opposite. Round the corner from the farm is the Heron Corn Mill, a working mill on a pretty stretch of the Bela, which is a famous brown trout stream. The mill is open in the summer, and by appointment at other times. It is remarkable to see how a modest stream can power such bulky machinery, and with so little apparent effort and noise.

From Beetham a road to the coast goes bang through the park of Dallam Tower, right in front of the house itself, which is a very pretty early eighteenth-century building, the home of many generations of Wilsons. There was a good deal of alteration work done at the beginning of the nineteenth century by George Webster of Kendal, including an elegant winter garden, an early example of a conservatory. Webster also designed some pretty estate buildings, including a Tuscan house for the Wilsons' fallow deer.

The road continues to the seashore near **Arnside**, which, before the county was abolished, used to be Westmorland's only seaside town. Loitering in order to enjoy the view south along the estuary can be hazardous to drivers since the prospect over the sands to the Lake District hills is apt to deflect the attention. It is wiser to stop and admire it. Under the sea wall sheep graze patches of grass, marking the progress of the tide by their movement. As they concentrate upon their sparse fodder they shift in a resigned fashion, moving only when the water begins to slosh over the bit of grass that has been engaging their attention. The Cartmel shore is not far distant, and invites a walk over the sands, but this necessitates a tricky crossing over the channel of the River Kent which is not to be advised. Only the most dedicated of birders would want to go far from the shore since most of the waders are obliging enough to come close inland and can be observed in perfect safety from the promenade. There are redshank, oyster catchers, sheldrake, and the odd curlew coming down from the moors for a plodge.

In the nineteenth century it was reported: 'Beetham sands are well adapted for bathing, and though there is only water sufficient for this healthy recreation during 3 or 4 of the highest tides in each fortnight, several visitors come here in the summer, the air being remarkably salubrious and the scenery in the neighbourhood beautifully diversified. There is said to be a dangerous eddy in the river called the Dallam Wheel: on one occasion three brothers were drowned here trying to save each other.'

I would not recommend swimming there at any time, but a cautious visiting trailer sailor can do something when the tides serve. Arnside has a sailing club, which would doubtless give advice; necessary advice, for Morecambe Bay is very much *Riddle of the Sands* sailing, with constantly shifting channels, only suitable for boats that like taking the ground. Arnside is a place for the retired and for quiet family holidays; no junketing, discos or hot dogs, but some good Victorian seaside villas, one of which is now the youth hostel, and what must be the shortest pier in England, built to accommodate railway steamers which never came. It has now been twice destroyed in storms, but each time rebuilt by Arnsiders anxious for the reputation of the town.

The great attraction is the view from Arnside Knott, the hill in the possession of the National Trust. From here, with the help of the orientation table, the view over the lake hills can be appreciated. It is a magnificent perspective. Black Combe is tucked away round the corner but Coniston Old Man stands out in the background with the precipitous crags of Whitbarrow Scar nearer at hand. Arnside Tower lies in the valley south of the Knott, and is something of an oddity among pele towers, being built well after the initial nervousness about the return of the Scots had passed, sometime near the end of the fifteenth century. It looks military enough, but was planned from the first as a reasonably commodious dwelling, and probably illustrates the ancient conservatism of Westmerians. Remains of a bear were found in a cave on the Knott; it must have been good bear country, very like the Cumberland hills in Tennessee and Kentucky.

It is remarkable how quickly the port of **Silverdale** has become inaccessible; as late as 1930 boats of quite reasonable size could land at the cove. Today the sea is a good half mile away, separated by some very permanent-looking saltmarshes. There are good reasons for this rapid change, for Morecambe Bay sands are renowned for their instability. In a recent storm the channel of the River Kent shifted entirely from one side of the bay to the other. It is therefore quite possible that Silverdale could become a port again. It has the essentials – a couple of pubs.

Apart from the remains of an abortive attempt in the 1860s to build a barrage across the sands to Bolton, Jenny Brown's Point, the southerly tip of the peninsula, is well preserved. The coast down there belongs to the National Trust, and looks very much as it must have done when it was Mrs Gaskell's favourite viewpoint. Mrs Gaskell, that still underestimated novelist, took her holidays at Lindeth Tower, just inland from Jenny Brown's Point, where she was able to look out over the 'bay with its slow moving train of crossers led over the treacherous sands by the guide, a square man sitting stern on his white horse (the better to be seen when daylight ebbs). The said guide, Carter by name, is descended lineally from he who guided

Edward I over on his march to Scotland, and was given by him a coat of arms, and a grant of land. On foggy nights the guide, (who has let people drown before now, who could not pay his fee, but who writes 'gentleman' after his name, thanks to Edward I) may be heard blowing an old ram's horn trumpet, to guide by the sound . . .'

Charlotte and Emily Brontë had a holiday from their school at Stone Bower, now a home for the elderly disabled. Apart from a few cottages going back to smuggling days the village is mainly Victorian holiday development, like Grange or Felixstowe. St John's church reflects Victorian prosperity: spacious and expensively finished, with thoughtful craftsmanship. The capitals of the nave columns, for example, illustrate verses from the Book of Revelation. It replaces a decent square building of the 1820s, described at the time as forming 'a pleasing object in the retired rocky vale in which it is situated', now well converted into small houses. The earlier church was apparently abandoned when the Methodists built a larger and handsomer chapel a few yards away: such presumption from the Wesleyans could hardly have been welcomed.

The passage to the Lakes over the sands only began to lose popularity in 1846, when the Furness Railway Company started its operations. The initial rail journey was short enough, a few miles from Piel Pier on Roa Island to Dalton, north of Barrow, but, in conjunction with a steamer service from Fleetwood, was enough to end the monopoly of the Sands route, although it continued to be used by poorer travellers: even eleven years later twelve men were drowned when crossing Morecambe Bay. In 1857 the railway link was completed with the opening of the Levens viaduct, connecting the Furness railway with the main Glasgow to London line. In spite of an annual payment by the railway company of £20 'to the guide for travellers across the Levens estuary' the communities which had depended upon attending to the needs of travellers over the sands began to decline and those now served by the new railways began to flourish.

Milnthorpe was one of the towns caught by the railways, when its modest prosperity as a port was terminated by the silting up of the River Bela caused by building the Kent viaduct. It had been intended to have an opening section in the viaduct to allow ships upstream, but this proved impracticable: the gap was closed, and the water traffic through Milnthorpe ceased. There must have been some relief among the inhabitants when this happened, since an important part of the trade was in gunpowder, carried downstream in barges which caused a number of nasty accidents. The 'Mil' bit of Milnthorpe originally referred to the water mills on the River Bela, but in the eighteenth century there was a quite important sheeting production carried out. There is little of interest now beyond a spiky, angular, nineteenth-century church dedicated to St Thomas in honour of its patron, Mrs Thomasina Richardson.

While Milnthorpe is still, in spite of the relief afforded by the motorway, bisected by the A6, **Heversham** has escaped dismemberment; it has been bypassed (just) and deserves a stop. St Peter's church was an important monastery as far back as the eighth century, and a relic of those times exists in the shape of a cross shaft fragment with work similar to those of Rothwell and Bewcastle. W. G. Collingwood calls this 'a most precious monument . . . as battered as a Parthenon slab, but no less classic in its art, you can tell at once that the sculptor knew his business . . . the grape bunches among their graceful stems, the "little foxes that spoil the vines" with bushy tails and pricked ears, are work of that first great English school of art taught by Italian masters in the eighth and ninth centuries', and deduces from this fragmentary evidence that Milnthorpe was a flourishing Dark-Age port: a bold assumption, but it is a good piece of carving. Tilred, Abbot in the early tenth century, seems to have found the place not to his liking and became anxious to move on, since he made a gift of some lands in County Durham in order to be consecrated Abbot of Borham and admitted to the cloisters of Lindisfarne.

Outwardly the church displays no signs of antiquity, since it was almost completely destroyed by fire in 1601 and very firmly restored in 1868. Inside, however, a bit of twelfth-century and later work can be seen, with some pieces of seventeenth-century glass, a huge fifteenth-century chest and a nice little effigy of Lady Dorothy Bellingham. An eighteenth-century achiever is commemorated: the Rev. William Preston, DD, who combined a fellowship of Trinity College, Cambridge, with being Rector of Oakhampton, *chargé d'affaires* at the courts of Vienna and Naples, private secretary to the Duke of Rutland, and Bishop of Killala and of Fernes.

A hundred yards away, on the other side of the A6, the Blue Bell is a road-house sort of pub with a restaurant attached: rather glossy but welcoming, and with respectable food. Heversham Hall, which has a fourteenth-century core, is almost opposite – another of the towers built for defence against the Scots.

On the other side of Heversham, up the hill from the church, are the remains of the original grammar school, and a well-preserved cock pit. Cock fighting is still, it is said, a favoured sport, if it can rightly be given that name, in certain parts of Cumbria: certainly game cocks are bred with great interest. 'Mains' were normally held in barns or public houses but, in the eighteenth century at any rate, some were out of doors. On a more elevated plane the Heversham village institute is called the Athenaeum, a name proudly chiselled in a slab of local stone.

Evelyn Waugh once said that all good houses lie on a road or river, by which he meant that they were not surrounded by parks in the vulgar eighteenth-century manner, and by this, or any other standards, **Levens** is a very good house. It has a road, a river and a park, and could never be called anything but well bred; it is everything an American tourist might wish to see in an English country house – ancient windows, oak panelling, huge chimneys, fine old furniture, an extraordinary topiary garden, several ghosts and a couple of family legends: and a collection of steam engines for eccentric good measure. Like Dallam and so many other houses it started off as a pele tower, and here the original construction of the house is still very obvious. The pele was expanded and rebuilt towards the end of the sixteenth century by one James Bellingham, who introduced the splendid plasterwork and panelling. His work, although later than that at Sizergh up the road, is bouncier and less sophisticated, the sort of thing that one thinks of as essentially northern-English sixteenth-century work. The jolliest is in the small drawing room, the overmantel of which depicts

> the Five Sences stand portrayted here,
> The Elements Foure and Seasons of the Yeare.
> Samson supports the one side as in Rage
> the other Hercules in Like Equipage.

The same room has some Narciso Diaz pictures and a nice Sickert, and all sorts of oddments, including the Duke of Wellington's watch and a clasp from Napoleon's cloak.

A century later the estate had to be sold when the great-grandson of James Bellingham lost his fortune through gambling, a fact which gave rise to the tradition that Levens was won over the card table. It was, however, bought, and for the not inconsiderable sum of £24,000, by a kinsman, James Grahme. Colonel Grahme was one of nature's survivors; although a staunch supporter of the Stuarts and having served in Louis XIV's army – he was one of those who accompanied James II on his last flight to Faversham – he made his peace with Dutch William after the Glorious Revolution. He was elected to Parliament after a decent interval in 1702, where he remained for a quarter of a century, dying in 1730 at the age of eighty-one. Colonel Grahme's service to James severely damaged his own fortunes but before that event he restored Levens in the handsomest of fashions. The dining room, perhaps the finest in the house, is all his work. It is hung with glowing Cordoba leather and contains a fine set of contemporary chairs, forming a perfect period piece.

Since then the house has remained very nearly unaltered, doubtless due to the fact that although Levens has been sold twice it has remained within the same family alliance of Redmonds, Bellinghams, Grahmes, Howards and Bagots, the latest of whom still live here. The Levens family have displayed consistently good taste, and as a result the house is full of fine things: an extensive collection of De Wints, a real Rubens, Chippendale candelabra, and some good china and silver. The most agreeable of all these must be the Levens Constables, twenty-inch-high long-stemmed ale glasses, from which the toast 'Luck to Levens whilst the Kent flows' was traditionally drunk in twenty-one-year-old Morocco beer.

Robin Bagot has now retired from running the estate, which has been taken over by his son Hal. Robin kept up the tradition of Levens craftsmanship by making his own harpsichords and starting a series of recitals in which some very distinguished artists indeed have performed.

The most extraordinary part of Levens is the topiary gardens. These, too, are due to Colonel Grahme, who sought the advice of one Jerome Beaumont, the great landscape designer of the day, who had served both Louis XIV and James II. All Beaumont's English work, and he did much, has now disappeared except for that at Levens. Three hundred years later, the topiary garden has grown beyond the point of anything Beaumont could have imagined. The effect is wild, surrealist and quite bizarre: huge abstract shapes, pyramids, columns, reminiscent of monstrous chess men, give the alleys and lawns the air of legends; one could imagine a unicorn appearing at any time round the next corner to lay its head in the lap of any convenient virgin. The original formal and precise seventeenth-century French garden has become English, and northern-English at that. It makes an entirely correct setting for the Levens ghosts which include a grey gipsy, a worrying figure who, being turned away from the house to starve, cursed the family, saying that no son should inherit the house until the River Kent ceased to flow and a white fawn was born in the herd of Levens deer: and convincingly since 1680 only once has a son inherited the house from his father. The pink lady is an altogether less malevolent spectre and pops out at any time for odd reasons. Nor is the black dog sinister, unless his sudden appearance on the stairs in front of people causes them to trip up. Robin Bagot, who is still happily with us, has been heard playing the harpsichord at a time when he was in fact miles away. He promised to attempt the same thing after death to see whether there might be anything in it. Although Levens is open to the public it succeeds in a way few relatively small country houses have done in retaining the true atmosphere of a house that has been lived in by the same agreeable family for centuries.

Like the gardens, Levens Park is a seventeenth-century survival: the walk down the superb avenue of trees takes you out near the Kendal link road, where a turn to the right will bring you to the tow path of the Lancaster canal. If this is followed for a few hundred yards the entrance to the Hincaster tunnel is reached, a fine piece of early nineteenth-century canal construction. The hall may be regained by taking the road from the entrance near the farm.

The Kendal to Lancaster canal was spectacular, fifty miles of canal with only one flight of locks at Tewitfield. Its closure to navigation upstream of the locks was one of the worst pieces of state vandalism of recent years. Rennie's remarkable engineering enabled fast packet services to operate between Kendal and Preston at the unprecedented speed of ten miles an hour. The canal boats, drawn by trotting horses, carried signs fixed to the forestay saying that they would cut the tow ropes of anything that did not get out of their way immediately. When the Tewitfield flight of locks was reached, passengers had to change boats in order to keep up with the schedule and were made to hurry up or down the flight.

The canal is in water south of Tewitfield, near Warton, but this section is out of the scope of this guide. North of Tewitfield there are still sections which can be used by canoeists, but from Stainton north, just after the Hincaster tunnel, the whole canal has been destroyed.

The Park also has an interesting ring cairn just by the river, not shown on the Ordnance Survey map, which marks a Bronze-Age dwelling, possibly a funeral hut, inside a circular perimeter. Thousands of flints were discovered here, suggesting a site of great antiquity.

The river in the park is not, as might be expected, the Leven, which is some way over to the west and nowhere near Levens, but the Kent, which waters Kentdale.

Sizergh Castle is only a short distance away, but a temptation in the opposite direction is constituted by the Hare and Hounds in Levens village – an ancient pub with solid food and a view across the Lyth valley.

Two famous sixteenth-century manor houses only a mile or so apart present an opportunity which should not be missed even if it puts a strain on the appetite. Both evolved in very much the same manner, and the contrasts are illuminating.

Castle is a bit pretentious as a description for Sizergh. Like Levens and Hutton John, it is a respectable large manor house built around a pele. No fortifications exist that would justify the name castle, or have ever existed, and until quite recently the house was generally known as Sizergh Hall.

Even more than Levens, Sizergh epitomizes the continuity of Westmorland life: it went as part of his wife's marriage portion to Sir William Strickland in 1239, and Stricklands have remained there ever since, although the estate was given to the National Trust in 1950. The house has grown with the family over the years; everything you see is Strickland work, from the massive pele tower built about 1350 to the rock garden laid out in 1926. About a century after the pele tower a Great Hall was added, and a hundred years after that two long wings. The southern one of these contained a single huge room, nearly 120 feet long, in which all the servants lived and had their being. When Walter Strickland, who was responsible for this work, mustered his men to fight the Scots, he took 290 mounted and fully armed men with him, the largest contingent by far of any in the county. Walter spent lavishly on the house and endowed it with what makes Sizergh pre-eminent among early Elizabethan houses, its magnificent woodwork. The quality is unmatched: nothing of the bucolic naivety that often characterizes carving of this period, but an elegant sophistication that seems much more French than English, especially northern English.

The entrance hall is the ground floor of the mid-fifteenth-century Great Hall, which originally extended the full present two storeys. This proved too much for Tudor tastes, and the present first floor was installed: the entrance screens of 1558 are the first one sees of Sizergh's fine woodwork.

The main rooms are on the first floor: the dining room is the first storey of the fourteenth-century pele tower, now divided in two,

Sizergh: the dining room

Lowther Village: what council houses *might* be like

Levens: the surrealist quality of the garden in winter

Kendal: a ginnel, close or wynd

forming this room and the adjacent Queen's Room. Both rooms have complete oak panelling with armorial overmantels, but it becomes apparent that the furnishings really do not equal the setting. There are some individually good pieces, but the effect is distinctly patchy. The drawing room, which forms the Tudor insertion into the Great Hall, is very pleasant, with a south-west aspect over the terrace, but the pictures are all family portraits of limited interest. At the other end of the drawing room the fifteenth-century tower has, like the earlier pele, been divided into two rooms; the stone parlour is a pleasant little sitting room, and the Elizabethan dining room has the finest woodwork in a house famous for it, together with some decent furniture.

A comparison with the dining room carvings can be made in the Linenfold Lobby, which is at least a generation earlier, and that on the overmantel of the Bindloss Room on the floor above, which is sixty years later.

The best room of this house ought also to be on this floor. Before 1891 the Inlaid Chamber had magnificent oak panelling in poplar and bog-oak, some of the finest in the country, but that year the family, stumped for cash, sold it to the Victoria and Albert Museum for £1000. But the plaster work on the ceiling and frieze could not be removed and is quite splendid.

The lavish carving of the public rooms forms a striking contrast to the stark grandeur of the pele itself. This is the largest and most complex of peles, having a couple of extra turrets that almost give it the air of a real keep. The second floor rises thirty feet to the roof, and contains a fine collection of sixteenth-century furniture, the most remarkable of which is a set of benches which may date from as early as 1530. A two-handed sword, which is mentioned in the earliest sixteenth-century inventory of Sizergh's contents, hangs on the wall. This may be genuine fourteenth-century, or a rather later copy, and is what the Scots would call a claymore – the *Claidheamh mòr* – the great sword. The term is often misapplied to basket-hilted broadswords, but the real claymore is just such a terrible weapon as this.

The most interesting objects in Sizergh may well not be on show until the National Trust solves their insurance and preservation problems. As well as a fine Meissen tea service these include some Stuart memorabilia: a Goanese bedspread, which belonged to James II (Bombay had just passed to the English crown as part of Catherine of Braganza's dowry), Queen Catherine's Privy Purse, and the records of Robert Strickland, Treasurer to the exiled Queen at St Germain.

The Strickland family were recusants, and remained faithful to the Stuarts, with consequent damage to their fortunes. Sir Thomas accompanied James II on his exile to St Germain en Laye, a relic of which is a pretty but amateurish painting showing the young Prince James hand in hand with little Francis Strickland, Sir Thomas's cousin. Another cousin was Admiral Sir Roger Strickland who, after a distinguished career, was sacked for provoking a mutiny by attempting to have mass said aboard his flagship. Sir Thomas's younger son, Thomas John Francis, was more successful. Brought up with his parents in France, he became successively Abbot of the rich foundation of St Pierre de Preaux and Bishop of Namur, but having an accurately unfavourable view of the competence and prospects of the House of Stuart did his best to reconcile English Catholics to the Hanoverian succession, and was actually employed as a British government agent at Rome, keeping an eye on the Pretender. Lord Hervey described him as being famed for dissolute conduct wherever he went, but Hervey ('the bug with gilded wings') is never an impartial observer.

More recently members of the family have been great figures in Malta. Commander Walter married a Maltese heiress in 1858; their son Gerald became prominent in both English and Maltese politics as the first and last Baron Strickland, Prime Minister of Malta. During the difficult days between the wars he fought against Fascist influence, and founded the *Times of Malta,* of which his daughter Mabel was outspoken editor for more than thirty years, and the best known and respected personage on the island, remembered affectionately by generations of service visitors.

Lord Strickland had the gardens laid out: the rock garden, which is constructed from local limestone, is particularly good. It is the work of the Hayes family of Ambleside, a firm founded in the eighteenth century, which still has a spectacular presence in that town. The weathered stone and water trickling through dwarf conifers is Japanese in scale, a secluded microcosm of the mountainous landscape a few miles off.

Apart from a handsome pair of gate pillars the only earlier feature of the gardens is an eighteenth-century 'hot' wall, limestone faced with bricks, and having a southern aspect. In the corner between the wall and the house a Brown Turkey fig flourishes, witnessing the mild climate of this part of the country.

On the other side of the main road, by the banks of the River Kent, is a well-arranged caravan site in the grounds of the old gunpowder

works. It was essential in planning such works, to site the manufacturing and storage buildings well apart, so that an explosion would
not lead to complete destruction. The buildings themselves were
given solid walls and light roofs, in order to direct the blast upwards.
The greatest risk ran in the movement of the finished explosives
down to the estuary at Milnthorpe.

Enough of the old plant remains, now mingled with handsome
trees, to make it a delectable spot, where rabbits and squirrels play
among the nearly invisible caravans. Fishing permits for this beautiful stretch of the Kent are obtainable from the caravan site.

Kendal

The A6 and the A591 divide between Levens and Sizergh, and a
difficult choice has to be made between diverting to the west and
exploring the historic Furness area, or pressing on to Kendal and
Windermere.

Kendal was described in 1793 as 'a remarkably neat and well built
marketing and manufacturing town, and stands in a pleasant and
healthy situation', a description still apt enough. It must be among
the best of towns in which to live, and is everything that a small
provincial centre should be. There are comfortable houses with gardens a couple of minutes' walk from the centre, shops which provide
the best coffee in Cumbria, and the biggest selection of books, local
industries, a lively arts centre, one of the finest galleries in the country and striking views wherever you look.

Kendal has always been cross that Appleby, a much smaller place,
was the county town, with such amenities as a habitable castle, two
Members of Parliament, and an execution chamber. But Appleby's
charter was thirteenth-century, and Kendal's only Elizabethan, and
Westmorland clings to its traditions. In due course economic facts
came to be reflected: Kendal recovered much more quickly from the
Scottish ravages of the thirteenth and fourteenth centuries; in the
1832 Reform Act Kendal got a Member of Parliament, while Appleby
lost both of theirs, and finally Kendal became the county town of
Westmorland, which the inhabitants always thought it ought to
have been. Their satisfaction was short-lived, since the 1972
reorganization which produced a united Cumbria then gave the distinction to Carlisle, right at the other end of the county and
considered, in Kendal, as a suburb of Newcastle. Kendal however did
at one time enjoy the dignity of having a duchess, which is more than
Appleby ever had, even if she was Melinisa von Schulenberg, the

unattractive, insatiably ambitious mistress of that unamiable monarch, George I.

Apart from an intrusive gasworks the Industrial Revolution left Kendal undamaged, and the best of the old town was preserved. The origins of its prosperity, like that of Lavenham or Sudbury, lay in the wool trade, but, unlike most East Anglian towns, Kendal managed to prosper when that trade declined. The products were different, which may have helped, for even at its best Kendal cloth could never be the equal of fine Suffolk broadcloth. Kendal Green was a workaday material, suitable for those 'knaves' whom Falstaff claimed to have set about him on Shooters Hill, its distinctive colour coming from a dye of woad and dyer's greenweed (*genista tinctoria*), which, in spite of its name, is yellow.

There is an etymological curiosity attached to Kendal fabrics. Although all woollen, they were generically known as Kendal cottons: this has no reference to cotton cloth, and indeed the derivation may be quite different; it is used to describe the napped surface of the cloth. This brushing together of the fibres is also the source of the expression 'to cotton (on) to' someone or something. Admirers of Kendal have tried to establish the existence of a superior sort of cloth on the strength of an order 'for X elne of Kentdale to be ane cote to the King'. But this was in 1505 when the King was that miserly Welsh upstart Henry Tudor, only too likely to require the cheapest sort of garments. No, there are too many references to Kendal cloth – the ironic 'His costly clothing was threadbare Kendal Green,' for example – to permit it to have been anything other than the most plebeian of fabrics.

A less famous Kendal fabric was bleached white, and sometimes decorated with coloured spots, when it was known as 'ermine'. According to a Flodden ballad, the Kendal archers wore white:

> The left-hand wing with all his rout
> The lusty Lord Dacre did lead
> With him the boys of Kendal stout
> With milk-white coats and crosses red:
> These are the bows of Kendal bold
> Who fierce will fight, and never flee.

For once the ballad was accurate. Surrey, who commanded the English forces, reported that the 'hardy Kendal men "went no foot back for them" '.

Kendal later became the centre for hand-knitted stockings, an industry which suffered a terrible blow when the army abandoned breeches for trousers. Much of the work was brought in from Dentdale, made by 'the terrible knitters of Dent'.

The town's importance stems from its geographical position at the end of the high road from the south. Going is easy as far as Kendal, on a long level stretch; indeed, when Rennie came to build the canal from Kendal to Lancaster he needed only one set of locks on a fifty-mile cut. Northwards things begin to get difficult, the choice lying between the Lune Gorge and Orton Scar, which is the route the M6 now takes as far as Tebay, or the terrible haul up Shap Fell. Any Lake District traffic going south by land found its way to Kendal over an intricate network of packhorse routes from the catchment area, the extent of which counterbalanced the relatively low value of the produce. In the eighteenth century 350 packhorses carried their wares every week into the town.

Kendal church is therefore as impressive a structure as any in Suffolk or Norfolk, with Great Yarmouth and Abingdon one of the widest in the country. Right at the southern edge of the old town, it makes a good place to start an exploration, with car parks convenient for both it and the museums. The west front is not spectacular – the view from the east, across the river, is better – but the interior is full of interest. A rectangular space, 140 feet by 103 feet, is divided by 4 arcades, with 32 columns. There is no great variation of either width or of height, apart from a clerestory level on the nave bay, and the effect of constantly changing vistas is fascinating, like a northern Cordoba.

There are no individually magnificent attractions, but lots of pleasing details remain even after a fairly thorough 1850 restoration. The west door leads straight into the Flemish aisle, built in the late fourteenth century to accommodate the Flemish weavers who had settled in Kendal. A series of chapels at the east end of the aisle starts with the Parr chapel, built by the family of King Henry's surviving wife – Aragon divorced; Boleyn beheaded; Seymour died; Cleves divorced; Howard beheaded; Parr survived. Katherine Parr was a tough little Kendal lass, who had seen off two husbands before she married Henry at the age of thirty-one. Even when Queen Regent, during Henry's absence abroad, she insisted on adding her maiden initials KP to her royal signature in a typically Border gesture of independence. She had not wanted to marry Henry – 'better to be his mistress than his wife,' she said, but coped with him remarkably well. Herself a woman of learning and culture, Katherine took pains to

71

encourage her stepdaughters, Mary and Elizabeth, and had a book of her own published, an unusual achievement for an English queen at any time. The female heads above the windows are her badge.

The Strickland chapel comes next, behind an early sixteenth-century screen; it contains a later table tomb of Walter Strickland of Sizergh, who died in 1656. Apart from some armorial glass in the Bellingham chapel, a crowned head in the window above is the only ancient bit of stained glass in the church. Among the rest is a pretty Virgin and roses by M. A. Scott, and a pair of windows by J. C. N. Bewsey, a pupil of Charles Kempe.

The biggest of the four aisle chapels is the northernmost, that of the Bellingham family, which also serves as the chapel of the Border Regiment, the 55th Foot. Alan Bellingham's brass of 1577, in full armour, is notable in an area thin on brasses, but those of Sir Roger and his wife are nineteenth-century replacements of lost originals. A Chinese flag and bell commemorate the storming of Chusan in the inglorious Opium War of 1839–42, which was sparked off by the arrest of Lancelot Dent, 'the greatest opium-smuggler of them all', whose family lived at Flass, up by Shap (see page 301).

Hanging on the north wall is a helmet and broadsword meant to have belonged to Robin 'the Devil' Philipson, who rode into the church in pursuit of his enemy, Colonel Briggs. The sword looks to be of the 1650s, but the helmet is of a century earlier, unlikely to have been used by so prominent a knight.

The nave is overpowered by an immense suspended wok-stand, overhanging the central altar; there may be a liturgical reason for this, but aesthetically little excuse. The twentieth century has also contributed a group, the 'Family of Man' by Josephine de Vasconcellos: many local churches have work by this accomplished sculptor, which is much admired, but I for one would prefer something a little more astringent. Flaxman's memorial to Zachary Hubbersty (the name should have been snapped up by Dickens, but wasn't) shows a bereft widow and six children comforted by an angel, and is in a similar vein.

There are some good inscriptions. To the Rev. Mr Tyrer, by himself, confusingly active and passive in mood:

> London Bred me, Westminster fed me,
> Cambridge sped me, my sister wed me,
> Study taught me, living sought me,
> Learning brought me, Kendal caught me,

Labour pressed me, sickness distressed me,
Death oppressed me, the grave possessed me,
God just gave me, Christ did save me,
Earth did crave me, and Heaven would have me.

And to Michael Stanford, a seventeenth-century rector, and F(
Christ's College, Cambridge, described by an admirer as '
Hooker' and *'Fanaticorum Malleus'*. The fanatics were Q
especially Richard Frankland, who ran the Natland Acade
whom, Stanford was extremely suspicious: 'What his de$
therein (in conforming) I cannot divine except it be to sue 1
scholars to pay to him.'

Social distinctions are preserved in the memorial to
Bateman, who married Roger, a clothier, but was herself daugh
a yeoman, and died 'aged 26 years 5 months and od days'.

Other details to watch for are the attractive painted angels ii
roof of the north aisle. Angel roofs are much less common in
north than in East Anglia, and this is altogether simpler than su
masterpiece as that of St Wendreda's, March; but the Kendal an,
are undeniably attractive. Their painting was the idea of the 'H
band of the church', who chose the colours to match the adjoin
window; however unauthentic this may be – the angels probal
were never meant to be painted – the dark ceiling is much enliven
by them.

Until the nineteenth-century restoration Kendal church was muc
more colourful, for its walls had been decorated two hundred yea
previously by the painter James Addison, who 'filled every availabl
space with texts of Scriptures, cherubim and seraphim, green hissin;
serpents and flying dragons, the whole garnished and embroiderec
with sundry quaint devices in green, yellow and black painted on the
whitewash. The exterior walls were likewise decorated in yellow and
black margins some five inches wide on the roughcast, extending
round all the doors and windows, up the angles of the walls and
buttresses, and completely round the steeple.'

Abbot Hall, next door to the church, but with its own car park, has
been since 1962 part of the Kendal Museum complex, now one of the
finest in the country, showing how much can be done with limited
resources. The core is the house itself, built in 1759 for Colonel
Wilson of Dallam Tower perhaps actually by John Carr, the architect
of Harewood House, but more probably in the style of that self-
taught genius. The ground floor is given over to the permanent

collection of furniture and pictures, which includes the largest collection of Romneys to be found anywhere. Capable of a much wider range than usually appreciated – his drawings can be powerfully savage – Romney learnt his craft in Kendal, painting portraits at 6 or 12 guineas according to size, before becoming a London success. There is also a magnificent Cotman watercolour of Norwich market, which must make them terribly jealous back in Norfolk.

Temporary exhibitions are housed in well-lit first-floor galleries, and are often distinguished and always interesting, largely due to the skill of Mary Burkett, curator from 1968 to 1986, who dragged Kendal into the mainstream of English artistic life. A surer mark of success than the awards that have flooded in is that the permanent picture collection is so large as to permit only a fraction of it to be shown; apart from topographical works there are enough good modern paintings to fill a major gallery, including many of the Glasgow School, and the best collection anywhere of Kurt Schwitters. Particularly interesting to Lakeland tourists are two big pictures by Philip de Loutherbourg, showing Belle Isle on Windermere in storm and in calm. The boat depicted is recognisably the Curwen yacht still preserved, two centuries later, in the Windermere Steamboat Museum. De Loutherbourg produced more square feet of painting than any other eighteenth-century painter – including scenery for David Garrick – but these are admirable works.

Distinct from Abbot Hall, but just across the courtyard in the old stable, is the Museum of Lakeland Life and Industry, which is just what it says it is. Among the things to look out for is a collection of horseshoes - seventeen patterns, adapted to suit different conditions, which show what a complex trade farriery is; photographs of the stupendous George Steadman of Asby who in the early twentieth century won the heavyweight title at Grasmere for fourteen successive years, the last time at the age of fifty-four; and Arthur Ransome's writing room, with his furniture, books and manuscripts. The elegant Tuscan portico has been lifted from the gasworks, as the inscription, 'Ex fumo dare lucem', might suggest. Between that and the stables are what remains of the old grammar school.

Hard by Abbot Hall and the church is the Ring o' Bells, the most individual of Kendal's pubs. Built on consecrated ground by the tintinnabulants themselves in 1741 it is almost unchanged, retaining its tiny snug.

Although Abbot Hall is an essential stop, which should not be missed by any visitor to the Lakes, the rest of Kendal merits

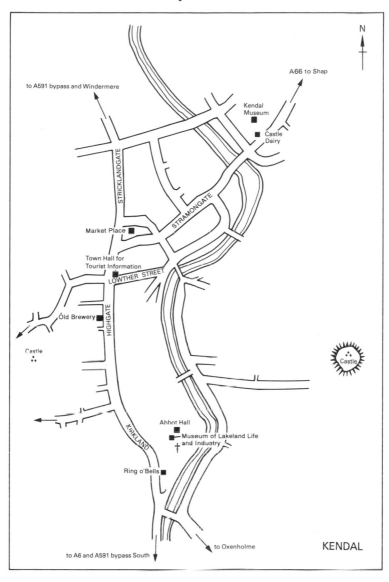

exploration. Kendal announces itself as the 'Gateway to the Lakes' and 'the auld grey town'; both are accurate enough, but hardly do justice to one of the country's most attractive small towns. It could have been even more attractive had they resisted the temptation to demolish many of the grey limestone buildings and replace them by well-intentioned but uninspiring municipal housing. Writing in 1968 Norman Nicholson was justifiably gloomy: 'What I have seen . . . does not give rise to much hope.'

But 1968 must have been the nadir; the authorities saw the error of their ways, and began a policy of rehabilitation rather than destruction, which has saved much of the peculiar charm of old Kendal.

The heart of Kendal is the long stretch of the old A6 known variously as Kirklands, Highgate and Stricklandgate, on either side of which dozens of yards, ginnels, crofts, lanes, courts and closes lead off, either towards the river or the steep fell side. During the forty years I have known Kendal many of these have been razed to provide car parking, but enough remain to make an exploration enjoyable, and in the last few years public conscience has pushed through some valuable preservation schemes. The most important of these is the conversion of the old brewery off the west side of Highgate into a flourishing arts centre, with exhibitions and a year-round programme of concerts, films and plays. One of the worst features of provincial towns has been the decline in performing arts as theatres have closed, and there is often a complete lack of any opportunities for young people to enjoy themselves. The north-west has been as bad as anywhere. In 1996 there was only one permanent theatre company between Glasgow and Bolton; by 1998 there should, all being well, be another when the Century Theatre at Keswick is rebuilt. In this deprived region the Old Brewery shines out like a good deed in a naughty world.

The Kendal Civic Society has shown also what can be done to preserve the best of the old town buildings in their work at Collin Croft. The remains of Kendal's older castle – it has two, which is something of a distinction – lie just above Collin Croft on Castle Howe. The outer bailey became a bowling green, and the original motte and ditch are well preserved, the motte now forming a suitable setting for an elegant obelisk commemorating the centenary of the Glorious Revolution of 1688. An added pleasure in wandering around the Fellside is the pleasant odour of mint emanating from Wilson's works in Cross Lane. Kendal Mint Cake has become a staple food for any Arctic or Himalayan expedition – solid sugar, packing an immediate kick, and one of the inevitable presents brought back from Lakeland; however detrimental to teeth, complexion or anything else, the original Mint Cake is uniquely comforting on a cold hillside. Other available comestibles may be respectable enough sweetmeats, especially the fudges, but all lack the primitive appeal of Kendal Mint Cake. Quiggins and Romney's also make mint cake; Romney's is the best known, but all recipes stem from the same original, although processed mint imported from the USA is now used.

One of Kendal's other surviving industries is snuff-blending, carried out by Gawith and Hoggarth's in Lowther Street, under a sign representing a Mozartianly romantic Turk. A poet must have lurked, or perhaps is still lurking, in Lowther Street, for Gawith and Hoggarth's snuffs include, as well as the prosaic 'Kendal Brown', 'Western Glory', 'Exquisite Fleurette', 'Jockey Club', 'Hyacinth', 'Sea Breezes' and 'Heliotrope'.

And their tobaccos are described with meticulous attention:

> 'Mixed Shag' affords a smoker a sufficiently strong yet smooth cool tobacco with the flavour of pure leaf gently stoved to enhance its best characteristics, 'Dark Bird's Eye' – whole leaf cut to give the 'bird's eye' effect particularly favoured traditionally by the Fisherman, together with the finer cut favoured under adverse conditions. Very strong, very cool.

All this is squeezed together in a series of narrow, sharply rising, twisting and thoroughly inconsequential passages. Thomas Gray observed, when he passed through on his way to make the Lake District famous, that 'all the houses seem as if they had been dancing in a country dance, and were out without intent or meaning'. You can live, work, pray, drink and amuse yourself within a hundred paces, making for a rare urban intimacy that is Kendal's greatest charm.

Kendal is not well off for pubs and hotels – not to be compared with Keswick or Penrith. The Old Woolpack Hotel has been modernized out of recognition, and few of the pubs are of great merit: indeed Kendal on a Friday or Saturday night is a good place not to be, although for those who like music and poetry with their beer the Old Brewery is an entertaining spot.

The Town Hall sits on the corner of Highgate and Lowther Street and deserves a closer look. Hidden underneath an absurd tower and dormers taken straight from a French architect's railway station pattern book complete with carillon, an elegant Regency building can still be made out. This is by Francis Webster, a local architect, who together with his descendants altered the face of the town: Kendal today owes almost as much to the Websters as Newcastle to Dobson and Grainger. Father Francis also designed the Castle Howe obelisk, Stramongate and Miller Bridges, and a number of town houses of which the best are 21 Stricklandgate, 134–6 Highgate, and Sand Aire House on Stramongate. Son George did at least one good house, but concentrated on churches – Holy Trinity, St Thomas's and St George's are all his, with brother Francis II in charge of the sculpture, but George's best building is the dignified Bank of Westmorland in Highgate, with its original title now barbarously concealed under a Midland Bank fascia.

The Friends' Meeting House in Stramongate houses an interesting series of tapestries 'celebrating the ideas and experiences of Quakers since 1652' built in 1816 – with central heating – the interior is magnificently spacious.

Highgate also has some fine shopfronts: Farrars, another Francis Webster building, which can be tracked by the smell of roasting coffee, and Titus Wilson (a sixteenth-century building altered by George Webster) which has been given an early nineteenth-century facelift. Both these, and others, contrast with some disgraceful twentieth-century shopfronts, inflicted on the town by great national concerns who really should know better.

Hidden away among the rest of the town are dozens more attractive spots: Sandes Hospital, the New Shambles, undisturbed for two centuries, and the surviving maze of lanes. Among them hides a charming eighteenth-century Unitarian chapel with an impressive later extension, in the shape of a Corinthian-pilastered schoolroom. Thomas Gibson is recorded on his tombstone as being of 'Rational Piety and inviolate Integrity' – excellent Nonconformist virtues.

Dotted around the town may be found the urban equivalent of the country house grottoes – the Kendal summer houses, which make an entertaining study.

Kendal is not the only Cumbrian town to have had summer houses – one or two remain at Ulverston and elsewhere – but it has retained enough to make something of a feature. Every man needs the equivalent of a shed in his garden where he can get away from his family and sit without anyone enquiring too deeply as to whether he is spending his time profitably. Geordie miners have them on allotments where they could be attending to their pigeons or leeks. Prosperous Kendal bourgeois of the seventeenth and eighteenth centuries frequently erected miniature cottages in their gardens where they could smoke, drink, eructate and behave in a fashion that would have been found unacceptable by their wives, while admiring the view both of the neighbourhood and their own properties.

The best of these can be seen around Castle Howe, two pretty octagonal Gothic structures. An earlier example remains at Bradley Field House, to the west of the town, as does the last of the Kendal summer houses, a fine Decimus Burtonesque two-storey edifice off Cliff Brow. For those citizens who did not possess their own, the municipal summer house in Serpentine Woods could be hired for picnics. This has happily been restored by the Kendal Society, but many other pretty little buildings have been sacrificed to supermarkets and car parks.

Over the river to the north of the town the third constituent of the Kendal Museum faces the old station buildings (Oxenholme, on the main line, is now the nearest manned railway station) in a converted mill. The Kendal Museum of Natural History and Archaeology is not a bad place for an introduction to Lakeland history and geography, although it has lost something of that delectable jumble sale atmosphere it once had (there was a most elegant mummified hand that, when I was fourteen, impressed me deeply). Almost as old as the Keswick Museum, it was founded by a Mr Todhunter in 1796 as an exhibition of curiosities, with an entrance fee of one shilling, 'children, workmen and servants 6d each'. It became a much more serious collection in the hands of the Kendal Literary and Scientific Society, but children will appreciate the stuffed animals and fourteenth-century soldiers. Cartmel Fell's crucifix is here, and some interesting Roman steles, but unfortunately not that of an officer, now in the British Museum, which has the warning: 'Anyone found putting another corpse in this grave will be fined.'

Just around the corner in Wildman Street stands the Castle Dairy; a misnomer, possibly a corruption of 'Dowry', since it is a fine sixteenth-century house, with a core two hundred years earlier. Open in the summer season, the interior has some excellent Elizabethan plasterwork and furniture.

Nothing much of interest is to be found east of the river except the second castle and the old canal basin. The gasworks, a pretty original building, dating from 1825, six years after the opening of the canal, has had its portico moved to Abbot Hall. Kendal was early in installing gas lighting, which was done with remarkable alacrity – just over a twelvemonth to finance, build the works, and install the piping.

Canal Head still has the original canal terminal buildings and Websters' 1818 showrooms at Bridge House.

The ruins of Kendal Castle sit on a convenient drumlin and offer a good view of the northern fells, but are of interest only to the castle enthusiast. In order to make sense of what is left one must understand that the castle was circular, with towers and the keep incorporated in the curtain wall. Quite the best thing on the Kendal left bank is the view of the church and Abbot Hall on the opposite side of the river. From here it becomes clear how the Bellingham chapel was originally an independent building which became digested by the church.

Many of those lucky enough to have been born in Kendal have chosen to stay there rather than to seek their fortunes in less agreeable spots. One who emigrated successfully was Thomas Shaw, son of a dyer, who went to Queen's College, Oxford, and became in 1720 chaplain to the English merchants in Algiers. From that base, over a period of thirteen years, he was able to make numerous expeditions as far off as Sinai, where he was frequently imperilled by lingering to botanize. Shaw was a true scholar, who described hundreds of species of plants, and won the admiration even of Edward Gibbon. He also seems to have been a clubbable fellow, who made an active and agreeable Principal of St Edmund Hall in Oxford, where he was responsible for building the new part of the front quad.

William Hudson, son of the landlord of the White Horse, was another émigré, who combined working as an apothecary with being the most distinguished Linnaean botanist of his time, and an FRS. He produced the *Flora Anglica* in 1762 and was in charge of the Chelsea Physic Garden. There was a strong tradition of such practical science in the north of England, which seems to have been particularly marked in Kendal. John Gough was an even more famous botanist, in spite of his having been blind from infancy. Everyone who met him, including Wordsworth and Coleridge ('the in every way amicable and estimable JG'), was struck by his remarkable facility in identifying plants by touch alone, using the lips and tongue to supplement his fingers. Gough was also a mathematician, and taught the most famous of Cumbrian scientists, John Dalton, and indeed took an active interest in anything at all odd, as becomes a Westmerian; the variety of voices, the ebbing well at Giggleswick, migrating birds, ventriloquism, the mathematical theory of the speaking trumpet, Scoteography and fairy rings, all were made subjects of scientific papers. Another pupil of Gough's was William Whewell, the nineteenth-century Master and benefactor of Trinity College,

Cambridge, who came to him from Heversham grammar school. And Kendal had, for a short period in 1818 and 1819, what must be the most distinguished editor of any provincial newspaper. This was Thomas de Quincey, who, with the backing of Wordsworth, ran the *Westmorland Gazette,* filling it with detailed accounts of murder and rape trials, 'metaphysing' articles on the theory of taxation, Kant, Herder and the planet Mars, a rich mixture. De Quincey was not flattering (or, on reflection, perhaps he was) about newspaper editors: 'low-bred mercenary adventurers – without manners – without previous education – and apparently without moral principle'. One could think of some current examples.

While in Kendal it is worth making for **Scout Scar,** the summit of the escarpment on the east bank of which the town lies. Almost opposite the entrance to Abbot Hall car park, on the other side of Kirklands, Gillingate leads west out of the town. A mile or so up the road signposted to Underbarrow, over the bypass, Scout Scar is reached. There is a car park on the north side of the road, and a footpath opposite which leads to the scar.

This is a wonderful place for getting one's bearings. Scout Scar is a precipitous limestone escarpment – a certain amount of care needs to be taken near the edge, since the cliff is pretty vertiginous, where it looks west over the undulating fields of low limestone farms, thickly wooded groves and becksides to that great block of limestone, Whitbarrow. To the south are the clear sands of Morecambe Bay and traversing from the west the most spectacular of the mountains can be seen, with the help of a sheltered panorama, generally vandalized but legible. Coniston Old Man, Scafell Pike, Great Gable, the Langdales, poke their craggy heads on the skyline, succeeded on the north by the smoother slopes of the High Street range.

Some of the best walking country in the Lakes lies just north of Kendal, not the tough walks of the high fells, but such pleasant strolls as the paths that lead up the Mint Valley from Burneside Hall to Garnett Bridge, or along from there past the little tarns by Birk Rigg.

Burneside Hall is notable for retaining some of the defensive works that commonly accompanied the larger peles – a gatehouse and parts of the curtain wall and moat. It was originally a Bellingham holding, but passed to the Braithwaites, of whom the best known is Richard, who wrote a very great deal of deservedly neglected work and one masterpiece: *Drunken Barnaby's Four Journeys to the North of England.* After an enjoyable time at Oxford, Cambridge and London – 'I knew what sinne it was to solicit a maid into lightnesse;

or to be drunken with wine, wherein was excess . . .' – he settled down, married and eventually moved off to Catterick where he became a Justice and Deputy Lieutenant, dying in 1673. *Drunken Barnaby* is the oddest of works, written in rollicking goliardic Latin, like that of the Archpoet and the other bawdy thirteenth-century writers preserved by Helen Waddell. In an autobiographical section Braithwaite writes:

> *Armentarius sum factus*
> *Rure manens incoactus*
> *Suavis odor lucri tenit*
> *Parum curo, unde venit;*
> *Campo, Choro, Tecto, Thoro,*
> *Canta, Sylva, Cella, Foro.*
> *Equi si sint cari, vendo*
> *Si sint minore pretio dempti,*
> *Equi a me erunt empti*
> *Ut alacrior fiat ille,*
> *Ilia mordicant Anguillae . . .*

Or, in the English translation where he explains his partiality for Kendal:

> Thence to Kendall, pure her state is,
> Prudent too her magistrate is . . .
> Here it likes me to be dwelling,
> Boozing, loving, stories telling.

It really does sound better in Latin!

Burneside itself is a decent industrial village, largely the creation of the worthy Cropper family who have been running the paper mills there for over a century. One member, Margaret Cropper, lived in the village and produced some distinguished, and distinctive, poetry. The mills are the only survivors of what was once a great centre of activity; at the turn of the nineteenth century the ratio of mills to population in Birmingham was 1:1380; in the Kent Valley it was 1:315. A good walk from the village goes along the River Kent past Cowen Head up on to the fells near Potter Tarn.

Going up the Sprint Valley, either on foot or by car, the narrow entrance to that excellent valley **Longsleddale** starts at Garnett Bridge. Ubarrow Hall, on the east side, is a massive pele, with walls eight feet thick and a small Victorian church nearby, but the real attraction of the valley is that it is natural, unspoilt and comparatively uncluttered, and affords access to some excellent high-level walks.

East and north of Longsleddale valleys radiate from the central High Street watershed. Bannisdale, Borrowdale (not to be confused with the Cumberland one), Crookdale, Wasdale (another), Wet Sleddale, Swindale and Mosedale are all unspoilt and almost uninhabited valleys, quiet places for hearing curlews and experiencing one of England's truly remote places, where the most marginal of farming shades into the wilderness.

Water engineers cast envious glances at these places. Their attempts to use Longsleddale as a pipeline trench and to flood Bannisdale completely were vigorously and, temporarily at least, successfully resisted. Norman Nicholson was instrumental in that last fight, and wrote:

> Bannisdale is a back-water in time – a shallow hollow lying between fleshy muscled hills with here and there a sparse, fluffy beard of oaks blond in autumn and black-stubbly in winter. There is no village, no church, no pub, no tales of the 'Kings of Bannisdale'; nothing, in fact to rouse romantic nostalgia. Yet this is not one of the deserts of England. It is a valley that has been lived in and worked for centuries. Every meadow and in-take, every wall and barn is the result of many generations of toil, struggle and grim persistence. As I said when the controversy about the proposed dam was at its height; if you drown Bannisdale, you drown history.

From the head of Longsleddale the old drove road is well marked, since it later became used for quarry traffic: it leads north to the Gatescarth Pass, which brings you out at Haweswater, and south to Wads How Bridge. Both this and Sadgill Bridge are fine examples of packhorse bridges; this route was until comparatively recently a major one, referred to in 1750 as the high road from Ambleside to Appleby.

A real walk can be made of this by going up the Gatescarth Pass almost to the reservoir and returning via Small Water and Nan Bield to Kentmere, then back to Longsleddale over the drove road from Stile End. This route gives splendid views of Mardale and Kentmere, and upper Longsleddale, and passes under the impressive crags of Harter Fells. It also enables you to sample Small Water, one of the handsomest tarns in Lakeland. Mrs Humphry Ward, in *Robert Ellsmere*, calls Longsleddale Long Whindale, and describes it thus:

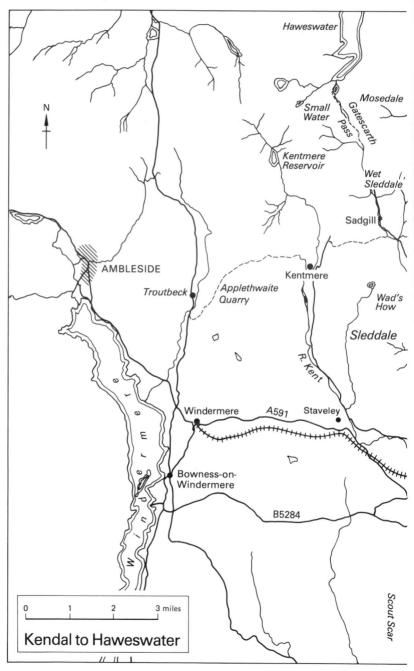

Haweswater

Mosedale

Small
Water

Gatescarth
Pass

Kentmere
Reservoir

Wet
Sleddale

Sadgill

N

AMBLESIDE

Troutbeck

Applethwaite
Quarry

Kentmere

Wad's
How

Sleddale

R. Kent

Windermere

A591

Staveley

Bowness-on-
Windermere

B5284

Scout Scar

0   1   2   3 miles

Kendal to Haweswater

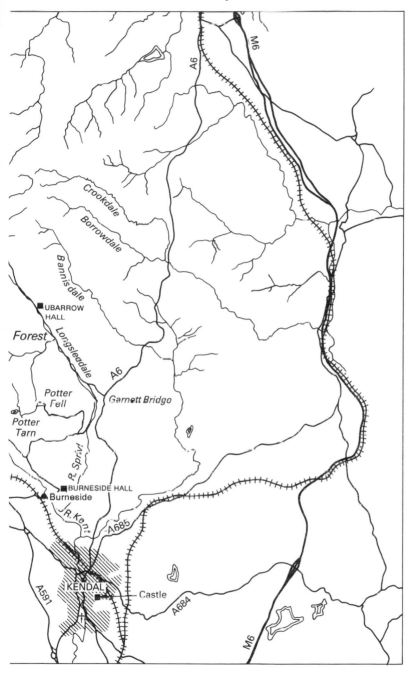

Summer in the North is for Nature a time of expansion and joy as it is elsewhere, but there is none of that opulence, that sudden splendour and superabundance, which mark it in the South. In these bare green valleys there is a sort of delicate austerity even in the summer: the memory of winter seems to be still lingering about these wind-swept fells, about the farmhouses, with their rough serviceable walls, of the same stone as the crags behind them, and the ravines, in which the shrunken becks trickle musically down through the debris of innumerable Decembers.

Longsleddale is properly best left to pedestrians since the single road gets very crowded in the summer and parking at Sadgill becomes difficult, but **Kentmere** is more accessible and one of the most delightful, unspoilt parts of Lakeland. The 'mere' bit is historic rather than actual, for the original small lake has now dried out, and provides Kentmere's only industry, the extraction of diatomaceous earth for filters, although further up the valley a small tarn has been made into a reservoir, which is kept stocked with brown and rainbow trout. The entrance to the dale from the south is memorable as one squeezes through between crags pressing in to enter a fertile valley, expanding on either side. Kentmere is but a hamlet, and not a great deal remains of the original St Cuthbert's church apart from the roof timbers, but there are two pretty bobbed blonde angels guarding the altar, and a good bronze repoussé art nouveau monument from the Keswick School of Industrial Arts to Bernard Gilpin, the 'Apostle of the North'.

Gilpin, who came from Kentmere Hall, seems to have been a good and humorous man in an age crammed with intolerant and sadistic divines. He narrowly escaped burning by Bloody Mary, and avoided promotion, living most of his life over in Durham as rector of Houghton le Spring, and attracting universal love and admiration (at least after Bishop Bonner was sacked!). His horse was returned by some thieves: 'For they knew that any who robbed Master Gilpin would go straight to hell.' It is not usual to find fortified houses up in the hills, and Kentmere pele marks the importance of the ancient route. It has been well restored, and preserves its bartizan turrets and bold parapets, original windows, fireplace and garderobe. The adjoining hall is also mid-fourteenth-century, with a pointed arch to its doorway; this, and the mullions, are of sandstone, supplementing the unworkable local slates which form the walls. Kentmere Hall Farm is a decent, well-managed farm, an operation which becomes rare as one goes further into the Lakes, where farming is almost overwhelmed by the demands of planning and tourism.

From Kentmere the old Garburn drove road to Troutbeck leads past the Applethwaite quarry. Hugh Hird of Troutbeck, passing over one day, found ten men trying to raise a new beam for Kentmere Hall; he lifted it up himself, and was sent off to London for young Edward VI to admire, but the valley folk were more impressed by his picking off Scots raiders at long range with his bow as they rode down Scots Rake. His preferred diet was 'thick porridge, that a mouse might walk on dry-shod, to my breakfast; the sunny side of a wether to my dinner when I can get it'.

4

Cartmel

The area south of the Lakes originally linked by the Sands route, and therefore joined to Lancashire, is composed of three peninsulas – Cartmel, Furness and Millom – pushing out into Morecambe Bay, and separated by the estuaries of the Rivers Leven, Kent and Duddon.

Each tongue of land has markedly different attributes: Cartmel is rural, with no towns, the remarkable village of Cartmel itself and Holker Hall, a quadrilateral with sides about seven miles long, giving a neatly defined area of unspoilt countryside for pottering about in. Furness was the ancient centre and is the modern, although hegemony has shifted from Dalton to Barrow, which is the only manufacturing town of any size in the Lakes area. Millom is occupied by the mass of Black Combe, an outcrop of Skiddaw slate quite cut off from the main hills around Keswick, with the town of Millom clinging to the edge.

The whole area of Furness, as far as the north end of Windermere, Hawkshead and Coniston, owes its pre-1974 status as part of Lancashire to the route across the Sands. Communications from Kendal to the west were either over precipitous roads or through swamps, and it was much quicker to get from any part of Furness to what, once one is there, still seems like the mainland, over the Sands. Furness therefore always looked to Lancaster rather than Kendal, and most certainly not to distant Appleby, as an administrative centre.

If a decision is taken to go west rather than north into Kendal the straight fast A590 from Levens ought not to tempt the motorist to pass the **Lyth** and **Winster Valleys** without stopping. These two valleys have no grand houses, nor much in the way of picturesque villages or dramatic crags, but are ideal places for wandering quietly along wooded paths, especially in the spring when the damson blossom is out, or later when the honeysuckle and roses are massed in the hedges (they keep hedges up properly in the north, a lesson to the money-grubbing, corn-growing vandals in East Anglia). Whitbarrow, a great limestone block, separates the valleys and dominates the scene, rising 700 feet sheer above the road, and can be got at either from Witherslack Hall on the west or Millside on the south. The top of the escarpment, Flodder allotment, is a nature reserve, run by the Lake District Naturalists' Trust, and a fine example of limestone pavement, with pale grey stone water-worn into ragged crevices and fantastic shapes. (Allotment deserves an explanation. Valley farms share out the fellsides between them; the share may be done by having a 'stint' of so many head – the right to graze that number – or by having a specified area allotted and enclosed.) The view from Lord's Seat, the summit, is worth the climb, which leads out of thick woodlands by way of steep cliffs to the turf and bare stone of the top. There is also a cave and an old mine at opposite ends of the scar, to add variety.

Scattered about the valleys are some often neglected examples of vernacular architecture. Cowmire Hall, a prosaic name for a down-to-earth building, is an unspoilt yeoman's house, three storeys high, six bays and a pele tower behind, looking dourer than it need behind grey rendering. There is a pretty footpath to it, leading past With-erslack Hall, and passing Pool Bank, where the farmhouse retains its wooden spinning gallery, an unusual survival. On the other side of Whitbarrow, Flodder Hall is more picturesque than Cowmire, and bears an entertaining inscription:

> *Si sapiens fore vis*
> *Sex serva quae tibi mando;*
> *Quid loqueris et ubi*
> *De quo cui quomodo cuando.*

'If you wish to be a wise man, do these six things I command; watch what you say, where, of whom, how and when you say it.'

Nether Hall used to serve as an overnight stop for pack ponies, and possesses a shed where pulleys were fixed to lift the loads on and off the horses, saving a lot of manhandling.

This is Mrs Humphry Ward country. That remarkable lady, the granddaughter of Thomas Arnold and niece of Matthew, aunt of Aldous Huxley, colleague of Beatrice Webb, the 'Mary Ward' of the University of London, was a prolific and popular novelist. Like Charles Reade and Zola (well, only a little like Zola, for she was an English middle-class lady, after all!) Mrs Ward was concerned with making social points through the medium of fiction. *Helbeck of Bannisdale*, which she wrote while staying at Levens, is by any standard a considerable work, and the description of Westmorland scenery as good as has been done. Better at any rate than that achieved by another popular lady novelist, Constance Holme, who

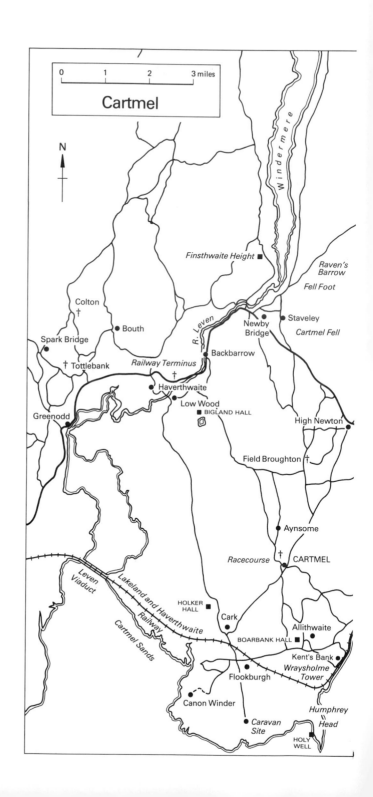

Cartmel

0 1 2 3 miles

N

Windermere

Finsthwaite Height ■

Raven's Barrow

Fell Foot

Colton †

● Bouth

R. Leven

Newby Bridge ●

● Staveley

Cartmel Fell

● Spark Bridge

† Tottlebank

Railway Terminus

Backbarrow ●

† Haverthwaite ●

● Low Wood

BIGLAND HALL ■

High Newton ●

Greenodd ●

Field Broughton †

● Aynsome

Racecourse † CARTMEL

Leven Viaduct

Lakeland and Haverthwaite Railway

HOLKER HALL ■

Cark ●

Allithwaite ●

Cartmel Sands

BOARBANK HALL ■

Kent's Bank ●

Wraysholme Tower

Flookburgh ●

● Canon Winder

Humphrey Head

● *Caravan Site*

HOLY WELL

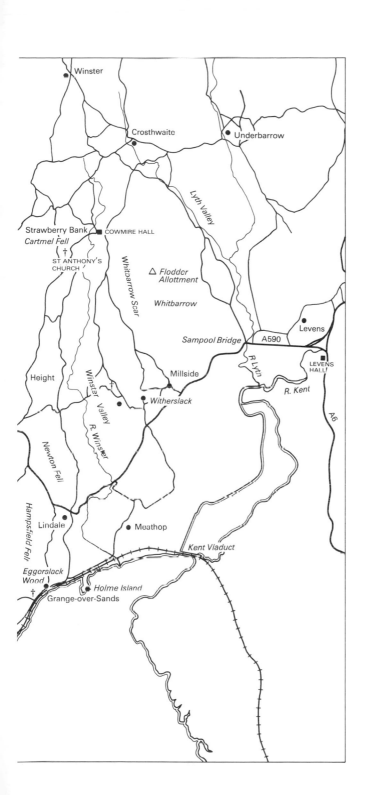

might be called the Mary Webb of Westmorland, although even she is sometimes perceptive and always less risible than Mrs Webb.

Witherslack village hides under Whitbarrow, and has to be sought out. The Derby Arms, a Wilson's house, with good pub food, is just off the main road at Town End, and marks the district as Stanley territory. Until well into the nineteenth century the Earl of Derby held manor courts in the pub, which marks its dignity by twin Tuscan porticos, on the second Tuesday after Trinity.

Witherslack church is a rarity, a Restoration chapel built to the orders of John Barwick, Dean of St Paul's, who was born in the village in 1612. Barwick was an active royalist, a secret agent of the king, and was imprisoned by Parliament. For several years he was fed only on bread and water 'which, however, had an effect contrary to that which his persecutors expected, as it conduced in a striking manner to the recovery of his health'. He is commemorated in elegant Latin by his brother Peter, a physician:

> *Afflictiones infracto animo toleratas,*
> *Res tandem, licit summe arduas, feliciter gestas,*
> *pro collapso regni & ecclesiae statu,*
> *Ad curam & dignitatem.*

The exterior, at a time when the classical was in vogue everywhere else, is traditional Westmorland Gothic, a style which seems never to have died out: the quite sharply battered walls of the tower are typical. But the interior was remodelled in 1768 and resembles nothing more than the ballroom of a country house of the period, with Ionic columns enclosing the sanctuary, inviting some sedate soirée.

The country house atmosphere is strengthened by the absence of any religious element: all is lay, even the east window with the original seventeenth-century armorial glass, forming a celebration of Stanley family glory: Earl of Derby, Lord – once King – of Man, linked with the Bourbons, Viscontis, de Tremouilles, and the Dukes of Bohemia.

The Barwick brothers' hatchments, which include the distinguishing red rose given to them by Charles II, are vigorous, and countered by a rather twee sleeping child, the young Geoffrey Stanley. A handsomely bound prayer book was given to 'Her Excellency Lady Stanley of Preston' – a doubtfully correct mode of address – by a Mr. Elligood, Rector of St James's in Montreal, 'in memory of Sunday 10 February 1889'.

Originally the church was pewed in the post-Reformation style, with seats running fore and aft across the church, the pulpit in the centre of the north wall, and the altar relegated to infrequent use at the east end. The old vicarage, near the church, is now a good small hotel and restaurant, one of the best in the area. Halecate House is half a mile outside Witherslack, and has its gardens open all the year round, specializing in the sale of spectacular plants that suit the alkaline soil of the district.

Particularly useful at busy weekends and offering an alternative route to Windermere, by which the lake shore can be reached well south of Bowness, the A5074 joins the upper Lyth and Winster Valleys. Leaving the A590 at Sampool Bridge, where the old causeway to Levens village can still be seen paralleling the main road, it skirts the villages of Underbarrow, Crossthwaite and Winster.

Lutyens liked **Underbarrow** church (1869) and called it a 'charming design'; Pevsner thought it naughty. They could both be right, since its tower over the porch, capped with a little spire, and gables on the apse, are hopelessly unauthentic, but certainly entertaining. Cunswick Hall belonged to the Leyburns, who took the injudicious side in 1715. Before that Katherine Parr lived in it for a time; there is a contemporary royal arms carved over a gateway.

Crosthwaite church, one of the few originally licensed by Bloody Mary, is next to the pub, the Punch Bowl – a convenient arrangement. William Pearson, who became a founder and first treasurer of the Astronomical Society of London, was born here in 1767.

Starnthwaite Ghyll school has been in its time a fulling mill, a paper mill, a bobbin, a corn and saw mill: water is a protean energy source. **Winster** church was rebuilt at the instigation of that Bishop Harvey Goodwin along whose avenue generations of Cambridge undergraduates have bicycled, to replace an earlier building, which although only a chapel of ease, served a great area. According to the Rev. Thomas Machell in 1692 it extended 'over the water into some part of Cartmell Fell (which may be more truly called Cartless Fell for there is not a cart used in this country)'. The font and the painted texts are left from the old church. There is a good modern window showing St Kentigern, with his robin, by Professor L. C. Evetts of Newcastle, and a pretty patchwork hanging by the Carmelite nuns of Presteigne.

The western side of the Winster Valley is formed by Newton and Cartmel Fells, of Silurian slate and therefore quite different from the eastern limestone landscape in every way. The contrast is striking and educational: black slate and white limestone, with the contours and vegetation changing uniformly and on the sudden. The climb up out of the valley, one in four, if you go from Witherslack, is a good test of the agility of a car on hills.

Near the top of Newton Fell, at Height, is a cottage which used to be a Quaker meeting house, and an early one, boldly bearing the date 1677, twenty-two years before William and Mary's Act of Toleration made such buildings legal: the old burial ground is opposite, on the other side of the road. The road from Newton to **Cartmel Fell** is at its best, like much else in the Lake District, in October. Newton Fell is rugged; scraps of rock poking through the turf, and a few scrubby trees. After Hare Hill, heightened with the vivid yellow of gorse, running along the eastern side of the escarpment, the woods close in. The deciduous trees have turned, the bracken is declining in rich golds, and the whole brown-yellow spectrum is punctuated by strong evergreen. In the middle of all this, a mile or more from the nearest village, is **St Anthony's Church,** a representation of Reformation history in stone.

It was built in 1504 as a chapel of ease to serve the scattered farms of the area, seven miles from the parish church at Cartmel. Apart from new pews being put in, it is still much as it was. Firmly and solidly built, it has not needed much in the way of restoration: out of sight, in a poor area, it has not attracted the attention of improvers.

The funds for building were provided under the will of Anthony Knipe, Lord of the Manor of Burblethwaite, from which circumstance comes the unusual dedication. The east window, which is contemporary with the church, has a rare figure of the saint, properly dressed in the white robes of a Coptic priest, with a Coptic tau cross and bell, looking very foreign in so English a surrounding. He was the patron saint of charcoal burners, which is suitable enough in this region, and like St Vitus gave his name to a disease, St Anthony's fire or erysipelas. Chaucer's parson refers to it in his diatribe against the 'sinful costlewe arraye of clothinge . . . than semeth it, as by variance of colour (of the hose) that half the partie of their privy members were corrupt by the fyre of seint Antony'. But the stained-glass saint, whose friendly boar seems to demand attention, is unmarked.

The central lights of this remarkable window illustrate the seven sacraments, linked by flows of blood to the wounds of Christ. Although damaged – baptism and confirmation are missing altogether – what is left gives a vivid idea of medieval life: a charming miniature of a priest blessing a penitent, the administration of extreme unction, marriage, ordination, and the Mass can all be made out clearly, due to

94

the clarity of the glass and its accessibility in the little church. What cannot be seen is a diamond inscription: 'William Brigg goeth to London upon Tuesday XIIth day of April, God send him.'

The Briggs of Cowmire Hall were later benefactors; they paid for the re-erection of the rood screen in 1571, when the Protestant reformers demanded the removal of such relics of popery. Clearly unwilling to part with their very handsome screen, the conservative parishioners converted it into a parish pew, to be used as a school. The master's desk, and the scholars' solid benches, incised with the work of many generations, are crowded inside. A previous generation of Catholic Briggs had paid for the stained glass in the pew, which shows Christ in the Garden of Gethsemane and St Loy, the patron of blacksmiths.

Another box pew, the Burblethwaite pew, faces it on the south side. The elegant columns are Jacobean, and the frieze, which matches surprisingly well, early nineteenth-century Gothic. These enclosures offer grand accommodation, fitting for middling grand gentry; one farmer's pew still remains, dated 1696, and marked WH, for William Hutton of Thorpinsty. It is suitably solid and modest. The parish spent a bit of money then – the three-decker pulpit is a similar date, and a window was placed above it to provide light – but after that nothing much was done until a conservative restoration before the First World War.

Almost anywhere else in England such a church would either have decayed to ruin or been altered to accord with new tastes, but St Anthony's remains almost unchanged, low and pebble dashed, a testimony to the care and conservatism of its few loyal parishioners. Perhaps some credit should be given to the incumbent at the time of the Civil War, who was described by the Parliamentary Commissioners as 'an old malignant not yet reconciled'.

In such a remote area the church was the centre of communal life; land sales and official businesses were carried out in the big porch; the long bench against the south wall provided a place for those who had come in from distant farms to rest and eat their meals, and watch the archery practice taking place in the churchyard. Burials only started here in 1714, and there are few memorials; the nicest one is in the nave, and commemorates young Miss Poole, who died at the tender age of three: 'Under this stone a mouldring virgin lies, who was the Pleasure once of Human Eyes.'

One of Cartmel Fell's treasures is now in Kendal's museum: a pre-Reformation crucifix, doubtless preserved by the 'old Malignant'.

Much knocked about, having at one time apparently been used as a poker, it is an object of historical rather than aesthetic importance.

Mrs Humphry Ward is good on Cartmel Fell church:

> From here, under a roof shaken every Sunday by Mr. Bayley's thunders, there stood a golden St. Anthony, a virginal St. Margaret. And all round them, in a ruined confusion, dim sacramental scenes – that flamed into jewels as the light smote them! In one corner a priest raised the Host. His delicate gold-patterned vestments, his tonsured head, and the monstrance in his hands, tormented the curate's eyes every Sunday as he rose from his knees, before the Commandments. And in the very centre of the stone tracery, a woman lifted herself in bed to receive the Holy Oil – so pale, so eager still, after all these centuries! Her white face spoke week by week to the dalesfolk as they sat in their high pews. Many a rough countrywoman, old perhaps, and crushed by toil and child-bearing, had wondered over her, had felt a sister in her, had loved her secretly.
>
> But the children's dreams followed St. Anthony rather – the kind, sly old man, with the belled staff, up which his pig was climbing.

A short walk uphill from the church takes you to Ravensbarrow Cairn, which affords a good view of the Winster Valley below, to the east.

Having got to Cartmel Fell it would be foolish not to press on another mile to Strawberry Bank. The Mason's Arms, described on page 153, is one of the best pubs in this part of England.

Back to the roundabout on the south side of the A590, a minor road leads to Lindale and Grange. This is where Cartmel proper begins: not that there is any impropriety about Cartmel Fell but the latter is more part of the Winster Valley rather than the peninsula. Meathop is an isolated rock rising from the marshes, a favourite spot for curlew gathering in the spring; I have seen fifty or more of those big birds together, making a chorus of their unmistakable cries.

Lindale, which is not to be confused with Lindal in Furness (see page 136), hangs on to the steep side of Hampsfield Fell. The church was built by George Webster of Kendal, in an off moment; the churchyard contains his elaborate grave. It used to have an even more impressive monument, the obelisk designed by John Wilkinson the ironmaster as his own monument, commemorating him whose 'life was spent in action for the benefit of man and, as he presumed humbly to hope, to the glory of God'. After falling into disrepair, the obelisk has been resited just above the road to Grange. Wilkinson was an extraordinary man, devious, foul-tempered, radical, father of three bastard children, and a manufacturing genius, devoted to exploring the potential of iron. His major memorial is the iron bridge over the Severn at Coalbrookdale; he built the first iron boat, a barge to carry peat moss to his Castle Head foundry, and insisted on being buried in an iron coffin. Although all his work was done in the Midlands – he moved there at the age of twenty – Wilkinson retired to Lindale and built himself a mansion at Castle Head, now St Mary's College, just to the south of the town. His father's more modest home, Wilkinson House, is in the village.

When John Wilkinson built Castle Head a number of Dark Age artefacts were found, including about seventy-five Roman and ninety-five Northumbrian coins. It has been conjectured that this signified Roman occupation, but this is improbable, given the total absence of any other archaeological evidence in the area. It is much more likely to be a lost Anglo-Saxon hoard; if the inhabitants of Cumbria were as tenaciously conservative then as they are now, Roman coins would have continued in use for a long time.

Holme Island is cut off more by the railway line than by the sea. Edwin Waugh, grandfather of the bad-tempered novelist, who visited it a century back, described it as 'a perfect marine paradise . . . he might easily forget it was the result of man's taste and enterprise, and fancy himself in some bowery nook of a wide part . . . sand-banks so smooth, so gently swelling and secluded, that fair Sabrina might sit there'. The 'enterprise' was that of John Brogden, one of the promoters of the Furness railways.

Grange-over-Sands was called into being by the railway; the winter climate is said to be the mildest in the north of England, and certainly supports those delicate plants which always feature on picture postcards – the pride of municipal gardeners. The well-preserved station was built to match the chief hotel, run by the famous Riggs of Windermere and described at the time as 'first rate, in a beautifully picturesque situation; very comfortable. Charges by tariff moderate; being well sheltered on NE is suited to winter as well as summer residence.' In 1866 the Westmorland Gazette found Grange 'not gay, not fast, not boisterous, nor overcrowded', nor has it changed much; it suits decent retired folk, blue hair, tweed hats, Grenfell jackets and pleated skirts: hairdressers and teashops flourish.

The architecture of Grange is pleasant rather than distinguished, a reminder of how difficult it is to build an ugly house in local stone,

and with plenty of foliage, while a horrible bare lavatory-tiled convalescent home on the outskirts underlines the importance of using the
right materials. The parish church, St Paul's, begun in 1851 to accommodate the newly arriving holiday-makers has some good
modern oak joinery in its friendly interior. Immediately outside is an
odd Germanic clocktower which would appear more at home in
Jugendstil Vienna than respectable Grange.

You can stand above the carefully tended flower beds by the
ornamental lake and look east – oddly enough, since Grange is after
all on the west coast – across the pastel-shaded sands to Arnside, or
south to Morecambe and Heysham power station. A short walk up
through Eggerslack Woods leads to the hospice on **Hampsfell,** which
must be visited. The limestone fell is crowned by a substantial stone
shelter built by Mr. Remington, a nineteenth-century clergyman with
a taste for versification:

> This hospice has an open door
> Welcome alike to rich and poor;
> A roomy seat for young and old
> Where they may screen them from the cold . . .

to which the response is:

> And if the rich and poor should meet
> I trust they will each other greet,
> And rich or poor and young and old
> Together screen them from the cold.

Which they probably do, since anoraks are great levellers. But Mr
Remington's fireplace is full of Coke tins and rubbish, which is a sad
commentary on his last verse:

> For no good man would think it pleasure
> To climb the fell to spoil your treasure.

The view from the top – there is a panorama, which is not much
help – is comprehensive: Black Combe is over on the west; Scafell
Pike pokes out beyond the Old Man of Coniston; the Langdale Pikes
are unmistakable, and so is the ridge of Helvellyn. And to the south
the view across the sands and out to sea is breathtaking. Literally, too,
for this is a windy spot, and the hospice provides a much-needed lee.

Down again at **Kents Bank** you see, at last, something of the
sands route. Just as at Hest Bank, by Lancaster, the end of the way

Morecambe Bay cocklers

Allithwaite Hall: Wyatt Gothick

Charcoal burning: Walter Lloyd emptying a finished kiln

Coniston foxhounds: a far cry from the accepted notion of fox-hunting

over the sands is found behind the railway station. Indeed, the stations must have been sited with an eye to serving those travellers who expected to continue to make use of the sands. A causeway leads temptingly off towards Lancashire, and the name of the guide is given; no longer a Carter as for so many centuries, the present incumbent, Mr Cedric Robinson, still lives at Guide Farm, Cart Lane, and should be contacted by venturesome parties. Refreshment to travellers used to be offered by an outpost of Cartmel monks, now a pleasant house, also in Cart Lane. Today one has to go further; the area of Grange is not well-pubbed.

Allithwaite church is kept locked. From the outside it offers a good view over the sands, and is reported to have a late Morris and Co. window.

Boarbank Hall once belonged to the Barrows, at least one of which family was a canon of Cartmel, and has his picture with the others in the stained glass of Bowness church. The elegant house built in the 1830s has now been largely altered, but the stables are original. It now houses, by a happy arrangement, nuns who follow the same discipline as that which the Cartmel nuns embraced, and provides nursing care.

Those bound for further west – Ulverston and beyond – went from Kents Bank to **Flookburgh** and **Cark**, where a second crossing to Ulverston canal foot crossed the Levens Estuary. There is not much to hold one at either Flookburgh or Cark itself, except for the possibility of buying fresh fish at Flookburgh. Those who have never eaten freshly boiled shellfish, which are uncommonly difficult to come by in England (you really need to buy them live, at the port, and steel yourself to the task of boiling the poor beasts alive, for fishmongers usually cook them too long), should certainly seek them out here.

The fishing is now done by tractor-hauled nets, but has an ancient history. Flookburgh was once famous for flat-fish (flukes) and cockles: it had an Edwardian charter, and still retains the civic regalia. Cockling, although an intensely competitive occupation, was regulated by the superstition that any quarrel would inevitably lead to the decamping of all the cockles. They are apparently perennially curious creatures; the usual method of luring them from the mud was to operate a 'jumbo' – a sort of upturned table which was tipped up and down. The vibrations attracted cockles to the surface to see what was going on.

Cockles continue, although falling out of public favour, but shrimps are still much in demand and sold at some of the houses in the village. Charles II once came to sample the cockles: in view of his tastes, and the well-known rhyme, he should have tried the shrimps. Bowling greens, too, admire the sea-washed turf found on Meathop Moss and much of it has been denuded in the service of that sport.

The Cavendishes of Holker have been patrons of the district, and built the church. Today the main contribution to rates must come from the huge caravan park on the site of the old airfield. Although highly developed with swimming pool, bars, shops and restaurants, it is discreetly tucked away behind the sea wall, and enables thousands of people to have inexpensive holidays without incommoding anyone else.

There is a real cliff, a rarity in these parts of the coast, just to the east. **Humphrey Head** has – of course – splendid views, but also an authentic cave, used as a place of refuge in Roman times and earlier. It was here that the last wolf in England was killed in the fourteenth century by Sir John Harrington of Cartmel, but judging from the number of other places where this is said to have happened it seems the animal must have made as many farewell appearances as Nellie Melba.

There was once a famous spa here, the Holy Well. Camden mentions it in his *Britannia:* lead miners used to come from Alston to recuperate with its aid, since the minerals were reputed to counter the poisonous effects of the lead. Holy Well water is reported to resemble that of Wiesbaden, and to be an aperient: the spring still flows, and tastes not unpleasantly salty, which is hardly surprising considering its position. Unlike many more modern remedies, it almost certainly has the merit of not doing any damage, even if it cures nothing.

Canon Winder, a handsome sixteenth-century house, is isolated on the marshes looking over the sands to Ulverston. It is said to be, as the name suggests, a retreat for the Cartmel canons, and is certainly on a generous scale, with surprisingly high ceilings. Wraysholme was a pele tower; one of the later models, being built about 1485 for the Harringtons of Gleaston Castle, it now has just been avoided by the railway, which at least gives a good view.

Flookburgh adjoins Cark, which is now the estate village of **Holker,** the grandest house in South Lakeland.

Since the death of Sir William Lowther, who left the estate to his cousin, a younger son of the second Duke of Devonshire, Holker has remained in the Cavendish family. Nineteenth-century Cavendishes were an industrious crew. William, one of the most distinguished scientists of his day, discovered nitric acid, described the composition of water, and was a recluse of extreme eccentricity; his microscope is kept in the library at Holker. Lord Frederick Cavendish became the most famous member of his family when he was stabbed to death by Fenians (the precursors of the IRA) in Phoenix Park. His father, the Seventh Duke, epitomized the best sort of Victorian aristocrat: educated, generous, decent and public-spirited. It was he who was responsible for the present house, designed by Paley and Austin of Lancaster.

Holker is a good house to visit: you can walk about quite freely, unattended and unfenced in. There is nothing of outstanding importance, nor any recognizable theme, just a pleasant collection of objects acquired through the centuries. The interior design of the house is worth attention, for Paley and Austin had access to some excellent craftsmen, at a time when craftsmanship was at its best. The falling off since is exemplified by the external downcomer some twentieth-century Goth has placed right by the entrance to the house.

The remarkable thing about Holker – at least the Victorian wing, which is part open to the public – is that it still exists. Most Victorian houses of this size are now hotels, old people's homes, or flats. Holker is preserved as a family house, albeit on a splendid scale, with its furnishings and decoration intact.

The layout of the house has made this possible, since there is a quite separate and almost private Georgian wing, Tudorized by the versatile George Webster in 1846, quite large enough to enable the present Cavendishes to lead a domestic existence, leaving the more magnificent parts to the tourists for most of the year. The life of less fortunate home-owners is not enviable. Either they pig it in the dower house or a converted stables, effectively banished from their ancestral home, or suffer the inconvenience of exposing their domesticities to the public gaze, keeping the rooms on view in apple-pie order, never leaving anything out of place, and generally being desperately uncomfortable.

Forty years later half this house was destroyed by fire, and a replacement was provided in a jovial Elizabethan style. If it were on a smaller scale it could be a Bradford millionaire's house, but as it is, Holker is more like a contemporary American great house, such as Biltmore: a resemblance increased by the similarities between the countryside of Furness and North Carolina.

The Holker guide book, in what may be charitably supposed to be a typographical error, quotes Pevsner describing Paley and Austin as 'the best architects living in the country'. In fact Pevsner says 'county' but, carping aside, Holker is a successful house, which manages to be impressive and comfortable at the same time. The estate only became Cavendish land in the eighteenth century. Originally part of Cartmel Priory estates, George Preston, who renovated the priory church, built the first house: for a short time, by marriage, the estate came into Lowther hands. Sir William was an ill-favoured, pug-faced bachelor, whose portrait by Reynolds in the dining room can be compared with a caricature of him, also by Reynolds, and a rarity, hanging in the billiard room.

Excluding hall and gallery, there are only four public rooms on the ground floor, all nearly in their original state. The library is handsomely fitted out, with a magnificent carpet and soulful portraits of Lord Frederick and his wife. They really were a virtuous and admirable couple: Lady Frederick sent one of her murdered husband's cufflinks to his assassin as a token of forgiveness. Among the other portraits is one of Oliver Cromwell, a reminder that the Cavendishes owe their strawberry leaves to their strenuous efforts on behalf of Dutch William.

The drawing room is hung with its original Macclesfield silk and has a particularly fine eighteenth-century marble chimney-piece. Oddly enough the billiard room is included in the range: in earlier country houses billiard rooms had tended to be sited at the end of a corridor, near an outside entrance, where men could smoke and be nasty all by themselves without polluting the more polite areas of the house. Either manners had improved or the Cavendishes were more than usually refined.

A romantic self-portrait of the young Van Dyck dominates the dining room. Upstairs the impressive scale of the long gallery contrasts with the comparative modesty of the Duke's bedroom, with its simple canopied tester and small writing table. The Seventh Duke, who made Holker his home, was a modest and retiring man, whose greatest work in a meritorious life was to establish the Cavendish laboratory in Cambridge, where thirty years after the Duke's death Rutherford first split the atom. In quite a real sense therefore the atomic age began in that pleasant room.

The previously conventional gardens are being transformed by Hugh and Grania Cavendish to include a wild meadow, formal parterres, a splendid Tivoli-like rill and an extensive range of trees and shrubs.

The estate cottages, designed like the earlier part of the house by

Webster, have windows with octagonal glazing bars which look very pretty but which must be the devil to clean. Cark Hall, in the village, is older. It has a magnificent portico, too magnificent indeed for even so substantial a residence, which was added about a century after the house was built by Christopher Rawlinson, a prominent antiquarian.

Mrs Fletcher Rigge, brought as a bride to Cark Hall in 1782, was so horrified by the inaccessibility of the place that she insisted on moving to Northallerton, a satisfactorily flat area. Her son Gray, toughened by Charterhouse and Trinity College, Cambridge, brought his family back, but by insensible degrees modified their name to Greyrigge which sounds better.

Cartmel Village

Cartmel village is unique. A bold statement that, but where else is there a race course adjoining the substantial remains of a medieval priory? Where are there more bookshops than souvenir boutiques, more pubs than estate agents, and a river with so impossible a name as Eea?

As well as being unique, Cartmel is very pleasant: the village, like that of Blanchland in Durham, is built around, and largely from, the priory, one of the finest churches in the region.

Cartmel's first appearance in history is in 677 as a gift, 'together with all its Britons', by King Egfrith of Northumbria to St Cuthbert. That interesting clause suggests that at the time the Celtic inhabitants were living in a state of bondage, but still surviving, having been neither wiped out nor absorbed into Saxon society. The priory was founded in 1188 by that remarkable man William Marshal, first Earl of Pembroke, Regent of England and servant to Henry II, Richard I, John and Henry III, who was the most powerful subject in England for nearly half a century. He established Cartmel as an Augustinian priory, 'with every kind of liberty that the heart can conceive or the mouth utter; and whosoever shall in any way infringe upon these immunities, or injure the said priory, may he incur the curse of God, of the Blessed Virgin Mary, and of all other saints, as well as my particular malediction' – which might have been last, but was probably not least; William was a bad man to cross. A particular duty of the canons was to ensure the safe passage of travellers over the Kent Sands, from Hest Bank to Kent Bank. For the next stage, over Cartmel Sands to Ulverston, they had to rely on the services of the Conishead monks.

Externally the Priory seems very odd: the structure is fundamentally

Norman, but the whole of the east end is occupied by a magnificent fifteenth-century window, and, most peculiarly, the tower is placed diagonally on the crossing. Norman Nicholson aptly likened it to a child's playing with building bricks.

What remains of William Marshal's building – the chancel and transepts and the nave north wall – was considerably altered in the fourteenth century. The structure aptly reflects the adventurous history of the plan. The chancel and transepts are original, the nave a curious addendum, cobbled together over the centuries, and the only part of it that has signal merit is the south door, a majestic portal protected by a later porch.

Cartmel was never as large, rich or important as Furness, and was run on different lines. Augustinian canons were less entrepreneurial than Cistercians, leading old-fashioned, claustral lives centred round the liturgical day and seasons. Limited by William Marshal to twelve in number, they could never have governed a large lay workforce, nor did they have the wealth in land to necessitate this. Apart from an odd holding in County Kildare, most of Cartmel's land lay down towards Lancaster. Their special function remained that of assisting travellers.

Medieval monks are usually anonymous folk, but some brethren achieved an unusual immortality in having their portraits preserved in the priory's stained glass, now dispersed, like much of Cartmel's glass, to St Martin's in Bowness: they are (in the east window) Thomas Hogson, William Baraye, William Purfoot, Roger Thwaites and a George (whose second name is missing).

At the Dissolution of the Monasteries there were ten canons and thirty-eight staff, forming a modestly prosperous house. It was a bloody dissolution for Cartmel, however, since encouraged by the initial success of the Pilgrimage of Grace the ejected canons reinstalled themselves and forcibly prevented their former goods being seized. In Henry VIII's eyes this was treason, and the monks and their men were duly apprehended and tried. Their punishment was exemplary. Fourteen, including four canons, were hanged at Lancaster; one, Brian Williams, who must have had some good friends, was not only acquitted but given the new Protestant living of Cartmel, a transition which was not as unusual as it might sound. Ex-brother Brian continued in possession for fifty years. The Prior, who had avoided participating in the repossession, also did well for himself: he was given a pension and allowed to stay in the priests' house.

The fabric of Cartmel Priory has survived rather better than did its former inhabitants. Unlike so many other remote monastic foundations the church was preserved, since it had – or part of it had – served also as a parish church. The rest of the conventual buildings, with a few exceptions, were demolished for building stone, but the church survived largely intact.

Internally, it must be admitted, things are a hotch-potch: nothing matches anything else, and bits have been removed or inserted, but this is no great fault in an English country church, especially one that so faithfully reflects the passage of years.

William Marshal's work is best observed in the richly decorated round arches of the chancel, which are among the latest examples of Norman work, contemporary with that of Hugh Pudsey at Durham.

Above them the triforium has been altered and below the whole concept changed by the insertion of a splendid fifteenth-century east window, brought over, tracery and glass together, from Yorkshire. Not a great deal of this glass remains; the best bits have found their way, as I said before, to St Martin's in Bowness and to Cartmel Fell, but here is a good John the Baptist and a handsome archbishop. An altogether less admirable alteration is the smashing of the sedilia in order to insert the Harrington tomb on the south side of the chancel. Not that the tomb is not very fine: Pevsner calls it one of the best of its date in England, and it is a good date (c.1350). Although knocked about at the Reformation enough detail survives to show the fine quality of the carvings; St Mary Magdalene, St Catherine, the Virgin and Child, and a number of male saints escaped the puritans. So did a charming frieze of the monks themselves, which includes the precentor beating time. The Harrington tomb is best seen from the southern chancel chapel, known as the Town Chapel, which also has the most easily seen glass, the earliest in the church, dating from about 1340. It depicts the popular subject of the Stem of Jesse, the genealogy of Christ, and is quite magnificent, contrasting with the later glass in the chancel: strength and simplicity moving to naturalism and elegance.

The chapel also has a rare effigy of one of the canons themselves, robed for the choir and holding a chalice, and housel benches in place of a communion rail.

The north or Piper Chapel retains the original vaulted roof, the only part of the church to do so. It has some small pieces of fifteenth-century glass still in their original settings, and a tablet recording the death of one William Myers on 30 February 1762: they like a joke in Cartmel.

The choir stalls equal the glass in splendour, and are equipped with a set of the finest misericords. Two to look out for are on the

north side. One represents an elephant leaning against a tree, reflecting the medieval belief that elephants had no joints in their legs, and
must lean against something in order to sleep. They could be captured by chopping down the tree, when they would find themselves
unable to get up again, like a beetle. This idea stems from Caesar,
who describes the great elk of the Hyrcanean forest in exactly these
terms, and typifies the medieval devotion to a classical authority.
Another classical theme is Alexander the Great being carried by
eagles. Then there is a spirited hunt, with three hounds chasing a
deer, flanked by a curious hedgehog and a monogram with hearts and
roses.

At first sight it might seem that the canopies are the same age as
the stalls, but in fact they are two centuries later, placed there by the
generous George Preston. The Prestons acquired much of the lands
both of Cartmel and Furness at the Dissolution, and proved to be
more conscious of their responsibilities than many of the Tudor 'new
men'. A handsome painted hatchment in the north wall of the nave
describes Preston's genealogy and records that: 'The said George
Preston, out of his zeale to God and at his Great charges, repaired this
Church being in great decay with a new roofe, and timber and beautiful within very decently with fretted plaister works, adorned the
chancel with curious carved woodworks and placed therein a pair of
Organs of Great Valewe.' The curious carved woodwork is an interesting mixture of classical and medieval motifs – Corinthian pillars
decorated with instruments of the Passion and flamboyant tracery on
the hinged screens. Pevsner takes this as proof of a Gothic revival,
but it is more in keeping with the notorious tenacity of local taste,
which has always moved with deliberation. Very probably this mixture of the fashionable and the traditional is exactly what they
wanted.

This conservatism is shown by a memorial tablet to Ethelred
Thornburgh, who died in 1596, which concludes: 'To whose sweet
soule heavenly dwellinge Our Saviour grant overlastinge.' Anywhere
else, in more progressive parts, prayers for the souls of the dead
would surely have been thought dangerously papistical; it was, after
all, only eight years since the Armada!

The interior of the church is more than usually well equipped with
monuments which reflect the aspirations and fashions of the times.
There is no praying for the souls of the departed after Ethelred's (who
was a girl, oddly enough, since that is the masculine form of the name,
as in the Unready king) death, but rather catalogues of virtues, as:

Hospitable to strangers, courteous to all
sweet in her temper, sincere in her conversation . . .
a pattern of Charity and Liberality as may raise
Emulation in some, Envy in others, but be out done by few.

Parishioners have their monuments, but the bodies of those washed up on the coast, most of whom died attempting the crossing of the sands, are buried here and recorded only in the parish registers. Not all even had a name: there is, for instance, 'One little mann Rownd faced which was Drouned at Grainge.'

The north-west crossing pier has a set of shelves hanging on it, carrying loaves of bread, that prove that the bequest of Rowland Briggs of five pounds 'to be laid out in bread and distributed to the most indigent housekeepers of this parish every Sunday for ever' is still being honoured.

A white Carrara marble effigy of Lord Frederick Cavendish, the Fenians' victim, a dull Victorian font which should be disposed of and replaced by the original one with its pretty blue cover (now relegated to a side chapel) and an engagingly twee group by Josephine de Vasconcellos, occupy a good deal of the west end. The problem with free-standing monuments is that they need a great deal of room in order for the interplay of mass and space to be properly appreciated: they therefore ought to be of the highest standard, which none of these are. Two large panels on the west wall, bearing the Creed and the Lord's Prayer and the Commandments, are surmounted by stern bearded figures, one of them incongruously wearing both a mitre and a phylactery.

The south transept has a cabinet of curiosities, of which the most impressive are the letters patent granted by Charles I (whose miniature portrait forms the initial) in 1641, which bear three magnificent seals – the Great Seal of England, and those of the Duchy and County Palatinate of Lancaster.

In the churchyard there is a memorial to John Berry, mariner, who died in 1762:

Tho' boystrous blasts and Neptune's waves
Hath tost me to and fro,
In spite of both, by God's decree,
I harbour here below
And here I do at anchor lie
With many of our fleet,

And must one day set sail again
Our Saviour Christ to meet.

The rest of monastic Cartmel has gone, absorbed in later buildings, except for the gatehouse, now kept up by the National Trust, and possibly a pretty cottage in the south-west corner of the square. Not that it is any the worse for that: like Blanchland, Cartmel is a jewel of a village, where everything is handsome, whilst remaining a working community. The racecourse helps, since Cartmel is transformed twice a year when the race meetings come. The course is neither large nor expensively equipped, but must have the most beautiful setting of any in the country. It might be even better (although worse for the riders) if the modern fences and stands were removed, and it was left as the eighteenth-century course it originally was.

Modern Cartmel is the square, the streets leading into it and the River Eea (although it's nobbut a beck) running straight through it. A slow walk produces a succession of memorable vistas, with nothing out of place, except parked cars. Like any Lakeland village Cartmel reflects the local geology, lying as it does on the border between the limestone of Hampsfell and the Silurian slates of Bigland. Both stones are used in the buildings, although a good number of these are rough cast and whitewashed against the elements.

The old lock-up (in the road to the right of the post office) is an uncomfortable place, fifteen feet high with one small lofty window. It must have accommodated many of the customers of Cartmel's pubs in its time, for the village has three in the centre, plus an hotel, as well as the Pig and Whistle on the main road. Of the pubs the Cavendish Arms is the oldest, and stands on the site of a monastic guest house. The Cavendish brews its own excellent beer and houses an iconographic portrait of Lord Frederick. In the next door house a cockpit was in use at least until 1926. Edwin Waugh was directed to the King's Arms by a man with a red nose: he 'found the place filled with a cheerful smell', and was given lobscouse, oatcake, cheese and watercress, 'the whole seasoned with a good deal of hearty fun'. Lobscouse, incidentally, is often appropriated to Liverpool, but is originally a North-Sea dish, common to Germany and Scandinavia as well as this country. It is a stew of the cheaper cuts of beef and mutton with whatever vegetables come in handy: salt meat was used by sailors, and it makes a comforting, easily absorbed meal that can be eaten with one hand on the tiller. Equally substantial meals can now be had at the Priory Hotel, kept by a local man, George Bodie, fell racer, hound and horse breeder, and crooner. Also in the square are two bookshops, the best possible companions to the pubs. Between priory, pubs and bookshops, Cartmel has everything to transform a wet Lakeland day into an interlude of delectation.

The countryside back over from Backbarrow to Cartmel is worth exploring. Bigland Hall dates from 1809, but there have been Biglands living there at least since the sixteenth century: Broughton is now time-sharing flats. Hampsfield Hall, where Ethelred Thornburgh lived, used to have a pele tower, demolished last century. What is left is pleasant but undistinguished.

Aynsome is one of the oldest settlements on Cartmel: the name signifies solitariness, and the manor is said to be on the site of the original one. It is now a pleasant country house hotel, where the guests eat in 'the royal room', built by Thomas Michaelson Machell, where the Duke and Duchess of Devonshire once dined. A piece of thirteenth-century masonry indicates that the mill was built by the canons.

Although Arthur Ransome is more associated with Coniston, the Ransomes spent much more time in Cartmel and Cartmel Fell. After Arthur's initial love affair with all the Collingwood family, the Ransomes' actual Coniston residence was limited to a bungalow called the Heald, where they spent some time during the first world war, and Lowick Hall, just outside Levens Bridge, which they sold at a loss after only a couple of years. But they lived at Ludderburn for ten years, and chose Hill Top at Haverthwaite for their final home. Ludderburn was their favourite: 'From the terrace . . . we could see forty miles away down into Yorkshire, to where the mass of Inglboro rose above the nearest hills', and in the other direction 'the best panorama of Lake mountains, from Black Combe to Helvellyn and the high ground above the valleys of Lune and Eden'.

From Cartmel the old packhorse roads run north, connecting the Sands route to the Lake villages. One of them passes through **High Newton,** which must have been a pleasant place in which to live before being sliced in half by the A590, putting the inhabitants of the southern part in peril of their lives when seeking restoration at the Crown Inn.

The old packhorse stables now form part of a superior antique shop, where the oak furniture appears to advantage on polished slate flags. There are some idiosyncratic bits of architecture among High Newton houses – triple arched Gothic windows, decent eighteen-panel sashes, and a fine doorway to Newton Hall. Newton's church is at **Field Broughton** (nowhere near Broughton, of course), and is a sandstone Paley and Austin building of 1894, with some pleasant Kempe stained glass. Dr Edmund Ransome has a tablet, commemorating his death in 1898 on the Gold Coast 'in the service of his country and of humanity'; this was presumably in the course of medical work following the Second Ashanti War the year previously, during which a number of troops died of fever, including Queen Victoria's son-in-law and Lord Louis Mountbatten's uncle, Prince Henry of Battenburg.

The main A590 road continues along the fell side to Newby Bridge, separating the limestone country on the west from the slate on the east, as the rugged outline of Newton Fell demonstrates, where outcrops of stunted trees make a dramatic backcloth against the shattered slate. Staveley is in slate land – this is Lancashire Staveley, not to be confused with the larger Westmorland Staveley up by Burneside. Staveley church, if you can get into it, is pleasant, a late-eighteenth-century restoration of an earlier fabric with later additions, including presumably the vestigial crockets on the pinnacles.

Nathaniel Hawthorne visited the Swan Hotel at **Newby Bridge** in 1855. 'It is a very agreeable place. A stone bridge of five arches crosses the River Leven close to the house, which sits low and well-sheltered in the lap of the hills: an old fashioned Inn, where the landlord and his people have a simple and friendly way of dealing with their guests . . . they load our supper and breakfast tables with trout, cold beef, ham, toast and muffins; and give us three fair courses for dinner, and excellent wine.'

It is all now rather smarter, with colour television and electrical trouser presses, a device surely of little utility in Lakeland, but they still feed you amiably and well. More practically the hotel reserves some boat moorings for visitors (rather shallow, though) so that you can sail up, dine, and sleep it off in your own cabin.

In 1651 the existing timber bridge was found to be 'in great decay, and very dangerous to passengers; and was builded about 30 years since with better timber than there is any now to be gotton; and it is conceived by the workmen that the pillars could serve to raise arches upon it . . . if it be made a stone bridge it will cost £90, if a wood bridge £60 and this wood therein not continue sound 20 years which we conceive will not be to the good of the country and commonwealth nor the credit of your worships nor your humble servants.' This petition of local notables to the bench of justices in Lancaster – it still comes as a surprise to find that this part of the country, which

110

seems so near to Kendal, should have been part of Lancashire: all due to the sands – was accepted, and the bridge built. It was immediately imperilled by contemporary juggernauts: only twelve months later – the bridge was built remarkably quickly – the same worthies were complaining about excessive strains caused by 'trailing of timbers', the work being 'all green and unknit'. The bridge survives today, five noble arches spanning the Kent, which then takes its short final course to the sea. Just below it a weir controls the level of Windermere; the river then rushes down the Backbarrow Gorge where it once powered an eighteenth-century industrial estate. The river is now famous for its game fishing.

The **Lakeland and Haverthwaite Railway** is a pathetic but proud remnant of that glorious nineteenth-century line that joined the new town of Barrow, with its great steelworks and prosperous shipyards, north to the heart of the Lakes, and south to Lancashire. At both termini steamer services took passengers onward to their destinations: you could go from Manchester to Ambleside on the system, and many did. Today only three and a half miles of track are left, but this does at any rate connect with the Windermere Iron Steamship Company's vessels at Lakeside pier. In the best Orient Express manner you alight from your steam train (after an eighteen-minute ride!) and cross the platform either to embark, or to visit the coffee room, with its panoramic view of the lake. No longer, unhappily, to embark on a steamer: the company's name is an anachronism, and their ships are diesel driven.

Tern, with her canoe bow and counter stern, is the prettiest of the craft, and has recently been given a replica of her original funnel, which has done much to improve her looks. She was built in 1891 at Wivenhoe in Essex, about as far away as one can easily get. *Swift* followed her in 1900, but is now lying laid up and forlorn, leaving *Tern* holding on as the only ex-steamer still plying on the lake. But an agreeable journey can be made if you take the first train from Haverthwaite, sail to Bowness, look at the church and steamboat museum before going to Ambleside, where a short walk will take you to lunch or tea at the Rothay Manor Hotel, which has one of the best restaurants in the district, after which an afternoon steamer will provide for a somnolent return to Haverthwaite.

As a preparation for more serious climbing, as well as a patriotic duty, you can scramble up **Finsthwaite Height.** Wainwright's advice on this walk may be neglected; there is a perfectly good, well-marked public right of way leading from the sharp turn past the railway

111

bridge. The first part of the climb is steep, but becomes gentler. One moves up through the remains of coppiced beeches, interspersed with Scots pines and birch. Coppiced woods, once neglected, have an untidy and abandoned air, but Finsthwaite has enough variety to make it acceptable. The woods are looked after by the Lake District Society for the Protection of Birds, which must be effective, since rarely glimpsed coal tits and long-tailed tits are easily spotted here as they accompany you up the hill, twittering happily. There are also signs of deer. Before turning left on the final stage of the climb to the tower, some outcrops offer a scramble up to a viewpoint. Not to be compared with Hampsfell, say, it has the great advantage of a sheltered grassy slope from which the lower reaches of Windermere may be admired with comfort, while you reflect on having climbed 400 feet in ten minutes – at this rate Scafell would only take an hour!

Up here the air is unpolluted and encourages lichens and moss: some of the former grow to science-fiction-film dimensions. The tower on the summit, now occupied by a pair of kestrels, was built in 1799 by James King of Finsthwaite House 'to Honour the Officers, Seamen and Marines of the Royal Navy whose matchless Conduct and irresistible Valour, decisively defeated the Fleets of France, Spain and Holland, and preserved and protected LIBERTY and COMMERCE'. This was, of course, after the victories of St Vincent, Camperdown and the Nile in 1797, the year of victories.

Finsthwaite is one of Walter Lloyd's favourite sites, providing a reasonable supply of coppice wood for his one-man revival of the charcoal burner's craft. Walter moves his plant around, in bow-topped living wagons and flat carts, drawn by his champion Fell pony stallion, Heydsel Charlie. The supply of timber is critical: it needs to be heavy hardwoods – oak is his favourite, ideally in diameters of not more than 6 inches. Lighter woods such as birch, although making good charcoal, are less economical.

Even a one-man operation using four kilns on a five-day cycle can consume a great deal of timber, and the resultant demand has meant that new areas of coppice can be developed.

Charcoal burning is a smoky, but not unpleasant life; one day's hard – and skilled – labour in loading the kilns, arranging the timber so that it will char evenly, a day's burning, a couple cooling, then grading and packing, give a rhythm to the week. In the quieter moments Walter attempts such other coppice crafts as handle-making and peg-splitting.

Finsthwaite got its church in 1724, but the present building is

Paley & Austin 1874. This firm produced original and imaginative designs, not attempting to be 'correct' but looking forward to Art Nouveau, and using traditional craftsmanship in an innovative fashion: their design for Finsthwaite won a competition for a small church in a mountain area, and it has an appropriate solidity, all thoroughly done. The church has some good Henry Holiday-ish windows, and a field communion set made from shell cases, used in the First World War on the Piave front, where Ernest Hemingway got his fighting experience. Barbara Sneyd lived at Finsthwaite House; *Riding High, 1896–1903*, the story of her childhood, is a lively account of country house life of that period.

Jacobites make the churchyard a place of pilgrimage, since a reputed daughter of the Young Pretender is buried here. Her name was Clementa Johannes Sobieska Douglas, and she was certainly the daughter of Clementa Walkinshaw. There are said to be some Jacobite relics still in the neighbourhood associated with her, but any real proof of her descent is lacking.

George Braithwaite of Stock Park is buried in the churchyard. In 1762 'he ended a vertuous and benificent life aged 92', which was pretty good going for that time.

Backbarrow was an industrial village with an extensive ironworks founded by John Wilkinson's father Isaac in 1738, clustered around the fast-flowing Kent which provided abundant power. Apart from a few ruins all this has disappeared, or been incorporated in Lakeland Village, a time-sharing enterprise with an associated hotel. To see what these works were like one should go over the Pennines to Sheffield, where an entire eighteenth-century steel works has been preserved at Abbeyside; but theirs, they will tell you in Sheffield, is real steel – owt else's nobbut clog iron. Backbarrow was distinguished by continuing to use charcoal for its furnaces long after everyone else had turned to coke: they only stopped after the First World War. There was also an indigo works, just as you come into the village, still at the time of writing marked by blue stains. Apart from its use in dying denim jeans the indigo was mixed with lime to make 'blue bags'. These were indispensable adjuncts to Monday morning washing along with wash tubs, mangles, poss sticks, dollies and Barnes airers, as giving that perfect glowing white that miners' wives insisted on. They were also meant to be good for wasp stings, although the medical reason for this was never made clear. But like iodine, they had the satisfactory quality of visibly distinguishing the sufferer, and attracting sympathy. The blue-bag works were originally the Ainsworth cotton mills, which developed a bad reputation for ill-treating child workers, who worked six days a week from 5 a.m. until 8 p.m. and sometimes later.

Backbarrow is now sliced off from its parent village, Haverthwaite, by the new road, and few people franchise that forbidding barrier, which is a pity, for Haverthwaite has much to offer. St Anne's church, from 1825, is clean and decent, but not distinguished. The churchyard, however, contains a memorial to William Fell, a soldier of the 52nd Light Infantry, who fought in the Peninsular Wars from Pombal to Vittoria, was at Ciudad Rodrigo, and Badajoz. In spite of being dangerously wounded at Ortez over the border in France, he survived until 1852. Mr George William Dickson, commemorated inside, was less fortunate: while walking at midday in Monte Video, 'he was struck by the musket shot of an assassin after it had passed through the body of its intended victim. He lingered for a few hours and died on the 24 May 1847.' There is another monument, to Jane Elizabeth, wife of Zachary Mudge, a good Dickensian name.

The Anglers Arms is a pleasant pub, and the nearest to the railway terminus. Further along, in the village next to the river, is an interesting industrial survival, the Low Wood gunpowder works. Most of the buildings are of 1849 -the central administration and stores block, with its impressive four-storey clock tower, and the isolated sheds where the powder was packed and stored. Gunpowder was made in various grades, the finest being used for small arms. Size of grain depended on the type of charcoal used; that coming from silver birch and alder was highly esteemed, but the best was 'Savin' from juniper bushes. (Savin is an interesting word; it is the 'Sabine herb' and appears in Anglo-Saxon before the Conquest, and well before 'juniper' became part of the language.)

The powder was removed by boats, the river then being navigable for quite sizeable craft to just below Low Wood Bridge, this being regarded as much safer than using roads or railways. Until quite recently the ammunition made at the Enfield factories was taken to Woolwich by specially built sailing barges, two of which still exist, used as yachts. They are considerably smaller than a Thames barge, although built on exactly the same lines; their dimensions needed to be reduced in order to enable them to pass the canal locks. Their attraction was, of course, that their wooden hulls and lack of engines minimized the risk of an explosion.

Today the Low Wood works houses glass engravers, antique dealers, and an incongruous electrical goods discount store.

Abbots Reading Farm Museum has, as its name suggests, a collection of vintage implements but also, more interestingly, a variety of native British livestock. Being a working farm opening times are limited; less understandably, so are those of many South Lakeland tourist attractions. Confirmation of these with the Tourist Board offices is essential.

5

Furness

The second of the South Lakes peninsulas, Furness, is quite unlike the first. Where Cartmel is pastoral and aristocratic, dominated by Holker and the Priory, Furness is industrial, and has been for centuries. It owes its present character to systematic development by the monks of Furness Abbey and their successors. For however wild and romantic it may often seem, this landscape is every bit as man-made, exploited for human ends, as the Black Country or Tyneside. Where it differs is that later stages of development have not obliterated the earlier, and the whole extent of eight centuries of industrialization still remains visible. Other abbeys, like Fountains, are now only noble ruins, divorced from the land that sustained them, land that was often spread over several counties in parcels of differing sizes. At Furness, although the buildings themselves are ruinous, the evidence of a recognizable medieval economic system can still be traced.

This is due to the isolation and singularity of the area, in which has been preserved much more evidence than can be found in more accessible and prosperous parts of the country. The fabric of the Abbey itself came through the nineteenth century by the skin of its teeth, threatened by the onset of the railways and the encroachment of Barrow suburbs, but the region once ruled by the Abbot has not altered beyond recognition since the foundation in 1122 by King Stephen, as recorded in the Latin verse of the Furness Coucher Book:

> *Anno milleno centeno bis duodeno*
> *Fourneys fundatem primo fuit et situatem . . .*
> *Hanc hac valle domum* Stephanus *comes aedificavit,*
> *Quem gens Anglorum Regem sibi post titulavit.*

The Coucher book, commissioned by Abbot William Dalton in 1412, was copied out by Brother John Stell, who included his own portrait as part of an illuminated letter, with the punning prayer: '*Stella parens Solis John Stell rege munere Prolis.*'

Although first occupied by Savignac monks from Tulketh, near Preston, Furness became Cistercian when the orders merged in 1147, and the county responded to the briskly efficient practices of the

116

white monks of Cîteaux. Their activities, taken together over a period, amounted to a methodical exploitation of all natural resources, employing the best technology available at the time.

The great forests, of which Grizedale is the best example, provided pannage for pigs (gris is from the Norse word for pig), fuel for all purposes, charcoal for smelting, coppice wood for joinery, bark for tanning, willows for basket making and timber for construction, shipbuilding and all forms of manufacture. Henry VIII's commissioners listed forest produce: 'Also there is another yerely profitte commying and growing of the saide woodes, called Grenehewe, Bastying, Blocking, Byordyng, making of sadel trees, Carte wheeles, Cupes, Disshes and many other things wrought by Cowpers and Turners, with making of Cloes and pannage of Hogges.'

The staple was, as elsewhere in England, sheep, although of a rougher and hardier breed here than those found in more favoured places. Granges staffed by *conversi* or lay brothers, with a choir monk in charge, were set up at outlying spots (Grange-over-Sands, Grange-in-Borrowdale and Hawkshead) to ensure the co-operation of the sometimes recalcitrant tenants and to administer justice – the Abbot had the right to a couple of his own gallows; and to act as a collecting centre for the wool. Hawkshead Hall gatehouse incorporates some of the medieval grange and was used as a courthouse. Piel Castle served as a wool warehouse. Packhorse roads connected the granges with the mother church, and with each other; the becks were crossed by bridges, of which examples may still be seen all over the dales.

Greenodd, at the mouth of the River Leven, can be reckoned as the boundary between Cartmel and Furness. It used to be a flourishing ship-building village, right into the second half of the last century, but there is nothing to show for it now. Building small vessels in wood requires nothing in the way of fixed installations beyond a few storage sheds; a level patch of land near the water's edge is all that is needed. Even at Beaulieu, in Hampshire, where large frigates were built, few traces of the past remain, beyond the attractive houses and little chapel. Greenodd has not even got these, the position of the quay only being identified by the Ship Inn. Until the bypass was built some of the old quays survived, but these were swept away by that tribe of twentieth-century vandals – road surveyors.

Greenodd church is at Penny Bridge, and just to complicate matters further is the parish church of Egton-cum-Newlands. In the

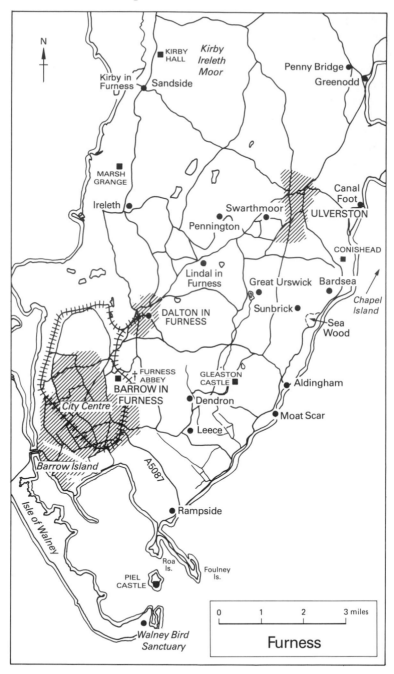

N

KIRBY
HALL

*Kirby
Ireleth
Moor*

Penny Bridge
Greenodd

Kirby in
Furness   Sandside

MARSH
GRANGE

Canal
Foot

Ireleth   Swarthmoor   ULVERSTON

Pennington

CONISHEAD

Lindal in
Furness   Great Urswick   Bardsea

Sunbrick   *Chapel
Island*

DALTON IN
FURNESS   Sea
Wood

FURNESS
ABBEY   GLEASTON
CASTLE

BARROW IN   Aldingham
City Centre   FURNESS   Dendron

Moat Scar

Leece

Barrow Island

A5087

Isle of Walney   Rampside

Roa
Is.   Foulney
Is.

PIEL
CASTLE

*Walney Bird
Sanctuary*

0   1   2   3 miles

Furness

spring the churchyard blossoms with early wild daffodils and cro-
cuses, with which it is profusely planted. The church itself is
pebbledashed and oddly domestic: it was built at the end of the
eighteenth century and rebuilt in 1864. Nothing remains of the earliest church except a couple of grotesques in the west porch.

Penny Bridge is named after the Penny family, one of whose
members in the eighteenth century formed a timber-owners' co-
operative to build their own furnace, the landowners being aggrieved
at the low prices paid for charcoal by the iron-masters.

The first intimation of approaching **Ulverston** is given by the
odd spectacle of a lighthouse rising from the top of a hill. The
monument was raised in memory of the second most famous Ulver-
stonian, Sir John Barrow (1764–1848). His connection with the town
was not of the firmest, since his father came from Patterdale, and
young John left Ulverston at the age of fourteen, never to return. The
local grammar school, which was run by William Walker, one of
'Wonderful' Walker's children, did so well by Barrow that he went on
to become Secretary of the Admiralty, a post he held for forty years.
A founder of the Royal Geographical Society, and one of the first
supporters of Arctic exploration, his name is commemorated in the
Barrow Strait, in Baffin Bay.

Barrow was a typical, tough, craggy-featured 'statesman', a fine
shot and able horseman, as he proved in earlier life during 3000 miles
of South African riding when he was charged with keeping the peace
between Boers and blacks. Although a staunch Tory he was, like most
Lakelanders, impatient of injustice, and saw through the 'brutality
and gross depravity of the boors' who persecuted the Kaffirs, 'a fine
race of men – powerful and vigorous in body, resolute and undaunted
in mind, and fearless in danger . . . [who] require their own land, to
make them a respectable and happy people'.

Since the Reformation and indeed as a result of it, Ulverston
displaced Dalton as the centre of Furness: due to its position as
terminus of the second stage of the sands route, from Cartmel to what
is now Canal Foot, it enjoyed a modest prosperity, but at the beginning of the nineteenth century it looked like becoming an important
town, a rival to Kendal. Between 1801 and 1841 the population
nearly doubled, to around 9000. This growth was due to the construction in 1795 of a ship canal, capable of carrying vessels of up to 350
tons, designed by John Rennie, to connect the town with the comparatively deep water of the Ulverston channel. The town's finest
buildings date from the period of affluence initiated by the canal. It

was short lived, for the coming of the railways brought Barrow, a much better harbour, into contact with the hinterland, and very slowly Ulverston relapsed into an agreeable sleepiness. It still, however, retains one of the best markets in the region: perhaps because of its Lancastrian origins, the cooked meats and pies are especially good.

Thomas West found the people of Furness in general, and of Ulverston in particular '. . . civil and well-behaved to strangers, hospitable and humane . . . The women are handsome, the men in general robust.' Two centuries on, they so continue.

A quiet potter around Ulverston will reveal some pleasant buildings, at least one good antique shop, and some decent coffee bars. Some of the town's – rather faded – handsomeness is due to its being built in limestone, an attractive material in itself. The Lancaster Banking Company's building in Queen Street is a good example of fine masonry, and of a dignified provincial bank. Shopping is untouristy, but bargains can sometimes be found at the Cumbria Crystal works where factory visits are arranged.

Medieval Ulverston was not much more than a site for a hospital for the leprous and indigent, served by the Conishead canons, which is why the parish church is at some distance from the modern town. Only a single arch remains of the original structure, which was rebuilt at the Reformation and much altered in the 1860s. Some good monuments were spared: John Braddyll a 'painfull and impartial magistrate', Wm Sandys, murdered in 1558, in courtly armour, and Myles Dodding, a couple of generations later, in huge top boots, contrast with a little girl kneeling at prayer, wearing an adorably mawkish expression. The windows are all nineteenth-century, and by many prominent makers; the church guide, unusually, includes an informative section on the stained glass.

The biggest tomb, that of William Sandys, is in fact a nineteenth-century work, with all respect to Professor Pevsner, who accepts the date of 1583 it bears. That troublesome figure, George Fox, who lodged at nearby Swarthmoor Hall, made at least three attempts to preach in the 'Steeple House' at Ulverston. On the third he was set upon by a mob incited by Colonel Sawrey, a JP from Plumpton Hall, and badly knocked about. His maltreatment apparently did not discourage Fox, who later married Margaret Fell, of Swarthmoor, when she was widowed.

Canal Foot where the canal locked into the bay is hidden behind a chemical works; the unpleasing smells produced by Glaxo have to mingle with the good beer sold at the Bay Horse. This must be one of the best places on the coast for birdwatching, not so much for the number or variety of wild fowl but for the fact that you can sit outside and sup your beer while doing it. It has recently been bought by John Tovey of Miller Howe and even better things are expected.

Rennie's sealock has been concreted up, but enough remains to make it evident that this was at the time the widest and deepest canal in England. The mole, a fine piece of mason's work, alongside which ships waited to lock in, still has its bollards, and a winding hole upstream of the lock indicates the size of the vessels that used it.

The guide to Leven Sands lives at Canal Foot: he still holds his office under the Duchy of Lancaster, and the present guide, Alfred Butler, has had the post for more than forty years.

Ulverston's two most famous recent sons are an unlikely pair: Norman Birkett, a hawklike six-foot three-inch judge at the Nuremburg trials, and little Stan Laurel, the other half of Laurel and Hardy, who was born in 3 Argyle Street, his father being an actor and playwright. There can be little doubt which is the most popular. Stan has both a public house and a museum, but no memorial of Birkett exists. Lord Birkett, a great friend of Lakeland – his last action before his death in 1962 was to lead a successful action to oppose the flooding of Bannisdale – is however commemorated by Nameless Fell, above Douthwaite Head, now no longer innominate, being now known as Birkett Fell. Birkett left an interesting account of the war crimes tribunal. He found Goering 'complete master' of the US prosecutor Jackson, who seemed ignorant of 'the first principles of cross-examination'.

The Laurel and Hardy Museum, run by the dedicated Bill Cubin, is in a little courtyard opposite a shop supplying the requirements of witches and warlocks, off Market Square. A lifetime admirer of the comics, Bill Cubin has made a unique collection of photographs, posters, letters, films and memorabilia. It is more than forty years since I saw them in the flesh at the Empire Theatre, Newcastle, and I can still remember an acute pain from my immoderate mirth; it is a rare comic talent that can excel on both stage and screen. If the museum is shut, Bill leaves his telephone number on the door and will open up at the drop of a hat.

Swarthmoor Hall, between Pennington and Ulverston, is a good Elizabethan house, and of great importance to the Society of Friends for it was here that George Fox, their founder, dictated his *Journal.* Quakerism began in 1652, when George Fox saw a vision on Pendle

Hill, in Lancashire, which led him to discover the Westmorland Seekers, loosely connected groups of honest folk searching for the truth. From these merged the 'valiant sixty', all locals, who formed Fox's apostles.

Within a couple of weeks of Fox's first great gathering on Firbank Fell, between Kendal and Sedbergh, he had found his way to Swarthmoor, installed himself there, and quarrelled with the local vicar.

This took place in the absence of Swarthmoor's master, Judge Thomas Fell, a noted upright and decent magistrate and a staunch Independent, who was at first 'very much afflicted and surprised' to be met at the sand's edge by an excited deputation, led by a wrathful vicar, especially when he was informed that his young wife was harbouring an heretical and impoverished itinerant preacher. But Judge Fell was a wise man, and let Fox speak for himself. Although not converted (he liked to sit in his adjoining study, the door open, listening to the Quaker meetings) the Judge became an admirer of Fox and a protector of the Friends until his death a few years later.

Unlike Thomas West, George did not think much to Ulverston, full of 'liars, drunkards, whoremongers, and thieves, who follow filthy pleasures', but appreciated the hospitality of the Fell household.

Mrs Fell's daughter Sarah kept careful accounts which have survived, and are fascinating. She bought a 'black alamode Whiske' (which is a neckerchief) for sister Rachel, for which she paid 2 shillings, and another for Susanna, which cost 4s 4d; she only paid, good girl, 1s 10d for 'a little black whiske for myself'. But the purchase of a vizard mask and a hat for herself must have embarrassed her, for the price has been deleted. When William Penn came to visit in 1673 a fattened sheep was killed for the founder of Pennsylvania, at a cost of 7s 6d, but Issa Newby was only paid a penny ha'penny a day for haymaking.

Widow Margaret Fell was a remarkable lady, an Askew from Marsh Lodge (see page 137), who threw herself into the defence of Quakerism, interceding personally with the Protector and Charles II, and publishing numerous tracts, many written while in prison, including one early feminist document, *Women's Speaking Justified, Proved and Allowed by the Scriptures.* Eleven years after the Judge's death she married Fox, and survived him for eleven years, dying in 1702 at the age of eighty-seven. By then she had been able to address William III, thanking him for the protection he had given the Quakers.

Fox himself bought a house and some land from his stepdaughters in order to establish a Quaker meeting house at Swarthmoor in 1668. As well as the house, he gave 'my ebony bedstead, with the painted curtains, and the great elbow-chair that Robert Widders sent me; and my great sea-case or cellaridge, with the bottles in it. These I do give to stand in the house as heir-looms, when the house is made use of as a meeting place; so that a friend may have a bed to lie on, and a chair to sit on, and a bottle to hold a little water to drink.'

He also gave instructions as to how the house – or the barn – should be converted. It must be slated, not thatched, with the floor raised, the yard paved (with stones got by 'poor men') and the walls laid in lime and sand and a proper porch. In particular the meeting place should be large, 'for truth may increase'. Fox did not, however, want the meeting house to come in to immediate use to the detriment of existing meetings: 'Ffriends are not to meet in it soe long as ffriends can meet at Swarthmoore Hall.'

The meeting house, with its porch, yard and substantial walls, still exists in Swarthmoor, although a good deal altered in the nineteenth century, but his cellaridge and ebony (actually lignum vitae) bed have been preserved in the Hall, which is now owned by the Society of Friends, who open it to the public during the summer. An essential pilgrimage for Friends, it is intrinsically interesting as a good seventeenth-century gentry house, a cut above the statesmen's homes, but less grand than Levens or Sizergh.

The three-storey-high mullioned bay and balcony indicate its standing, although all the outbuildings and some of the main house have disappeared. Internally the most interesting feature is a four-post newel, running the full height of the stair, like a miniature lift shaft, supporting the stairs from the centre; for at least three centuries it has done rather well, although in the spring of 1988 rather too stout a party of Townswomen contrived to collapse one tread. Mr and Mrs Fell's rooms have their original beds, and fireplaces carved by the sons of the Flemish carvers who did the work at Cartmel Priory. All is very simple, Quakerly substantial, and lovingly tended. A quilt made by a Fell daughter covers one bed; decent girls apparently made twelve, of varying thicknesses, to accord with the seasons.

After his marriage to Margaret Fell, George contrived to live at Swarthmoor long enough, between constant journeying and imprisonment, to dictate his *Journal*. He has an excellent direct style, perhaps because he was uneducated, which preserves the spoken language of the seventeenth century.

A different religious group, although one that shares attractive Friendly features, now owns 'The Paradise of Furness'. **Conishead Priory** is one of the most splendid houses in Lakeland, but has had its vicissitudes. Founded by Gamel de Pennington, of whom we will hear much more, in the twelfth century as a leper hospital, it became an Augustinian priory, the canons of which continued medical work until the Dissolution. By the early nineteenth all remains were cleared away and an enormously costly Mysteries-of-Udolpho Gothic residence, complete with hermit in his cell, contractually obliged to refrain from haircuts and too-frequent washing, was built by Philip Wyatt, one of that prolific tribe of architects, for Colonel Bradyll of the Coldstream Guards. Impossible for modern domestic use, even Colonel Bradyll found it too extravagant to keep up and the Priory became firstly a hydropathic hotel and then a convalescent home for Durham miners. It is now the home of a friendly set of Buddhists, the Manjushri Institute. Without the Buddhists, Conishead would have perished as did Lowther. Faced with galloping dry rot and prodigious repair bills they have met the challenge manfully. The scale of the place is palatial – 100 foot-high turrets, 40 foot windows, a cloister corridor 170 feet long – and enough of the detail remains to prove what a magnificent home it was. The studio and the dining room have preserved their original ceilings, the oak room with its delicious caryatids, the Wailes stained glass, the linenfold panelling and the seventeenth-century screen are still cherished, although the pictures and the furniture have gone.

Outside the prayer flags flutter, and visitors can walk round Bradyll's gardens – they are welcome in the house too on summer weekends, and to stay at any time of the year, although preferably if they are attending one of the Institute's courses. After a century and a half's growth the American garden has developed some majestic firs, redwoods, hemlocks and maples. The beech wood is later, planted with native hardwoods, growing to the water's margin. The woods serve as habitat for squirrels both red and now intrusively grey, although these are being combated and numerous birds including kestrels, owls, long-tailed tits and tree-creepers. You can go right down to the beach which gives a far view to Coniston in the west and Helvellyn in the east and a near view of waders and herons.

Chapel Island lies offshore, over a long stretch of sand. Vestigial elements of an original chantry were absorbed by Colonel Bradyll into a romantic ruin, which used to be a popular picnic spot. The east gable with its lancets is said to be original, part of the Priory outpost on the sands themselves, where travellers at risk from the tides could be plucked to safety, and where a light marked the edge of the channel.

Wordsworth was impressed by it in 1794, when he walked to it across the sands from Rampside:

> . . . All that I saw or felt
> Was gentleness and peace. Upon a small
> And rocky island near, a fragment stood
> (Itself like a sea rock) the low remains
> (With shells encrusted, dark with briny weeds)
> Of a dilapidated structure . . .

and observed the guide leading travellers over the sands:

> Not far from that still ruin all the plain
> Lay spotted with a variegated crowd
> Of vehicles and travellers, horse and foot,
> Wading beneath the conduct of their guide
> In loose procession through the shallow stream
> Of Inland waters . . .

Bardsea is a compact village, clustering on a small hill, with the Bradyll Arms giving a good view over the bay as well as more substantial nourishment. The name commemorates the family that built Conishead, and started to build Bardsea Church, but ran out of money: the church was bought at auction by Mr T. E. Petty, who completed it, and became its first priest. Pevsner finds the church by George Webster 'without poetry' but he can never have gone inside, since the east window is by Wilhemina Geddes, one of the finest stained glass artists in recent times. Her much earlier glass at St Luke's, Wallsend, is powerful work, which would alone justify a visit to that not very prepossessing town. Martin Harrison, in his authoritative work on stained glass, commented that this 'must have been a severe shock to the genteel supporters of the liturgical movement . . .' Bardsea is more relaxed, but still commanding. The woods were once Crown property, planted to provide oak for ships' timbers. Now a country park, with free access, there are still fine stands of oak and ash, together with some large wild cherry trees. The Hospitallers were established at Bardsea, but there do not seem to be any traces of them left, although a much earlier monument survives just above Sea Wood on the slopes of Birkrigg Fell. The stone circles there – almost certainly two, but only one is clearly discernible – were used over a period of many centuries, which at least included the early Bronze Age, since a pot from that era is in the Barrow Museum.

There are more Bronze-Age burials, nearby at **Urswick,** as well as both neolithic and Romano-Celtic settlements, but nothing much to see on the ground except for the Quaker burying plot at Sunbrick, a moving, isolated sepulchre. Great Urswick Church, however, has plenty to offer – if you can get inside it, for like so many others nearby it is kept locked. Perseverance is needed, but the results of it are worthwhile, for the interior is full of interest.

The antiquity of the place is attested by two tenth-century cross fragments. The larger, the Tunwini cross, has an Anglo-Saxon inscription: *tunwini setae: aefter torohtred bekun aefter his baeurn; gebidaes ther saulae*, which, I am told, means 'Tunwin set up (this) in memory of Torhtred, a monument to his lord; pray for his soul'; and 'Lyl wrought this.' The quality of the carving of Adam and Eve, shows how much Anglo-Saxon sculpture had degenerated since the eighth century. (The subject is discussed in detail on pages 298–9.)

No criticism can be levelled at the modern carvings, which proliferate, the work of the Camden Guild of Handicrafts, mainly by Alec Miller. A most elegant sounding-board, by W. F. Nelson, in the shape of a scallop shell supported by putti, serves an eighteenth-century three-decker pulpit, and matches it perfectly. There is a fine roodloft, and engaging choir stalls. The heraldic glass deserves examination. Some parts of the south chancel windows are ancient, probably originating from Furness Abbey, since the Arms of Furness and those of Citeaux, the mother house, appear in the lancet window, together with a lion's head (Harrington) and a small bird. The other window, towards the east of the chancel, has the arms of Furness notables – Coupland, Kirby, Pennington, Broughton and le Fleming.

James Cranke, who is said to have taught Romney, painted the *Last Supper.* Many of the 'Gainsboroughs' and 'Reynolds' proudly exhibited in north-western homes, and on one occasion at least sold as such, are really by Cranke, a competent workman who practised at Warrington, but retired to Urswick, his native place.

St Mary's and St Michael's church is basically thirteenth-century, very straightforward with a big square tower and no crossing. High up in the west wall of the tower there is a fifteenth-century *Pietà*, a rarity in these parts. James Barwick of Bardsea Hall, now demolished, has a brass, the inscription on which starts:

> Fool man, why art thou such a sot
> To dote on that which soon is not?

Leave thy sinful lusts and pleasure,
Which thou delight'st in beyond measure . . .

The church was founded by Michael le Fleming (hence the dedication) whose descendant Daniel became its first vicar, some time during the twelfth century. The Furness monks claimed the right to present to the living, as indeed they claimed possession of all Furness. But this was disputed by Michael, who had been given the eastern part of the peninsula by Henry I: he successfully maintained his claim, and his descendants prospered, living on to worry Wordsworth seven centuries later.

The village pub is the General Burgoyne, 'Gentleman Johnny', who was one of the most literate officers the British army has seen, wrote plays with Sheridan, surrendered to the Americans at Saratoga, and has the best part in Shaw's *The Devil's Disciple.* Burgoyne married a Stanley and was MP for Preston for many years; he had literally to fight his first election, going to the polls with a loaded pistol in each hand.

Urswick also has a tarn in the centre of the village famous for its bream (permits from the nearby Derby Arms) of which it is very proud. Although of modest dimensions it adds much to the pleasantness of the place. And to the north of the village antiquarians will be able to make out the remains of a medieval field system.

Aldingham is wonderfully situated, right on the beach, lapped by the flood tides. A much less interesting building would be spectacular in such a setting, but the church of St Cuthbert is one of the best in the area. The oldest work is twelfth-century, like Urswick due to Michael le Fleming, and is to be found in the south arcade of the nave. Something over a century later the chancel and the west tower were added, the last as a fortification after the Scotish raid. It is an impressively solid piece of work. The timbers of the chancel roof have oddly scarfed ends, which seem to suggest their original role as ships' timbers.

The memorials include two restrained early-nineteenth-century examples, side by side, one in the classic, the other in the Gothic style. A poignant relic of imperial responsibility is a tablet commemorating the deaths of four grandsons of a nineteenth-century incumbent: one dead in Waziristan, one in Transvaal, and two on the Western Front. The east window is modern, and undistinguished; it should be compared with that at Bardsea to understand what contemporary stained glass should be about. St Cuthbert himself, complete with otters, is represented by a statue just inside the west door, given to the church by Durham Cathedral, where the saint is buried.

Aldingham Hall, a collected composition by Sir Matthew Digby Wyatt, very well preserved, is opposite the church. It was built for Dr John Stonard, who died before it was finished and left the house to his butler. The Wyatts were a complicated family: Matthew Digby's father was Philip's great-uncle; and just to make things more confused Philip's cousin Jeffrey changed his name to Wyattville in order to sound grander.

Aldingham and Bardsea beaches are good places to see the cocklers at work, driving their tractors far out to sea and returning at full pelt just ahead of the tide. Since the beds are the property of no-one in particular, 'foreign' cocklers, from Lancashire and Wales, sometimes make sallies, sweeping the beds clean, which is much resented by the locals.

A little further along the coast, Moat Farm and Moat Scar indicate where Michael le Fleming's first motte and bailey castle was built, perched like the church on the very edge of the sea. Some erosion has taken place in the intervening time and the bailey is now gradually relapsing into the sea. Between the footpath, the road and the beach itself, it is possible to walk all along the coastline here; painters should find it particularly attractive and un-Lakelandish, with tremendous opportunities for great broad washes and interesting architectural detail.

Gleaston Castle, possibly earlier a le Fleming hold, is ruinous and perhaps always was. It was started in a fit of nervousness after the Scots raid, but when Edward III asserted himself, after his fool of a father had been disposed of, confidence – presumably rightly enough, for that was the last trouble Furness ever had from the Scots – returned, and the building was never finished.

Dendron church was first built in 1642, by Robert Dickinson, a citizen of London, but born in Leece, to serve also as a school 'to have children brought upp in learning and taught therein'. The present structure is late-eighteenth-century, spare, but pleasant. Romney was one of those children 'taught therein' and Fox preached there on his first visit to Furness.

Norman Nicholson calls these Low Furness villages 'among the least self-conscious spots in Greater Lakeland' and so they are. Decent houses and properly looked after farms – short on black plastic, unburied sheep and binder twine, those infallible marks of a lazy farmer, and long on good hedging and well-maintained buildings.

Cartmel: the route over the sands

The improbable river Eea at Cartmel

Furness Abbey: the chapter house

While the east coast of Furness had been acquired by the le Flemings, the western part of the peninsula was Abbey land, starting at the Abbey Brook. Its history is interlinked with the prosperity of the Abbey, and the dispersal of its possessions after the Dissolution.

Based upon its solid holdings, from Walney Island to Hawkshead, **Furness** became one of the richest abbeys in the county, setting up daughter establishments first on Calder, then progressively further afield at Swineshead in Lancashire, Rushen in Man, and Iniscourcy and Abingdon in Ireland. The Abbey's prosperity was damaged by the Scots invasions of 1316 and 1322, after which its income was reduced from £176, at which it stood in 1292, to a meagre £13 6s 8d. By the time of the Dissolution this had recovered and increased to over £800, while the monks also ran a school, hospital and alms-houses, and provided free meals for their tenants, labourers and children.

Unlike those of Cartmel, the Furness brothers accepted the Disso-lution without too much struggle, and escaped their unhappy fate. The Abbey buildings, like Holker and so much else of the area, went first to the Prestons before passing to the Lowthers, ending up with the Cavendishes. The fabric of the conventual buildings has survived tolerably well, except for the church. They are in the unmistakable local red sandstone that forms the whole of that coast from Walney to St Bees, and crops up again in the Eden Valley. Like all Cistercian houses, Furness is beautifully set in a secluded spot, sheltered and well-watered, although bearing the unpromising name of the Valley of the Deadly Nightshade.

The best preserved, and most striking, is the great arcade of the chapter house, five deep, richly decorated round arches surmounted by a rank of lancet windows. The interior of the chapter house, which dates from around 1240, about the same period as the arcade, differs in character, less massive with slim, multi-faceted pillars, and more elegant, although still preserving the simplicity of the earlier times. The dormitory ran south of the chapter house; it was some 225 feet long by 40 feet wide, which gives some idea of the size of the establishment. The infirmary was 126 feet long, and wider than the dorter; its chapel is intact. Unlike the hospital at Beaune, where the beds were arranged in a line parallel to the wall, here the bed heads fitted into recesses along the wall, in the manner of a modern Night-ingale ward. The chapel, which has odd triangular-headed windows, contains a number of effigies and tomb covers, difficult to examine closely. Some of the better ones are visible in the gatehouse, including two strange forbidding knights in armour, with their helms closed, among the earliest of their kind, and found mainly in the north of England.

A good deal of amusement for children can be had poking about in the foundations of the octagonal kitchen, which is built over the beck, and identifying the sluice and hearths. As befits so large a community, there was a capacious privy and reredorter, discharging into the same beck, *upstream* of the kitchen, which can hardly have been the most pleasant of arrangements in a dry summer (they do happen!). There is also a nine-man-morris board to be identified in the floor of the guest house.

The ruins of the church are still impressive, and taken with what exists at Cartmel give some idea of how much was lost to English art at the Reformation. The single undamaged part is the sedilia on the south wall of the chancel. These, much later than the rest, are of the same period as King's College Chapel and of exquisite workmanship. They flank a piscina, and are all topped by the same cornice, with separate pinnacled canopies. The priests who used them must have had to struggle against the temptation towards pride.

All else is ruinous. The tracery of the east window is gone, as is of course the glass, which must have been magnificent. It was done by Sir John Petty of York who died in 1508, and a visit to York or even to the remnants of the York glass at Cartmel gives some idea of what has been destroyed.

One holiday from Hawkshead, Wordsworth and some other boys hired horses from the innkeeper and rode to Furness and back, a fair day's work for the animals. One wonders what the innkeeper said when they returned the next day, after:

> Lighted by gleams of moonlight from the sea
> We beat with thundering hoofs the level strand.

They did not behave too well in the Abbey either: after experiencing that

> ... more than inland peace,
> Left by the west wind sweeping over-head
> From a tumultuous ocean, trees and flowers
> In that sequestered valley may be seen,
> Both silent and both motionless alike

they galloped off,

> Our steeds remounted and the summons given
> With whip and spur we through the chantry flew
> In uncouth race, and left the cross-legged knight,
> And the stone abbot, and that single wren
> Which one day sang so sweetly in the nave . . .

After a buffeting from the elements on Roa one knows exactly what Wordsworth meant by 'that more than inland peace'.

Towards the end of his life he got most indignant, and rightly so, at the idea of the railway being built right through the Abbey precincts. He contrasts the reverent behaviour of the navvies, taking time off in the ruins, with the meanness of the capitalists only concerned with selecting the cheapest route. The opening is Wordsworth at his most ludicrous:

> Well have you Railway labourers to *This* ground
> Withdrawn for noon tide rest . . .

but ends with a still-relevant couplet:

> Profane despoilers, stand ye not reproved,
> While thus these simple hearted men are moved?

It would be fond to imagine that **Barrow** might ever become a tourist favourite, but having got as far as Furness Abbey the town which now surrounds it has something to offer, and the unprepossessing flats of the Barrow Islands, Foulney, Roa, Piel and Walney are of prime importance to birdwatchers.

But W. G. Collingwood found 'abundant poetry and picturesqueness, for anyone who does not travel in blinkers', and D. H. Lawrence described 'the amazing sunsets over flat sands and the smoky sea . . . the amazing, vivid, visionary beauty of everything, heightened by the immense pain everywhere': he was there in August 1914.

There was not much to Barrow before the nineteenth century beyond a few scattered hamlets, including the uneuphonious Stank: Barrow itself is the creation almost entirely of two men, Henry Schneider and John Ramsden. In 1839, when Barrow was a hamlet of a couple of dozen houses, Schneider bought the Whiteriggs iron mine and began to export ore from a jetty at Barrow. He followed this up with the development in 1851 of the rich Park ore deposit near Askham. Six years later, when the railway connection to Lancaster was complete, it became feasible to import Durham coal to make steel. Furness haematite proved eminently suitable for the new Bessemer process, and Schneider and Ramsden combined to found the Barrow Haematite Iron and Steel Company. Ramsden arrived with the railway as manager of the engineering department in 1846, and pushed through the Schneider deals, the construction of docks, the establishment of a shipbuilding industry, and, with active support from the seventh Duke of Devonshire at Holker, the development of an entirely new city. Not the most attractive of towns, with few good buildings (the working men's club in Abbey Road is the best, a meticulous Picardy château), it is still not without a rugged charm. You feel it does very well to be there at all, still battling it out.

It has been a battle, too, with the collapse of the steel industry. Barrow has been saved by one of Ramsden's initiatives, the Barrow Iron Shipbuilding Company. Although it built fine merchant steamers to start with, it was bought by Vickers at the turn of the century and became an important warship yard, with a unique record in building submersible craft. Their first were two steam-driven Nordenfeldt boats: a hundred years later they are building nuclear-powered submarines, which can be seen by the public on special occasions. Their huge sheds, dominating the town, are strikingly impressive. Vickers built airships, too, on Walney Island, and although these were not successful one of the Vickers engineers, the young Barnes Wallis, developed his revolutionary principles of geodetic construction, which have yet to be fully developed, from the work he did at Barrow.

A new and architecturally admirable museum has been built over one of the nineteenth century docks. Sensibly and informatively arranged, although still awaiting the arrival of many items, and with a new sea-lock giving a permanent basin, the Barrow Dock Museum is a credit to the town.

Whatever the limitations of Barrow itself, its location makes the environs interesting. **Piel Castle** – the pele of Foulney – on a small island has been there since the fourteenth century as a coastal defence, protecting the fine natural harbour behind Walney Island. The castle is not much more than a pele tower – hence its name – with an outer wall and some domestic building, including a chapel, but it makes a good ruin. The pele was built by the monks of Furness, after the Scots raid of 1322, in order to protect their shipping and to provide a secure store for goods awaiting transport. The Abbot had a number of ships – the *Sea Lewe* and *Mari Cogge* are listed – and in 1324 the Abbot was ordered to prepare all his vessels of over forty

132

tons burthen (i.e. capable of carrying forty tuns of wine, the origin of ship carrying capacity measurement). Some early cannon, of the late fourteenth century, were recovered from a wreck off Walney, and are kept at the Artillery Museum at Woolwich. One of them is about ten feet long, which sounds too big for a ship of that period and might have been meant for coastal defence.

By the sixteenth century Piel had fallen into disrepair: 'Castle and haven lying both nowe and in tyme of warre w'out strength or garde.' A particularly dangerous state of things when the population were 'so voyde bothe of the feare of God and of Her Majesties laws', and 'all ynfected with . . . Romish poyson', and the deputy steward Thomas Preston was a 'Papishe Atheiste'.

But Piel was not restored, and is now a popular place to visit in the summer, not least because the island also houses a pub, the Ship Inn. You used to, and still may, be able to be dubbed Knight of Piel. This involved paying for drinks for everyone in the bar, and undertaking that 'if there are any sports taking place on the island, such as boat racing, cock-fighting, bull-baiting or pigeon shooting, to help the King of Piel with your assistance'. If a Knight were ever wrecked and drowned off Piel he was entitled to go to the Inn and demand a night's lodging and as much as he could eat and drink. You can certainly still have a night's lodging, or more, if you telephone beforehand to make sure that the ferry is operating, but you are expected to pay!

Piel became famous, for a moment in June 1487 when Lambert Simnel landed there 'with a great multytude of stranngers with force and armes, that ys to saye, swerdys, speris, marispikes, bowes, gounes, harneys, brigandynes, hawberkers, and many other wepyns and harnes defencible', in his attempt to expel the new King Henry VII.

Although Simnel's rising, and the man himself, were the objects of later derision, he had been taken seriously enough in Ireland, where Lambert was crowned, in Christ Church, Dublin, as Edward VI. Even if few in England believed his claim to be either Richard, one of the Princes said to have been murdered in the Tower, or Edward of Warwick, son of the late George, Duke of Clarence – he of the butt of Malmsey – his backing was solid enough. Duchess Margaret of Burgundy had paid for a powerful expeditionary force of German professionals led by Martin Swart, who were joined by Irish, making a force of 8000. The choice of Piel owed something to the fact that Sir Thomas Broughton of Broughton had taken an active part in the previous rising against Henry Tudor.

Simnel's force did not meet much in the way of opposition, but raised few recruits, the people not being minded to have a king 'brought in to them on the shoulders of Irish and Dutch'. The Earl of Lincoln was in command, and eventually met the royal army south of Newark. The Germans and the Irish fought well, but the latter were no match for armed men, and were killed 'like dumb and brute beastes' as were Lincoln, Swart and probably Broughton, although a tale went about that he escaped to live in hiding near Witherslack. Simnel was an object of derision: not punished, he was given a job as turnspit, and later as falconer. He outlived Henry, and died in 1525.

A contemporary ballad had the refrain: 'Martin Swart and his men, sodledum sodledum bell!'

Piel is reached by a boat from **Roa** island, now joined to the mainland by a causeway. Roa is the home of winds, a collection of cottages and the remains of a villa, built by Schneider, and protected by a row of cannon. The Furness line originally started from a pier at Roa, before Barrow was developed, but was then abandoned, and Roa has ever since had a neglected aspect, as though its *raison d'être* had evaporated. On the mainland end of the causeway is **Rampside,** one of the ancient villages. The pub there is the Concle, which is meant to be derived from 'Conc Hole' – concs being whelks. It has been there for some time, but Knype Hall has been there longer. A newly restored, restrained seventeenth-century house, the roof line is entirely taken up by twelve identical chimneys, set askew like the tower of Cartmel. There are other examples of this oddity in the area but this is the best.

Wordsworth stayed at Rampside, in what is now the Clarke Arms in 1794, and later wrote:

> I was thy neighbour once, thou rugged Pile
> Four summer weeks I dwelt in sight of thee:
> I saw thee every day; and all the while
> Thy form was sleeping on a glassy sea.

It must have been an extraordinarily good summer!

Foulney island is not really an island either, but tenuously joined by an embankment. It is a good, if uncomfortable place for observing sea-birds – terns, those remarkable dive-bombers, nest there, and the amicable cuddy ducks, or eider ducks traditionally associated with St Cuthbert.

Walney island has birdwatching more highly organized. The southern part of the island is a sanctuary, with observation hides, which are particularly rewarding in the winter and early spring, when literally tens of thousands of oyster catchers, knot, dunlin and curlews can be seen, as well as merganser, scoter and golden plovers. Gulls' eggs are delicious with smoked salmon or Morecambe Bay shrimps, but difficult to come by locally. George Fox did not have much luck on Walney: on his first visit 'the people were something rude' and on his second 'as soon as I came in to land there rushed out about forty men with staves, clubs and fishing poles, and fell upon me, beating and punching me, and endeavoured to thrust me backwards in to the sea'.

Dalton used to be very much the capital of Furness, the chief town of the Abbots, who had their courthouse – and a gallows – there. The only court records come from after the Dissolution, when the existing cases were being cleared up by Royal Commissioners. Nothing too grave was under judgement: the only hanging was that of a dog, proved as a 'shepeworyer'. But some people were fined for not keeping proper hedges, and they still ought to be. In other parts of England greedy landowners have butchered their hedges, or grubbed them up entirely, in the quest for a few more square yards. In Furness they look after them properly, and the young hinds are trained in layering fences decently.

The courthouse stands, a rare example of an unaltered pele tower. It is at one end of the car park, the other being marked by an engaging nineteenth-century cast-iron fountain. St Mary's church is also Victorian, although with a very much longer history, since there was a church on the site in 1195. As late as 1825 the floor was still earthen, and there was little trace of the original work remaining when the present church was designed in the 1880s by Paley and Austin. It is a fine example of confident High Victorian architecture which makes full use of the variety of colours found in local stone, and has some good local craftsmanship apparent in the carvings. Romney is buried here, in his native town, and the vicarage garden is built over a plague pit.

Even before Barrow emerged, Ulverston had taken over from Dalton as the chief market-place, so there is not much else of consequence in the town. Two centuries ago West described it as 'a miserable antiquated vill, once the pride now the shame of Furness'. This is a bit hard, for there are many worse places than Dalton, which now also boasts a swimming pool and a Wildlife Animal Park. David Gill runs this primarily as a conservation project, with animals kept as freely as possible. Parrots fly around, and lemurs lurk in the trees, and with such rarities as a Siberian tiger, the park is worth finding. One small, but decisive Civil War action took place in Dalton in the summer of 1644 in which the Parliamentary sympathizers were soundly beaten, routed by a single volley and a charge. Two hundred prisoners were taken, besides those killed; the only Royalist casualty was Sir John Preston, who got a kick on the head by which 'his perfect sense and understanding he recover'd not for half a year'. The Prestons were 'Papist and Delinquent' and had paid for their defeat at Lindal the previous year (see below) by having the profits of their Cartmel and Dalton livings sequestered, so this must have been a pleasant revenge.

Lindal in Furness is not to be confused with Wilkinson's Lindale, over in Westmorland. What there is to see in Lindal, which is not a great deal, is of less interest than what might be found there one day. Lindal formed a temporary terminus of the Barrow railway, when at some time towards the end of the nineteenth century an engine failed to stop and careered right to the end of the line where it disappeared into an old mine shaft. Since the crew had jumped to safety and the shaft was so deep as to make salvage impossible, the locomotive still lies buried there to await the attentions of steam enthusiasts.

In 1643 Lindal was the scene of another modest battle, between a Royalist force of about fifteen hundred under Sir William Hudleston, and a rather smaller Parliamentary army led by Colonel Rigby. It cannot have been a very bloody affair, for Rigby, clearly a tough professional, refused to call it even a skirmish. The Royalists were quickly routed, and over three hundred prisoners taken, together with their ammunition and supplies.

Pennington church has a real *sheela-na-gig,* a medieval fertility figure, an unusual feature anywhere, but even rarer in these Puritan parts. She owes her survival to having been buried in the east wall, and only revealed during the rebuilding of 1925, the last in a series since the church's establishment. The workmen were understandably embarrassed. 'They would not like the parson to see it' and wanted to smash it up. But, happily, she survived and is shown triumphantly in the porch.

Less sensational, but even rarer, is a tympanum discovered early this century in a farmhouse, now set in the south aisle. Crudely sculptured from the local sandstone, it shows a primitive Christ, with a runic inscription in old Norse: 'Gamel built this church, Hubert Mason wrought this stone.' This, unbelievably, records the foundation of the church by Gamel de Pennington about 1170. The date is extraordinary: a century after the conquest, just about contemporary with the wonderful Latin verses of the Arundel manuscripts, the Norman-named inhabitants of Furness, and presumably their feudal lords, still used Norse – and in runes – even for ecclesiastic inscriptions. (The survival of Norse as the spoken language is also attested further north; Coniston is 'King's town' and the received opinion is that the king in question was Stephen. Anywhere else in England it would then surely have been simply Kingston.)

Gamel de Pennington's successors moved to Muncaster Castle in about 1240, and are there still. Gamel's own home was Pennington Castle, the earthworks of which are visible on a hill about half a mile off.

The remainder of the church is unremarkable, except for the old font and the functional oil lamps, first installed in the 1826 rebuilding. The churchyard is ancient, judging from its circular enceinte.

The road from Pennington back to the west coast traverses fells full of old iron workings, and is not the sort of place to wander on a foggy night. At first sight the West Furness coast looks rather dull; certainly the main road from Dalston to Grizebeck passes little of interest, apart from the perennially spectacular view up towards Coniston and across to Millom, which appears quite romantic from a distance. But there are discoveries to be made just a little way off the beaten track. **Marsh Lodge,** almost on the edge of the sea, is the ancestral home of the Askew family, and was once a fine seven-bay William and Mary house. The gateposts, palatial in size and detailing, and the splendid doorway, witness this, but it needs a little imagination to restore the decayed seventeenth-century wings, in the middle of which a straightforward nineteenth-century house has been planted, retaining the original fenestration. Another hint of past greatness is the stone arcading on a large detached barn up the lane.

Footpaths cross the marshes a little further along at **Sandside,** where the last stage of the sands route began – again just behind the railway station – and where you can walk with safety at least all over the salt marshes. Sandside has a Ship Inn of 1671, which boasts a curious stables, the slate blocks of which have been carved by a master letterer; a variety of beautiful nineteenth-century styles record 'Come Again', 'Young Orville', 'Wait for the Waggon' and 'Galloway Jock and Robert Burns'.

Kirby Ireleth Moor has been a centre of quarrying for a long time. The mineral rights belonged to the Earl of Burlington – hence

Burlington Slate quarries. Before the railway came the slate was sent sliding off to the ships down inclined planes. It is a good blue slate, less gloomy than the Welsh equivalent, and rather expensive. The Earl used to have the right to hold a court in the Punch Bowl Inn at Beckside, which must have provided some profitable trade to the innkeeper. Ireleth's parish church is a few miles away at Beckside, and has a good Norman doorway and other traces of early work, but, as Mannex's guide regretted in 1853, 'exhibits as alas do many other of our country churches, the *refined* tastes of modern churchwardens, who have superimposed a nondescript set of additions'. Things were not improved by a later restoration, which destroyed some wall paintings which may have been similar to those at Kirby Hall.

The churchwardens left some good bits of thirteenth-century glass in place in the chancel: to the north a pretty grisaille window and on the south a wild-eyed Christ wearing what seems to be a huge orange bow tie. The clarity and vigour of the colours prove that this was among the best of the stainer's work. Some enterprising craftsman has recently provided a carved and painted door in the chancel, with incidents from the life of St Cuthbert, the patron saint. Cuthbert also features in a pleasant modern window, with his duck and his otter. Among the church's silver is a paten given by Colonel Kirby in 1698, 'taken from the French who had plundered Cartagena in New Spaine' in the famous sack of the year before. The gift may have been in the form of a penitent gesture, for the Colonel was himself accused of pillaging, and was actually hanged for murder a few years later.

It is easy to miss Kirby Hall entirely, as Pevsner did. This now decayed but clearly once-splendid fifteenth-century house lies just off the main road, surrounded by modern farm buildings. The roof of one wing has collapsed, and the mullioned bay is only a single storey, but lying about outside are some carved grotesques and gargoyles that indicate its history. It does not seem to have been built as a pele, but as an early manor house. Inside on the first floor, reached through a trapdoor, is the chapel, which was once decorated with handsome sixteenth-century frescoes. Most of these have been destroyed by the damp, but enough remains to show what a treasure it must have been; black letter texts run along the coving, with a large repeated pattern of birds and flowers below.

The house belongs to the Holker estates, who, with the support of English Heritage, are about to restore the roof, which will preserve the chapel and its murals.

6

Bowness and Windermere

In spite of growing year by year more like the Serpentine on a busy Sunday, Windermere is after all the biggest of the lakes, and the most famous, and the one presenting the most spectacular views, so it deserves a thoughtful approach. The worst way of getting there is the most usual; straight off the M6, onto the Kendal bypass, up the A591, to arrive at the outskirts of Windermere in a line of traffic. Ranks of Victorian buildings, dark in random slate, lie below, presenting the immediate dilemma of finding somewhere to park while registering the views across the lake.

It is not Windermere's fault that like Bowness, and now Ambleside, its only *raison d'être* is tourism. Kendal has its industries, Cockermouth, Keswick and Penrith still have important markets, but Windermere exists only because that is where the railway ended. Writing in 1940 Doreen Wallace was very stern about Windermere: 'It is made of horrible Victorian gothick houses that disfigure most Lake District towns and villages . . . the houses of the gentry and near gentry are as if a Swiss chalet and a London suburban villa committed miscegenation and the offspring was made of a peculiarly dark, unyielding, slaty stone, and inherited three stories, and at least two gables from the other, there you have the typical Lakeland lodging house.'

Tough stuff, and while it is true that the slates are gloomy, we have seen since 1940 how really bad modern building can get, and are ready to embrace even Lakeland lodging houses.

An alternative previously mentioned is to branch off the A590 and take the A5074 up the Lyth Valley, from which a number of minor roads branch off to lead to the Windermere shore; or to take the left-hand fork at the Kendal roundabout on the A591 and follow the B5284 via Crook to Bowness. This skirts the historic ground of **Rather Heath,** where the Westmerian yeomen made their stand against Stuart oppression. Kendal was one of the centres of disaffection in the early seventeenth century when the landlords attempted to extinguish Border tenants' rights, the system by which tenants, in return for mustering to arms against the Scots, were assured of their tenure being inherited by their successors. In this the landlords were encouraged by James I, who, as an émigré Scot and a despot, detested the idea of independent, well-armed tenant farmers always ready to lay waste to a few Scottish villages. The Kendal men gathered on Rather Heath, which lies between the two roads, to present their petition. They did not leave their weapons at home. The hint was taken, and tenant right continued in being although avaricious James succeeded in obtaining a monetary recompense for having given up his claim.

But if the direct route has to be taken then both Staveley and Ings are worth stopping at. **Staveley-in-Westmorland** is bigger than Staveley in Lancashire (see page 110), and has in St James's church, a little way off the main road to the right, one of the most magnificent Morris & Co. windows imaginable, designed by Sir Edward Burne-Jones, and a miracle of dark blue beauty which is unnoticed by most guide books. Nothing remains of the old church, St Margaret's, but the fourteenth-century tower, now becoming derelict.

A decent pub, the Eagle and Child, is named after the crest of Lord Derby, but the story of the lord who arranged to have his natural son 'found' in an eagle's nest is an ancient one (wrongly reputed to be in Domesday Book). The sign of the Duke William shows the solid figure of the Hanoverian Duke on his white horse, another proof of local admiration for the hero of Culloden.

The obelisk on the right on the way in to Staveley was erected in 1814 by James Bateman of Tolson Hall to commemorate the endeavours of William Pitt, 'the pilot that weathered the storm', now that the Corsican tyrant was safely confined on Elba. Bateman was so discouraged by the Hundred Days that he did not attach the plaque, which was done only a century later by Charles Cropper. On the other side of the village it is easy to miss Ings, hidden behind a big petrol station and Little Chef restaurant. Ings Church was built in 1743 by Robert Bateman, forelder of James:

> He was a parish-boy – at the church door
> They made a gathering for him, shillings, pence
> And halfpennies, wherewith the neighbours bought
> A basket which they filled with pedlar's wares;
> And, with this basket on his arm, the lad
> Went up to London . . .

Wordsworth, of course. Bateman prospered as a Leghorn merchant, and repaid the parish by building a new church, on a bucolic Georgian idea, with pinnacles that look like flaming torches, and a fine Italian marble interior. Dorothy and Mary Wordsworth visited it in 1802, and described it as a 'neat little place, with a marble floor and a marble communion table, with a painting over it of the Last Supper . . . The woman told us that "they had painted them as near they could by the dresses as they are described in the bible" and gay enough they are.' He also built himself a new house, Reston Hall, off the road back towards Staveley.

Peter and Jeremy Hall have been making fine furniture at Staveley for a quarter of a century. They see themselves as continuing the Gillow tradition of simple elegance and restoring antiques to the most exacting standards.

A road opposite the church leads past Grassgarth to a prehistoric settlement, and serves as a pathway on the east side of Applethwaite Common to Kentmere. The names of Ings and Grassgarth record the old Norse system of land use. A 'grass' – about eight acres – was a unit sufficient to support a holding of one horse, three cows, seventeen sheep and twenty geese in winter grazing off the fog or aftermath together with hay; the animals being loosed up on the fell *saeters* during the summer months to allow the hay to grow, fertilized by their winter droppings. *Ings* is similar – a well-watered meadow. The whole of the area to the south of Ings and Staveley, the watershed between the Gowan/Kent and Lyth Valleys, is pleasantly broken country, with little woods and tarns, well away from the bustle of the main roads.

Inevitably, however, by whatever route, one comes at some time to the **Windermere** conglomerate, and since it is not without attractions – especially at Bowness - and since most of the hotels and many of the best and worst restaurants are there, the Bowness-Ambleside strip has to be considered.

The tourist office just on the left in front of the railway station – a pretty building – is invaluable. The staff will save the whole business of tramping about looking for accommodation by arranging it over the telephone for a modest fee. Although they are efficient, and have an extensive register of beds, it is plain daft to leave things till the last minute on a summer weekend, when this part of the Lake District becomes jammed. The time must come soon when traffic will have to be turned away from Kendal, and tourists will have to sneak in round one of the back doubles.

The Windermere Hotel, opposite the station, was famous as Riggs', built in 1847 and one of the few remaining early hotels

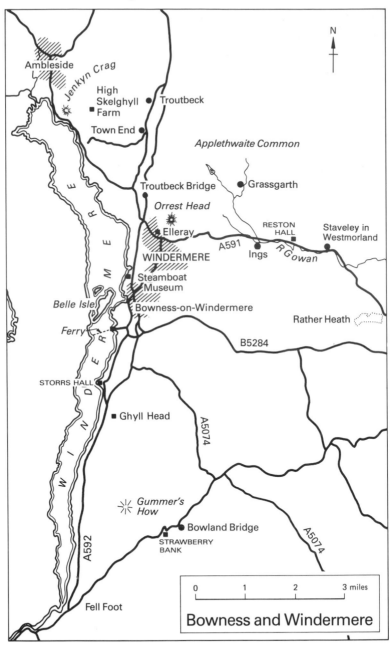

N

Ambleside

Jenkyn Crag

High
Skelghyll
Farm ■

● Troutbeck

Town End ●

Applethwaite Common

● Troutbeck Bridge

Orrest Head

● Grassgarth

● Elleray

RESTON
HALL ■

Staveley in
Westmorland ●

A591

Ings ●

R Gowan

WINDERMERE

Steamboat
Museum

Belle Isle

Bowness-on-Windermere

Rather Heath

Ferry

B5284

STORRS HALL ●

■ Ghyll Head

A5074

W I N D E R M E R E

*Gummer's
How*

● Bowland Bridge

A5074

STRAWBERRY
BANK

A592

Fell Foot

| 0 | 1 | 2 | 3 miles |

Bowness and Windermere

especially built to serve the tourist trade. 'A prince of hotels; one of the best and most moderate in England,' Herman Prior called it in 1860 in his *Pedestrian Guide to the Lakes;* the Riggs family were prominent hoteliers, and ran the first big hotel at Grange as well. Behind it Orrest Head, a notable viewpoint, rises, and gives an opportunity to get one's bearings, helped by a panorama on the crest. The important hills lie to the north, looking up the lake. Scafell appears in the gap between two nearer hills; just to the north the Langdale Pikes are unmistakable; Wansfell Pike rises above Troutbeck, and Ill Bell on High Street is round to the north-east. Wordsworth wrote of the view from Orrest Head:

> Standing alone, as from a rampart's edge,
> I over looked the bed of Windemere,
> Like a vast river, stretching in the sun.
> With exultation, at my feet I saw
> Lake, islands, promontories, gleaming bays,
> A universe of Nature's fairest forms
> Proudly revealed with instantaneous burst.

The difficulty now would be to 'stand alone' on Orrest Head, but the prospect still deserves enthusiasm. The walk can be prolonged, with the benefit of some good views, to the Low Wood Hotel. The path crosses the Trout Beck neat Townfoot, and continues via High Skelghyll Farm and Jenkyn Crag.

Just below Orrest Head is Elleray, the home of John Wilson in the early years of the nineteenth century. A multifaceted character, elected Professor of Philosophy at Edinburgh although he took his duties tolerably lightly, Wilson was a great cult figure in the literary society of the time. As a contributor to *Blackwood's Magazine* under the name of Christopher North he showed his insensitivity by attacking Keats, and demonstrated his own incompetence by writing some of the worst poetry ever to get into print. It can read like a parody of Gray:

> Sylph like with graceful pride
> I saw the wild Louisa glide

or Coleridge:

> Why sits so long beside yon cottage door
> That aged man with tresses thin and hoar . . .

or Wordsworth:

143

I wander'd lonely, like a pilgrim sad
O'er mountains known but to the eagle's gaze

But it was all meant seriously and seriously applauded. Wilson's series of essays, *Noctes Ambrosianae,* formed the base of his contemporary reputation and power, but although lively enough, now only indicates how transient are journalistic reputations. But what impressed his contemporaries, and much later continued to impress Norman Nicholson, was the zest for living that John Wilson/Christopher North exhibited.

> Instead, let us recognize in Christopher the first man to respond, with the whole of his bodily being, to the challenge of the Lakes. To him what the Lakes offered above all else was the physical stimulus of air, sunlight, space, and water. The gush and growth of bracken and grass, the bubble and bounce of becks, the whirl and withering of the wind – all this made a clean challenge to lung and muscle . . . His pastimes, admittedly, were not quite the same as ours; wrestling, jumping, swimming, shooting, riding, chasing bulls through the meadows in the hours just before dawn – 'a sixteen stoner who has tried it without gloves with the Game Chicken, and got none the worse, a cocker, a racer, a sixbottler, a twenty four tumblerer, and out and outer, a true, upright, knocking-down, poetical prosaic, moral, professional, hard-drinking, fierce-eating, good-looking honourable, straight forward Tory,' said one of his own clan. In his *Letters from the Lakes* which he wrote (under the character of a foreign visitor) in imitation of Southey's Don Espriella he gives an account of an excellent two days tour which included all the then little known western dales. But for the most part his pleasures were more dashing, releasing the pressure of those spirits which as a young man hurled his body across streams, and, as an old man, made him weep bucketfuls at the sound of his own rhetoric. For Wilson was no clerk, or mechanic or factory hand, no inhabitant of working class street or suburb, no product of a century and a half of industrial urbanization. He came to the Lakes superb in physique, insatiable in appetite, and unlimited in funds, and if his gusto was in part an impersonation, a loud laugh to cover a timid heart, it was also immensely and endearingly uninhibited.

The portrait in the Wordsworth museum at Grasmere shows a handsome long-legged young fellow, full of confidence. One can understand how, even in pre-Thatcherite days, when Tories really were Tories, such a man stamped his personality on a whole generation.

St Mary's, Applethwaite – really Windermere, but Applethwaite is the parish's name – is a sparse church with some good modern glass in the west end of both aisles. The adoration of the Magi and the shepherds, and Christ among the doctors, include some spirited characters; the shepherd playing pan pipes is particularly agreeable. There are also a couple of good Victorian windows in the north and south aisles. The north window is either by or closely after Henry Holiday, and shows two attractive Morrisy girls, Hope and Patience. An arsonist caused extensive damage in 1988, which has been well, and doubtless expensively, repaired.

The other church, St John Evangelist, now disused and boarded up is said to have a screen carved – and well carved – by the vicar and parishioners, and some decent Holiday glass.

A peculiar little tower, on the opposite side of the road, is a monument to M. J. B. Baddeley, author of the *Thorough Guide to the Lakes,* who made himself the authority on the subject; for many years Baddeley was to Lakeland visitors as Baedeker was to travellers in Germany. He has probably still the best series of panoramas, and his orotund style can be entertaining: 'Thanks to the philanthropic policy which, since its initiation by the Midland Company in 1872, has become all but universal throughout the kingdom, the tourist need only reckon the number of miles from his home to the portals of the district, and lay aside a corresponding number of pence, to ensure being conveyed there with an amount of comfort and expedition unknown to any but first-class passengers on the continent . . .' He could hardly say the same today!

Although Windermere did not exist before the railway (there were a few cottages know as Birthwaite), **Bowness** is a place of some antiquity, as being at the narrowest part of the central lake and the most suitable place for a ferry, a service that has been operating at least since the fifteenth century. St Martin's church dates from 1483, although there was an earlier building on the site. The interior was given a thorough going-over in 1879 and might benefit from an irreverent coat of whitewash, but there are some good things, of which the finest is the east window. This is very fine indeed, worthwhile sitting down and studying with a pair of field glasses, if you happen to have them handy – in fact this is one of many churches where an enterprising parochial church council might invest in the sort of coin-operated binoculars you find on piers, and which children love. Some of the glass came from Cartmel, including the panels along the bottom, one of which shows a group of Cartmel canons, and another with the Prior himself; this was originally recorded as being 'William Plo . . . Prior of Cartmel', but the inscription has now vanished. The coats of arms, all of local families, visible in the upper part of the window, include those of John Washington of Warton, who died in 1407, and was great-great-great-great-great-great-great-great-great-great-grandfather of George. These Washingtons came to Warton at the end of the thirteenth century, and were a cadet line of the Wessyngtons of Wessyngton (now Washington), in County Durham. Although originally Scots, from the Hirsel in Berwickshire, now the home of Lord Home, one William had the good sense to move to Durham about 1180, when he acquired Washington from Bishop Pusey of Durham. The existing Washington Old Hall was started some time in the fourteenth century, and my mother being born there gives me a personal interest in it. (Being born in the village myself, my passport has always confused the US immigration service, 'Oh, yes, you have a town of that name, too?' one asks them innocently.) The arms are of course the stars and stripes (or, to be heraldically correct, mullets and bars) and are not easy to spot, being part of a group of four. There are Washingtons still about in the neighbourhood, led by the elegant Colonel Washington of Dacre.

The central part of the window was probably made for the church; it shows a Crucifixion with attendant saints and angels. On the right-hand side there are some earlier fragments of other saints, including St Lawrence and St Stephen, and one even earlier, a little green Virgin and Child of circa 1260.

There is an odd panel in a window in the north aisle, showing the emblems of the carriers' trade. The difficult roads of the Lake District made the carrier an important part of rural existence right into the twentieth century. Mrs Thornburgh in *Robert Elsmere* (one of Mrs Humphry Ward's best) has her tea party ruined when the carrier forgets to pick up the cakes she ordered from Kendal. The implements in the window are a Wantey hook, a coil of rope, and a bunch of packing pricks.

The texts on the walls are Victorian but those between the arches are from about 1600; one is a set of questions and answers from a book written by Robert Openshaw in 1548, and uncompromisingly Protestant they are, the Reformation equivalent of Stalinist posters: 'Is the breade and wine turned into the boddie and blood of Christ?' Answer, firmly, 'No.' So much for transubstantiation. Equally anti-papistical is a set of Latin hexameters on the soffit of an arch of the south side of the nave; written by one 'Christopherus Philipson,

Junior, Generosus', of Calgarth in 1629, they commemorate the Gunpowder Plot. The original Latin is difficult to elucidate, but I have seen it translated as: 'This is a day more famed as each year brings it round. Rejoice, good men. The mischief conspired in Stygian gloom has been made an empty tale at the hand of Providence. England, which was to be conspicuous by the greatness of its ruin, may now sing hymns, since she has remained free by the grace of Heaven.'

The best monument is that of Bishop Watson of Calgarth. It is an eccentric Flaxman piece, and reminds one that Flaxman had a streak of the surreal, even if to a lesser extent than his contemporary Fuseli. The Bishop's crozier is superimposed right across the tablet, projecting beneath the bottom. It is a highly inappropriate piece of symbolism, since Watson was anything but a faithful shepherd to his sheep: appointed Bishop of Llandaff, he lived in Westmorland and visited his see once every three years. The Bishop's father, who was Master of Heversham grammar school, was born in 1672: the Bishop died in 1816, father and son therefore spanning nearly a century and a half between them – the Restoration to the Regency, Dryden to Shelley. Watson was what the Scots call 'a lad of parts', who made his way to Trinity College, Cambridge, and, at the age of twenty-seven, was appointed to the chair of Chemistry, knowing, as he admitted, nothing whatsoever about the subject.

He nevertheless made himself one of the more distinguished scientists of his time, an FRS, and the author of some classically significant papers. Seven years later, equally ignorant of his new subject, he was created Regius Professor of Divinity, getting himself a sham degree the day before election. Once again, he made himself a very respectable political theologian, taking the best side on all questions – anti-slave trade, Tories and Bonaparte, pro-ecclesiastical and agricultural reform, and a dedicated tree planter.

From 1789 he lived in his new house at Calgarth Park, now a hospital. He bothered Wales, where he was known as the bishop who lived in Westmorland, not at all, but kept nagging at the Whigs to help him to a better job; he was once very nearly made Archbishop of York, and would probably have stayed away from there just as contentedly.

The bowl of the font, with little heads on the angle, is a relic of the first, thirteenth-century church. Adjacent to it is a nice seventeenth-century statue of St Martin of Tours, in his characteristic act of slicing his cloak in two and giving half to a beggar.

Rasselas Belfield is buried in the churchyard outside the east window, with the epitaph:

> A slave by birth I left my native land,
> And found my freedom on Britannia's strand.

He was a black servant, named after Dr Johnson's Abyssinian prince. Black servants were not uncommon in eighteenth-century Cumbria; one Suffolk Stockdale from Cartmel attacked his master in a murderous frenzy. The attack was averted, and, since Cumbrians never like bringing the law into personal affairs, Suffolk was bundled into a chest where he was kept until a convenient ship could be found to return him to the West Indies from whence he had come. Thomas Ullock, who died in 1791, is opposite:

> Poor Tom came here to lie
> From Battles of Dettingen and Fontenoy in 1743 and 1745.

Very properly, St Martin's is encircled by pubs of which the Hole in t'Wall is the best. The Royal, formerly White Lion, was kept by another Ullock, 'whose face was the index to an excellent cellar', as a traveller recorded in 1820. The Crown 'patronized by royalty, by American presidents, and by the aristocracy' is another well-established house. Indeed the whole of the town is given over to pubs, hotels, eating places and shops. Bowness underlines the point that Lakeland is already saturated. On summer weekends the place is impassable: and nigh impossible. In spite of what might seem to be common sense the planning authorities have allowed many new developments, including some large time-sharing complexes, which add to the transient population. There is little or no local industry, nor anything much for the tourists to do apart from wandering from shop to café and back again. There is one cinema for when it rains, and a putting green and tennis courts for when it doesn't. Herman Prior described Bowness in his *Pedestrian and General Guide* as having 'something of a Margate flavour': that was in 1860, and on a summer Saturday. The flavour remains.

Windermere, like any lake, is best appreciated by being on it. Views of mountains may be very fine but large sheets of water are rare indeed, and therefore meant to be properly used: sailed on, if big enough, and rowed on if not, preferably with someone else doing the work. Steaming is also good and motor vessels, if slow and quiet enough, admissible. Water-skiing, diving and swimming are something else. They may or may not be pleasurable in themselves, but

148

they do not add to one's enjoyment of the lake, for they can as well be carried out in gravel pits or swimming baths. But the lake itself, in spite of commercialization and exploitation, is sometimes serenely beautiful and contrives always to be pleasurable one way or another.

The ferry itself is half a mile away from the church, a pleasant walk through Glebe Park, where there are live cows, coming down to the lakeshore to drink and looking uncomfortable in the middle of the modern holiday industry. The ferry pulls itself across on a rope, and carries eighteen cars. Since the round journey takes some quarter of an hour, the queues in the season are considerable. There used to be a second ferry, crossing from Millerground landing to Belle Grange. Millerground is now National Trust property, and provides parking, picnicking, boating and sailing. The ferryman's cottage, which is a good early seventeenth-century vernacular building, with an external circular stairwell, has an adjoining turret which might have housed a warning bell. Queen Adelaide's Hill is in memory of William IV's wife, who stayed at the White Lion Hotel in 1840 (the name was changed to the Royal in her honour) and was 'charmed with the panorama of splendid beauty which was here spread before her view, and testified her admiration in a manner highly gratifying . . . to the feelings of Mr. and Mrs. Fleming'. The Queen took tea with the Flemings, who lived in Rayrigg Hall, a favourite resort of William Wilberforce, who used to row out to an island for his early morning prayers and meditations. Wordsworth as a schoolboy visited the White Lion . . . this . . . splendid place, where he had 'Refreshment, strawberries, and mellow cream.'

On 19 October 1635, a wedding party returning from Hawkshead was capsized and forty-seven people drowned, but since then the ferry has been rather safer. Much of the lakeside between the ferry and the town has been developed, and used to house, besides the usual shops and cafés, the Windermere aquarium. This engagingly ramshackle institution has gone to be replaced by the more sophisti-cated Amazonia World of Reptiles. Although this is all to the good, one misses the introduction the old aquarium provided to the Win-dermere char.

The char is *the* Windermere fish. Celia Fiennes described it in 1698: 'Big as a small trout rather slendere and the skin full of spotts. Some reddish, and part of the whole skinn and the finn and taile is red like to finns of a perch, and the inside flesh looks as red as any salmon.'

If the aquarium specimens were anything to go by char have

grown since Miss Fiennes's day, or trout shrunk: they are fine big fish, and voracious eaters. Liable to leap out of the tank at the food, char have sharp teeth, and can inflict some nasty bites. I have not tried char potted, as they used to be, but poached or grilled they are certainly excellent; a mild sorrel sauce is a good accompaniment.

Char are fished between May and October by plumb-lining, trolling with several spoons using long Burma cane rods with a weighted line. Most of this is done by locals, who have the right equipment, but anyone can try their hand with a spinner, hiring a rowing boat for the purpose. Char also crop up in Wastwater, Ennerdale, and Coniston, where I would imagine that fishing would be safer, since Windermere is much used by water-skiers. There is no speed limit on much of the lake, and one of the least attractive aspects of the summer is the number of fast motor boats travelling at terrifying speeds in a lake used by yachts, lake steamers, rowing boats, anglers and swimmers, who may not be accustomed to being on the water. It must be something of a tribute to the discipline of the water-skiers that there are so few accidents.

Tragically, since this passage was first written, the inevitable happened, and a young girl was killed by a water-skier. It was said that as many as 70,000 craft may be on the lake at the same time: a huge new marina near the ferry makes this figure look plausible. In the first edition of this book, published in 1989, I wrote 'Something surely must now be done to enforce sensible rules of navigation on the lake.' An inspector was indeed appointed to report, who recommended that a speed limit be enforced. Although clear and unequivocal, the recommendation was rejected by the government minister, John Selwyn Gummer, at least thereby establishing who can be blamed for the next death.

Windermere Aquatic sells a range of really caddish motor boats, seemingly painted in tinsel, that doubtless go very fast to the danger of all other navigators. You could equip a small armada in the chandler's shop, with everything required in order to attempt the passage of the ten and a half miles of Windermere: anchors, echo sounders, maroons, navigational systems, computerized compasses, bunting, including the Jolly Roger, Scottish lion and a cocktail flag, and a whole variety of clothes from sports jackets to lurex dresses and large plastic earrings. Shepherd's still build traditional wooden boats; their latest, in an example of Cumbrian continuity, was for the late Mr Curwen of Belle Isle, successor to that shown in the de Loutherbourg paintings at Abbot Hall.

Rowing boats, elegant skiffs, are hired from the bay near the steamer pier: motor boats, both nasty plastic ones and nice old tubby varnished clinker-built craft, can also be had, but these have the disadvantage of – strictly speaking – not being allowed within a hundred yards of the shore, so that if you are planning to visit islands, or one of the National Trust-owned plots where landing is permitted, you are better off with a skiff. Bold spirits may also hire sailing dinghies, and it is possible to charter sailing cruisers for longer holidays.

To appreciate the lake one starts, as usual, with the geology. The hills surrounding the head of Windermere, of which the Langdales are the most prominent, are Borrowdale volcanic, steep and rugged. South of Ambleside a narrow band of Coniston limestone marks the demarcation to lower, rounded Silurian slates. Looking up the lake, northwards, therefore gives the dramatic prospects; down water the landscape is more domesticated.

Two glaciers joined to make the present lake, one forming the northern part, and continuing into the Winster Valley, the second flowing down the Langdales to form Esthwaite and southern Windermere. The middle part, opposite Bowness, is a shallow bridge, only 10 feet deep in parts, while both ends are very deep, 209 feet and 137 feet; the bottom of the deep northern sector is indeed 80 feet below sea level.

This makes the Bowness area the best for pottering. A dozen little islands are within easy reach: most belong to the National Trust and can be landed on for picnicking.

The one big island, **Belle Isle**, was until recently owned by the Curwen family, who built a beautiful and unusual house on it. Actually John Christian Curwen, who completed it in 1781, was born a Christian, cousin to Fletcher of the *Bounty*, but changed his name on marrying the lovely Isabella, heiress of the Curwens, after whom the island is named. The house had actually been started earlier, by a Mr English, and designed by John Plaw, the architect of St Mary's church in Paddington Green, and an accomplished neo-classicist. Belle Isle is often compared with that other round house, Ickworth in Suffolk, built some twenty-five years later. Ickworth is really quite different, much grander and lacking Belle Isle's idyllic setting; and all Belle Isle is round, while at Ickworth the domestic quarters are accommodated in the adjacent wings. It is a beautiful house, compact and elegant, in a superb setting; the great portico and double staircase

151

look out towards the Bowness shore, but from most other angles the house is hidden in the surrounding trees.

A disastrous fire in 1994 gutted the house, which is being carefully restored by its new owners, fittingly enough an insurance company.

In addition to a more serious career as a reformer (see p. 320) J. C. Curwen was a pioneer of the Windermere regattas, and an enthusiastic sailing man. His first yacht, built in 1789, recently discovered serving as a hen-house in Southport, is now preserved at the Windermere steamboat museum, but his best-known vessel was the *John,* one of the first boats to be fitted with an iron keel. In between came the *Barton,* designed by one Captain Joshua McRock, who wrote to Curwen: 'I have heard of her celebrity in 2 long epistles from spectators who have described not only her glorious career but the beauty, variety, and pleasing appearance of the sailing and surrounding scenery, all of which has been drawn with such brilliancy of colouring that the most adept imagination can fancy nothing more sublime or seducing.' The successors of Curwen Yachts are the Windermere 17-foot day boats, first introduced in 1904 and still raced by the Royal Windermere Yacht Club.

The most famous Windermere regatta was that of 1825, organized by John Bolton of Storrs and Jock Wilson. Wordsworth, Southey, Walter Scott and Canning, who were both staying at Storrs, all came. Lockhart, Scott's biographer, described the event:

> There was 'high discourse', intermingled with as gay flashings of courtly wit as ever Canning displayed and a plentiful allowance, on all sides, of those airy transient pleasantries, in which the fancy of poets, however wise and grave, delights to run riot when they are sure not to be misunderstood . . . the weather was as Elysian as the scenery. There were brilliant cavalcades through the woods in the mornings, and delicious boatings on the Lake by moonlight . . . the bards of the Lakes led the others that held Scott and Canning; and music and sunshine, flags, streamers and gay dresses, the merry hum of voices, and the rapid splashings of innumerable oars, made up a dazzling mixture of sensations as the flotilla wound its way . . .

One would have liked to hear Wordsworth 'run riot' with 'airy transient pleasantries'.

Bolton was not the sort of man with whom Wordsworth should really have been associating. His fortune, and Storrs Hall, were built on the Liverpool slave trade, and unpleasant stories are told about his carly career. Storrs Hall is still there, a couple of miles down the lake from Bowness, and now an hotel. The building retains enough of the original features to give some idea of its original elegance. It is by J. M. Gandy, whose work we saw at Lancaster Castle. Gandy was a pupil of Sir John Soane, there are some Soanean touches in the use of internal lighting.

Down by the lake there is an octagonal belvedere, 'the Temple of the Heroes', built a little earlier than the house to honour England's admirals Duncan, St Vincent, Howe and Nelson.

The most prominent of Bowness hotels are the Old England, which has been there since 1859 but is now a large characterless Trust House Forte establishment, catering for coach parties, and the Belsfield. This was built in 1845 for the Baroness de Sternberg, and bought twenty-five years later by H. W. Schneider, the Barrow iron magnate. Schneider did things well: every morning he walked down to his private pier, preceded by his butler, Pittaway, carrying the breakfast before him on a silver tray. They then boarded Schneider's yacht *Esperance,* where Schneider breakfasted during the voyage to Lakeside. There a special train, containing Schneider's secretary who had collected the morning's post from Barrow, met them. On the train the letters were answered, enabling Schneider to arrive at the works with a fair proportion of the day's work done.

Esperance was Clyde-built, of Schneider's own iron; very elegant, with an icebreaker bow and twin screws. She remained on the lake until 1941, when she sank, but before doing so served Arthur Ransome as a model for Captain Flint's houseboat in *Swallows and Amazons.* The pier used by Schneider is still known as Esperance Pier and, surprisingly, the boat itself has survived. By a laudable piece of initiative Captain T. C. Pattinson, DFC, managed to raise her, and she is now housed in the Windermere Steamboat Museum, without her engines, but the oldest boat on Lloyd's Register of yachts.

A little further down the lake, below Storrs, as steep road leads left on to Cartmel Fell – and to the Masons Arms, a fact of no less importance. The Masons Arms, mentioned on page 96, is at Straw-berry Bank, on an old packhorse route, a modest pub, but one that dispenses an unparalleled range of beers, including some vintage, and lethal Belgian and German specimens, and provides really good food. On the way there the watershed between Windermere and the Winster valley is crossed, and one looks down on the pretty hamlet of Bowland Bridge, where there is another pub. The road round the back towards the lake – it is the old turnpike road, from Newby Bridge to Kendal, via Crosthwaite, that replaced the packhorse trail – passes a good walk up Gummer's How, the highest bit of land about here, owing its elevation to being a lump of gritstone pushing through the slate. Wainwright describes it as 'a fell walk in miniature, a little beauty, with heather, a few rocks to scramble on, soft couches for repose, a classic view, and a rustic ordnance column'. You can get to it from a car park at Astley's plantation, a couple of miles on from Strawberry Bank.

The road gets back to the lake at **Fell Foot,** a National Trust property, a charming park, handsomely landscaped, with a children's adventure playground.

Fell Foot House has disappeared: it was built by one Jeremy Dixon, about 1800, and bought by the Ridehalghs of Staveley. At the Reformation there were ironworks here, as Henry VIII's commissioners reported: 'The Abbots of the sometime late Monastery have been accustomed to have a Smythey, and sometimes 2 or 3, kepte for making of Yron to those of their Monastery.'

The boat-houses survive, not to be missed, an array of Gothic fantasy castles, with portcullis, water-gates, castellations, and huge inlays of weathered limestone causing the whole to resemble more closely Sarastro's castle than any mere garage for navigators. They were built in 1860 by Colonel Ridehalgh to house his steam yachts *Fairy Queen* and *Britannia.* The sixty-six foot *Queen* was built on the Clyde, sailed to Parkhead, on Cartmel, and hauled from there to Windermere on a trailer pulled by twenty-five horses; the journey took nine days. She was one of the first vessels to be provided with her own gas generation plant. *Britannia* was even more opulent: 110 feet long, with painted glass lights, and equipped with specially designed china and silver. The only remnant is now a saloon skylight, found in Barrow serving as a greenhouse roof, and preserved in the Windermere Steamboat Museum. Plans are afoot to house a collection of vintage motor boats there; it would be hard to find a better place.

The road back to Bowness passes Ghyll Head, a good piece of seventeenth-century vernacular architecture, and by contrast Broadleys and Moor Crag, on either side of the road, which Pevsner describes as two of Voysey's best houses. Voysey's style, which usually featured pebbledash, battered walls and stone mullions, is in keeping with local styles, and Broadleys, which is the home of the Windermere Motor Boat Racing Club, and featured in the final

Town End bank barn, Troutbeck

Town End, Troutbeck

Ambleside: Stock Beck

scenes of the film of John Fowles' novel, *The French Lieutenant's Woman,* is a very good house indeed. It was built for a Yorkshire coal owner, who must have been a man of discernment, since he also employed the architect to design some colliery buildings. Voysey at Broadleys was responsible for much of the furniture and fittings, right down to the toast racks, but none of this has survived. The members of the Windermere Motor Boat Club are a hospitable lot, at least to other motor boaters, and allow visits to their magnificent clubhouse by those interested, but not at weekends, and only with notice. They differentiate between motor boaters and real sailors, which I suppose is fair enough.

On the northern side of Bowness is that excellent institution, the pride of Bowness, the **Windermere Steamboat Museum,** on Rayrigg Road, which runs to Ambleside along the lake. George Pattinson, its founder, is one of the great benefactors of Lakeland: he has given it a museum of national importance – and one which transforms a damp day at Bowness. George was brought up in the mainstream of Windermere life; his father was that Captain T. C. Pattinson who recovered *Esperance,* and his grandfather, also G. H., owned both steam and electric launches, and operated the steam tugs *Powerful* and *Iris.* The oldest vessel in the collection is not, however, a steamer, but a sailing yacht, an open dipping lugsail clinker-built twenty-seven-foot boat launched in 1780. This is the very boat painted by de Loutherbourg and raced by J. C. Curwen in the Windermere regattas against the famous *Peggy,* still preserved in the Isle of Man where she was built. *Dolly* is the oldest steam launch, built in 1850 or thereabouts. Oddly, her preservation is at least partly due to her having sunk in 1895, lying at the bottom of the lake bed for sixty-five years. Had she remained in service, the cost of keeping her going would probably have led to her being scrapped, like so many other early boats, and mud is an excellent preservative. In 1960 the remains of *Dolly* were found; in a most creditable piece of diving work she was salvaged and brought to George Pattinson's for renovation. Amazingly, her engine and boiler, after sixty-five years of immersion, still worked perfectly. The boiler has now been replaced, but her 1850 engine still propels *Dolly* at a sedate pace, and makes her the oldest mechanically powered vessel in the world.

Branksome is the most elegant boat in the museum. Built in 1896 by Brockbanks of Windermere she is fifty feet long, teak built, with walnut panelling. Her velvet upholstery, leather seats and carpets are original, as is the solid marble washbasin in the galley, and her tea kettle which boils a gallon of water in ten seconds. *Otto,* built the same year, is mechanically more advanced with a Sisson triple-expansion engine. She was built at Wivenhoe, Essex, knocked down and sent in parts for re-erection on Windermere. *Bat* is not very glamorous to look at, although she has a most elegant hull, but was the subject of an early experiment in wireless control when in 1904 she was steered by radio from a mast on Queen Adelaide's Hill. Jack Kitchen, a local inventor, and Isaac Storey contrived to direct *Bat* around the north lake by wireless, although they prudently left a stoker on board as back-up.

George Pattinson rescued S.S. *Raven* in the nick of time from the breakers, where she had been consigned by her unnatural owners. Now steaming under her original Furness Railway Company's colours, with her Campbell's of Glasgow engine, *Raven,* built in 1871, is the second oldest mechanically propelled vessel in Lloyd's Register of Yachts, and the oldest still to be working with her original machinery.

The museum condones motor boats, the earliest of which, and one of the earliest surviving anywhere, being a pretty sixteen-footer with her original single-cylinder four-stroke engine and an ingenious hand-operated variable-pitch propeller. *Canfly,* owned by the Windermere Motor Boat Racing Club, is extraordinary. Another Pattinson, Major E. H., bought a 1917 Rolls-Royce Hawk engine from a scrapped Royal Navy airship and fitted it in his launch, giving her a top speed of thirty knots. She has direct drive and no gear box, and is therefore only capable of going ahead; the sole method of stopping is to cut the engine, steer, and hope.

One unassuming object is Beatrix Potter's rowing boat, a little double ender, Jeremy Fisher skiff in which she paddled around Moss Eccles tarn, upon the Claife Heights, interviewing ducks, and Arthur Ransome's original *Amazon* of *Swallows and Amazons* is here in person.

Ambleside, Rydal and Grasmere

If Bowness and Windermere are the places for families with children, the northern end of the lake, including the Rothay valley, Rydal Water and Grasmere, is the best centre for those of a literary bent who do not care too much for the more strenuous high-level walks, but appreciate some modestly extended rambles in the heart of the Wordsworth country.

The Miller Howe, on Rayrigg Road, a little further along towards Ambleside, is another of Lakeland's institutions. Beautiful views and delicious food have made John Tovey's restaurant the standard which others emulate, and Tovey-trained restaurateurs spread this influence (the excellent Uplands Hotel at Cartmel describes itself as being in the Miller Howe manner, and so it is, a little less theatrical but with just as good food).

There are a couple of useful National Trust parking and picnic spaces on Rayrigg Road, which give good views, before getting to **Troutbeck Bridge**, a useful and neglected place. Useful because it has one of the few public swimming pools, open after school hours and in the holidays (there *are* a few days most years when it is pleasant to swim in a lake, but it really is only for the hardy), and a respectable pub, and Troutbeck Bridge offers a record of industrial history not easily matched.

There was a fulling mill built here in 1274 to serve the locality as the power plant for the local cloth industry, which performed all the operations from the sheep to the finished cloth: relics of all these stages can be seen around Troutbeck eight hundred years later. Wool was first carded – getting the strands straight – and then spun; spinning galleries can still be seen on the sides of farmhouses further up Troutbeck Valley. After weaving the cloth was boiled with a potash soap, made from burning bracken; potash kilns are again still visible up the valley, on the right-hand side of the Kirkstone road. After dyeing, if this were done (and as late as the mid-eighteenth century Richard Watson caused a sensation by first appearing at Cambridge in a 'mottled' – presumably undyed Herdwick – coat), the cloth had to be coaxed into shape. Originally this was done by 'waulking' the cloth in a trough, a custom that survived into this century in the Hebrides, but in more progressive parts since the eleventh century water-driven fulling mills were used, which hammered the cloth into a reasonably straight piece.

Like corn mills, fulling mills represented a considerable capital investment, and served a whole community industry. The last stage was the drying of the cloth, stretched out on tenterhooks in tenter fields, which at Troutbeck have now been built over. Troutbeck Bridge fulling mill was on the south bank of the beck just behind the present location of Fell's engineering works. In 1390 it was converted into a corn mill, using the same motive power; in 1673 it became a paper mill; by 1829 it was a bobbin mill: its last function was to generate electricity. The old mill is now used by a firm of monumental masons, the latest in a series of industrial activities going back over seven hundred years. The mill-wheel has gone, but the head and tail races still exist. Some of the mill cottages, near the post office, have grinding wheels in their gardens.

There are two roads from Troutbeck Bridge to Troutbeck, and it is not a bad idea to go by the one that is on the south side of the valley and return by the northern route. The first road, reached by turning up by the Sun Inn, passes the Lakeland Horticultural Society's gardens at Holehird, which has some very good flowering shrubs, a handsome rock garden and a knowledgeable staff.

Holehird is a prosperous brewer's idea of a Lake District cottage, now a Cheshire Home for the Disabled. The gardens are open and worth a visit, if only for the splendid handkerchief tree, said to be the largest in the country, whose pale green leaves and white bracts are stunning. The alpine garden is naturally good, but it is a pity that the kitchen garden has been lost; there are few of these labour-intensive survivals of a bygone era kept up. As well as the views, it is a scholarly place, well labelled, and well tended.

Jesus Church, Troutbeck, has an unusual dedication, shared as far as I know by only one other church in the country, at Enfield. It probably owes this distinction to its origin as an oratory – a place set aside for prayer rather than one where masses were said – attached to St Martin's at Bowness. In 1562 the chapel was rebuilt, and consecrated as a church for the first time. The original beams remain, but little else of that building, which by 1736 had become so ruinous as to be rebuilt.

What is now striking, and which makes a visit to Jesus Church essential, is the splendid east window, which forms a memorial to the

Arts and Crafts Movement, with contributions by Burne-Jones, William Morris and Madox Brown. The Burne-Jones angels are celestial centrefolds: his Christ is elegantly blond, with a tiny moustache, almost epicene, and looks oddly out of place in the sturdy commonplace dales kirk. Brown's contribution (the lower south lights) is animated, and Morris's (higher central lights) suitably decorative. There is another Burne-Jones window in the centre of the north wall, full of pretty red angels.

In the gallery, an unusual feature in a lakeland church, there is a Hanoverian coat of arms, which includes the lilies of France. This records the claim of the English monarchs to the throne of France, a claim only renounced at the time of the Treaty of Amiens. George III was the last monarch to be King of England, Scotland, Ireland and of France.

The pretty churchyard is worth walking around. It has three gates and a number of eighteenth- and nineteenth-century tombstones with very fine lettering, a shaming contrast to brutal modern machine-cutting. Some of the largest of these are erected in memory of faithful servants by their master. One is to the Reverend Mr Sewell, an incumbent who built the pub on the summit of Kirkstone, a deed for which his name ought most certainly to be perpetually remembered.

This Troutbeck is in what used to be Westmorland and must not be confused with the other Troutbeck under Saddleback, which is in what used to be the other county. Incredibly, Pevsner, in his *Buildings of England,* does just that. The reference to Troutbeck (in Westmorland) is only comprehensible if you happen to know that the last two entries refer to the other Troutbeck (in Cumberland), where there are indeed Roman camps, on the road from Old Penrith to Keswick: you could spend a lot of time ferreting about for them in a different county!

The junction from the road down from Kirkstone Pass and the old drove road that ran from Hawkshead to Kendal, Shap and Appleby was used until the eighteenth century as the high road out of the Lakes to the east. The Garburn road is still well defined, and makes a pleasant walk, over to Kentmere and back down to Ambleside. There are one or two places where the ground falls away sufficiently steeply to make for good photography or sketching, and some interesting bits of geology; the top of the Garburn Pass is a good spot for identifying the narrow band of Coniston limestone that cuts across the countryside, and Badger Rock on the way down into Kentmere is one of the largest boulders in the Lake District.

Logically enough the village of Troutbeck starts at Town Head and finishes at Town End, which is a National Trust property, but quite unlike their grander country houses. It is a 'statesman's' house, belonging to one of those independent yeomen who held the land by border tenure, laying on them the duty of mustering fully equipped to repel the Scots, or to take part in the 'hot trod'. Their duties were defined in one of the first Acts of Queen Elizabeth I's reign: 'All tenants between the ages of 16 and 60 are to serve the Queen in their most defensibel array for war at all times on horseback as well as on foot at the West borders of England for anent Scotland . . .'

What distinguishes Town End from other unspoiled houses, such as How Head at Ambleside, is that it continued as the home of the Browne family from the date of its erection until 1950. The furnishings, and many of the objects, are therefore just those that a prosperous farming family might have acquired over three centuries.

The Brownes were yeomen going on for gentry. George Brown was High Constable in 1667, and his son Benjamin succeeded him in the office. In 1715, when the Jacobites threatened, Lord Lonsdale, as Lord-Lieutenant, wrote to Benjamin Brown sounding just like the Reverend Ian Paisley: 'I doe not doubt but you have heard that a great many people in Scotland and Northern England with a design to fill the nation with Blood and bring in Popery have taken up arms against the King and Government and every honest man . . .' One contemporary of George and Benjamin Browne was Thomas Hoggart, 'old Hoggart', reputed to be an uncle of William Hogarth. This 'mountain Theocritus' wrote verse dramas, acted out in the open, which included 'The Destruction of Troy' and 'The Lascivious Queen'.

Town End is by no means the only piece of distinguished local architecture in Troutbeck: indeed the whole long village is a textbook example of vernacular building. Among those particularly worth looking for just opposite Town End is the great barn, a bank barn, i.e. one with access at two levels, the upper reached by a ramp, with a gallery, and mullioned windows. Low House, further along on the same side, has another gallery, and corbelled chimneys. There are more fine barns, houses with oriels and mullioned windows, and Jowniewife House, almost a little hamlet, conveniently next to the Mortal Man. This pub retains some early features, but is best known for its old sign, of a fat and a thin man, painted by Julius Caesar Ibbetson, no less, with the rhyme:

O mortal man, that livs't on bread
How comes they nose to be so red?
Thou silly ass that look so pale
It is by drinking Sarah Birkett's ale.

Ibbetson, who lived in Ambleside for some years after 1800, is one of the livelier painters of animals, rather in the style of Morland, a distinguished watercolourist, and not at all the sort of person to paint inn signs, although he spent some time enjoying their products. The Queen's Arms, on the road past Jesus Church, is an entertaining pub: it incorporates an ancient four-poster in the bar, and has a spinning gallery, now blocked in.

Briery Close, where Charlotte Brontë stayed with the Kay Shuttle-worths, is just down the road. It was there that she first met Mrs Gaskell, who was to be her biographer. Charlotte had the right ideas about the Lakes.

'I discovered that the Lake country is a glorious region, of which I had only seen the similitude in dreams, waking or sleeping. Decidedly I find it does not agree with me to prosecute the search for the picturesque in a carriage . . . I longed to slip out unseen, and to run away by myself amongst the hills and dales. Errant and vagrant instincts tormented me . . .'

The Town End road back to the lake gives one of the best views over the head of Windermere, and passes Lowwood. There were plans in the 1840s to bring the railway from Oxenholme to Low-wood, a proposal which aroused Wordsworth's ire. How could 'the imperfectly educated classes benefit from visits to the lakes'? The promoters had their eyes rather on 'the merchant princes of Liverpool and the cotton-lords of Manchester', but were successful only in getting the railway as far as Windermere. That they were stopped there might have been due to a sonnet fired off by Wordsworth which began:

Is there no nook of English ground secure,
From rash assault? . . .
. . . How can they this blight endure . . .

Looking at Bowness on a Bank Holiday, it is hard not to feel he had a point.

Lowwood Hotel has accommodated many famous guests – Wordsworth, of course, but also Shelley, with Harriet, John Stuart

Mill, and E. M. Forster, who found the charge of 12/- a day some-what high 'but I must admit they do you prettily there . . . no beastliness'. The Hotel used to be popular with honeymooners, 'the resort, during the season, of countless *neogams*' according to Prior, 'by common tradition sacred to Hymen' as Baddeley put it, but also catered for others 'who are not too much preoccupied with the beau-ties of each other to admit those of nature to a share of their admiration'.

The views from the front of the hotel are still good, but honey-mooners now probably prefer something a little quieter, unless they are taken by the idea of water-skiing, which can be done from the Low Woods Watersport Centre opposite the hotel, which also runs PADI skin-diving courses, that can lead one to qualify as a *urinator* (two can play at Prior's game). You can hire boats as well, and learn to sail, at Low Wood; a useful place, for landlubbers. Stagshaw Gar-dens is up the hill, a National Trust property open only in the spring and early summer, when the rhododendrons and azaleas are out.

Stagshaw is the creation of Cuthbert Acland, National Trust re-gional agent, over the twenty years he lived in Stagshaw cottages from 1959 to 1979. It is therefore very much a late twentieth-century garden, designed to make the most of shrubs and trees, with year-round appeal. Inevitably, given the location, there are many rhododendrons, which look spectacular in the spring but allow noth-ing to grow beneath and afford no habitat to wildlife, and they are more at home here in conditions resembling their native Himalayas, under tall pine trees on a steep slope with the lake glinting through their branches, than in cottage gardens. There are also splendid ca-mellias, azaleas and a great variety of trees, so well arranged that the native bilberries flourish, and the mosses are irreproachable.

Brockhole is a bit back towards Troutbeck Bridge. This house, built in 1899 for a Manchester businessman, is now the Lakeland National Park Visitors' Centre, an active place, which has daily lec-tures and audio and visual shows, displays, geological and natural history demonstrations, and full-day courses in dry-stone walling and water safety and rescue. There are many nature trails, Teddy Bears' Picnics and guided walks which take you up to Town End.

Waterhead is the northern terminus of lake steamers, and is an agreeable spot, well provided with pubs. The Wateredge Hotel, sand-wiched between the road and the lake, is particularly attractive, and the Waterhead Hotel has some nice wrought-ironwork. The road to Ambleside forks, the left-hand route going past the Roman fort of

Galava to Langdale and Hawkshead. The lakeside here is elegantly manicured with pretty well-groomed rocks, but you have to be keen on Roman forts to make anything much of Galava, in Borrans Field. ('Borrans' is often found in the district: it derives from a Norse root meaning 'stone piles', and generally signifies Roman remains.) Hardknott is much more rewarding.

'**Ambleside:** This Town or Market Village was formerly perhaps more rich in picturesque beauty, arising from a combination of rustic architecture and natural scenery than any small Town or Village in Great Britain – Many of the ancient buildings with their porches, projections, round chimnies and galleries have been displaced to make way for the docked, featureless and memberless edifices of modern architecture . . . Yet this town if carefully noticed, will still be found to retain a store of picturesque materials.'

Architecturally speaking Wordsworth is still right. Ambleside offers a fair number of diversions: the nurserymen, Hayes, have a miniature Crystal Palace and an adventure playground in the garden centre, one of the largest in the north; glass is blown before your eyes by Adrian Sankey; and Zefferelli's combines a repertory cinema with a decent café, gallery and shops. The best bit of Ambleside is up the hill away from the commercial centre, where the old church is a respectable if uninspired 1821 design, now converted, but How Head, opposite, is a stark dramatic piece of Lakeland vernacular at its best. More so even than Town End which has been whitewashed, added to and has something of a cottage aspect, How Head represents how a prosperous statesman's family lived. It is something of a rarity, since most similar houses were transformed by their owners into fashionable Georgian mansions. How Head, being in the middle of the old town, was allowed to remain unaltered, apart from being divided into separate units.

The Braithwaite family, who built the house, also owned Borrans Field, and it is thought that they used some of the Roman masonry in their new building. Certainly some of the stones, especially on the front facing the church, are noticeably different from the random slate used elsewhere. Other bits of Galava met a humbler end, when the sandstone was used by local housewives for cleaning their pans. A detailed inventory of the contents of How Head was made in 1657 on the death of Gawen Braithwaite, and provides a rare insight into seventeenth-century Cumbrian life. The furnishings of the parlour contained, among much else including chairs, both wood and leather and three tables,

2 little greane stooles
Quisions xi of which one is haire
a box wh. drawers in it for antiquities
a cabinett for hott watteres
a stone bow and a crossbow (A greate old crosbowe).

The real treasure of Ambleside is the Armitt collection, a remark-able assembly of books and articles of local topography, history and geology, a full range of Lake District guide books, letters and papers from eminent Lakelanders, including the Wordsworths and the Ar-nolds, Harriet Martineau, Ruskin, both Collingwoods and Beatrix Potter, who also bequeathed several hundred of her drawings of fungi and of archaeological specimens and mosses. The Armitt Trust was founded in 1912, but incorporated both the Ambleside Ruskin Society, established with the active support of Ruskin himself, and the Ambleside Book Club, of which Wordsworth was a member.

The whole valuable and extensive collection bursts the bounds of a single room above the public library, supported by enthusiastic residents and by the British Library. It is hoped that more extensive premises can be found, since at the moment, although visitors are welcomed, if more than three are there at a time they have to breathe in turn. Among the pictures there are, as well as the Beatrix Potter drawings and the topographical prints and watercolours, a magnifi-cent portrait by Kurt Schwitters of his friend Dr George Ainsly Johnston.

In retrospect, the attitude of the Dadaists, who saw the conduct of twentieth-century affairs as truly insane, the one sane reaction to which was artistic madness, seems eminently reasonable. Through-out many vicissitudes, which must have fortified his beliefs, Schwitters applied his considerable talents to upsetting the norms. He fled first Germany and then Norway just ahead of the Nazis, ending up in that temporary refuge of genius, the British internment camps on the Isle of Man, where his behaviour continued to mock the authorities. He built a kennel in his room, in which he slept, and before retiring fell into the custom of barking for some while. A kindred spirit, who happened to be a banker – to the eternal credit of that trade – took him up and barked back.

At the end of the war, Schwitters moved to Ambleside and began a productive period, which included the construction of the third and last Merzbau. A concept invented by himself – in the 1920s, half a century before those ridiculous rows of bricks and heaps of rubbish cherished at our expense by the Tate Gallery – Merzbau is a huge three-dimensional collage. 'Merz' is a symbolic nonsense word, derived from 'ComMERZbank', and *bau* is simply the German for building or construction; Schwitters was a gifted professional painter, but this was his most original and important work, which has never been equalled. His previous two Merzbau, in Germany and Norway, having been destroyed, he set about, in the last year of his life, the creation of a third. This was in a barn at Elterwater, given to him by a landscape architect, Harry Pierce; it was intended, as Schwitters said, 'to stand close to nature, in the midst of a national park, and afford a wonderful view in all directions,' but it has now been dismantled and is preserved in the University of Newcastle's Hatton Gallery. Some of Schwitters's pictures can still be seen in Cumbria, in the Armitt collection and in the Abbot Hall, although theirs are mostly kept in reserve.

The centre of Ambleside is the Stock Beck, which in the past provided power for a whole series of mills, the fabric of most of which remains, making for a picturesque view up the beck. A footpath from behind Barclays Bank (and past Ambleside's civilized bookshop) leads up through Stock Park to Stock Ghyll Force, which Harriet Martineau admired: 'It is the fashion to speak lightly of this waterfall . . . but it is, in our opinion, a very remarkable fall (from the symmetry of its parts) and one of the most graceful that can be seen.'

The beck is not only figuratively but literally the centre, too. Until 1674 Ambleside above Stock was in Grasmere, and below Stock in Troutbeck. The division is marked on the bridge, but the marker is half buried under tarmac, and needs to be replaced.

Most people never see the marker, for they are too busy admiring Ambleside's best-known building, Bridge House, a two-room, two-storey edifice perched on a bridge by itself. It was probably built as an apple room and a summer house of the local manor – we had a not dissimilar two-storey structure over in Westmorland, with the two rooms known as the upper and lower apple rooms: apples need a good deal of room for proper storage.

St Mary's church is an expensive mid-Victorian piece of work by Giles Gilbert Scott. Although it probably did not set out to be entertaining and Scott is said to have been disappointed with it, it turned out to be one of the jolliest churches in Lakeland. Part of this is sheer badness: the windows in the Wordsworth chapel can hardly fail to provoke a giggle, while that of the Presentation, 'A Mother in Israel', ought to have them falling about in the north aisle. The monument to Commander Lutwidge, RN, is an exuberant Gothic piece, and the big

mural on the west wall by Gordon Ransom is guaranteed to elevate the spirits. It is the Ambleside Rushbearing, and is lively, beautifully observed and very pretty. Flanking it are a couple of good windows by Holiday, but the whole of the west end is in danger of being engulfed by chairs, tables and tracts.

Ambleside has its own rushbearing, as have many other parishes in Westmorland and Yorkshire. It seems to be a specifically northern festival, and has been linked to St Oswald, the Northumbrian King who died fighting the heathen on 5 August 642. Grasmere is the most widely known, and is dealt with fully, but to my mind the flavour of the thing is best caught at the less touristy Eden Valley villages.

At the time of its construction there was a tremendous fuss made about the new church, which was thought to be quite out of keeping with the neighbourhood, being too big, and especially in having a steeple. Today this seems all a little misplaced, for Ambleside has lost any rural simplicity it once had and become a holiday town of shops, villas and hotels into which the church fits well enough.

Rothay Park is down by the River Rothay, which joins Rydal with Windermere; a good place for picnics, it has the best children's playground in an area that does these things well: rope bridge, stockades, Roman forts, swings and climbing walls all provide anxious parents with heart-stopping moments. The grown-ups' part of the park is dotted with picturesque *roches moutonnées*, with trees clinging to them. About here you come across evidence that you are in slate country, for large upright slates are used for boundary walls, a practice unknown where slates are not abundant.

Harriet Martineau built the Knoll, past the car park on the Grasmere Road. That lively 'sparky' woman exercised the minds of Victorians for over forty years with her intelligence and clarity of thought. She loved her 'pretty house . . . nearly covered with ivy roses, passion flowers and other climbers, and the porch a bower of honeysuckles'. Wordsworth approved and she records that unpoetical poet as saying: ' "It is the wisest step in her life; for . . ." ' and we supposed he was going on to speak of the respectability, comfort and charm of such a retreat for an elderly woman; but not so – "It is the wisest step in her life; for the value of the property will be doubled in ten years." '

In much the same way as 'good lifers' have been more recently, Harriet was concerned to demonstrate that a working man's family could subsist on two acres of decent land. (At the same time the Chartist Land Society was attempting to set up a model community just outside Watford where some of the original houses can still be seen.) Harriet's project was more restricted, but more convincing; she imported a labourer and his family from her native Norfolk and set him up in the grounds of the Knoll, enlarged by a rented half acre, with such success that 'my good farm-servant is a prosperous man'. She was right to get an East Anglian, for Cumbrian men have never been great hands at growing things, leaving that to the womenfolk and engaging themselves with the stock and the foxes.

The oldest pubs in Ambleside are the Salutation, from 1656, the Black Cock, now advanced in the world as the Queen's Hotel, and the White Lion. It was at the Salutation that horses were changed for the journey to Keswick. The Cock was at one time bought by Bishop Watson: the landlord, seeking to flatter his new owner, changed the name and the sign to 'The Bishop'. A rival pub picked up the abandoned name, and The Bishop's trade began to fall off. Rather than go to the expense of changing his sign the landlord wrote under the Bishop's portrait, complete with wig and bands, 'This is the Old Cock'.

Clappersgate used to be classified as a port since it had a wharf where slate from the quarries was loaded. The port was subsumed into the boat-house and harbour of Croft Lodge, the prominent house demandingly visible at the head of the lake. It was built about 1830 for a prosperous Liverpool merchant, who built in a style described by Hartley Coleridge as one 'which neither Vitruvius, Palladio, Inigo Jones, Piranesi nor Sir Jeffrey Wyatville ever dream'd of, even in a nightmare, or under the influence of opium'. Charles Lloyd, who wrote *Edmund Oliver,* a novel with Coleridge as an equivocal hero, lived at Brathay Bridge and the Redmaynes up at Brathay Hall. Giles Redmayne built Trinity chapel, of which Wordsworth approved. His taste would now be accounted odd; the chapel is a stuccoed Italianate edifice, which would be much more at home in South Kensington. Mr Redmayne made his fortune in the Italian silk trade, which may account for it; but it has a pleasant graveyard, with fine views to the west.

A little earlier John Housman, author of a guide published in 1817, promised a view of 'the little white seats of Mr. LAW and Miss PRITCHARD' at Brathay and Clappersgate.

The National Trust has a camping ground, small but beautifully situated, at **Low Wray,** a convenient place to swim or launch a canoe.

'Pile' is the only apt word to describe **Wray Castle.** Built in 1840 by Dr. James Dawson, another rich Liverpudlian, at the enormous cost of £60,000, it is a Cecil B. de Mille fantasy of medieval architecture – turret after turret poised on towers, corbelled machicolations, castellations, barbicans, arrow slits, and every cliché of the medieval revival characterized by the Eglinton tournaments loom up magnificently. Overpowering close to, it appears splendid from the other side of the lake. Herman Prout was lukewarm: 'a modern antique . . . really might be much worse. The site is admirable', but the Potter family, who rented it for their holidays, thought it wonderful. Today, bathetically, Wray is a school for radio operators. You can walk all around it, but not inside.

The church, of which Canon Rawnsley, founder of the National Trust, was once incumbent, is less dramatic, but has some nice

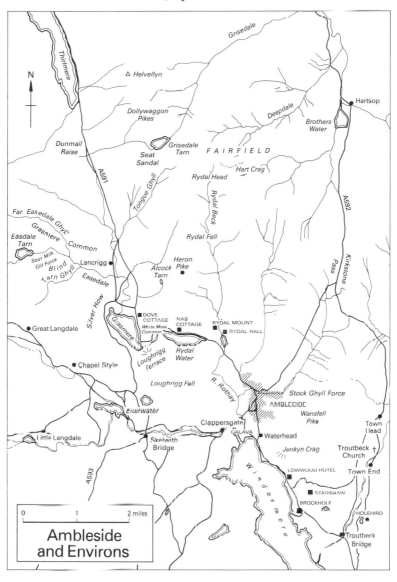

N

Thirlmere

Grisedale

△ Helvellyn

Dollywaggon
Pikes

Deepdale

Hartsop

Brothers
Water

Dunmail
Raise

Grisedale
Tarn

F A I R F I E L D

Seat
Sandal

A591

Hart Crag

Rydal Head

Tongue Ghyll

Rydal Beck

A592

Far Easedale Ghyll

Grasmere Common

Easdale
Tarn

Rydal Fell

Sour Milk
Gill Force
Blind
Tarn Ghyll

Lancrigg

Easedale

Heron
Pike

Alcock
Tarn

Silver How

Kirkstone Pass

DOVE
COTTAGE
White Moss
Common

NAB
COTTAGE

RYDAL MOUNT

Great Langdale

Grasmere

RYDAL HALL

Chapel Style

Loughrigg
Terrace

Rydal
Water

Loughrigg Fell

R. Rothay

Stock Ghyll Force

Ellerwater

AMBLESIDE

Wansfell
Pike

Town
Head

Clappersgate

GALAVA

Waterhead

Little Langdale

Skelwith
Bridge

Jenkyn Crag

Troutbeck
Church

A533

Windermere

LOWWOOD HOTEL

Town End

STAGSHAW

BROCKHOLE

HOLEHIRD

| 0 | 1 | 2 miles |

Troutbeck
Bridge

Ambleside
and Environs

woodwork. From here a path leads along the shore under Claife heights as far as the ferry; a pleasant stroll. The heights, and the hinterland, are described in Chapter 10.

Rydal and Grasmere

The worst way of going from Ambleside to Rydal is the most obvious one: the A591 has been too busy for nearly a century, and is not improving. There is a very pretty motor (just) road from Rothay Bridge that follows the stream and passes Fox Howe, where Dr Arnold spent his holidays from Rugby. On foot, a circuitous but attractive route is up through Rothay Park and Loughrigg, coming into Rydal via the Loughrigg Terrace, which has a famous view and seats from which to admire it. The third, more direct, branches up off the main road towards Rydal Hall, for many years the home of the le Flemings, who started over in Furness in the twelfth century. Daniel le Fleming, who built the first Rydal Hall in the late seventeenth century, wrote a Polonius-like letter of advice to his son, which gives a nicely realistic feeling for Restoration mores:

> Marry thy Daughters in Time lest they marry themselves; and suffer not thy sons to pass the Alpes, for they shall learn nothing but Blasphemy, Swearing and Atheism. Towards thy Superiors be humble, yet generous; with thy Equals familiar, yet respective; towards thy Inferiors show much humility, and some Familiarity, as to bow thy Body, stretch forth thy hand, uncover thy head, and suchlike popular Compliments.

It would be difficult today to better his psychologically acute advice on deportment, which could be written straight into any management textbook.

The interior of the Hall – not usually open to the public – which starts at the back being seventeenth-century and ends up early-nineteenth at the front, has been much altered, but the policies have some interesting features of which the most notable is the grotto or summerhouse, built by Sir Daniel, when it was described as being 'one little room wainscotted round'. It became ruinous and has been partly restored. You need to climb around a bit to savour the view up the last of Rydal Falls, which are, it must be admitted, inconsiderable watercourses by other standards, but incontestably worth looking at. They also give an opportunity of comparing the Constable sketch with the more or less unchanged object itself. Wordsworth observed, about Rydal Falls: 'What an animating contrast is the ever-changing of that, and indeed everyone of our mountain brooks, to the monstrous tone and unmitigated fury of such streams among the Alps.'

The game larder, around the back, is a rare survival. Cumbria has always been a good place for living off the land, with abundant fish and game. Even today an average moorland shoot will produce partridge, grouse, migrating pheasant, snipe, hare and of course quantities of rabbit. Far from being much of a luxury, Cumbrian country house diet in the autumn gets tediously monotonous as pheasant succeeds shattered pheasant.

Rydal Mount, over the way, is more rewarding, for this is the house to which Wordsworth moved in his period of affluence, after eight years of the simple life in Dove Cottage, and five years of renting first Allan Bank and then Grasmere Old Rectory. Neither of these had been happy homes: Allan Bank was cold, and the chimneys smoked; the Old Rectory was no better, and rendered insupportable by the deaths of his two children Catherine and Thomas. The Mount is an unremarkable sort of house except for its position. Wordsworth always had an eye for a view, and Dove Cottage had afforded only a restricted aspect, but the Mount, more elevated, has wide-ranging prospects over both Grasmere and Rydal. It is possible that the knoll in front of the house could have been used in Anglian times as an observation point, from which warning might be given of anything menacing that might be moving up on Dunmail Raise.

The year 1813, when the Wordsworths moved into the Mount, was a watershed; it was in that year that William was given the job – in both senses of the word – of Distributor of Stamps in the County of Westmorland, and thereafter the family was able to live in security. It was from here that his beloved daughter Dora was married, to Edward Quillinan, the Irish soldier of whom Wordsworth did not approve (but few fathers are unreservedly enthusiastic about sons-in-law). Wordsworth's disapproval might have been the whole idea of dragoons who wrote verse: Quillinan tried his hand at this and produced a quite professional epitaph on Southey, the 'Robin's Requiem':

> As the bearers bear the dead
> Pacing slow with solemn tread,
> Two feathered choristers of spring,
> To the dark procession sing
> Heedless of the driving rain
> Fearless of the mourning train . . .

171

At Rydal Wordsworth lived out the rest of his long life, revered as the grand old man of English letters, but in fact having already completed his greatest work. A good deal of the house is still largely as the Wordsworths left it, although the Turkey carpet has gone. Dorothy was delighted with it: 'I must tell you of our grandeur. We are going to have a Turkey!!! carpet – in the dining room, and a Brussels in William's study. You stare . . . and you are tempted to say: are they changed, and are they setting up for fine folks . . .?" '

Wordsworth's taste in art was patchy – he was a great admirer of Haydon, that exponent of the bombastic, and there is a lithograph by that artist of Wellington, leaning against an enormous Copenhagen, which is dedicated to Wordsworth and accompanied by his sonnet. None of the rooms are large: the drawing-room and the library, originally separate, were thrown together recently – but the Wordsworths had a lively time: 'We had three days ago a dance, 40 Beaus and Belles besides Matrons, Spinsters and Greybeards – tomorrow in this same room we are to muster for a venison feast.'

Margaret Gillies, who did the small portraits, took the poet's fancy. On the day she left he was heard enquiring of his wife, 'My dear, would it be considered very indecorous or profligate if I gave Miss Gillies a kiss on parting?'

There is not the same sense as at Dove Cottage of being in a shrine when you visit Rydal Mount: it is a lived-in family house, with such convenient improprieties as wash-basins in the bedrooms. Only the isolated room inhabited by the unfortunate Dorothy, who by then was suffering from the mental illness from which she never recovered, conveys a powerful sense of the past. And of course, although William built the study himself, about 1838, he left his greatest mark in the garden which he created. At various times he observed that had he not been a poet he would have liked to be a pedlar or a gardener, and it was out of doors that most of his creative work was done, 'wi a girt voice bumming awaay fit to flayte aw the childer to death ameiast'.

Lacking a cheerfully extroverted personality, nor having much commercial spirit, Wordsworth would have starved as a pedlar, but Rydal Mount garden is a wonderfully romantic creation: in four acres or so it gives a feeling of infinitely varying space, combined with careful detailing.

The Mount was rented from Lady le Fleming next door, and when at one time it seemed that she might call in the lease, and turf out the Wordsworths, much to the poet's distress:

> The doubt to which wavering hope had clung
> Is fled, we must depart, willing or not;
> Sky piercing Hills must bid farewell to you . . .
> . . . to your paths,
> and pleasant Dwelling, to familiar trees . . .

Wordsworth bought the field immediately below the house, now known as Dora's Field, where he might build himself another house, but Lady le Fleming relented, and the neighbours remained on sufficiently amicable terms for Wordsworth to write an adulatory ode to her when she provided funds for building Rydal church. It contrives to be banal, but at the same time incorporates a wonderful ascent in the last six lines from the pedestrian to the magnificent:

> Nor deem the Poet's hope misplaced,
> His fancy cheated – that can see
> A shade upon the future cast,
> Of time's pathetic sanctity;
> Can hear the monitory clock
> Sound o'er the lake with gentle shock
> At evening, when the ground beneath
> Is ruffled o'er with cells of death;
> Where happy generations lie,
> Here tutored for eternity.

But even then he did not really approve of the building. 'It has no chancel; the altar is unbecomingly confined; the pews are so narrow as to preclude the possibility of kneeling; There is no vestry . . .' etc.

In view of his worry at the prospect of having to move from the Mount, Wordsworth would doubtless be happy to know that the house is safely in the hands of his own great-great-granddaughter, Mary Henderson, who is not so very far removed from personal knowledge of him, since her grandfather John, who died when she was ten, was a teenager when Wordsworth himself died.

The church is not disagreeable – a little fussy without, and prim within. Except, that is, for the charming and explicit *fin de siècle* Henry Holiday cherubs in the Quillinan window, hardly really suitable for the man Dora called her 'dear heavy dragoon'. In Wordsworth's time social proprieties were observed; the Wordsworths and the Arnolds from Fox Howe were allowed the front pews, but the le Flemings had the gallery, with their own fireplace to themselves: distinctions between baronets and mere immortals had to be preserved.

Nab Cottage, now a guest house, is on the north side of the main road. This belonged to the family of Margaret Simpson, who became Thomas de Quincey's wife, although only after she had borne him a son, which annoyed the Wordsworths who frowned on such things (even though Wordsworth's own illegitimate daughter was by then in her twenties). After the de Quinceys left, Coleridge's son, Hartley, lived there for many years. Although Coleridge and Wordsworth were distant from 1810 onwards, L'aal Hartley remained a close friend of the family, and indeed of anybody who knew him. Hartley took to drink, schoolteaching, and writing verse, but in spite of all these faults was taken to the hearts of the tolerant and affectionate Cumbrians.

I do not count any stretch of water that cannot be sailed on or rowed in a proper lake, and consider Rydal Water to be an upstart pond, whose only duty is to form the centrepiece of a series of famous views, which it does very well. It is too small for boating – which is not allowed – and too popular for peaceful fishing. Once Sir William le Fleming started to build an ornamental summerhouse on the island, but, rather sadly, did not persevere with his project, perhaps because Wordsworth described it as outrageous.

Thomas Gray found **Grasmere** 'one of the sweetest landscapes that art ever attempted to imitate. Not a single red tile, nor flaring gentleman's house, nor garden wall breaks in upon the repose of the unsuspected paradise, but all its peace, rusticity and happy poverty in its neatest and most becoming attire.' From a distance – Loughrigg, for example – Grasmere still looks to be a place of beauty such as Gray found it, but its situation astride the main north/south route in the region, and its own tourist importance, mean that it is commonly thronged. The principal attraction is Dove Cottage, where William and Dorothy set up house together in 1799, and is now, together with the adjoining Wordsworth Centre, a museum, and a place for serious students. The museum is very well arranged, and makes the most of what it has, but it is difficult to represent graphically an essentially psychological phenomenon. If one comes armed with some knowledge of the early nineteenth century and the romantic movement there are many interesting points to be made (Hazlitt's portrait of the radical – even revolutionary – John Thelwall shows how competent a portraitist the essayist Hazlitt was, and reminds us of the young Wordsworth's sympathies). In writing the first edition of this book I found that children were given a sanitized biography of the poet: 'After hearing about the Revolution in France, he sailed to Calais to begin a walking tour. He made new friends and became a supporter of the revolution.' Making new friends included, of course, falling in love and having an illegitimate daughter! Today's versions are more sophisticated, but the imagination is led to boggle by one item, a picture of a Westmorland Volunteer of 1803 presenting arms, a reminder that the patriotic Wordsworth was then drilling, in just such a dress, in readiness for a French invasion.

Dove Cottage itself has been preserved as a shrine and attracts both the devout and the merely curious. To those who have learned to love those unevenly brilliant geniuses Wordsworth and Coleridge, and to admire the other nineteenth-century writers who came to Grasmere – de Quincey, Hazlitt, Scott and Southey – Dove Cottage is an illuminating experience. The cosy straitened rooms still seem to harbour ghosts of lost felicity. Between them the Wordsworths and their friends made a very fair job of recording life at Dove Cottage – and one can easily imagine Walter Scott jollying William along, or Coleridge's flashes of illumination. But many English visitors turn up ignorant of William and all his works: it is a place billed as an attraction and somewhere to go out of the wet. Beatrix Potter is more popular, especially among the Japanese: 'If only Wordsworth had long furry ears we'd be top of the pops', one staff member lamented. Some visitors attempt to invest William with Beatrix's attractions, and ask when exactly Wordsworth married Beatrix Potter; the Americans are no better – one group insisted that this was the home of Henry Wadsworth Longfellow, and that the guide was mistaken; another asked if Shakespeare came to visit Wordsworth. They leave perhaps a little wiser, impressed by the touching simplicity of the place, a world apart from the family home at Cockermouth, or even from the comfortably middle-class Rydal Mount. It is all very well done; the original furniture, fires in the grate, and the bedroom papered by Dorothy with newspapers, but unless you have succumbed to some extent to the Wordsworth lure there is nothing very illuminating, and even from that point of view there are limitations, for that seminal romantic book, *Lyrical Ballads,* was not written here, but by Wordsworth and Coleridge while they lived in Somerset; and the poems William did write in Grasmere were composed for the most part out of doors. But Dove Cottage is inseparable from Dorothy Wordsworth, and the *Journals* she wrote there are among the finest diaries ever written. Dorothy is pure gold; she is incapable of clumsiness or pretentiousness, both of which her brother too often exhibited. Her eye for detail is immaculate:

175

(Wednesday 30th June.) We met an old man between the Raise and Lewthwaites. He wore a rusty but untorn hat, an excellent blue-coat, waistcoat, and breeches, and good mottled worsted stockings. His beard was very thick and grey, of a fortnight's growth we guessed; it was a regular beard, like grey plush. His bundle contained Sheffield ware. William said to him, after we had asked him what his business was, 'You are a very old Man?' 'Aye I am eighty-three.' I joined in, 'Have you any children?' 'Children? Yes, plenty. I have children and grand-children, and great grand-children. I have a great grand-daughter, a fine lass, thirteen years old.' I then said, 'Won't they take care of you?' He replied, much offended, 'Thank God, I can take care of myself.' We amused ourselves for long time in watching the breezes, some as if they came from the bottom of the lake, spread in a circle, brushing along the surface of the water, and growing more delicate as it were thinner, and of a paler colour till they died away. Others spread out like a peacock's tail, and some went right forward this way and that in all directions. The lake was still where these breezes were not, but they made it all alive. I found a strawberry blossom in a rock. The little slender flower had more courage than the green leaves, for they were but half expanded and half grown, but the blossom was spread full out. I uprooted it rashly, and I felt as if I had been committing an outrage, so I planted it again. It will have but a stormy life of it, but let it live if it can.

The immediate area of Dove Cottage, a few yards from the busy main road, is so crowded with cars and coaches as to make it impossible to recapture the sense of tranquillity that the Wordsworths experienced. But merely moving a couple of hundred yards up the side road is enough; this is the old turnpike road from Grasmere to Rydal, before the lakeside route was made, which comes out at White Moss Quarry, where there is a car park. It is worthwhile walking up to the path that leads past White Moss Tarn to see, almost unaltered, what was effectively the Wordsworths' backyard, and places that inspired many poems affectionately named; Mary Point, Sara Point, The Wishing Gate, and John's Grove. If you want to go from Dove Cottage to Rydal Mount, which is the chronologically correct order, you take the White Moss Tarn path, which leads on along the contour to Rydal Mount.

What with Dorothy's *Journals* and William's letters, there are not many other episodes of early nineteenth-century life that have been recorded so clearly. But in addition Coleridge was a frequent visitor who kept voluminous notes. Together they make an unrivalled collection, for these were all people of genius, at the most fruitful time of their lives, analysing thoughts and experiences with unwearying energy.

Life at Dove Cottage, with Coleridge dropping in from Keswick, where he had followed his friends after their joint residence, the excitement of continuous creation, William's marriage, the constant succession of friends, still seems, a couple of centuries later, to have been idyllic. Dove Cottage had been an ale-house, the 'Dove and Olive Bough', until not long before the Wordsworths rented it. In his marvellous comic poem 'The Waggoner', which should be re-read every time one is infuriated by Wordsworth's pomposity, Benjamin the carter passes it nostalgically:

> For at the bottom of the brow,
> Where once the Dove and Olive-bough
> Offered a greeting of good ale,
> To all who entered Grasmere Vale;
> And called on him who must depart
> To leave it with a jovial heart;
> There, where the Dove and Olive-bough
> Once hung, a Poet harbours now,
> A simple water-drinking Bard;
> Why need our Hero then (though frail
> His best resolves) be on his guard?
> He marches by, secure and bold;
> Yet while he thinks on times of old,
> It seems that all looks wondrous cold;
> He shrugs his shoulders, shakes his head . . .

After the Wordsworths left, first for Allan Bank and finally via the old Vicarage to Rydal Mount, de Quincey took the cottage over and demolished the summerhouse, which began the disenchantment between the family and de Quincey, who had come there at first in order to be near his hero: Dorothy in particular deplored what she thought to be careless destruction.

As a lake, Grasmere is only modestly exciting, but boats can be hired, and it is possible to picnic on the island, just as Wordsworth did. The great merit of taking a boat is that it separates oneself, at least to a modest extent, from the incessant motor traffic, which otherwise makes Grasmere often intolerable.

Grasmere church was dismissed by Murray's guide as 'a heavy hideous building'. Baddeley called it 'one of the humblest specimens of ecclesiastical architecture ever in Westmorland'. It is, in fact, a remarkable, if odd, Cumbrian church. Serving three parishes, the churchyard has a separate entrance for each: an unassuming little gate for Langdale, a plain lych-gate for Grasmere itself, and an arch surmounted by a lamp for Rydal and Ambleside. The Langdales have half the church to themselves, since the north aisle, which is almost as big as the nave itself, was built around 1500 in order to house them. It must have caused problems, for in 1562 John Benson of Baisbrown left money 'so that the Roofe be taken down and made oop again'. Above the existing arcade another was built, with the arches springing from the centre of the lower, supporting the centre of a third roof built above the lower two. The result is decidedly odd. Wordsworth described it:

> Not raised in nice proportion was the pile,
> But large and massy; for duration built;
> With pillars crowded, and the roof upheld
> By naked rafters intricately crossed.

The Reformation communion table is now used as a credence table; the le Fleming box pew remains, as does an interesting survival, an offertory box inscribed 'S Oswaldes Poor Box'. St Oswald, the Northumbrian king killed fighting the heathen Mercians in 642 at Hexham, is the patron saint. His hand, which was reported incorruptible, is seen on the churchwarden's staff; his head is buried in Durham Cathedral alongside St Cuthbert.

William, Mary and Dorothy are buried in the churchyard, together with Hartley Coleridge, Dora and the two infants who died in Grasmere. Just outside the churchyard is Sarah Nelson's famous gingerbread shop, which was originally the village school. The gingerbread, still made according to the original secret recipe, is a delectable confection, which keeps well, and, like Penrith fudge, finds its way all over the world. There is also Rushbearers' gingerbread, which is made to sustain those taking part in the Rushbearing ceremony.

The regional differences in gingerbread have never been properly discussed. Northern gingerbread really is bread, of varying degrees of softness, right down to crumbly cake; in the south it becomes ginger biscuit, cut into shapes of men with buttons, and, god help us, even teddy bears. Not at all a serious article of nourishment. What gingerbread really should be can be regarded as settled by the article in *Chambers' Encyclopaedia,* 1749, for Chambers was a Westmorland man, and would know what he was talking about:

. . . a richer kind of bread, the flavour and taste whereof are heightened and improved with spices and particularly ginger. We shall content ourselves with the following one, which is well recommended. Into a pound of almonds, grate a 1d white loaf, sift and beat them together: to the mixture add 1 oz. ginger, scraped fine, and liquorice and aniseed in powder, of each ¼ oz, and make the whole into a paste, with ½ lb sugar: mould, and roll it, print it and dry it in a stove. Others make it with treacle, citron, lemon and orange, with candied ginger, cardamom and carraway seeds.

The old inns in Grasmere are the Red Lion and the Swan. Harriet Martineau recommends staying at the Swan, still reasonable advice. Of the Red Lion she said: 'The driver must stop at the Red Lion to order dinner . . . an old fashioned place, where the traveller's choice is usually between ham and eggs and eggs and ham.' Things were better fifty years earlier, when you could get a dinner there for ten-pence consisting of 'roast pike, stuffed. A boiled fowl, veal cutlet and ham, beans and bacon, cabbage, pease and potatoes, Anchovey sauces, parsley and butter, plain butter, Wheat bread and oatcake, three cups of preserved gooseberries, with a bowl of rich cream in the centre.'

When staying with the temperate Wordsworths in Dove Cottage, Sir Walter Scott accustomed himself to dropping in for a drop of something stronger at the Swan, without, of course, mentioning this to his hosts, which led to a contretemps when, appearing for once in company with the Wordsworths, the landlord offered him his 'usual'.

The Rushbearing is the oldest of Grasmere's three annual events: the Rushbearing, the Sports, and the Lakeland Artists' Society Exhibition. Rushbearings are northern festivals, famous ones also taking place at Warcop, Urswick and Ambleside – although the latter is an offshoot of Grasmere itself. They date from at least medieval times, before church floors were commonly flagged and the naves pewed. Named graves in churchyards are comparatively recent: before the seventeenth century the eminent were buried in the church itself, under the earthen floors, and the polloi in unmarked graves outside. Church floors were covered with rushes, renewed once a year in the summer, on which the people knelt or stood. How the practical necessity of renewing the rushes became an annual festival is not recorded, but Rushbearings have been held in Grasmere since 1680, and annual payments for new rushes were made at St Margaret's, Westminster, in 1544 which included sums for the provision of ale.

Almost everyone in the village now takes part, and makes

'bearings' from, fresh rushes to be carried by the children. Some of them are traditional – a cross decorated with yellow flowers, *Levavi Oculos* and *Cantate Domino,* St Oswald's Hand, a Maypole, a Serpent, and many others, but whatever combination of flowers and rushes ingenuity suggests is acceptable. The central figures are six girls from the school, in green frocks and white blouses, who carry bundles of flowers on a sheet. The whole village processes, accompanied by the school band playing the Rushbearing March. It is the greatest of fun, and the weather almost always keeps fine.

The same cannot be said of the Sports, but it matters less since the wrestling, which is the main event, is even better in the mud. Cumberland and Westmorland wrestling, taking place between well-matched men, in such a setting, is captivating. Size and weight are important, but not critical; skill is. Clad in traditional dress, long drawers and velvet pants, the wrestlers embrace, heads on each other's shoulders, and try for a grip: they may circle for minutes, disengaging their arms, feeling for an advantage. Then they move; the bout then may be over immediately, and it rarely takes more than a minute, as they push for a throw. It may look simple, but an informed commentator will explain the intricacies of hypes and swinging hypes, and buttocks and cross buttocks, hanks, backheels, outside strokes, and both inside- and cross-clicks.

Although the Guides Race is international, with competitors from as far afield as New Zealand and from even France, the Wrestling is very much a local event: a far comer may join in from Northumberland, but most contenders are Cumbrian and tend to come from the same families. The Brocklebanks have been in the forefront for years, and in 1986 there were no fewer than five St Michael's Thretfalls out of the thirty-one entrants in the open class. It is something of an honour even to challenge these great men, and our family still congratulates its youngest member in having been thrown by a Brocklebank half his size.

The Guides Race is not the best of spectator sports. A body of lithe and agile men line up, dash off up the hillside, where they are soon indistinguishable, and return ten minutes or so later. Nor is the hound trailing much different, except that the dogs are even less visible than the men; their proud owners may spot them, but not the layman. Hound trails have the advantage that the dogs do not damage the countryside as much as people do. The Guides Race is an élite event, but mass fell races are causing apprehension as runners anxious to make time ignore the zig-zag paths and take a straight line, carving up the ground as they go. A correspondent to the *Westmorland Gazette* (L. M. Neeson, 31 July 1987) complained that mountain marathons had turned Wansfell into 'an ugly, worn, sludge-ridden scar, running with water'. Such things as bicycle races nowadays attract much attention, but they will not engage mine.

The art exhibition is no ordinary amateur show, for the region is prolific in painters and sculptors and standards are high. It goes on throughout August, overlapping with Rushbearing and Sports, and shows the work of some talented local painter, and sculptors. The Heaton Cooper Gallery is open throughout the year, and has always some good watercolours on offer.

Grasmere is a good centre for fell walking, both the less strenuous and the tough. Two more sedate walks that should be essayed are up Easdale and round Silver Howe. Easdale was a favourite of both the Wordsworths and de Quincey, who called it 'one of the most impressive solitudes amongst the mountains of the Lake District'. The footpath, which leads up the south side of the valley to the tarn, is clearly marked. Sour Milk Gill Force up near the tarn is a worthwhile waterfall. Returning by Far Easdale you pass near Lancrigg, now a vegetarian hotel, just above the youth hostel; walking about there was where Wordsworth composed most of the *Prelude*, that most remarkable of autobiographical poems.

Wordsworth liked round chimneys and since Lancrigg was built by a friend of his, 'the beautiful Mrs Fletcher', round chimneys it has. One of Mrs Fletcher's daughters married John Richardson, who is buried in the churchyard at Grasmere. Sir John had a most eventful life; he fought with Nelson at Copenhagen, in America during the war of 1812, went with Franklin to the Arctic, and on expeditions of his own (during one of these the Indian guide took to eating his companions, and had to be shot by Richardson) and was commissioned to lead the search for Franklin's last expedition. This he organized so well that, although they found only traces of Franklin's men, the expedition returned safely without casualties, in heartening contrast to that of which he was in search, the best equipped and most lavish of Arctic history, lost to the last man.

Evidence for Wordsworth's partiality for round chimneys is given by Canon Rawnsley, who heard from an old man who had helped with the building of Fox Howe, Dr Arnold's house, that 'Wudsworth was a girt un for chimleys, had summat to saay in the makkin' of a deal of 'em hereaboot. There was 'maist all the chimleys Rydal way built efter his mind. I can mind he and the Doctor had girt argiments

181

aboot the chimleys time we was building Foxhow, and Wudsworth set he liked a bit o' colourin 'em. And that the chimley coigns sud be natural headed and natural bedded, a lile bit red and a lile bit yallar.' Wordsworth certainly did not approve of whitewashed buildings, feeling that these stood out too starkly; a stone colour, as described by the old man, was his preference.

A similar house, up Blindtarn Gill, on the left, was the home of the unfortunate Greens, who died on Blea Rigg in a snowstorm, leaving six children. Both Dorothy and William were much affected by this accident, which inspired Wordsworth to a valedictory poem, illustrating again his remarkable capacity for moving from the ridiculous:

> Who weep for strangers? Many wept
> for George and Sarah Greene;
> Wept for that pair's unhappy fate,
> Whose grave may here be seen . . .

to the sublime:

> But deeper lies the heart of peace
> In quiet more profound
> The heart of quietness is here
> Within this churchyard bound.
>
> And from all agony of mind
> It keeps them safe, and far
> From fear and grief, and from all need
> Of sun or guiding star . . .

Silver Howe has no such solemn connections, but is a delightful hill to walk on and around. The views from the top include the Langdales, Saddleback, Helvellyn and High Street tops, and give a clear idea of the lie of the land.

The sterner stuff is on the other side of Grasmere. Fairfield Horseshoe is the classic walk, beginning and ending at Rydal which is convenient, but it is more entertaining to make straight across to Patterdale by way of Cofa Pike, Deepdale House, and St Sunday Crag. Even so this is not the best way up Helvellyn; the approach from Patterdale is to be preferred.

Wordsworth's way up the mountain starts, naturally enough, from Grasmere, up Little Tongue Gill to Grisedale Tarn. This is the old packhorse route from Grasmere to Patterdale over Grisedale Hause, turning off the high road at Mill Bridge, north of the Travellers' Rest. It was near Grisedale Tarn that William said goodbye to his brother

John for the last time, before John, the great hope of the family, seeming to be bound for wealth and fame as captain of an East Indiaman, was drowned when his ship was wrecked off Weymouth. The whole family was deeply shocked by this and Wordsworth, 'with floods of tears', wrote the elegiac verses which contain that profound couplet

> Here did we stop; and here looked round
> While each into himself descends.

The 'Brothers' Parting', which Wordsworth went to pains to pinpoint '2 or 3 yards below the outlet of Grisedale tarn, on a foot road by which a horse may pass to Patterdale', is now marked by a commemorative stone.

The single essential literary pilgrimage that must be made from Grasmere also starts from the main road behind the Swan Hotel and is the short walk up Greenhead Gill to Alcock Tarn in search of Michael's sheepfold. Somewhere up there is the spot where Wordsworth, with much travail, composed the finest of his early long poems, 'Michael', which appeared in the second (1800) edition of *Lyrical Ballads*. In his preface, Wordsworth advanced those ideas of poetry that changed the whole course of English writing and concepts of poetry, and in 'Michael' he proves the rightness of his views.

Exactly where Michael left his unfinished sheepfold has been a matter for literary detectives. The owners of Michael's Nook, a civilized hotel, claim that it is built on the site of the fold, and they may be right, but it is hardly worth bothering about. It is better to take the poem somewhere up towards the tarn, out of the wind, read it, and go back down to the hotel to recover from the experience.

8

Thirlmere, Keswick and Derwentwater

Thirlmere and Keswick

Dunmail Raise has always been a focal point: the pass on the only north-south route traversing the Lake District and the watershed between Morecambe Bay and the Solway Firth. In tourist terms it marks the boundary between the southern and northern lakes, of which Derwentwater and Keswick form the centre, with the largest concentration of accommodation in the region. The Raise is meant to be the site of a battle in 945 between King Edmund of England and the Cumbrian leader Dunmail, in which the latter fell. Since in fact he did not, but lived a good while and died peacefully on a pilgrimage to Rome, it seems rather perverse to name the place after him. Dunmail is more usually Donald, and this Donald was, like the present monarch, a descendant of the first Scottish king, Kenneth MacAlpin, and the son of that Eugenius who signed the treaty of Dacre. It is a bleak cold spot, and the modern motor road – dual carriageway in places – deprives it of any romance.

Thirlmere, one of the largest lakes, was the subject of intense controversy when in the late nineteenth century it was appropriated by the Manchester Water Authority as a reservoir, and the valley flooded. It is now nearly a century since the waterline of Thirlmere has been 'adjusted', which gives time to evaluate what has happened. Criticism has focused on the landscaping, and especially the heavy plantation of the east side with conifers. This is not to everyone's taste, but it can be said that the backside of Helvellyn has no great beauty, and is if anything improved by the plantation. A more serious criticism was that by using the valley as a reservoir the whole lake is sterilized – none of the things that ought to be done on lakes can be. Until quite recently Thirlmere could only be admired from afar, but now, after the better part of a century, the water engineers have seen the light: there is more joy in heaven over one sinner that repenteth. . . . Accepting that Mancunians need clean water for at least some purposes, it does seem that the present compromise is sensible: some money has been spent on water treatment, four miles of lakeside

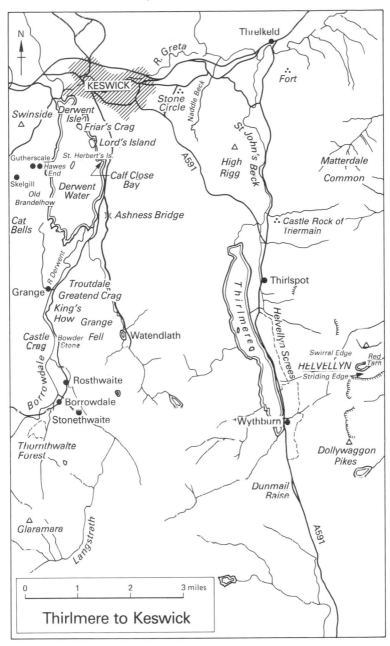

Thirlmere to Keswick

paths have been built, public toilets established, and a nature trail up Launchy Gill signposted. Most importantly, rowing and sailing boats are allowed, providing they can be launched from a single access point, which effectively restricts usage to dinghies. No matter, day boats are all that are needed, for no one is going to press for cruisers on Thirlmere. Another lake, and a decent-sized one, is open to sailors. Care will need to be taken to allow for the wind-tunnel effect, for this is a very narrow valley, but in view of the north-south orientation sailing should be less susceptible to sudden gusts than on Ullswater.

So far there is no great scope for parking, but the lack of amenities such as pubs and cafés on the accessible, west side of the lake will probably help to restrict demand. Improved access also enables the water men to be given credit for something they perhaps did not mean to do. Their plantations were built not for decoration, but to protect the catchment slopes against erosion. Starting with Douglas firs by the lake, they progressed through spruce to larch and beech, and on the hitherto bare upper slopes planted Scots pine. Now that these trees have matured the results are striking: formerly naked screes have become stable, with thick ground cover; fenced off from sheep the native birches, hazels and oaks have regenerated, and in the fullness of time will supplant the beeches and shorter-lived conifers. This regeneration of a worn-out landscape is exactly what is needed over great areas of the Lakes, but is most easily brought about only when commercial interests can also be served.

It is easy to miss **Wythburn** church, up above the Grasmere road. It was built as a chapel of Crosthwaite in 1554, but what exists today is 1640 with an apsidal extension of 1772. Its lonely position, intensified by the inundation under Thirlmere of the neighbouring buildings, attracted the attention of the Romantics. Hartley Coleridge described the chapel:

> Humble it is, and meek, and very low,
> And speaks its purpose by a single bell
> But God himself, and he alone, can know
> If spiry temples please him half so well.

and Wordsworth :

> . . . Wythburn's modest house of prayer
> As lowly as the lowliest dwelling.

The glass, by Hugh Arnold, 1896, is good, and there is some nice bronze repoussé work, presumably by the Keswick School of

Industrial Arts. It was in Wythburn church that Parson Sewell of Troutbeck lost his sermon which dropped down between the pulpit and the wall. Unable to retrieve it, he apologized to the congregation: 'T'Sarmonts slipt down i't'neuk and I can't git it out; but I'll tell ye what – I'se read ye a chapter o' the Bible's worth ten of it.'

There used to be a pub at Wythburn, the Nag's head, and the Manchester Water Board cannot be blamed for its disappearance, since it stood well above the water level, by the roadside, just past the church. Lower down, and now irrevocably drowned, stood the Cherry Tree, where Benjamin the Waggoner and his hitchhiking sailor got drunk in Wordsworth's poem, 'The Waggoner', verses which prove that, at least in his earlier days, the poet had a sense of fun.

> Blithe sould and litesome hearts have we,
> Feasting at the CHERRY TREE!
> This was the outside proclamation,
> This was the inside salutation;
> What bustling – jostling – high and low!
> A universal overflow!
> What tankards foaming at the tap!
> What store of cakes in every lap!
> What thumping – stumping – overhead!

But if the Cherry Tree has gone the King's head at Thirlspot remains a convenient oasis on an otherwise dry road.

St John's is a pretty little valley, and a direct route from Ambleside to Penrith. It starts, at the junction of the A591 and B5322, with the Castle Rock of Triermain, which does in fact look suitably fortified if viewed from the right angle. Walter Scott used it in his 'Bridal of Triermain':

> . . . a mound
> Arose with airy turrets crowned,
> Buttress, and rampire's circling bound,
> And mighty keep and tower.

'Rampire' sounds invented, a combination of 'rampart' and 'vampire' which would suit a Dracula film, although it is in fact a perfectly good if archaic word. There are actually vestigial ruins on the rock, which was known as Eadulf's Castle in the thirteenth century, but can never have been much more than a watchtower.

St John's church is right up on Naddle Fell, in the old track over

187

towards Keswick. The church is probably on the site of one of the hospitallers' chapels, then a chapel of Crosthwaite (see also pages 196–9) but the fabric has been rebuilt, the last time in 1845 with a tiny tower looking like a salt cellar. It makes a good base for a quick walk up to High Rigg, especially worth making towards sunset on a bright day, when the great ridges of Blencathra stand sharply out. There is said to be a holy well in the churchyard, which is perhaps the explanation for its original siting, but I can find only a modest drain of no apparent sacredness.

Those bound for Keswick, however, take the left-hand fork at Stanah. Wordsworth nearly met his end here when the Keswick coach, careering down the slope on the wrong side of the road, caught the wheel of his gig and threw both the poet and his son John over the wall. The guard, fearing the worst, was greatly relieved when a dishevelled and furious poet emerged, expostulating vociferously. Approaching the town, a narrow path on the left takes one to **Castlerigg Stone Circle,** which competes with Long Meg and her daughters as the most impressive neolithic monument in the region. A quite distinct entrance between two large portal stones faces due north. It is also possible to discern a rectangular enclosure within the circle, aligned to the east, which suggests the inner sanctum or altar of a temple.

Like Long Meg, Castlerigg is set on a plateau surrounded by hills, visible for miles around from any direction, which suggests the imperative of being seen, or seeing, but does not contribute to solving the mystery of the site's original purpose. But at least to the redoubtable Iris Cambell, who reported on Long Meg, all is clear. Her 'psychometric projection' explains Castlerigg to be: 'A central Meeting Place where Priests would come from surrounding Centres – but of a funereal nature; performing their funeral rites by weaving different cosmic colours around the bier in order to speed the departure of the passing Soul.'

John Keats did not have the benefit of this explanation when he wrote in 'Hyperion' of:

> . . . a dismal cirque,
> Of Druid stones, upon a forlorn moor,
> When the chill rain begins at start of eve
> In dull November, and their chancel vault,
> The heaven itself, is blinded through the night.

Since **Keswick** has now lost its railway, and is accessible only by

Bowness: a summer evening storm

SY '*Gondola*': apart from the unsightly new bridge, a perfect Victorian yacht

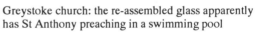

Greystoke church: the re-assembled glass apparently has St Anthony preaching in a swimming pool

Crosthwaite church, Keswick: Thomas de Eskdale's font

road, car-parking arrangements have been drastic, demolishing chunks of the town centre to make way for the tourists. However regrettable, this has been essential, for Keswick now depends entirely upon the tourist trade. Not that this was always so, for Keswick has experienced waves of prosperity and recession, superimposed on its existence as an important-ish market. The sixteenth century saw the miners, the eighteenth the black-lead industry, and the nineteenth the tourists, added to in the twentieth by the Evangelicals. There may perhaps have been a Roman fort, or at least a signal station, at Castlerigg, and certainly the Roman road passed near by, but Keswick itself is a late medieval development. The two original centres were at Castlerigg up the hill, and round the church at Crosthwaite on the other side of the River Greta. A lively market opened up there, so much so that the burghers of Cockermouth in 1306 complained that it was taking away their trade, by selling 'corn, flour, beans, peas, linen, cloth and meat' – a wide selection of merchandise. Their pressure, combined with the energetic promotion of the Derwentwater family, who owned the land on which Keswick stands, and received a market charter for it, ensured that the new development went on in Keswick rather than round Crosthwaite church, but wherever the actual location of the market the general area was bound to be a centre of trade, situated as it is at the convergence of important routes.

Keswick's first era of prosperity dates from 1564, with the formation of the Company or Society of Mines Royal, an Anglo-German enterprise given royal permission to extract and process metallic ores in the Lake Counties, York, Cornwall and Devon, Gloucester and Worcester, and Wales. The German – and largest – part of the shareholding was the firm of Haug, Langnauer and Co. of Augsburg, who provided both the lion's share of the capital and all the qualified staff. Haug, Langnauer kept their books with good German thoroughness and their records give a unique picture of sixteenth-century Lakeland life. Luxuries – Dutch chairs, warming pans, tools, drugs, linseed oil, clothes 'for Robin our messenger' – had to be brought from London. More basic commodities were fetched from Newcastle – Rhenish wine, Malvoisie, Muscatel and candles – great quantities of the last, to illuminate the workings. Kendal could be relied upon for the necessities – feather beds, Claret at a shilling the gallon, Spanish wine considerably more: the expatriates clearly needed some stimulants to survive the Cumbrian climate.

The German workers must have brought high standards with

them; they insisted on having a bath-house built, the cost of which could be docked from their wages. *'So Inen den knappen his allain permemoria gehalton, und teglich wid'bej inen einbracht wirdt.'* English observers were suspicious; Fynes Morison recorded that: 'The use of Bathes is frequent in Germany . . . And this frequent sweating is used by the men to repayre their health caused by immoderate drincking as the women use it for clenlynes.' Given the quantities of Rhenish, Malvoisie and Claret, to say nothing of the local beer, Fynes may have had a point.

Many of the workers were educated men. When Rochius Franck returned home his books were sold: they included 'a fine new Dr Martin Luther's Bible, printed in Franckfurt, with the beautiful figures', Munster's *Cosmographia,* and a Vitruvius. Franck also disposed of his surplus clothing, among which were 'a good dressing gown, "color de Roy", a Turkish jerkin, and one lined with fox fur'.

Native labour was confined to the less skilled trades – walling, domestic service, transport – and paid accordingly, very much less than the craftsmen. Later some English were given more responsible jobs: by 1571 John Bunting is described as a 'smelter'. In spite of this superiority and the unpopularity it brought with it at the time, some at least of the Germans were induced to settle and raise families. There are many descendants of German miners, Tullys, Bankes, Calverts, in the area still; the Rawlinsons and Nicholsons all have German blood.

Few traces of the miners are left in Keswick itself, and not much can be seen in the Newlands Valley, although Goldscope continued to be worked until late in the nineteenth century. Coniston and Tilburthwaite offer much better opportunities to wander, with due circumspection, around ancient workings.

Plumbago brought the next onset of riches to Keswick, and to Keswick alone, for this useful substance is found – or was, for all accessible deposits have been exhausted – only in Borrowdale. Plumbago, also known as black lead, graphite, or locally, wad, has a variety of uses 'both medicinal and mechanical. It is a present remedy for the colic; it easeth the pain of gravel, stone and strangury – it operates by urine, sweat and vomiting – to glaze and harden crucibles – by rubbing it upon iron arms, as guns, pistols and the like, and tinging them with colour, it preserves them from rusting', but the two most widespread applications were in the manufacture of pencils and of moulds for casting, especially in cannon foundries, where the regularity of bore and shot was of critical importance. As for pencils, Keswick has been making pencils, in the sixteenth century merely

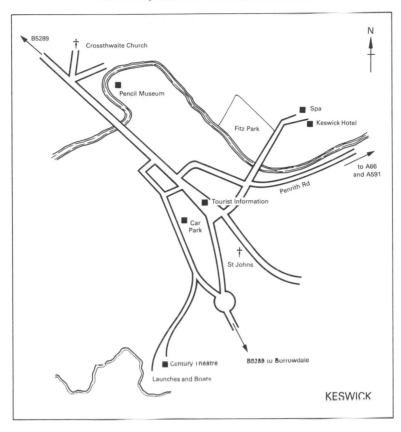

chunks of graphite in a suitable holder (the word pencil was at the time, and for a couple of centuries after, also used as a synonym for brush), for at least four hundred years and still continues although the graphite is now imported from Sri Lanka, Korea, China or Russia.

While it lasted the plumbago boom led to temptingly high prices – thirty shillings and upwards a pound – and smuggling, always a favourite occupation in Cumbria, flourished. In spite of the penalty for stealing or receiving graphite being transportation, the George Hotel prospered as the headquarters of the smuggling trade.

It might be said that the pubs, of which the town has a fine selection, are the best connection with Keswick's past. Thomas Gray stayed at the Queen's Head, with which he was tolerably content. Southey preferred the George, which was originally the George and Dragon, where the sixteenth-century German miners paid over their

191

royalties to the Queen's officers, before the plumbago smugglers made their illicit deals there. Some of the best bits of the George have been retained – panelling, fires and no juke boxes. In what must have been a Freudian slip, a brochure refers to there being 'no guilt and glamour at the George'. The Royal Oak was first a packhorse, then a coaching inn, visited by Southey, Coleridge, Wordsworth, Shelley and de Quincey, Tennyson and Robert Louis Stevenson, all of whom, together with John Peel, are commemorated in stained glass. William Hazlitt, who was here in 1803, has no monument, since he left under a cloud, having propositioned a girl who 'refused to gratify his abominable and devilish propensities' whereupon 'he lifted up her petticoats and *smote* her on *the bottom.*' The Four in Hand, as the name indicates, was also a coaching inn. The Packhorse, up a little ginnel, commemorates another trade route. The Pheasant, the Odd-fellows' Arms, and the Queen are pleasant, but my favourite, out of season at any rate, would be the Dog and Gun, where they have a selection of the Abraham Brothers' climbing pictures, which a century on have never been bettered. George and Ashley Abraham were not only superb photographers, with their studio in Keswick, but pioneers in the art of rock climbing; the images of Lake crags, especially that of Edwardian ladies poised on Napes Needle, which are to be seen on innumerable sepia postcards, are their work.

Apart from the pubs, and sweet shops, the main cultural diversion of Keswick is the Fitzpark Museum, still recognizably that 'repository of curiosities' that Peter Crosthwaite established in 1779 in his native place, although now housed in a building that might well be mistaken for a cricket pavilion. Crosthwaite, 'Admiral of the Keswick Regattas and Hydrographer to the Nobility and Gentry', had served in the navy – with what rank he did not specify, but probably as master, and in the Preventative Service. His cartographical experience was used to produce maps of the area – not bad maps either – which served as the base for a tourist industry; Crosthwaite was anxious to offer every amusement and all guidance to the 'persons of rank and fashion' who were beginning to discover the Lakes, and the first essential was to enable them to find their way around.

Unlike the Kendal museums, that of Keswick is never going to achieve international acclaim, but it is a useful resource on a wet day, being an amiable enough collection, with an ancestry longer than more famous institutions. Having set himself up as Keswick's equivalent to a Master of Ceremonies, Crosthwaite made it his business to amass sufficient curiosities to keep the 'Nobility and Gentry' entertained. As well as Thomas Gray's Claude glass he collected antiquities and fossils, arranged the making and repairing of tourist paths, and invented things: 'A machine that will measure distances . . . a machine for saving people from fires . . . a swinging machine for the benefit of health . . . a portable bathing machine . . . a machine for saving ships and men in tempestuous weather'.

The most striking exhibit today is post-Crosthwaite. The Rock, Bell and Steel band was played by Joseph Richardson, its inventor, and his three sons for Queen Victoria in 1840. It is the sort of instrument Mozart would have loved – twelve feet long with super-imposed ranks of local stone and steel keys, and a series of bells, all struck with hammers of varying sizes by the energetic Richardsons. Since it seems to be still in reasonable condition, or could easily be made so, it should surely sometimes be used. Concerts, recordings, competitions, portable instruments, could all initiate a new Keswick industry.

Not much mileage can be had from another exhibit. Inside an oak chest, which you are warned to open carefully, a 500-year-old cat being therein, is a veritable mummified cat. There used to be the Wild Dog of Ennerdale, too, but it has disappeared.

The more serious, but to non-literary visitors less entertaining, exhibits are the extensive selection of manuscripts and letters left to the museum by prominent Lakeland writers. The Southey collection is particularly important, reasonably enough, since Southey made Keswick his home. Hugh Walpole's are the most illuminating; carefully written – they could go straight to a publisher's editor without typing –with hardly a correction to be seen; he nevertheless wrote extremely quickly, sometimes as much as a thousand words an hour. Equally illuminating are the photographs of his house; his taste clearly leaned heavily in favour of the male nude.

Southey's family life, and indeed Southey's conduct generally, cannot be criticized. Southey is just a bit too good to be entertaining. Like Walpole, he wrote too much too easily and, although one of the best-known literary men of his day, and Poet Laureate before Wordsworth, his reputation has become almost entirely submerged: no American universities vie eagerly for manuscripts, and even the pronunciation of his name is a matter of question (if Byron is to be trusted it was 'Sowthy'). Part of the trouble is that his best work was in history and biography, than which nothing dates more quickly: who reads even Macaulay today, much less Morley or Monypenny? But this neglect is not entirely fair, since some of Southey's poetry is more than respectable. 'After Blenheim', for example, is one of the best anti-war poems:

'Now tell us what 'twas all about'
Young Peterkin he cries;
And little Wilhelmine looks up
With wonder-waiting eyes;
'Now tell us all about the war,
And what they fought each other for.'

'It was the English,' Kaspar cried,
'Who put the French to rout;
But what they fought each other for
I could not well make out.
But everybody said,' quoth he,
'That 'twas a famous victory.'

'My father lived at Blenheim then,
Yon little stream hard by;
They burnt his dwelling to the ground,
And he was forced to fly:
So with his wife and child he fled,
Nor had he where to rest his head.'

'With fire and sword the country round
Was wasted far and wide,
And many a childing mother then
And newborn baby died;
But things like that, you know, must be
At every famous victory.'

'They say it was a shocking sight
After the field was won;
For many thousand bodies here
Lay rotting in the sun:
But things like that, you know, must be
After a famous victory.'

'Great praise the Duke of Marlbro' won
And our good Prince Eugene';
'Why 'twas a very wicked thing!'
Said little Wilhelmine;
'Nay ... nay ... my little girl', quoth he,
'It was a famous victory.'

'And every body praised the Duke
Who this great fight did win.'

194

'But what good came of it at last?'
Quoth little Peterkin:-
'Why, that I cannot tell,' said he,
'But 'twas a famous victory.'

Another amenity on a wet day is the Pencil Museum attached to Rexel's pencil factory, which traces the history of pencil-making from the use of plumbago to present techniques, and, unconsciously, the degeneration of packaging design from beautiful art nouveau cases to the present fussy objects. Boys are taken by the escapers' pencils provided to pilots flying over Germany, with tiny compasses and maps concealed in the eraser heads.

Even better news for parents is Keswick Spa, a new leisure pool opposite the Keswick Hotel, a once grand establishment that housed the Emperor of Brazil on his visit to Keswick, now a Trust House Forte hotel, but retaining some of the agreeable furnishings, including no fewer than seven barometers in the hall, presumably for the better satisfaction of guests eager to obtain confirmation from at least one source that the rain would not last. The Spa is open all the year round and has waterslides, wave-making machines, palm trees and artificial sunlight for those days when the natural product is absent. The truth about Keswick is that it is nearly twice as wet as the driest parts of England, but on the other hand a good deal drier than some other parts of the Lakes. Fifty-one inches a year may be expected in Keswick or Kendal, but 70 inches or more at Windermere.

Coleridge tried to persuade himself that the climate was not as bad as it was made out to be, and in spite of John Dalton's advice – a man Coleridge described as 'devoted to Keswick' – that there was '5 times the duration of falling weather at Keswick than in that of Midland counties, and more than twice the gross quantity of water falling', Coleridge was able to write that 'I have every reason to believe Keswick (and Cumberland and Westmorland in general) hold as dry a climate as Bristol. We have fewer rainy days, taking the year throughout.' But this was in 1801, in the first flush of enthusiasm for the Lakes: three years later, writing from the Kings Arms, Kendal, in January 1804, he recorded a walk from Grasmere: '19 miles through mud and drizzle, fog and stifling air, in 4 hours 35 minutes', and noted his 'peculiar susceptibility' to changes in weather, which eventually persuaded him to try more reliable climates.

It is – just – worth visiting the church in the centre of Keswick. In the nineteenth century Keswick decided it ought to have a church of its own, in addition to the old church at Crosthwaite, and had Salvin build St John's. It is typically severe, and has a steeple, which never seems to have attracted the derision that Scott's effort at Ambleside provoked. In view of the chastity of the church it must be galling that its two most famous adherents – Myers and Hugh Walpole – were of off-centre sexual proclivities, for it was at St John's that Canon Harford Battersby started the annual Keswick Convention, the evangelical gatherings, that now bring thousands of earnest visitors every July. They perhaps pass over the whimsical guide to St John's church, which remarks with pursed lips that 'F. W. Myers, was a famous minor poet. A scandal is attached to his name' and, disappointingly, says no more. A memorial in the chancel commemorates some members of the Myers family, Frederick Myers being the first vicar of Keswick, but casts no further light on the matter. It was in fact his son, Frederick W. H. Myers, who was described as having 'a great number of sexual quirks'; one of the more entertaining was insisting on accompanying his friend Edmund Gurney on his honeymoon to Switzerland, in spite of the bride's objections. While here it is worth taking a look at Cars of the Stars Motor Museum to admire the Batmobile and other automotive fantasies.

Although as a town Keswick is nowhere near as entertaining as Kendal and has no buildings of great merit, it does retain pleasant enough collections of Victorian villas, but redevelopment has accounted for most of the little ginnels that once led off from the main street; those that survive testify to the price that has been paid for the huge car park that adjoins the main street.

St Kentigern's, Crosthwaite, is one of the few large central Lake District churches – Hawkshead and Bowness are the only ones of similar size, but Crosthwaite has a much longer history than either of them. It is probable that it was one of the places visited in the mid sixth century by St Kentigern – or Mungo – the Celtic missionary, and it is quite true that there are six other examples of this otherwise unusual dedication, including Mungrisdale – Mungo's pig dale – from Caldbeck to Aspatria, which constitute a feasible route for a missionary saint to have followed. Unlike some fearsome Celtic clerics Kentigern was an attractive saint; his other name is Gaelic, Myn Ghu (dear friend), and was given to him by his mentor St Servanus. He is often represented with a robin, the pet of St Servanus, which had been accidentally killed and restored to life by Kentigern – a minor but pleasing miracle.

A little later – but historically much more certain, for Bede relates

196

it, and Bede was writing of that which he knew, and Bede can be relied upon – one Herbert, a close friend of St Cuthbert, lived on an island on Derwentwater as an anchorite. The tradition is that this was the place now known as St Herbert's Island, where there are indeed ruins, but of indeterminate date. Crosthwaite – the cross-clearing – gives a likely tenth-century date, by which a preaching cross had been erected, with a church being built some time before 1181. As it stands, the church is mainly sixteenth-century, apart from the earlier north chapel, and the type that was common at the time, single hall nave and chancel, in one, with no transepts.

The most unusual feature, though not very prominent, is the collection of Consecration crosses that can be seen both inside – nine – and outside – twelve. These mark the place where on the dedication – in this case of the rebuilding – the Bishop anoints the fabric with holy water. Usually these places were marked only by painted crosses, which have long since disappeared, but in some regions – Dorset for example – it was the fashion to incise the crosses into the stonework. This external marking is peculiarly English, a tangible reminder that, even before the Reformation, the English church had developed its own separate rites and traditions.

Keswickians took to the Reformation only slowly, and a generation later were still praying upon 'beads, knots, portasses, papistical and superstitious Latyne Prymers' and congregating on such 'abrogate holidays' as the feasts of St Thomas Becket and 'the Conception, Assumption, and Nativity of our Ladye'. Bishop Barnes's precise list of the 'popish reliques and monuments of superstition and idolatrye' that had to be done away with illustrates both the terrible loss of medieval work that occurred throughout the kingdom, and the prosperity of Crosthwaite at the time:

> 'Two pixes of silver, one silver paxe, one cross of cloth of gold which was on a vestment, one copper crosse, two chalices of silver, two corporase cases, three hand bells, the scon whereon the Paschall stood, one pair of censures, one shippe, one head of a paire of censures, xxix brasen or latyne candlesticks of six quarters longe, one holy watter tankard of brasse, the canopies which hanged and that which was carryed over the Sacrament, two brasen or latyne christmatories, the vaile cloth, the sepulcher clothes, the painted clothes with pictures of Peter and Paul and the Trinity'.

Although all these have gone, local piety and the influence of the families fortunately preserved the monuments: two damaged but very fine alabaster figures of fifteenth-century civilian Radcliffes, and brasses of the next generation, Sir John and Dame Alice Radcliffe, Sir John in full armour. Both are wearing tau crosses, indicating their membership of the Guild of St Anthony.

A depiction of that saint with his own tau cross occurs in one of the fragments of early glass; the best of these is a head of Mary Magdalene with an elaborate and fetching coiffure.

Crosthwaite is very much Southey's church, and was restored as a memorial to him. Southey lived for many years at Greta Hall, on the hill, a pleasant square Georgian villa, now part of Keswick School. Coleridge, his brother-in-law, was the first literary offcomer to set up in the lakes: understandably horrified at the news that Mrs Coleridge was about to produce another infant, he sought refuge with Wordsworth before finding a place of his own. Greta Hall had been bought by a prosperous carrier, who let off part of it to the Coleridges. (The carrier, as it happens, was the Mr Jackson who employed Wordsworth's waggoner, Benjamin.) Coleridge kept nagging at Southey to take the remainder of the house, and after some time Southey complied. From then on it was Southey's house and Coleridge quite soon departed for the south.

Southey has a large white marble effigy by John Lough, a Hexham stonemason's apprentice, who made his way to London on a collier brig, was taken up by Haydon, and studied in Rome. Lough was a better artist than usually realized, capable of vigorous and dramatic work, which includes the statues of Queen Victoria outside the Royal Exchange and George Stephenson in Newcastle, and the best of which bears comparison with any nineteenth-century work, even in France. Henry Ewarts is given a verbose memorial, which contrasts with the extremely simple stone of Edward Stevenson, late governor of Bengal; but he was governor only for a day, so brevity is suitable. The font is a most decorative piece, commemorating the vicar Thomas de Eskdale, who as canon lawyer was sent to Rome to settle the argument which persisted between the Furness and the Fountains monks about the boundaries of their Borrowdale lands.

Thomas Martin, a weaver by trade and a calligrapher by inclination, wrote out the instructions to bellringers preserved in the tower when aged eighty-six:

> You Ringers all observe these Orders well,
> He eight pence pays who overturns a Bell;

He who presumes to ring without consent,
Shall pay one Shilling and it shall be spent;
And he who rings with either Spur or Hat,
Shall pay his eight pence, certainly for that:
He who in ringing interrupts a Peal,
For such offence shall pay a quart of Ale:
In falling Bells, one Penny must be paid,
By him who stops before the signal's made,
And he who takes God's Holy Name in vain,
Shall pay one shilling and this Place refrain,
You Ringers all take care, you must not fail,
To have your forfeitures all spent in Ale.
With Heart upright let each true Subject ring
For Health and Peace, to Country, Church and King.

There ought to be a feast day in the calendar to celebrate Canon Rawnsley, vicar of Crosthwaite for many years, during which he made an indelible mark on the Lake District, and indeed upon the whole country, by founding the National Trust in 1893, with Octavia Hill. The first Duke of Westminster, Bend Or's grandfather, was the initial president, with Rawnsley as secretary. It was Rawnsley who was the engine that powered its expansion, from the following year when it acquired its first piece of land to his death in 1920. In his spare time, besides his pastoral duties, he was a county councillor, chaplain to George V, founded the Keswick School of Industrial Art, was a friend of Ruskin and Tennyson, published nearly forty books, established memorials, parks, schools, and forced through many laudable conservation measures. He must have been quite impossible and completely invaluable. He is buried at Crosthwaite, but his local memorial is Friar's Crag, together with Lord's Island and Great Wood, preserved by the National Trust in his memory.

There is no memorial to Coleridge in the church; the only potential English rival to Goethe in the prolixity of his genius is buried in Highgate, where he spent the last twenty years of his life in the care of Dr Gillmer. Yet Coleridge's reaction to the Lakes, and his appreciation of them, was much more sensitive than that of Southey and even possibly than that of Wordsworth. Certainly Samuel Taylor Coleridge, 'Gentleman-poet and philosopher in a mist,' as he described himself, produced accounts of his travels a good deal livelier than any of William's; although those of Dorothy are another matter. Take his description of his scramble – a perilous scramble, since it seems to have been down Broad Stand, a route nobody could recommend – off Scafell, which is the first record of such an experience:

> . . . I passed down from Broad Crag, skirted the Precipices, and found myself cut off from a most sublime Crag-summit, that seemed to rival Sca'Fell Man in height, and to outdo it in fierceness. The first place I came to, that was not direct Rock, I slipped down, and went on for a while with tolerable ease – but now I came (it was midway down) to a smooth perpendicular Rock about 7 feet high – this was nothing – I put my hands on the ledge, and dropped down. In a few Yards came just such another. I *dropped* that too. And yet another, seemed not higher – I would not stand for a trifle, so I dropped that too – but the stretching of the muscle of my hands and arms, and the jolt of the Fall on my Feet, put my whole Limbs in a *Tremble,* and I paused, and looking down, saw that I had little else to encounter but a succession of these little Precipices – it was in truth a Path that in a very hard Rain is no doubt, the channel of a most splendid Waterfall. So I began to suspect that I ought not to go on; but then unfortunately, though I could with ease drop down a smooth Rock of 7 feet high, I could not *climb* it, so go on I must; and on I went. The next 3 drops were not half a Foot, at least not a foot, more than my own height, but every Drop increased the Palsy of my Limbs. I shook all over, Heaven knows without the least influence of Fear . . . My limbs were all in a tremble. I lay upon my Back to rest myself, and was beginning according to my Custom to laugh at myself for a Madman, when the sight of the Crags above me on each side, and the impetuous Clouds just over them, posting so luridly and so rapidly to northward, overawed me.

His stay in Cumberland marked the end of his great productive period with the completion of 'Christabel', a poem full of Cumbrian resonances. There is nothing in English literature more chilling than the appearances of Geraldine, the serpent woman, in that poem.

> And Geraldine in maiden wise,
> Casting down her large bright eyes,
> With blushing cheek and courtesy fine
> She turned her from Sir Leoline;
> Softly gathering up her train,
> That o'er her right arm fell again;
> And folded her arms across her chest,
> And couched her head upon her breast,
> And looked askance at Christabel –
> Jesu, Maria, shield her well!

A snake's small eye blinks dull and shy,
And the lady's eyes they shrunk in her head,
Each shrunk up to a serpent's eye,
And with somewhat of malice, and more of dread
At Christabel she looked askance! –
One moment – and the sight was fled!
But Christabel in dizzy trance,
Stumbling on the unsteady ground –
Shuddered aloud, with a hissing sound;

I wonder whether the girls of Keswick react to that earlier, vividly sensuous, coupling of Christabel and Geraldine. It has to be admitted that Coleridge needs to be got to grips with; his thought is often difficult to follow, but the seldom-made effort is greatly rewarding. There ought to be no question of what to do in Lakeland on a wet day; you take Coleridge's letters and journals to a comfortable pub and stay there till the weather clears.

Coleridge was at Greta Hall for only four years, although his wife lived there for longer, but Southey, who came in 1803, stayed till his death in 1843. On the day of his own arrival Coleridge enthused:

> Our house stands on a low hill, the whole front of which is one field and an enormous garden, nine-tenths of which is a nursery garden. Behind the house is an orchard, and a small wood on a steep slope, at the foot of which flows the River Greta, which winds round and catches the evening lights in the front of the house. In front we have a giant's camp – an encamped army of tent-like mountains, which by an inverted arch gives a view of another vale. On our right the lovely vale and the wedge-shaped lake of Bassenthwaite; and on our left Derwentwater and Lodore in full view, and the fantastic mountains of Borrowdale. Behind us the massy Skiddaw, smooth, green, high, with two chasms and a tent-like ridge in the larger.

The view is still the same, and the constantly changing light still astonishing.

But one does not come to Keswick to see the town, but to use it as the most convenient centre for exploring the surrounding country-side. Only Bowness/Windermere have comparable numbers of bedrooms, and they are sufficiently far away from the best walking areas to make it difficult to manage without transport; and it is one of the best features of a day on the fells that one should be able to walk back to a bath, dinner and bed, with perhaps a little bragging in the bar about the distance covered and the perils encountered. With Keswick as a starting point, Skiddaw and Saddleback, the Derwent Fells and Newlands Valley, Grassmoor and Grisedale Pike, Watendlath and Walla Crag are almost on the doorstep, with the Borrowdale Fells only a little further off.

Derwentwater

The great majority of visitors approach Keswick from the east, but the best views are from down the lake, looking up towards Skiddaw. This was the aspect that impressed the eighteenth-century visitors. Sensibilities have become blurred since, and it is hard to be as impressed by the tame bulk of Skiddaw as was Mr Arnison, organist at Newcastle and a great man in his day, whose compositions were compared with those of Handel, who described **Derwentwater** as 'Beauty lying in the lap of Horror!'; or as deeply as was Dr Brown, who found 'rocks and cliffs of stupendous height, hanging broken over the lake in horrible grandeur, and the woods climbing up their steep and shaggy sides, where mortal foot never yet approached. On their dreadful heights the eagles build their nests . . .'

Joseph Pocklington, a prosperous banker, on the other hand, seems to have had a more relaxed attitude towards the landscape, and bent his energies on making Derwentwater decorative. Vicar's Island, formerly Hestholm, and now Derwent Island, became Pocklington Island, embellished not only with an Inigo-Jonesy villa, but a fort and battery – one nine-pounder and five four-pounders – a romantic boat-house, and his own private circle of megaliths. Since the island was then almost treeless, these embellishments looked particularly stark, and infuriated many including Wordsworth, who devoted a full page of his *Short Guide to the Lakes* to a sarcastic description which concluded: 'The taste of a succeeding proprietor rectified the mistakes as far as was practicable, and has ridded the spot of its puerilities.' All have now, rather sadly, disappeared, swept up by back-to-nature romanticism.

The fort came in useful, not only as a set piece in Pocklington's Regatta, organized by Peter Crosthwaite, in which the main entertainment was its attack by a fleet, but in banging off cannon to provoke echoes, a fashionable phenomenon. The most successful place for doing this was at Lodore Falls, where the innkeeper offered a small cannon at a shilling, or a larger at half-a-crown.

A rather jolly poem offered in celebration of the regatta was published:

Scarcely had day's bright god begun his course,
And chas'd the misty vapours from the lake,
When, ardent for pleasure, forth there spring
A bright assemblage of firm, active youths,
And virgins blushing like the opening bud.
Nay, some there were who sought the sportive scene
Whom frozen age had bow'd with iron hand,
Drawn by the force of curiosity
Or by the workings of parental care
To watch and guard their blooming daughter's steps.

Lake festivities today centre around the Century Theatre in the car park by the launch pier. This extraordinary collection of lorries and trailers, once mobile, became permanent when no longer roadworthy, frozen in a structural art form. It was a bold and laudable enterprise, bringing a repertory company to a theatre-starved region, and was rewarded in 1996 by a grant of £3 million from the National Lottery to provide a properly-equipped theatre; but the 'blue box' will be missed.

Like any lake, Derwentwater should be enjoyed for itself, and it is, together with Ullswater, the most generally accessible. No water-skiing is allowed, so conditions for everyone else are much more pleasant than on Windermere. Nichol End Marine at Portinscale hire out sailboards and dinghies, and both there and at the Keswick boat landings skiffs and motorboats may be hired. You can, if a suitable spot is found, launch your own trailed sailing boat, but the parking problem makes this difficult anywhere, other than at the Boat Club at Portinscale, where this is permitted. Small boats may also be launched (but not if they have an engine) from the car parks at Barrow Bay and Kettlewell, on the east side of the lake.

For exploring the islands, all conveniently situated, a skiff is best, since you can land more easily than from a motor boat. St Herbert's Island is the best for picnicking, with shingly shelving beaches, although the smell of wild garlic can make itself felt. St Herbert, now almost forgotten away from his native place, was the friend of St Cuthbert who, according to Bede, visited him every year. Herbert built himself a cell on the island, of which some scattered stones, doubtless used for other buildings since the seventh century, still survive to serve as barbecue pits.

The other islands are Lord's, Derwent and Rampsholme. Derwent – Pocklington's – Island is inhabited, no landing permitted, and since 1951 has been owned by the National Trust, who allow only very limited access. Pocklington's follies have gone, except for the chapel – boathouse, but some of his house remains, enlarged by Salvin in an Italianate mood. (Pevsner, unaccountably, thought this substantial building no longer there!) Lord's Island is locally claimed as the seat of the Radcliffes but in fact James, the second Earl of Derwentwater, only visited his Cumbrian estates once; the short time, five years, he spent in England was passed at Dilston. Joining the Northumbrians who led the 1715 rebellion, he was captured, and in spite of his youth – he was twenty-six – beheaded. His younger brother Charles, who was caught with him, managed to escape from the Tower, and joined the Stuarts abroad, but he was captured in 1745, with a shipload of weapons, before he had a chance to join the Young Pretender; and like his brother lost his head on Tower Hill.

Gray wandered up Derwentwater viewing the perspectives through his Claude glass which 'played its part divinely' especially at a 'place called Carf Close Reeds; and I chose to set down these barbarous names, that anybody may enquire on the place . . .'

Calf Close Bay was where Gray stood, just inland of Ramps-holme, looking out over the lake, with Walla Crag behind him; and the Crag does rise precipitously nearly a thousand feet above the lake, making Dr Brown's apostrophes not unreasonable. Barrow House, the Youth Hostel, is the last Pocklington survival, and still looks unmellow and 'flaring'.

All good visitors will wander down to Friar's Crag; John Ruskin declared it to be one of the three or four most beautiful views in Europe, and the first thing he remembered in life, when his nurse carried him up there. Ruskin was typical of his time in grading views, awarding stars to them as though they were hotels, but it is really a bit of silliness in so perceptive a man, at best a parlour game; where would you put Durham from the railway, or the Cuillins, or the Hradzany from the Charles Bridge, or Artemisium from Evvia? By this sort of standard Friar's Crag is a bit pedestrian, although it must be admitted that, in the early morning, before the traffic is moving, the sight of the rising sun lighting the top of Cat Bells, with Skiddaw looming off to the right, is a moving experience.

9

Derwentwater to Cockermouth

The region around Keswick is hard to fault as a centre for walking: within a few miles are some of the most entrancing places in the Lakes, including the sometimes neglected Newlands Valley and Grassmoor; and a short journey to Borrowdale can set you off on the best of the High Fells. But in selecting expeditions two may be omitted; **Skiddaw** is fine to look at, but boring to walk up – Saddleback wins hands down – and the fells running south to Grasmere are best left alone. The first observation is made in the teeth of Wainwright, who says: 'Heed not the disparaging criticisms that have been written, from time to time, often by learned men who ought to have known better, about this grand old mountain.' But I stick to my guns.

Skiddaw owes its reputation to the fact that at 3053 feet it is one of the highest summits and that it forms a convincing backdrop to the view over Derwentwater. But it is really not worth bothering about dragging up the quite easy approach. Quite as good a view, if not better, is obtainable from Saddleback, or for that matter from the much easier view point of the car park at the top of Hartside on the A686. This opinion is not fell snobbism – easy = dull – but a sober assessment of relative merits. Climbing Cat Bells is even easier but still very enjoyable.

Saddleback-Blencathra, on the other hand is not as high, missing the magic figure of 3000 feet by some margin, but is a must for anyone who can manage a reasonably strenuous walk. A casual glance at the mountain will show its main attractions – the three parallel buttresses rising steeply to the final ridge – and the best way, by far, is up the central one of these. The path is not shown on the Ordnance Survey map but leads from Gategill, where the Blencathra Hounds have their kennels, pretty much straight up Hall's Fell. The ridge proper begins at about 2000 feet, and resembles nothing more than the plates on a stegosaurus's spine. But the real excitement comes when having reached Hall's Fell top and gone north over the saddle to Foule Crag you see Sharp Edge, described by Wainwright as 'a rising crest of naked rock, of sensational and spectacular appearance, a breaking wave carved in stone. The sight of it at close

205

quarters is sufficient to make a beholder about to tackle it forget all other worries.' Ruskin went up there with his two manservants, and rendered them notably nervous; but Sharp Edge is not really too bad, and the relief once it is over is incomparable.

The walk may be taken the other way round, when you can practically smell your way back to Gategill, but in either direction it should only be attempted in good clear weather, having read, marked and inwardly digested Wainwright and the maps, and being properly shod and clad. The eastern flanks of **Blencathra** look out over Greystoke forest, rather bleak and exposed, and Mungrisdale is unexpectedly charming. Another Kentigern/Mungo church, quite possibly originally founded by the saint himself, is now as it stands a simple early-Georgian chapel with a contemporary three-decker pulpit, a pub, and a few cottages with never an intrusive note. Mosedale, the next village, is even smaller; the Quaker meeting house there is hard to spot, but quite distinguished inside, with Tuscan sandstone columns and good panelling. You climb Carrock Fell from Mosedale to see the Celtic hill fort, which is tolerably distinct. The position of the gate towers is clear, and some of the masonry intact, although the fortifications have obviously been deliberately slighted, presumably by the Romans.

Since many parts of the Lake District are overcrowded it is just as well that some places, like **Threlkeld**, remain relatively neglected. Threlkeld must be one of the best places to live, where one can wake up in the morning and look up at Blencathra rising magnificently above, sheltering the village from the north, and know that one can get on with one's own affairs, park where one wants and rely on a comfortable seat near the pub fire being vacant.

Hunting ranks high among Threlkeldean concerns, since the Blencathra have their kennels here, and some of their best runs have been almost on the doorstep. Tangible evidence of enthusiasm for hunting is evinced in the churchyard, where the 'fox hunters' pillar' records that 'a few friends have united to raise this stone in loving memory of the undernamed who in their generation were noted veterans of the chase'. There follow forty-five names, including that of John Crozier, Master for sixty-four years, and a verse by John Gay:

> The Forest Music is to hear the Hounds,
> Rend the thin Air, and with a lusty cry,
> Wake the drowsy Echo, and confound
> Their perfect language in a mingled cry

which might have been written especially of a pack 2000 feet up on the mountainside. The Horse and Farrier, next to the church, is a good straightforward foxhunter's pub.

Threlkeld itself is, like Coniston, a mining and quarrying village, with no particular objects of interest beyond the church of St Mary, a well-mannered Georgian chapel with a pleasantly oak-panelled sanctuary. The east window was obviously designed – using a chocolate-box palette – by someone who knew not Threlkeld. The Shepherds are wearing night-shirts and walking barefoot, against authentic Cumbrian backgrounds.

One of the first – 1904 – English sanatoria was built at Threlkeld, so that the tubercular patients could have lots of fresh – and cold – air; some survived. The sanatorium is now the Blencathra Holiday Centre, and is the starting point for a geological expedition up the Glenderaterra Beck. First the path passes an old lead mine, where there are plentiful samples of quartz, galena and barite lying about, but the usual cautions about keeping clear of adits and shafts apply. Next the bridge over Roughten Gill is musical; the slates, lightly tapped, emit musical notes; carefully selected, just such slates form the huge set of musical stones exhibited in Keswick museum. Finally, the next beck, Sinen Gill, cuts through a curtain of granite; this is the last stage in the change the slate has experienced as it became hardened by volcanic heat. As one walks up the rock changes from slate through quite distinct stages to granite.

While at Threlkeld it is worthwhile taking a look at Clough Head over to the south, which has something for everybody – a view of Blencathra, a good scramble (up Fisher's Wife's Rake), crags, quarries, steepsided gills, and a well-defined Celtic settlement, all reasonably clear on the Ordnance Survey map.

The river that runs past Threlkeld is the Glenderamackin; the name is, like Glenderaterra and Blencathra, a Celtic survival. If you feel like sorting out Pevsner's confusion about the Troutbeck camps, it is here in Cumberland Troutbeck that you will find the series of Roman camps at the end of the identifiable part of the road from Old Penrith. They are not easy to spot. You have to slip off the new A66 onto the old road, where the revetted banks are visible a few yards off, near the path to Field Head.

Wainwright's authority can be invoked in aid of my second reservation, that of avoiding the fells going south to Grasmere. I cannot speak from personal experience, but Wainwright and Walter

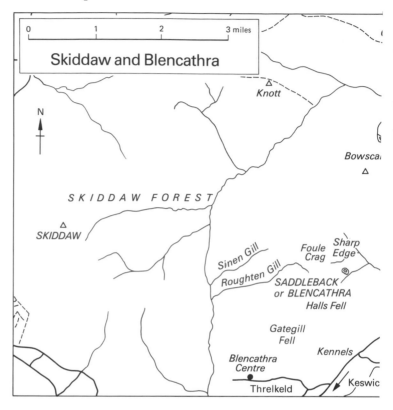

Unsworth both agree that this bit is both boggy and boring, and I am not going to quarrel with such authorities.

Most visitors to Keswick, however, will content themselves with less serious strolls in the immediate vicinity, and there are plenty of those. You can walk all around Derwentwater in an afternoon, but it seems a waste to walk when you could sail, or row. A compromise could be made by taking a launch from the town pier to High Brandlehow and walking along the west side of the lake, which takes in Lingholm Gardens and Portinscale. At Lingholm you come across traces of Beatrix Potter, which have now been analysed in some detective work by Wynne Bartlett and Joyce Irene Whalley. In their little book *Beatrix Potter's Derwentwater*, these ladies have shown how to enhance already pleasant walks by tracing the steps of Lucie in *Tale of Mrs Tiggywinkle* and the unregenerate Squirrel Nutkin. Lucie started from Skelgill farm – Littletown in the book, but still quite clearly identifiable as Skelgill in the picture of Lucie addressing

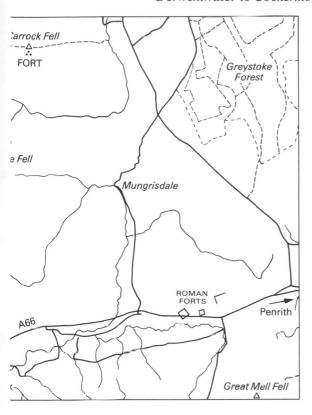

the cat – and went up to Cat Bells, where she came across Mrs Tiggywinkle. The washerhedgehog's house was one of the disused mine drifts that can be seen on both sides of Cat Bells and the view from there over to Skiddaw appears in the picture of Mrs Tiggywinkle distributing the nice clean clothes.

Cat Bells is a walk, not a climb, accessible to all, and very popular, since it has superb views and enough excitement to make things interesting. Naturally enough it is crowded on summer week-ends as it is a great point for hang-gliding as well, but this hardly matters since Cat Bells is a sociable place. The best way up is from the Gutherscale car park, straight up the ridge, or to take the same route but from Hawse End landing, where the launches stop. Having reached the summit (1481 feet, which Wainwright describes as an after-dinner stroll), you can drop down to the real Little Town, where the real Lucie's father, the Reverend Mr Carr, Vicar of Newlands, lived. A footpath runs direct to Skelgill, or an alternative longer route

209

to the right takes you past some old lead workings and spoil heaps. From Skelgill, after comparing the picture with the actuality, it is a few hundred yards back to the car park, or on to the Swinside Inn.

If that can be resisted, Lingholm Gardens is equidistant, by a pleasant path through the woods. The gardens are open during the summer, but are best early on when the rhododendrons are out; and there is a good café there, to sustain the faint. The Potter family made their holidays at Lingholm for nine years around the turn of the century, and the gardens are where the squirrels in *Squirrel Nutkin* disembarked on their expedition to visit Old Brown the owl, who lived on St Herbert's Island, quite clearly recognizable in front of Walla Crag.

Newlands chapel is beautifully situated at the habitable head of the valley, a plain little dales chapel with a tiny schoolroom at the west end. The old mineworkings, which in the sixteenth century were a centre of disciplined German industry, have been overgrown, although the largest of these, Goldscope (a corruption of Gottesgab, God's gift), is still identifiable, and the valley has reverted to a serene beauty. The motor road that passes over Newlands Hause to Buttermere, separating the Robinson group of fells from Grasmoor, is not too much used.

A prudent examination of the old mineworkings can be combined with a reasonably strenuous walk by going up Scope End to Hindscarth and down Scope Gill, or vice versa. Scope End is the prominent toothed ridge above Little Town and the mine lies above Low Snab, the last farmhouse, past the church. By now the original adits look so much like natural phenomena that they are best distinguished by the spoil heaps. Once up the ridge that leads to Hindscarth, a left turn goes up to Dale Head (extensive views from both, of course) and then down either by Dale Head Tarn or by an old miners' track leading off the summit, over Far Tongue Beck, which falls through a splendid ravine. Dale Head Mine is obvious enough, since the ruins of old buildings are prominent, as well as some small spoil heaps, but further down the valley more adits and water-courses need a little more detecting.

All this constitutes quite an expedition, and enough time needs to be given to admire the mine, the views, and the precipitous crags, which attract a good number of climbers. A fact that is borne heavily upon one in the later stages is that there is no pub nearer than Swinside. There was an hotel there once, now a private house, a very peculiar mauve-painted, wooden edifice on the road to Stair. This

210

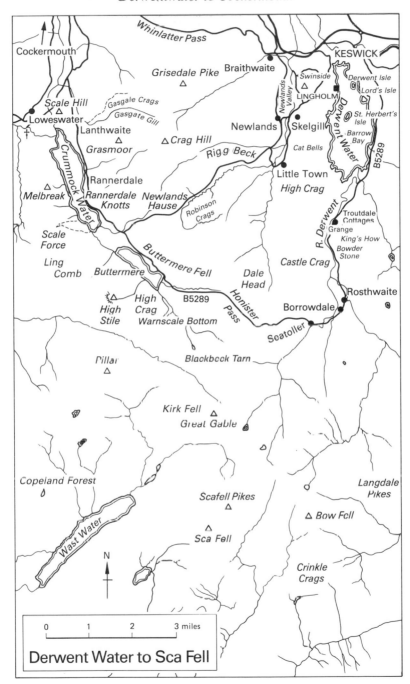

Derwent Water to Sca Fell

lack of pubs is the only defect of the Newlands Valley, otherwise a paradise, but it is a grave one. Apart from this single fault the area is good walking country. Causey Pike has an unmistakable profile from the valley, looking for all the world like a monstrous version of the cupolas on the Negresco at Nice, but Grisedale Pike and Grasmoor are best approached from other directions.

Back at Braithwaite the Whinlatter Pass road comes in to the left. Both here and on the other side of Bassenthwaite lie the Forestry Commission lands of Thornthwaite Forest and Dodd Wood. The Whinlatter Visitor Centre is a great place for children of all ages, with an imaginative exhibition and a stunningly good computer game. For those not too sure of their navigating skills the forest walks are marked, and provide well-graded choices. Braithwaite and Thornthwaite are useful villages, but without much architectural interest, although Thornthwaite church, on Chapel Beck, has a Georgian core and Little Braithwaite manor is a pretty Georgian house.

The interest begins on the west side of the lake with the Swan Hotel, just under **Barf**, which is the impressive pyramid rising apparently straight from the lake. There is indeed a path straight up, which rises 1200 feet in as many yards, and has everything to make a casual walker avoid the place – screes, scrambles, nasty ridges and, naturally, everywhere steep. Great fun, if you feel up to it, but if not a well-behaved – though still steep – path takes you up through the woods. Either way you pass the Bishop of Barf, a slate pinnacle kept whitewashed. The episcopal resemblance is not overwhelmingly obvious; he is not in his robes and mitre, but has to be imagined in his shovel hat. His clerk stands below, an unassuming individual who usually does not benefit from the Bishop's coats of white paint.

Given a choice, the road on the other side of the lake is better, since it takes you to Dodd, Mirehouse and the church of St Bega, as well as giving a view of Barf from across the lake. The Dodd Wood car park, where the old sawmill serves as a tea room (their home-made cakes are worth trying), is also the Mirehouse ticket office.

Although neither the largest nor architecturally the most distinguished house in Lakeland, **Mirehouse** must be the best, in the sense of being the pleasantest in which to live – apart from other considerations it is on the shores of a lake, a very considerable advantage. More than anything else Mirehouse resembles a large vicarage, where you might expect to find a family of Grantlys living in not excessively modest style, and there is something Trollopian about the

Spcddings who have lived there; indeed, in the nineteenth century, Mirehouse was visited by even more distinguished writers than that novelist.

The Spedding family fortunes were established by two gifted brothers, Carlisle and John, chief stewards to the Lowthers. Carlisle in particular was a man of first-class abilities, recognized even by one antagonist who called him a 'Tiriant' and a 'non such'. The family acquired the estate at the beginning of the nineteenth century, following which the house was pretty much rebuilt. James Spedding is the great name, a close friend of Tennyson, Carlyle, Froude and Fitzgerald, and editor of what remains the standard edition of Francis Bacon's writing. Immortalized too by the voluminous letters of his friends, Spedding stands out as a man of great charm as well as ability. Hc rcfused eveiy honour and post (including that of Regius Professor of History at Cambridge), and it is typical that when Tennyson was desolated by Arthur Hallam's early death he sought refuge at Mirehouse, selling his Chancellor's gold medal in order to be able to get there. That Spedding was a man of discernment is proved by his sly reflections on publishers:

> Judging by what publishers say to authors, and to each other, it would seem that the arrangements usually adopted . . . are not satisfactory to either party . . . I have heard of authors whose enjoyment of their publisher's champagne was marred by the reflection that it had been extracted out of themselves.

The house is only open during the summer, April to October, on two days a week, and so remains a family home, but one full of the sort of entertaining objects that accrue over a couple of centuries of civilized life, more concerned with the mainstream of cultivated existence than any other Lakeland families. For this reason the pictures are more varied than most; there are family portraits, it is true, but also a Sartorius, a Morland and a couple of Constables, with a quantity of literary memorabilia, among which are some revealing early photographs and drawings: big James Spedding next to tiny F. D. Maurice: Newman and Pusey (weasel face and ferret face) by Carlyle. My favourite object is not Spedding at all, but a portrait of General Sir John Fryer, who captured Yakub Khan, thc Emir of Afghanistan, at the conclusion of the second (successful) Afghan War in 1879. Before parting with his distinguished prisoner Colonel John, as he then was, of the Carabineers, prudently obtained a rcccipt, which is preserved in the same room. James Spedding was one of the

213

first of the Cambridge 'Apostles', a society recently of somewhat equivocal reputation. Another Apostle lived over at Grasmere – Henry John Robey, the only man ever to be ejected from the society, for some nameless offence. As a punishment it was decided that he should be deprived of capital letters and known henceforth as henry john robey.

Mirehouse gardens are good for children to wander through: they have four adventure playgrounds concealed in the wood, and a garden with plants selected for their attractiveness to bees; fractures, abrasions and stings can all be dealt with quickly at Keswick hospital.

Dodd Wood, which is part of the Mirehouse estate, marks the conversion of the Forestry Commission from the insensitive factory afforestation to reasonably sensitive landscaping. The light on their road to Damascus apparently shone in 1960 when they realized what an affront to the landscape was offered by great blocks of single species of conifers, slashed through by ruler-straight rides. In another ten years all will have changed to softer, more natural and less studied effects. A stiffish but well-marked climb to the top is rewarded by a really good panorama from Helvellyn, through the Langdales, Great Gable and Scafell to Grasmoor and the lake. Since it doesn't take too long to get to the top – a brisk hour – you can see before you start whether the view is likely or not to be clear.

A little further along towards Cockermouth a track turns off to Scarness which also leads to the old Bassenthwaite church of **St Bega**, isolated in parkland by the lake shore. (You can also get there as part of the visit to Mirehouse.) St Bega – if she existed, for she is not well documented – is also St Bee, of St Bees, and of Ennerdale; since these are only three churches so dedicated there may be something in the story of an Irish princess washed up on the Cumbrian coast. It is certainly recorded that up to the thirteenth century an ancient silver arm ring was kept in St Bee's church on which litigants had to swear, in a christianization of what must have been an originally pagan rite. Bits of the church exist from before the Conquest, and a fair amount of Norman work, but the whole was thoroughly restored in 1874, which at least removed 'Mr. Highmore's Seat' to which Bishop Nicholson objected in 1703 as having a 'Fuyrbaloe'd canopy which hinders the congregation from seeing the Elements Consecrated at Sacraments', and caused the communion table to be 'thrown into a corner'.

The Victorian restoration also provided a beautiful wrought-iron

Hawkshead: the monastic grange

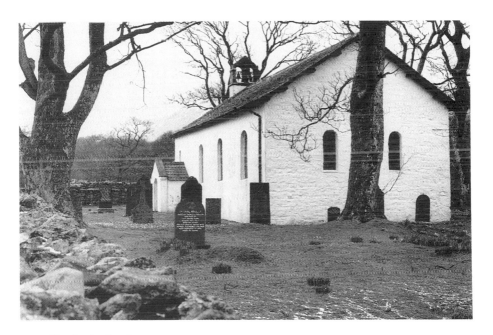

Newlands church

Grange in Borrowdale: the popular Bowder Stone

Bridekirk: St Bride's; the ruins of the old chancel

Spanish lamp, and discovered a fourteenth-century lead crucifix, now hanging over the pulpit.

It was whilst staying at Mirehouse that Tennyson wrote some of *Morte d'Arthur,* and it seems generally agreed that his idea of Excalibur's lake originated here where he sat outside the church by the old cross steps, looking across Bassenthwaite. It certainly sounds like

> ... the Chapel nigh the field,
> A broken chancel with a broken cross,
> That stood on a dark strait of barren land.
> On one side lay the ocean and on one
> Lay the great water, and the moon was full.

Bass Lake, as it is locally more generally known, has a good reputation for perch and eels, and is the only lake hereabouts where ospreys are seen. Perch are good only for pulling out of the water and putting back, but eels and pike, which flourish here too, deserve more attention than they get. Both are excellent smoked – pike are often given away by anglers – and pike baked in a fish brick and served with watercress or sorrel sauce cannot be faulted.

Boats can be hired from **Piel Wyke** at the north-west end of the lake – where there is also a hill fort – and make a good way of pottering about. Even if there are no islands, and the road does run close to the west side, there are enough secluded bays to be able to land for a picnic or even a swim, for, being shallow, Bass Lake is less cold than most. Members of sailing clubs may, if they ask politely, be allowed to use the launching slip of the Bass Lake sailing club. Bass Lake escaped Mr Pocklington's building activities (although he would surely have approved of the Bishop of Barf), but he did hold what must be the oddest horse-race on its waters. This was managed by towing the starters out to the middle of the lake on a raft and sinking the raft. The first horse to swim ashore won.

Bassenthwaite village has some pubs, but nothing much more; pubs and hotels cluster quite thickly round the north of the lake. Armathwaite Hall, where the Speddings lived before moving to Mirehouse, has been rebuilt and is now a hotel.

Starting back once more from Keswick, and moving off to the south, **Walla Crag** is worth climbing for the sake of its view, and possibly of following the path running along the hill below the Falcon Crags, which are impressive precipices.

One should start at Castlerigg – not the stone circle, which really ought to be called Godwell, but Castlerigg on the other side of the

A591, where the television mast is. Crags line the east side of Derwentwater all the way to the Jaws of Borrowdale, and give modest walkers an opportunity to admire the climbers without moving far from their cars or the Lodore Hotel. A summer weekend on Shepherds Crag is a fine time to take really deceptive photographs that give the impression that you yourself are clinging by fingertip, intrepidly operating the camera, while in fact doing so from the perfect safety of a decent path. The path that leads up to King's How from Troutdale, under Greatend Crag, is just such another place, although the walk is a trifle longer.

Watendlath is one of those places that has to be visited, but on foot, and not in the summer. The road from the lake is only just practicable, and ought to be closed to private non-resident traffic. Nor is Watendlath the sort of place which ought to be visited by car. More than any other inhabited Lake District place, it is silent, isolated and peaceful. In the winter, with snow about, the starkness of the landscape is double impressive; the still tarn, pollarded ashes and stunted thorns convey an entirely accurate impression of bleakness; here even the Herdwick sheep are brought under cover for lambing.

Winter is by far the best time of year to visit Watendlath, for in summer it is invaded by tourists, fretting as they try to pass on the narrow road, wandering aimlessly about the hamlet, and leaving litter. Hugh Walpole did not help matters by making Watendlath the home of Judith Paris, heroine of the first few hundred pages of his interminable Herries saga. Somewhere in Walpole there lurked a fine story-teller, but his amazing facility for churning out words resulted only in the production of dozens of eminently readable, but essentially second-rate novels. If they could be reduced to comic strip simplicity, and well illustrated, they could still be sensationally successful.

A good way to get to Watendlath is to climb up from Rosthwaite and go down the track on the east side of the beck to Ashness Bridge. Alternatively a path from Grange leads to Troutdale, which is a most attractive little valley over the top of King's How, but it faces you with some tricky navigation before striking the track that starts from Rosthwaite to Watendlath. Anyone not too sure of their orienteering should just wander about in Troutdale, especially since there are pubs nearby and none in Watendlath, or indeed, anything much anywhere before getting back to Keswick.

Grange-in-Borrowdale is actually just outside Borrowdale, in the flood plain of the River Derwent, at the head of the lake. It is this geographical position that explains Grange's most famous feature, its great double-arched bridge, stretching more than a hundred yards over what in summer appears to be a modest stream. When the floods come, however, the stream becomes a torrent, and the bridge comes into its own: unless of course the whole valley is inundated, which, as the flood markers indicate, is not unusual.

The little church at Grange is an oddity. 'The architect must have been an aggressive man,' Pevsner believes, and the saw-toothed spikes of the beams are at first sight alarming. But the Miss Heathcote who had the church built liked it, and the parishioners have kept it up so well, with all the original oil lamps, that the interior is in fact pleasant enough. Miss Heathcote knew what she wanted; having built the church the presentation was hers, and the rapid turnover of incumbents in her time – seven in eleven years – indicates an impatient decisiveness.

Eighteenth-century sentiments of horror were most often expressed when arriving at the Jaws of **Borrowdale** where the River Derwent flows through a wooded gorge under steep and craggy cliffs. Castle Crag (given to the National Trust in memory of John Hamer and ten other men of Borrowdale killed in the First World War) is the famous viewpoint, easily reached by a path from Grange. The valleys below, where they widen out to separate into Langstrath and Seathwaite, contain all the classic examples of glacial action – moraines, roches moutonnées, corries or cwms, and drumlins.

On the other side of the valley from Castle Crag the Bowder Stone, an enormous delicately poised granite mass brought to its present position by the glacier, was a Victorian delight and featured on many sepia postcards. The egregious Mr Pocklington built a cottage there, and bored a hole through the base so that visitors could shake hands through the stone. More recently, for the further delight of tourists, steps have enabled them to get to the top.

King's How has a memorial to King Edward VII erected by his sister Louise, one of the last surviving children of Queen Victoria, who only died in 1939:

> Here may all things gather strength, and find in scenes of beautiful nature a cause for gratitude and love to God, giving them strength and vigour to carry on their work.

A laudable sentiment, but the idea of the corpulent old King struggling to the top of King's How is curiously inappropriate.

Even King Edward would have had no difficulty with the riverside path from Grange, much the pleasantest way of passing the Jaws, alongside a sparkling stream cascading over a rocky bed, and through the oakwoods that are the peculiar glory of Borrowdale. Branching off from this path another leads off up Broadslack Gill, on the other side of Castle Crag, and continues along the foot of some impressive crags as far as Seatoller. Borrowdale came into the possession of Furness Abbey in 1209, and the monks promptly set about arranging their estates to the best advantage, rounding off their purchase a generation later with the acquisition of Brotherikeld, which gave them an unbroken stretch of land extending south from Keswick right in to Eskdale. To the north their territory marched with that of Fountains Abbey, a fact which led to inter-abbatial disputes, one of which was that settled by the Thomas de Eskdale commemorated in the Crosthwaite font.

Until recently Borrowdale was very isolated; the track to Keswick led through Watendlath and it was not until 1842 that the road was cut through the Jaws. Sarah Yewdale, who died in 1869 at the age of 101, recalled the first time she had ever seen a wheeled conveyance:

> There was no wheeled thing in Borrowdale in my youth; we used to carry o'nag back. We had peats and sticks but no coal; we wore home-spun cloth and clogs. People were very particular about going to chapel, and afterwards met in t'chapel garth for news. Joss Harry came frae t'Watendlath with his dog. [The dog continued to come on its own after Joss died.] There were fiddler and fellows for t'Christmas dance; servants, statesmen's sons and daughters were aw alike. We had chimney hams, bacon, mutton: rows of breet pewter plates on t'dresser. Weddings, to Kirk o'nag's back . . .

As a result of this isolation the natives had a reputation for stupidity. Other Cumbrians tell Borrowdale stories as the Irish do of Kerrymen, the French of Belgians, the Indians of Sikhs and so on. It would be tactless to talk of cuckoos in Borrowdale as of monkeys in West Hartlepool, since the Borrowdalians are said to have built a wall across their valley, to immure the bird, and thus ensure perennial spring.

Isolation has not saved Borrowdale from modern pollution. Acid rain (which everyone except the CEGB knows perfectly well is caused by not cleaning the stacks of coal-burning power stations) is destroying the lichen communities, some of the world's finest. At least one species – *Lobaria scrobiculata* – is already extinct. Nor is

Borrowdale any longer isolated. The narrow valley of Seathwaite becomes a linear car park on fine weekends, and fell walking is now a communal and quite jolly activity. It would be hard today to emulate the sad fate of Charles Gough, whose neglected body lay for three months under Helvellyn. Concerned first-aiders would be clustering around within seconds, and the mountain rescue teams would be on their way. There are comfortable advantages in this, and if the free spirit is urged to untrodden paths there is plenty of room elsewhere.

Borrowdale church, which is at Rosthwaite, has had any interest restored out of it, except for its actual location, which marks the boundary between the Fountains and Furness lands. Rosthwaite is where the valley forks, south-east to Stonethwaite and Langstrath and the Stake Pass, south-west to Seathwaite and Honister. Like the other old passes, the Stake makes a rewarding walk, especially if the original, well-marked route is followed, and all modern short-cuts avoided (as well as being more tiring – the old road-builders knew what they were doing – indiscriminate short cuts lead rapidly to damaging erosion). The route takes you beneath some spectacular crags (Eagle Crag, on the east side of the beck, is one of the best, and can be climbed if Wainwright is followed carefully) and eventually down into Langdale, not too far from the Dungeon Ghyll hotels. A longer and considerably more strenuous walk is to take in Bow Fell, either by diverting via Angle Tarn or going along the stony ridge of Rossett Crag.

Rosthwaite is the best-provided centre for Borrowdale, having more hotels and guest houses than anywhere else. In one of these Wordsworth spent a night in 1812, on which occasion he had to share a bed with a Scottish pedlar; unexpectedly he was said not to mind. Rogue Herries is claimed by one hotel, the Hazel Bank, but internal evidence would make me think he was meant to have lived near Scathwaite, towards which a side road leads off.

A mile past the village, at Seatoller, there is a National Park visitor centre, in a converted barn, open from April through September, with displays and information; a useful spot to visit before exploring the valleys further.

Seathwaite has the doubtful distinction of being the wettest inhabited place in England, with an annual average rainfall over 130 inches; not the wettest place, which is upon the fells round Esk Hause, which delivers over 150 inches (and in 1928, 250), but the wettest *inhabited* place. This is the micro-est of climates, however.

Six miles away, at Grange, the rainfall is only two-thirds that at Seathwaite, and less than half at Keswick, which is about the same as at Windermere. To get these figures in perspective, the Eden Valley has just over 30 inches (which is one reason why sensible people prefer to live there). This is not to say that Lake District weather is very much worse than that of elsewhere; it is more that when rain comes there is a deal more of it, but the average number of rainy days is not nearly so much higher.

To make up for its weather Seathwaite has what remains of the Borrowdale Yews, which Wordsworth admired as being even then of great antiquity:

> . . . those fraternal Four of Borrowdale,
> Joined in one solemn and capacious grove.
> . . . [where] ghostly shapes
> May meet at noontide; Fear and trembling Hope,
> Silence and Foresight; Death and Skeleton
> And Time and Shadow . . .

The old plumbago mines are found on the fellside above the yews, and scraps of the once much sought-after material are said still to be lying about: certainly the spoil heaps are obvious enough. Such ruins of mine buildings that remain are to be found at the mouths of the adits, of which there are several at different stages leading up to the 1100-feet contour.

It was from Seathwaite that Dorothy started her expedition to Scafell, accompanied by her friend poor Miss Barker (see p. 295). Miss Barker was always 'poor Miss Barker', since she was enticed, the Wordsworths considered, into marriage by a much younger man who – scandalous to relate – had been forced to live in Boulogne.

In spite of its weather, Seathwaite is very beautiful, sheltered by wooded hills with crags above. Most of the land together with the farm buildings is owned by the National Trust, who have kept it up as a typical Cumbrian farm with its cobbled yard, now a rarity. Even if no mountain expedition is intended, it is worthwhile walking a mile or so up the beck to look at Taylor Gill Force, very fine when it has been raining, and Stockley Bridge, a well-preserved packhorse bridge. Sour Milk Gill, near the farm, also has a good waterfall. But the reason most people go to Seathwaite is to climb some of the splendid fells that surround it; Great Gable, Scafell, Base Brown, Bow Fell and Glaramara are all within a couple of miles and all easily (as far as any such climb can be easy) attained from the Seathwaite car park.

From Seatoller the main road leads on up the **Honister Pass**, a bleak and craggy place, culminating in the old quarry workings at the summit. Honister Crag, which rises in all over a thousand feet from the valley, is directly in front, and mightily impressive. It was described in 1749 by one George Smith, in a letter to the *Gentleman's Magazine* as:

> terrifying . . . the horrid projection of vast promontories: the vicinity of the clouds, and thunder of the explosives in the slate quarries, the dreadful solitude, the distance of the plain below, and the mountains heapt on mountains that were piled around us, desolate and waste, like the ruins of a world which we only had survived, exercised such ideas of horror as are not to be expressed.

Mr Smith did not much exaggerate; on a dark winter's day Honister is a bleakly menacing spot. Getting the slate down from the heights at which it was quarried was done by sleds – dragged up empty, and guided in a controlled slide down – or simply by men carrying the slates on their backs; ponies could not manage the steep slopes except on well-prepared paths. Traces of these can be seen alongside the modern road, on a rather higher level, from Seatoller to the summit.

The contrast between the rugged treeless crags and the green level valley of **Buttermere** is breathtaking, one of the great sights of the region, recorded in Turner's great picture in the Tate Gallery. The village of Buttermere, sitting on the level meadows between Buttermere and Crummock Water, looks like a collection of toy houses. Even when close at hand, the impression of innocent seclusion and miniature scale remains. The tiny chapel, above the village at the junction of the Honister road and that leading up to Newlands Hause, its size reflecting the paucity of worshippers, was rebuilt last century and given a pretty Holiday window and some pleasing angels. Wordsworth said of it: 'A man must be very insensible who would not be touched with pleasure at the sight of the chapel of Buttermere.' Buttermere must have always been a community where everyone knew everyone else, and everyone's affairs were common knowledge.

Common poverty must have been a help: until the eighteenth century Buttermere church was served by a reader, being too small to warrant a clergyman. The reader's emoluments were 20s a year, a

pair of clogs and a hodden sark (or thick shirt). In addition he had the
rights of goosegate – to run his geese on the common – and whittle-
gate. This last, not uncommon on the dales, was the freedom to eat
(using his whittle) in sequence at the farms in the parish.

Eighteenth-century visitors were particularly struck by Buttermere,
seeing in it something of the natural state of man in which disciples
of Rousseau so firmly believed. It was the despoliation of this inno-
cence that made the story of the Beauty of Buttermere so popularly
affecting at the time (and, as Melvyn Bragg has proved, still has
power to enthral). The facts were simple enough: Mary Robinson,
daughter of the landlord of the Fish Inn, who had already been
'discovered' as a perfect type of rustic (and by all accounts ample)
beauty, was seduced into a bigamous marriage by an imposter; he
was unmasked and hanged – for forgery, not bigamy. And Mary, like
Charlotte in Thackeray's verse 'a well conducted person, went on
cutting bread and butter', seemingly unaffected by her experiences.
Anywhere else such a story might have been banal enough, but set in
Buttermere it still has a peculiar poignancy. The Fish Inn is still there,
as is the Bridge, both decent pubs.

The contrast between the valley and the crags has of course good
geological reasons, for the head of Buttermere valley lies on a join
between Skiddaw Slate and Borrowdale volcanics. Haystacks, High
Stile and High Crag are all volcanics; the lower slopes of these fells,
and Robinson on the other side, are Skiddaw slate, with the glaciated
valley lying in between. From the valley floor this junction is clearly
visible if you stand on the Gatesgarth path near Wanscale Bottom and
contrast the lumpy craggy brows of Haystacks with the smoother and
more regular slopes to the north.

Buttermere Lake (the description is of course tautological, but
differentiates it from the village) is small enough to stroll round in an
hour, by a path that in most places is very near the water's edge and
gives a succession of magnificent views. From water level
Buttermere seems a totally enclosed valley, shut in by the great crags
of High Stile, High Crag and Honister to the south and east, by
Robinson to the north and due to the curve of the valley by Melbreak
to the west and Rannerdale Knott. If you have brought a windsurfer
or dinghy it can be launched over the National Trust beach at
Gatesgarth end.

Only a few feet of elevation prevent Crummock Water and
Buttermere from being the same lake, but the two are quite different.
Crummock Water is considerably larger and more open than

Buttermere, without dramatic crags, although Rannerdale Knott is a good well-defined hill. Behind it lies the hidden valley of Rannerdale, running parallel to the lake behind the Knott. This is said to be the site of a great battle between the Saxons and Normans: a story made into a short novel, *The Secret Valley*, by Nicolas Size, who was landlord of the Bridge Hotel in Buttermere. Rannerdale used to have a Magdalene chapel, which has now disappeared, its stones doubtless purloined for some convenient cottage.

A good path leads right up the south-west edge of Crummock Water, between Melbreak and the shore, but most people branch off before Melbreak to visit Scale Force, the highest of local waterfalls, with a clear drop of over one hundred feet. It owes much of its popularity to Wordsworth, who called it 'worthy of being visited both for its own sake, and for the sublime View across the Lake, looking back in your ascent towards the Chasm. The Fall is perpendicular from an immense height, a slender stream faintly illuminating a gloomy fissure'. Melbreak itself is a perfect French goat's-cheese shape, and gives its name to the local hunt, the Melbreak Foxhounds. Grasmoor dominates the other side of the lake, looking a peaceful enough fell from the shore, but further on, by Lanthwaite Green, it presents an altogether sterner aspect.

Boats may be launched near Rannerdale over a little beach, or hired from the farm, and Crummock Water is just big enough to make for an entertaining sail with plenty of access points to the shore. There is said to be a good bathing spot at Low Ling Crag, an isolated roche moutonnée sticking out into the lake, which certainly makes a fine viewpoint, but bathing in any lake calls for a hardness and firmness of character that is not altogether common. Wordsworth admired the view:

> It must be mentioned also, that there is scarcely anything finer than the view from a boat in the centre of Crummock-water. The scene is deep and solemn, and lonely; and in no other spot is the majesty of the Mountains so irresistibly felt as an omnipresence, or so passively submitted to as a spirit incumbent upon the imagination.

The full majesty of Grasmoor is only appreciated when you get past the end of the lake to Scale Hill, when the range of crags that forms the north face of Grasmoor comes into view. The fell's name does not refer to grass, although in fact it has a well-grassed top, but to 'gris' the Norse swine. To see this other side you turn right at Lanthwaite Green farm and walk a mile up Gasgale Gill, where

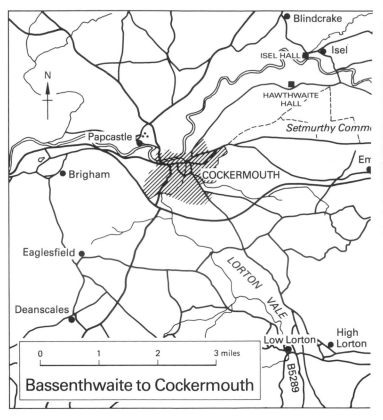

Bassenthwaite to Cockermouth

between Gasgale Crags and Dove Crag on Grasmoor, you are in the wildest and most desolate of ravines. By contrast, if at the farm you take the path to the lake and go down through the woods to the lakeside, you are in pleasant green Vale of Lorton countryside, as affable a place as could be imagined and conveniently near to Scale Hill Hotel, 'a roomy Inn, with very good accommodation', one of the few to be commended in Wordsworth's guide. Father West, the doyen of all Lake District guidebook writers, chose Lanthwaite Hill as one of his viewpoints and rightly so. Especially if you have come from Honister, it enables you to look back at the mountains rising in series and in all directions behind the lake, one of the finest prospects in the region.

Loweswater is only separated from Crummock Water by a mile of flat land, but lies in an entirely different landscape, escaped from the heights, surrounded by lower smoother fells, and encircled by trees.

224

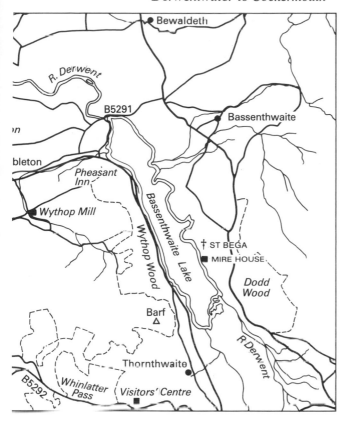

Holme Wood has the best of these, down by the lake, where the planters have held their collective hand and allowed the native trees to flourish.

Loweswater village is an ancient settlement; it has had a chapel since the twelfth century, but the present building is an 1884 reconstruction, pleasant enough, and beautifully situated. One of its eighteenth-century incumbents had a taste for verse and wrote:

> Honour the idoll which I most adore
> Receives no homage from my knee
> Content in privacy I value more,
> Than all uneasy dignity.

An appropriate sentiment for this secluded spot. Not the least pleasant prospect from the church is that of the Kirkstile Inn, a long-reputed pub. It may be that the earthworks to the south of the village are the remains of a Dark-Age church, associated with St Ninian. They are rectangular and have the correct orientation, but seem too large – 150 feet by 80 feet – for a church of that time. It is possible that there might have been a sacred enclosure, perhaps with a preaching cross.

Fell walkers lose interest at Loweswater since the Lorton Valley, which leads north to Cockermouth, has no rugged hills for them to tackle. It is instead a farming valley, with good meadows in the bottoms and pastures on the slope, scattered farms, and the extended village of **Lorton**. Aesthetes may jeer at the east window in the church, which Pevsner called 'really indefensible', but which has its admirers – and there is a good collection of heraldry on corbels, pews and pulpit. Wordsworthians come to try to find the Lorton Yew, which is at High Lorton, on the banks of the Whit Beck in a field next to the telephone kiosk. Wordsworth wrote of it in 1804:

> There is a Yew tree, pride of Lorton in the vale,
> Which to this day stands single, in the midst
> Of its own darkness, as it stood of yore . . .

Approaching two centuries later it is still there, still of vast circumference, but now showing signs of decay. Lorton Hall has a large pele, reflecting the fact we are now back in open country, out of the protection of the hills, and a handsome seventeenth-century wing, traditional in style but with pediments at least acknowledging the beginnings of a classical influence. At High Lorton the Roman road from Papcastle turned east to ascend the Whinlatter Pass. Its route is now followed by the minor road that goes through Boonbeck to join the main road at Blazebridge.

Whinlatter used to be the route taken by the turnpike between Cockermouth and Keswick, which was described in 1794 as 'the steep and Alpine passes of Whinlater, [which] form an ascent of five miles, up stupendous heights by a winding path, contrived in an excellent manner . . .'

The main road continues to **Cockermouth**, which is often compared to Penrith as a market town on the fringes of the Lake District, but one that has shown more initiative in developing tourist attractions. Penrith's steam museum has gone, but Cockermouth has acquired three new ones, as well as an art gallery and a live sheep show. It is here that the River Cocker joins the Derwent, the two streams helping to make Cockermouth an agreeable town to stroll around, with some decent Georgian houses and a wide, tree-lined and

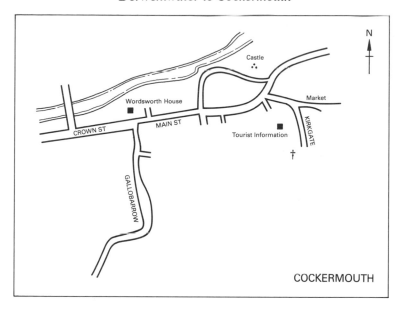

pleasant main street with a majestic statue of the Earl of Mayo, who formerly represented the town in Parliament and later distinguished himself by being the only Viceroy of India to be assassinated – in 1872, by a convict in the Andaman Islands. It is a large and solid memorial, as was proved in 1964 when a petrol tanker knocked it over; the tanker was wrecked, but the statue is intact.

Wordsworth spent the first thirteen years of his life in Cockermouth, and the family's house there furnishes many clues to an understanding of the poet. It is by some way still the finest house in the town – and possibly in any Lakeland town; nine bays of elegantly appointed early-Georgian façade, it is a *town* house; John Wordsworth was not a country gentleman, but Sir John Lowther's agent, a man of position, but not of rank, an attorney and son of an attorney, due a good salary (often not paid: he died with over £10,000 due from the Lowthers which was paid only nineteen years after John Wordsworth's death). Wordsworth was brought up in an atmosphere of some comfort and ease – the contrast with his poverty and plain living at Dove Cottage is the more striking. When he prospered, and moved to Rydal Mount, he was regaining something of the status he had known as a child, and quite clearly appreciated it, but the poet at Dove Cottage was, in modern terms, a social drop-out.

The finest room is the first-floor drawing room, with its handsome raised and fielded panelling, architraves and cornices, and its range of tall windows, the whole large enough to enable the Broadwood grand to retreat into the background. Wordsworth's own bookshelves and glazed secretaire, both good pieces from Rydal Mount, fit into the library as if they belonged there. The National Trust, who look after the house, run a coffee room in the kitchens, and arrange occasional concerts in the drawing room.

Cockermouth's parish church is undistinguished, but its castle is more interesting than the ruins at Penrith. It was in Percy hands from the fourteenth century, passing to the Wyndhams in the eighteenth when the Percy direct line died out (the present Dukes of Northumberland were originally Smithsons, and changed their name when Sir Hugh Smithson succeeded in right of his wife, who was a Percy). During the Civil Wars the castle was held for Parliament by the Percies, and was subjected to a Royalist siege; this can hardly have been very professionally carried out, since the besiegers suffered ten fatalities, and the besieged only one.

The outer gatehouse, which can be seen from Castlegate, is a Percy building of 1400 with a row of heraldic devices above the arch. Most of the rest of the castle is also Percy work, including the massive inner gatehouse and kitchen tower and the flag tower; the round tower, right at the other end of the castle, is earlier, from about 1250. The vaulted basement of the kitchen tower is locally known as 'Mirk Kirk', suggesting that this may have been the castle chapel, but this is inherently unlikely. The castle is now an Egremont home, open only on special occasions during the July Cockermouth Festival.

The three new museums are founded and funded by private individuals. Rod Moore's Toy Museum is a paradise for children of all ages, well organized and presented – and funded entirely privately. So is David Winkworth's Printing House Museum, with working examples from printing equipment.

Wood block presses, through the magnificent Columbia machines of the mid-nineteenth century to an automatic Heidelberg press; and a second-hand bookshop, make the establishment in Main Street a place in which to linger. Given the omnipresence of rock in the Lakes, William Creighton's Mineral Museum also merits a visit.

Just outside the town adjoining the new Shepherd's Hotel – cheery and unpretentious – is the Lakeland Sheep and Wool Centre, which stages exhibitions of real sheep, a score of well-behaved examples of different breeds from the lordly Merino to the rugged Herdwick.

Engaging dogs deign to herd geese (not enough room on the stage for perambulant sheep) and at every show one sample animal is expeditiously sheared. Performances take place all the year round (but times should be checked with the Tourist Offices) and should not be missed.

When to all these attractions are added a good art gallery in Castlegate House, Jennings Brewery, offering guided tours, a swimming pool and some respectable pubs, Cockermouth now unquestionably has Penrith beaten.

Rather than rejoining the A66 bypass it is better to take the minor road running parallel to the River Derwent, which is a lovely stream, but difficult to get near to before coming to Isel.

Hewthwaite Hall, on the north side of the road, is a rare survival, a late-fifteenth-century house, with a handsome coloured inscription above the door recording the date 1581 – a refurbishing rather than the original building. It is oddly pretty; two shields, one reversed, flanked by figures of bishops in niches, underneath the inscription, also flanked by niches:

> John Swynburn Esquire and Elizabeth his wyfe
> did make cost of this work in the dais of ther Lyfe
> Anno Domini 1581   Ano Rae 23

St Michael's, **Isel**, is beautifully situated by the River Derwent, very pretty thereabouts. Like Torpenhow, down the road, it is Norman, and looks it, with its numerous slit windows. Isel used to be de Morville land, but was given by Hugh, one of Beckct's assassins, to Hexham Abbey. The Leighs, and then the Lawsons, succeeded as Lords of Isel, and the church is now almost a Lawson chapel. All the Lawson eldest sons were called Wilfred, and the greatest of them was the nineteenth-century baronet, a humorous, fox-hunting Liberal, a teetotaller but unfanatic, whose bald head, long beard and twinkle made him idolized by the locals, as well as a favourite of cartoonists. Many of Sir Wilfred's sentiments sound uncommonly advanced, and highly pertinent. He said of the Afghan War, in a letter to his nephew, Lord Curzon, that we would have to explain 'that it was only "children" who were meant to "love one another" and that adults are to spend their time preparing machines and armies for blowing to pieces all with whom they have any difference of opinion'. Of the Boer War, when jingoistic fervour was at its height, he said: 'The nation was gradually inflamed and I really believe considered that there was something noble and patriotic in sending out troops, exceeding the

Boers in number by about five to one, to complete the overthrow of their freedom.' And, in reply to Kipling:

> The flannelled fool at the wicket
> In a frivolous pastime may revel
> But the khaki-clad brave in the thicket
> Is playing the game of the devil.

John Betjeman thought Isel 'a perfect English harmony of man and nature – a setting for Jane Austen . . . the tree-hung stream near the church flows past the lawns of a delightful old vicarage. All around stretches a lost landscape of pasture and river. *O fortunatus nimium . . .!*'

Inside the church are a couple of fragments of tenth-century crosses, part of the crudely worked *oeuvre* of a local sculptor who has been given the name of 'Untidy'. The church's treasure, the Triskele stone, has now been stolen, and is represented only by a photograph. Possibly pagan and very ancient, it bore a series of religious symbols – a swastika, two triskeles (the Isle of Man's three legs are a refined triskele), Thor's thunderbolt, and a sun-snake. Like many other churches Isel was built on a site already hallowed by religious custom.

The black marble tablet in the chancel bears a verse that stands out by its poetic merit from the common run of encomia and gloom:

> Hic jacet ille cinis qui Modo Lawson erat.
> Even such is Time which takes in trust
> Our Youth, and Joyes, and all we have;
> And payes us but with Age and Dust
> Within the Dark and Silent Grave
> When we have wander'd all our Wayes
> Shuts up the Story of our dayes:
> And from which Earth, and Grave, and Dust
> The Lord will raise me up, I trust.
>
> Wilfridus Lawson Miles obijt 16 die
> Aprilis Anno aetatis suae 87. Annoque
> Salutis 1632.

The beauty of the verse is not surprising when it is realized that this is in fact Sir Walter Raleigh's own epitaph, written by himself.

Isel Hall is more baronial than baronetal, a great range stretching over the river, culminating in Isel pele. The whole presents a façade a hundred yards or so long, all in a similar style, in date between the mid fifteenth century for the pele, to the late sixteenth/early seventeenth for the part furthest away. The present owner, Mary Burkett of Abbot Hall, opens the house once a week in the season, and at other times the impressive front can be admired from the road.

From Isel a road round Setmurthy Common will lead back to Embleton and over the A66 to Wythop Mill, a restored corn mill which offers teas. More substantial refreshment is available at the Pheasant Inn, marked on the Ordnance Survey map, which is really an hotel, well furnished in a peaceful setting on a wooded hillside. Before visiting the Pheasant one should look in at Higham Hall, an adult education centre. They are happy to let visitors look at their handsome house, with elegant Gothick detailing – cast-iron mouldings providing an unusual feature. You can book in for one of their courses of which there is an amazing range, from silverwork to flyfishing, Roman history to whisky appreciation, together with a number of musical events. From there one can return to Keswick along either side of the lake: the road on the west is considerably faster.

10

High Furness

In 1163 a squabble between the Baron of Kendal and the Abbot of Furness about who owned what in High Furness was settled by arbitration. 'The Fells of Furness are divided from Kendal by these bounds as it was sworn at my command upon the oath of thirty men.' And the thirty men duly attested the division, by which the monks gained all the land between Coniston and Windermere from *Wreineshaw* – Wrynose – south.

There is a bit of everything in High Furness: one of the best lakes – Coniston; the prettiest miniature town – Hawkshead; a dignified mountain – Coniston Old Man; undemanding attractive country walks; and, in the Langdales, some of the most dramatic scenery. Add that the whole is well-pubbed and the desirability of High Furness becomes clear. This chapter deals with the lower part, roughly south of Coniston and the Windermere ferry.

Nowhere in England is history written as clearly on topography as in Cumbrian place-names: two millennia of settlement are recorded on the map. Original Celtic names – Lyvennet, Carlisle, Blencathra, have survived; Saxon settlements surviving only on the eastern borders – Inglewood (the English wood), Heversham, and Westmorland itself; the odd Norman barony such as Egremont, but everything else is overwhelmingly Norse. W. G. Collingwood made a brilliant analysis of many patterns of Norse settlement, that of **High Furness** being particularly detailed. Coniston Water was originally Turstini watra – Thorstein's lake – only getting its present name after King Stephen's time. Thorstein's own home should have been somewhere near Lowick, in the region of the first settlement:

> Thence going up the eastern valley into the fells we find Finn's field (Finsthwaite), Hroald's or Hrolf's land (Rusland), Satterthwaite, and another Grisedale (pig valley). Just north is Hauk's satter (Hawkshead) which became the headquarters of that valley, but at first was only a dairy or sheep-cote. Going up the Crake valley we find Bethoc's erg (Bethecar), marking another Gaelic retainer; Old and New Booth-thwaite (Nibthwaite); Torfi's erg (Torver); the 'thwaite in a hole' (Hoathwaite) and Tilberthwaite) means the land

round a rock-ridge where traces of habitation suggest the refuge of somebody who had a reason for keeping himself to himself in pre-Norman days. And as the Vikings brought Gaelic thralls with them we can understand why Glenscalan ('dell of the huts'?) was so named even in the twelfth century. As in Iceland, a few Gaelic words crept into the Norse.

After that the monks made their mark with Granges, Monk Coniston, Priest Pot. Medieval industries are recorded in Tenter Hill, Ealing-hearth, Force Forge et cetera.

Wordsworth recommended approaching High Furness from the south, since it is seen to most advantage on entering the county over the Sands from Lancaster. 'The stranger, from the moment he sets his foot on those Sands seems to leave the turmoil and traffic of the world behind him; and, crossing the majestic plain when the sea has retired, he beholds, rising apparently from its base, the cluster of mountains among which he is going to wander, and towards whose recesses, by the vale of Coniston he is gradually and peacefully led.' The Sands crossing would have brought the stranger out at Foxfield, just south of Broughton, which is a good reason for beginning at **Broughton in Furness.** The detour taken by the A595 to the coast at Foxfield can perhaps be ignored in favour of Broughton, which is village-sized but has a spacious market-place grouped around an obelisk, all worthy of a real town, which is was on the way to becoming in the eighteenth century. Broughton market, which it has had only since that time, was a collecting place for wool and coppice wood products, which could be barged out of the Duddon estuary.

Broughton church, St Mary Magdalene, is outside the village on the left-hand side of the road going west. It is an odd edifice, with a massive Norman-style nave, a smaller south aisle, originally the nave, and an eccentric tower. Bits of original Norman – a crude south door and some adjoining wall – remain. The church guide says that the 1874 rebuilding was due to 'the energy, inspiration and generosity of Richard Assheton Cross of Eccle Riggs'. These laudable qualities might have been better applied, for the result is gloomy, but there are a couple of good Charles Kempe windows.

Broughton Towers, at the top of the market-place, was the pele of the Broughton family, the last of whom made the fatal mistake of joining Lambert Simnel. Since his day the house was acquired by the zealous Puritan Colonel Roger 'Praying' Sawrey, who founded the Tottlebank conventicle.

The triangle of land between the A590, the A593 (Broughton to

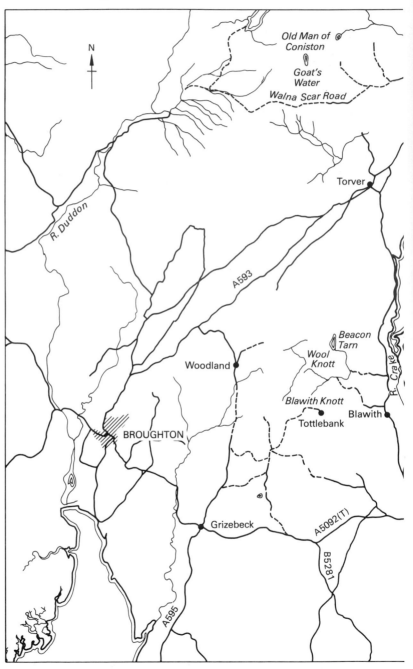

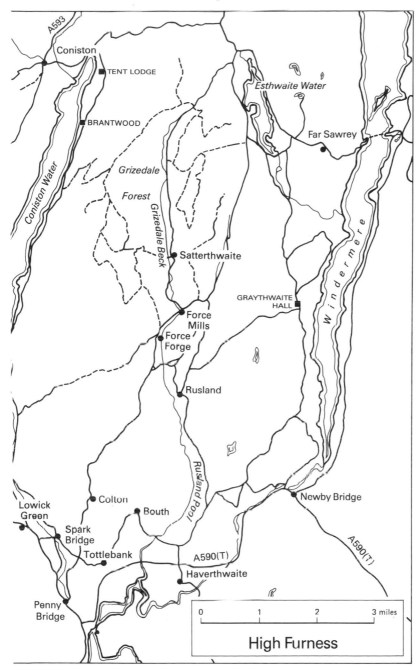

High Furness

Torver) and the A5084 (Lowick to Torver) is a good place to spend summer weekends away from more popular spots. This is all ragged Silurian slate, bristling with outcrops, gorse and juniper giving way to heather and bilberry, for which last reason it is also worth careful attention in July, when the bilberries are ripe. There can be no comparison between wild berries and domesticated blueberries, and even if it is finicky work to collect them the resultant pies or summer puddings are ample reward. If it is a year for juniper berries, these should be picked, being excellent with roast pork. The whole area is criss-crossed with footpaths and unfenced roads, which make possible a variety of round walks; perhaps the best of these is one that takes in both Woodland church and Beacon Tarn, highly recommended by Wainwright: 'a connoisseur's piece, every step an uninhibited joy, every corner a delight'. Woodland church is not easy to spot on the Ordnance Survey map or to approach from the A593. The best way of finding it is to strike due north from Grizebeck about two and a half miles. The chapel is modern, in typical dales style, but with an apse.

Wainwright's walk starts up the road to the north via Yewbank and Beacon Tarn to Wool Knott, but it is worth making two small detours, one to the south along the path to Blawith to White Borrans, the other in the opposite direction to spot an old bloomery. White Borrans (the noun denotes a heap of stones, and is used also for the site of Roman remains) are two large cairns, quite impressive in size. Any bloomery site is recognized by a heap of slag, hardly impressive, but a vivid illustration of how the Industrial Revolution transformed the face of England. If one abandons Wainwright there and strikes off via Tottlebank to Blawith Knott, you can take in a good view and some more Romano-Celtic remains at the junction of the path and the unfenced road leading back to Woodlands. These consist of quite an extensive complex of interlinked enclosures with substantial walls, with nearby burial cairns, some of which have been excavated.

The road from Lowick runs via Blawith to Torver through the pretty Crake valley, the River Crake being the outlet from Coniston, entering the estuary at Greenodd. Blawith and Lowick have a history of separatism that matches that of the two divisions of Ireland, and has been going on for almost as long. Lowick had its church first, but Blawith (which is pronounced 'Blaith', by the way) got its at least by the sixteenth century. In 1645 the parishioners of both decided for unification, and petitioned that a third church be built, at their own cost 'in an indifferent place'. The parishes were united, but no church built. In 1786 they were officially divided. By 1841 another attempt at unification was made, but resisted; it only lasted for five years. In 1928 it was announced that when the livings fell in they would be once more united. Lowick did not approve, especially since this would encourage the Nonconformists. Now, as throughout the country, the parish has been even further extended, with one hardworking parson dashing about between all the churches.

Towards the end of the eighteenth century, when Blawith was feeling self-assertive, the parish decided to go one better by building a steeple, which would be paid for by selling off some church land, which gave rise to the rhyme, doubtless coming from Lowick:

> Blawith poor people
> An old church and new steeple
> As poor as hell
> They had to sell
> A bit of Fell
> To buy a bell,
> Blawith poor people.

Since then both churches have been rebuilt. Such is hubris, within a century Blawith had to abandon its church, and build anew; so did Lowick, whose parishioners indulged themselves not only with a tower, but also with a vestigial steeple as well, while those of Blawith had to content themselves with a mere bell cote. Blawith has at least the ruins of its old church, which are more picturesque than either of the new buildings, but Lowick has the Red Lion, frequented by Arthur Ransome.

Torver church is by Paley and Austin, and may, as Professor Goodhart-Rendel describes it, be very fine, but since it is impossible to get into it — or even into the churchyard — it can be ignored in favour of the Church House Inn next door.

A footpath from Torver towards **Coniston** leads along the lake shore, past the site of a bloomery, to the Old Hall, whose massive chimneys are conspicuous. It was rebuilt in the sixteenth century and forms a very complete late medieval hall, in spite of its period, with a screens passage and dais, and a courtroom, built for the Flemings, whose main seat it was between the thirteenth and sixteenth centuries after they moved from Aldingham, and before they elected for Rydal. This moving twice in only four hundred years looks very like restlessness in a Lake District family. The collection of enormous chimneys indicates its original status as being something higher than

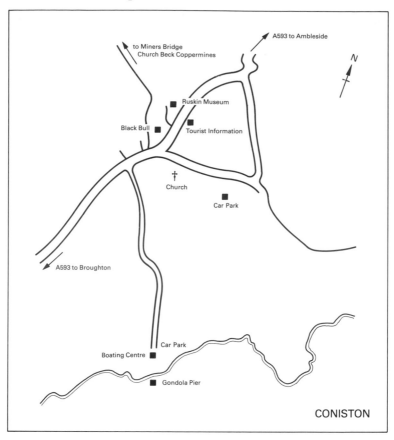

that even of a substantial farmhouse. The great hall on the first floor, with its screens, daïs and withdrawing room, just as in a Cambridge college, was fifty foot long, with the courtroom wing another sixty foot. The new sixteenth-century rebuilding was thorough, with all modern conveniences, the old pele having been completely removed, unlike most other local manor houses, where the towers were incorporated into the later building.

Coniston has been for centuries the most industrialized of all lakes; the Romans had bloomeries by Nibthwaite, the Furness monks developed mining and forestry, and in the nineteenth century Coniston itself was as much a mining village as Esh Winning or Witton Park. It is unfair therefore to expect the Coniston settlements to have the charm of Hawkshead or Broughton, and they do not. Coniston village, in spite of its setting, is a dreary place, with no building of distinction, and the local slate not looking its best. The church is a banal structure, devoid of merit, and the churchyard enlivened only by a memorial to Ruskin in the shape of a Celtic cross, designed by W. G. Collingwood, which boasts among its decorations both a swastika and a menorah.

Coniston is nevertheless well worth a visit for it has several, and varied, attractions. A guide of 1862 records that 'a steam gondola provides a daily service on the lake'; it had then done so for three years, and, thanks to the National Trust, still does, the only steamer in regular service on the Lakes now that the unhappy Ullswater and Windermere boats have been perverted to diesel engines.

Gondola is absurd and magnificent. Her rakish bow ends in a figurehead composed of a ducal coronet surmounted by a bifurcated serpent. Her forward cabin is magnificent in red plush, buttoned ceiling and twin gilded mahogany pilasters separating the large windows of the saloon. She glides through the water with an imperceptible silent smoothness inspired (powered is too downright a term for so ethereal a motion) by her twin cylinder, sixty horsepower engine. Her life has not been without incident. Built in 1859 by Jones and Quiggan of Liverpool for the Furness Railway Company, of which the Duke of Devonshire was chairman – hence the coronet – she continued in service until 1937, when her engine was removed and sold to a sawmill, her hull being relegated to the status of a house boat. In 1963 she broke her moorings and was washed ashore in a terrible state, where she might yet be, had not the National Trust, in a most meritorious work, undertaken to restore her. There is something about ships that preserves the characteristics of their time more clearly than do houses. It may be that people quickly adapt houses to themselves, pulling a wall down here, putting a window in there, or merely rearranging the furniture. A boat, in which so much is dictated by the necessity of surviving on water, is much less amenable to change. To sail in a replica *Golden Hind*, or a surviving sailing trader, is to live almost precisely as they did in the sixteenth or nineteenth centuries without any need for pretence. Going further back, when we tested our fifth century BC trireme replica in the Aegean, we found that in a few days our mixed late-twentieth-century crew were displaying most of the characteristics of ancient Athenians.

So *Gondola* – especially if you charter her for a private party, and arrange things properly – can be a near-perfect evocation of Victorian Lakeland.

Ruskin used to charter her every spring to remove his household to the Lake Bank Hotel where he, sensible man, stayed to escape the upheaval of spring cleaning.

There is little enough to intrude on the shoreline; unlike Windermere, Coniston, saved perhaps by the mining industry which continued to flourish, never became popular with nineteenth-century magnates, and the buildings that are visible fit in well enough.

Gondola is not the only historic craft preserved at Coniston, for Brantwood has Ruskin's *Jumping Jenny,* designed by the master himself after the pattern of the boats he had seen on Lake Garda. But the most famous and most tragic of Coniston boats must have been the last *Bluebird.*

Sir Malcolm Campbell chose Coniston for his attempt on the water speed record in 1939, which he achieved at over 141 miles per hour. On his death in 1949, his son Donald, with Leo Villa, his father's old mechanic, took up where Sir Malcolm left off. Donald moved between Coniston and Ullswater. His first world record of 202 miles per hour was made on Ullswater, but four years later he exceeded 260 miles per hour on Coniston. His aim was to better 300 miles per hour, and on 4 January 1967, he did this on his final dash down the lake, when suddenly *Bluebird* shot up into the air, and disappeared into the lake in an explosion of spray. Campbell's body has never been found, and the memory of that last brave attempt still hangs over the water.

The road down the east side of the lake passes Tent Lodge, which is where, in 1805, a tent was placed to allow the consumptive Elizabeth Smith to die in the enjoyment of the view she loved. Only twenty-nine when she died, Elizabeth could have been one of the most remarkable women of the nineteenth century. A prodigy of learning – she read French, Italian, Spanish, German, Latin, Greek, and Hebrew, and had some knowledge of Arabic and Persian – she was also, as befits a girl born in Durham, Surtees' county, a lively observer of humanity. Her powers of observation had been sharpened since, after her father's bank failed, she accompanied her parents on their posting around Ireland, where he served in the army. She never extended herself in prose, although she made a new translation of the *Book of Job,* but was capable of meritorious verse – on ice-bound Patterdale, for instance:

> . . . All nature stands aghast
> Suspended by the viewless power of cold.

She was also, apparently, a very pretty girl.

Brantwood was bought for its view, which Ruskin, a connoisseur of such things, held to be the best in Europe. The house was begun towards the end of the eighteenth century, as a substantial cottage, and extended in the next century when its best known owners were the English republicans William and Eliza Lynn Linton. Before the Lintons Brantwood had harboured another radical in Gerald Massey, who is said to have been the model for George Eliot's *Felix Holt the Radical,* and whose verse Tennyson admired. Why, one cannot imagine:

> Pleasant it is, wee wife of mine
> As by my side thou art,
> To sit and see they dear eyes shine,
> With bonfires of the heart!

or

> Nature at heart is very pitiful
> How gentle is the hand doth gently pull
> The coverlet of flowers . . .

Mr and Mrs Linton were a badly assorted pair; she married him, it was said, to test out her educational theories on his six ready-made children. He was a tolerably good engraver, an ardent propagandist and a close fried of Mazzini; she was a novelist, once well-known but now forgotten Judging by the extracts provided by Grevel Lindop, her works merit attention. The marriage lasted only a few years, even in the idyllic surroundings of Brantwood, before he sold out to Ruskin for £1500, who found the house to be shabby and needing repair – a not uncommon state of things when high-minded literary folk of left-wing views have been in occupation – and faced the task of tidying and expanding it to be a residence suitable for a sage, which is what Ruskin by then had become. It is by no means a grand or even a large house; Ruskin was content with a bedroom, study, sitting room and dining room, the rest of the accommodation being taken up by the Severns, Ruskin's niece and her husband, who acted as housekeeper and secretary and who seemed to have had a lively eye for the main chance; Arthur had a commodious studio built for himself to paint his indifferent watercolours and, after Ruskin's death, in defiance of Ruskin's expressed wishes, broke up the estate and possessions.

In spite of what the guide book says, Ruskin was not one of

England's finest watercolourists, but he was capable of some remarkable, almost surreal, work, and Brantwood has some good examples. By far the oddest is Ruskin's deathbed portrait of Rose la Touche, the object of his elderly and chaste passion (all Ruskin's passions were chaste! – he makes an interesting psychological study). But in spite of Ruskin's weaknesses and prolixity, he was a great influence in the development of England; he might be the last of the utopians – his Guild of St George has the ring of Southey and Owen about it – but he saw with appalled clarity the horrors brought about by industrialization and could be admitted as the first of the 'Greens', a century before his time.

The view across the lake to Coniston Old Man is certainly superb; Coleridge described it as 'an admirable junction of awful and of pleasing Simplicity . . . its boldest parts . . . two black peaks, perfectly breast-shaped . . . the whole Bosom of a Brobdingnag Negress . . .' Norman Nicholson added an eloquent caution:

> It is futile to assess such country in terms of views. The view flattens the scene to a man-made dimension; it measures the landscape from the borders of an imaginary picture frame; it reduces like to a post card . . . Coniston Old Man is not just a design in shape and colour seen from this or that angle . . . it is also the man-made screes beside the quarries; and whitewash on the Copper Mines Hostel, a stone playing ducks & drakes on Leverswater, making the black tarn throw up waves like a magician's steel rings; a small dog nosing its way alone up the track from Low Water to the summit; a scrap of silver paper curled round a stone like lichen; dirty snow in a culvert of rock; rowan berries, the red-green of mouldy raspberry jam, making the end twigs bend under their weight; wheatears; the split and spit of thin ice; a pulled muscle in the thighs; herdwicks; the smell of cut bracken; clouds; handkerchiefs.

A nature trail has been marked out on the hillside above Brantwood: it is not too easy to follow, but if persevered with leads through varied woodland up to Crag Head, passing an identifiable bloomery site and pitstead.

At Coniston, perhaps more than anywhere else, the right way to explore the place is on the lake itself, since this is where the Swallows and Amazons began. Ransome spent his own boyhood holidays here, near Nibthwaite, sailing in the heavy farm boat, in company with such colourful persons as Tsau-Chee, nephew of the King of Burma, and the only member of the family to escape when

242

the king, believing himself to be poisoned, shot all the other guests at a dinner party.

But the *Swallow* itself belonged to the Collingwood family, who practically adopted Ransome when he met them during a later holiday at the age of twenty. He was very fortunate in this, for the Collingwoods were a remarkably talented group.

W. G. Collingwood wrote one of the most felicitous guides to the Lake District, *The Lake Counties,* first published in 1902 and revised by Collingwood himself thirty years later. This work is based upon the unparalleled scholarship of W. G. and his son Robin, an intimate knowledge of the area over half a century, and the perspicacity of an artist, which he was. Robin, who was a contemporary of Ransome's, became Wainflete Professor of Philosophy at Oxford, and both the accepted authority on Roman Britain and the most influential historical thinker of his sadly brief day. His autobiography has been continuously on the Oxford University Press list for nearly half a century, and his *Idea of History* influenced a generation of historians.

The Collingwoods lived at the other end of the lake, at Lanehead, near Tent Lodge, where Mrs Collingwood played Mozart before breakfast, and the whole family settled to a morning's work, followed by sailing on the lake, walking or merely happily pottering. Ransome's account of these halcyon days in his autobiography is a most affectionate passage.

Of all lakes, except perhaps Ullswater, Coniston is the best for messing about on. Any sort of boat is permitted, but a ten miles per hour speed limit effectively bans water-skiers and motor-boat racers. The Coniston boating centre in Lake Road will arrange trailer-launches, and small boats (but not power boats) can be launched from the car parks at the north and south-west ends of the lake. Boats can also be hired there, including sailing dinghies, and landing is possible on most parts of the lake. A pretty 1920s launch runs a shuttle service to Brantwood from the Gondola pier. Where the Hoathwaite Beck meets the lake there is the site of an old bloomery to be looked for, but it takes a very careful examination to find any lakeside pubs, the absence of which is the sole real defect of Coniston as a lake. Anglers will be happy, however; Coniston is the second-best source, after Windermere, of char, and fishing either from the shore or by boat is much easier and pleasanter. There are also brown trout, eels and pike, as well as the inedible perch.

The Black Bull is the oldest pub in Coniston. 'The Little Rustic Inn', it was kept in the late eighteenth century by Tom Robinson who

243

had married one of the Wonderful Walker's daughters (see p. 268). Turner and de Quincey both stayed there, de Quincey during an Oxford vacation when he was fearfully making up his mind to call on Wordsworth. Coleridge ate there in 1802 '. . . Oatcake and Cheese with a pint of Ale, and 2 glasses of Rum and water sweetened with preserved gooseberries.'

Just round the corner is the Ruskin museum, a single room crammed with miscellaneous objects: a cabinet of curiosities, in no recognizable order, but with some good drawings by Ruskin himself. The Ruskiniana includes a pair of the great man's silk socks – very desirable – and a John Varley print of the naked two-year-old Ruskin having a thorn pulled from his foot by an attendant satyr. Among other exhibits is a collection of photographs of Donald Campbell during his record-breaking attempts, including a horrifying shot of the fatal accident on 4 January 1967.

Coniston is, naturally enough, one of the places to see the belt of Coniston limestone. It is most accessible in Church Beck, on the way up to the mines, and anyone interested in fossils would find it rewarding to fossick, since the limestone is particularly rich in fossils. The dramatic view, that Ruskin and so many others admired, is due to the contrast between the Old Man – Borrowdale volcanics – and the lower, rounded Silurian hills that encircle the lake.

Church Beck has another curiosity in the shape of an old mine shaft, right under Miners Bridge, by the waterfalls, and the opposite side of the Miners Road, which starts by the Black Bull. If the water is too high, the tunnel will be inaccessible, but the spectacular nature of the force will compensate. If you can get in, there is nothing much to see, but the floor is at least intact. In other mine entrances the floors can be both deceptive and extremely dangerous, and casual exploration should be strongly discouraged.

They had trouble with industrial pollution in Church Beck at least as far back as the seventeenth century when the parishioners complained that 'meadow and cornlands is decayed and wasted by reason of the stamphouse and braying of the copper ore and such rubbish . . . doth so muddy and corrupt the water . . . there is utterly decayed and wasted of the hay and the after grass . . . fishing is utterly destroyed and banished'.

The laudable decision that the polluter pays was quickly enforced and the German miners duly made 'Recompense, Resolution and Payment'.

The Miners Road can be the start of an instructive walk if you

The Kirkstone Pass and Brotherswater

Langdale

Watendlath in Winter

Ratty at the Boot Terminus

push on up to the plateau where the old copper mineworking buildings, now a youth hostel, sit, surrounded by bleak levels of spoil
heaps. Keeping right behind the cottages, up the Red Dell, the remains of the buildings are prominent, enabling the water-courses to
and from the wheels, remarkable pieces of engineering, to be clearly
identified.

A turn right of the track will take you over Hole Rake to
Tilberthwaite Gill, returning to Coniston down the unfenced road
along Yewdale.

Tilberthwaite Gill (National Trust land) is a wonderful ravine,
with ferns and mosses enjoying a damp seclusion, the now-aban-
doned green slate quarries and their buildings adding a dramatic note.
Ruskin's grave cross came from here, and there are meant to be
traces of the original Norse settlement in the wood near Holme Ground.
I have not identified these, but the valley is a grand spot for picnics.

You can of course climb Coniston Old Man; lots of people do, and
there is a fine view from the top. But any available time would be
better spent essaying the ridge of Dow Crag, or, more prudently,
merely admiring that great rock face from Goats Water: the view is
almost as good and the going more entertaining. This walk which
Geoffrey Winthrop Young, the great mountaineer, thought the most
beautiful in Europe, is done on the Walna Scar road, an interesting
track, developed as a pack-horse road to Ravenglass, and leading
over first into Dunnerdale (see also p. 269). The start of the scar road
is the second turning past the Sun Hotel. Coniston Old Man is nobbut
another hill, but Dow Crag – or Dhu or Doe – for opinions differ – is
unique. There are crags as dramatic on Scafell and Pillar, but Dow is
both more accessible and more imposing; a solid and enormous block
of stone, lying across the dark surface of Goats Water. It apparently
offers a rich variety of experiences to climbers, of which I am in no
position to speak, but it is simplicity itself for the walker to get to the
top by safe, even sedate, paths, although mere pedestrians should not
be deceived by Easy Terrace, which isn't. The right way is up to
Goats Hause, along the top and down at Walna Scar pass or vice
versa.

Blind Tarn, alias Torver Tarn, which is only a pond, since it has no
outlet, has free fishing for brown trout and small char.

Grizedale

The area between Coniston and Windermere is usually approached
from the Bowness ferry, which makes a good place to start.

The Sawreys, Near and Far (Near is naturally the one furthest from the ferry), are indelibly associated with Beatrix Potter, who lived at Hill Top, **Near Sawrey**. Now owned by the National Trust, and open to the public (at considerable expense and only in the summer months), it is nothing more than a small Lakeland farmhouse, somewhat altered by Beatrix during the thirty years she owned it. Although the permanent home of the Heelis's – she married William Heelis, a local solicitor, in 1913 – was down the road at Castle Cottage, it was at Hill Top that she wrote most of the famous books. Some of her alterations look odd – a large and handsome marble chimney piece inserted in a tiny parlour – but those brought up on the horrifying tale of Samuel Whiskers will experience an agreeable sense of *déja vu*: here is the veritable landing along which the ferocious Whiskers trundled the rolling pin; there the old dresser skirted by Anna Maria hurrying with the stolen dough. Everything is authentic, and preserved exactly as Beatrix Potter instructed in her will, down to the minutest details.

It is a pretty spot, with an unspoilt cottage garden (seen in the illustrations to Jemima Puddleduck and Tom Kitten) but I prefer the nearby Tower Bank Arms, also owned by the National Trust, open all the year round, with an interior undisturbed by brewery decorations, where the price of entrance to Hill Top will buy a pint of decent beer and a ham sandwich.

One of Mrs Heelis's favourite walks was up a bridleway to Moss Eccles, Wise Een and Three Dubs Tarns which are in fact manmade, like all these little tarns on Claife Heights. She kept a little boat on Moss Eccles tarn, in which she used to paddle about, sketching and observing the birds; it is now preserved in the Windermere Steamboat Museum. The road is not well kept, and the copious use of black plastic in a National Park, on National Trust property, is distressing, but once reached, the woods are pleasant. These represent the first attempts to reafforest the land burned out in the provision of charcoal: the planting was done by the energetic John Christian Curwen, and at the time was not unanimously well received: Wordsworth took particular exception to the larches. The old packhorse road ran from Hawkshead to Belle Grange, and thence on the ferry over to Millerground Landing. You now follow this across Claife Heights, where a footpath then follows the lake shore to the remaining ferry.

Adjoining the landing stage is Ferry House, the headquarters of the Freshwater Biological Association, a research institution that concerns itself with all aspects of lakes, rivers and their population. At a time when the Lake District environment is seriously threatened from many sources, the existence of a research and monitoring body of international standing in the heart of the region is particularly valuable. And it is often forgotten what a very popular sport fishing is; more people go fishing than attend football matches, and do it more quietly.

To the south, and a hundred yards off the road up a path, are the remains of the eighteenth-century viewpoint, generally known as The Station. While still at school, Wordsworth 'led thither a youngster of my own age, an Irish boy, who was servant to an itinerant conjurer. My motive was to witness the pleasure I expected the boy would receive from the prospect of the islands below and the intermingling water. I was not disappointed . . .' A conversation between the young Bill Wordsworth and an Irish conjurer's servant lad provokes an exercise of imagination.

Wordsworth grew a little cynical about the gushing enthusiasm with which later visitors greeted the same view, when he found that Lord and Lady Darlington, Lady Vane, Miss Taylor and Captain Stamp 'had pronounced this Lake superior to Lac de Geneve, Lago de Como, Lago Maggiore, L'Eau de Zurich, Loch Lomond, Loch Katerine, or the Lake of Killarney,' he wrote one of his rare comic verses beginning:

> My Lord and Lady Darlington
> I would not speak in snarling tone . . .

and continued to say that, having seen most of these places –

> And wished, at least, to hear the blarney
> Of the shy boatmen of Killarney,
> And dipped my hand in dancing wave
>
> Of Eau de Zurich, Lac Geneve
> And bowed to many a major domo
> On stately terraces of Como . . .

in short telling the distinguished visitors that they were talking rot. Today it is impossible to make one's own judgement, since trees obscure the view, the bay is full of Tupperware boats and the shore opposite crowded with pedestrian and pretentious buildings.

Far Sawrey has St Peter's church, a pleasantly situated nineteenth-century church with a St Cecilia window in the south wall presenting a little problem to those who can read music (which bit of

Beethoven is it?), and the Sawrey Arms, which has some good views from the garden. South of here the lake shore is mostly privately owned, and the only place of public interest is Graythwaite Hall. There are in fact two Halls, Graythwaite Hall and Graythwaite Old Hall. Not that plain Graythwaite Hall is all that new, since the earlier parts are from the sixteenth century, since which date it has been the home of the Sandys family. The south wing, and the back of the house, are in the local vernacular manner, but the main elevations have been rebuilt twice in the nineteenth century. Only the gardens are open to the public, Thomas Mawson's first work, of the early 1890s and still much as he left them, wildly romantic. The formal gardens have sundials and handsome gates by the local architect Dan Gibson, who designed Birket House.

Old Graythwaite Hall next door was built by the Rawlinsons at the same time as Graythwaite Hall, and is less altered, with Levens-like topiary work making a striking feature of the front.

If Windermere shores are not easily approachable the hinterland certainly is, for the greater part of the land between Windermere and Coniston belongs to the Forestry Commission, who have made it all intelligible to the visitor. People often find **Grizedale** forest gloomy, but properly understood the area demonstrates better than anywhere else I know how man used natural resources before the Industrial Revolution.

One starts from the visitors' centre at Grizedale Hall – or rather in what is left of Grizedale Hall, which is the stables. The Hall itself had one of the shortest lives of any modern country house; built by the Liverpool Brocklebanks in 1903, it was demolished only forty-nine years later. During the Second World War it served as a POW camp for German officers, and was the place which housed Franz von Werra, the hero of *The One Who Got Away.* Von Werra, a Luftwaffe pilot, made an escape from Grizedale, but was recaptured and sent to Canada. He tried again and was successful in escaping to America, eventually returning to Germany to meet his end on the Russian front.

Small trees and shrubs are available from the nurseries, and the forest centre sells books, provides refreshment and has a splendid children's playground, with huge forest animals: the frogs and hedgehog seem tame enough, but the fifteen-foot pheasant is the stuff shooters' nightmares are made of. These creatures are made from real wood by real people, a world removed from the plastic monstrosities that pass elsewhere as 'kiddies' attractions'.

Apart from the various uses of timber in construction and of providing pannage for swine (Grizedale means pig valley), the forest industries were charcoal burning, smelting, and wood turning. The remains to look for in the forests are pitsteads – the traces of the charcoal ovens – charcoal burners' huts, and bloomery sites. A pitstead can be seen on the trail leading west of the road just north of Satterthwaite: it does not look much, being only an earth platform about fifteen feet in diameter. The stone structure nearby is a potash pit, where bracken was roasted to make 'pot ash' which was then mixed with limestone and boiled with tallow, the result being the soap used in cleaning wool.

Such great quantities of timber were needed for iron making that it was necessary in Elizabethan times to limit the trade. A more economic method, ealing, was developed in Grizedale, and is commemorated in Ealinghearth in the Rusland valley (or so I believed, but George Booth of Ealinghearth mounts a powerful case for 'ealing' being a method of producing lye). In spite of contemporary conservationists' efforts most of the Furness forests were denuded by the end of the sixteenth century, and a century later a census showed that just over twelve hundred timber trees were left in the whole of the extensive parish of Windermere.

The method of iron making at the time was that which had been used for three millennia in the smelting of copper, by melting ore in clay crucibles, a system which left a great deal of slag lying about on the smelting sites (the Egyptian copper mines in the Negev are still conspicuous in this way), and these bloomery sites can be so identified in a number of places. The easiest one is probably that just off the road from Hawkshead to Newby Bridge at Dale Park Beck, which, together with other sites, is marked on the Grizedale forest guide and map. Hand-operated bellows were supplemented from the sixteenth century by water-powered bellows, still using the bloomery method. At Force Mills on the southern end of the forest, a number of bloomeries availed themselves of the Grizedale Beck, which falls steeply there, and also at Force Forge.

Bloomeries themselves were succeeded at the beginning of the eighteenth century by blast furnaces, which also used water power to drive huge bellows, raising the temperature in the furnace, and enabling two tons or more of iron to be made at a single charge. An extensive complex of structures – water-wheel, furnace and storage buildings – was needed, and remains of these are scattered all over Furness.

Outside the forest area, where the Causey Beck, which is the outflow from Esthwaite, joins Windermere, there are the remains of a bloomery which was modernized into a blast furnace. The remains of blast furnaces are also visible at Nibthwaite, Duddon Bridge and Backbarrow.

After being made, the brittle cast iron, if it were to be used for working, had to be converted into wrought iron, which was done in a finery forge, one of which has been excavated at Stoney Hazel, Rusland.

As a forest, as distinct from a document of industrial archaeology, Grizedale is a little too organized and tidy, but it does offer an instant study course in tree recognition. Trails are clearly marked, and the habitats preferred by different species are differentiated. Spring, when the bluebells, wood anemones and daffodils are out, is a good time to come, but at any time of year the forest sculptures can be enjoyed. These are the outcome of an imaginative piece of patronage by which residencies of up to six months are given to artists who work in natural local materials. Their productions are then sited in appropriate spots near one of the forest trails. 'Sculpture' is a loose word, since many of the constructions are not what one understands by the term – bits of drystone wall, complex Wendy Houses, and basket fences – but there is range enough to please anybody. I find the standing figures of 'Private Meeting' impressive, and 'Shooting Moose' great fun, but everyone is bound to admire 'The Fort', in the grounds of Silberthwaite School, whose pupils have co-operated with the artist, Don Rankin, to create a fairytale castle. As well as the modelled animals – which include a charming hedgehog – there are plenty of real animals in the forests, roe deer, of course, but also red deer, for this is one of the few places where they are free to roam. It is said that there are pine martens too, but you would need to be very lucky to spot one of those rare creatures.

Another engagingly dotty aspect of Grizedale is the Theatre in the Forest. Inconveniently located miles away from any centre even of a transient population, this fully-equipped theatre manages to attract audiences for plays, concerts and a range of odd shows, the highlights being the visits by members of that excellent orchestra, the Northern Sinfonia.

Satterthwaite is part of the Forestry Commission's estate, and has a pub, a church, and a pretty situation on the Force Beck. As it flows south, the Force Beck turns into Rusland Pool, and passes **Rusland** church and Rusland Hall. Rusland church's tower is Georgian, but the rest was rebuilt last century. Arthur and Eugenia Ransome are buried in the churchyard. Rusland Hall is Queen Anne, spare and elegant, with the open outlook that is possible in the sheltered valleys of the southern lakes. In the more exposed north you can be almost on top of a house before realizing it is there, so completely are they hidden from the elements; no one wants a view at the expense of warmth and dryness. The Hall is said to have been the headquarters of the eighteenth-century gang who manufactured 'golden guineas' from the local copper.

The whole aspect of the Rusland valley over to the Crake valley, which drains Coniston, is unspoilt and largely untrodden. Just along from Rusland church, near the road junction, is Rookhow, a good example of a Quaker monthly – as differentiated from weekly – meeting-house, built to accommodate Friends from all the Swarthmoor meeting, an area that covered the whole of Furness. Since so many came, and from such a distance, the house was provided with stables and a gig house as well as accommodation for those who wanted to pass the night. It was built in 1725, and is still very much as it was then, interior woodwork and all, an admirably straightforward piece of work.

Whitestock Hall, half a mile further on, is another handsome house with an open prospect over the Rusland Pool.

This is an area of country houses and tiny villages. Bouth is the largest but until recently **Colton** used to be the administrative centre. Colton church is quite removed from the village, up on the hillside through a road gate. It is rather larger than usual for a dales church, and served a considerable parish, which stretched from Coniston down to Haverthwaite and over to Windermere. The fabric is sixteenth century, although a thorough Victorian restoration has drastically altered the interior, which is when the present glass was installed. The Dickson memorial window, which I take to be Holiday, features local birds and flowers, including a curlew, and another later Dickson window has some handsome lettering. Less accessible, but of interest to campanologists, is one of the church's bells, a fine medieval piece probably from Conishead. Also medieval is the font, a monolithic sandstone which for two centuries had been used as the base for another.

Outside, the old school, with the handsome mounting block, forms a quite independent church community centre, a necessity when the Sunday services formed the most regular meeting place, where families could pass the whole day.

251

On a more puritan note the chapel house at **Tottlebank** half a mile south-east of Spark Bridge, up a farm road, is a peaceful spot. Isolated for a very good reason, since the Five Miles Act forbade the construction of a conventicle within that distance of a town, it was founded in 1664 and rebuilt in the eighteenth century. The chapel is still complete, with the benches arranged laterally, in the old style, and the graveyard, now, happily, better-tended, an evocative place.

Stott Park Bobbin Mill is a little further along, and is the only remaining one still in working order. Set in rural seclusion it constitutes a time capsule; this is what mills were like at the very start of the Industrial Revolution, rural, secluded, water-powered, far removed from the Dark Satanic imagery. (But then William Blake meant Oxford and Cambridge when he wrote that verse.) Bobbin manufacture grew with the cotton trade, and Lakeland found itself well placed to meet the demand for turned reels and bobbins, which were needed in tremendous quantities, up to ten million a year in a single mill. Plentiful water power, sometimes formerly used to drive wool-fulling or paper mills, was adapted to turning lathes. The raw material was those trees previously coppiced for charcoal burning, which could also be used for turning and slicing into bobbins. The production of charcoal demands plentiful supplies of small, regularly shaped pieces of wood that will char at controlled temperatures; large trees are useless. Suitable wood was obtained by coppicing: cutting young trees back so that they produced straight and regular shoots – hence coppices. These coppiced woods tend to look rather messy, without great trees, and with a lot of straggly undergrowth.

Stott Park, during the century and more of its existence, depended for the most part on water power. At first this was tapped in the uneconomical fashion by conventional water-wheels, geared up to run a number of lathes from a central shaft. When the steam became available many mills simply hitched the central drive to a steam engine, but at Stott Park the cheapness of water constituted an irresistible attraction. A small steam engine was installed, to be fired using offcuts and turnings, but later water power returned harnessed to turbines – still the most effective and elegant power source: nuclear submarines use steam turbines, but Sir Charles Parsons rarely gets the credit he deserves for his invention – until replaced by individual electric motors during the Second World War. All this machinery was designed and made locally: Fells of Troutbeck Bridge made the lathes; the turbines were supplied by Williamsons of Kendal; and two interesting machines, among the first semi-automated machine tools in existence, were designed by Henry Braithwaite of Crook.

As the English cotton trade declined and the demand for bobbins fell off, Stott Park turned to making handles for axes, spades and small tools, and any turning jobs that came up. It was only in 1971 that the mills finally closed. All this is now kept in working order, with wood, bobbins, carefully maintained machinery, and the last of the old bobbin turners still available to throw off the odd bobbin or two.

11

Hawkshead and the Langdales

Hawkshead is today the only surviving Lakeland market town: a town rather than a village, although one of the smallest in the country, complete with a town hall and a good number of pubs. Bowness and Keswick have become overgrown, Ambleside is largely a nineteenth-century invention, Coniston a mining village, Kendal and Penrith both on the periphery and part of the world outside, but Hawkshead-extra-car-park is very much as Wordsworth knew it. He went to school here, and made his reputation as a poet at an early age.

'How is't, Bill?' a schoolfellow asked, 'thou dost write such good verses? Do'st thee invoke Muses?'

Hawkshead is *Hauk's Saeter,* a saeter being, as readers to *The Three Hostages* will recall, a Norse upland summer meadow, which is just what the head of such a valley is. It provided everything a medieval community might need: good low land, abundant timber, and plentiful fish from the small lake, Esthwaite. The monks of Furness brought it under their control, and built a manorial hall to act as a local centre of administration. The town flourished under the prudent monastic rule and became a collecting and processing centre for the woollen industry, the foundation of late-medieval English prosperity. As might be expected from the nature of the land, Hawkshead woollens were ordinary, everyday fabrics, described in the seventeenth century as:

> Coarse cloathes, and such as ne'er did Alnage take,
> Yet 'tis commodious to the Common-weale.

But although prosperous, Hawkshead did not much expand. With the decline of the staple industry continuing in spite of governmental support, it remains today in its seventeenth-century form – a long street off which led a couple of squares and a number of passages and tunnels, meandering in an inconsequential way. Dr Alexander Graig Gibson, a pioneer collector of dialect, described Hawkshead:

A quaint old town is Hawkshead,
    and an ancient look it bears.
Its church, its school, its dwellings,
    its streets, its lands, its squares,
Are all irregularities – all angles,
    twists, and crooks,
With penthouses, and gables over archways
    eaves, and nooks.

The town is now faced by a huge car and coach park, as big as the rest of the place put together, and separated from it by a *cordon sanitaire* of woollen goods and souvenir shops, lavatories and a large eatery, all decently and tidily kept, but very Milton-Keynesey. By this method the town itself has been spared: without traffic except for essential and local services, or intrusive shop fronts, Hawkshead remains unspoilt. But it is rather like a stage set, with visitors wandering happily around looking as though about to burst into a hearty chorus from the *White Horse Inn*. Once the curtain has, so to speak, gone up, and the initial delighted gasp of appreciation subsided, the centre of Hawkshead is something of a disappointment. What there is to see of the town – and it is spectacular – has been seen. You cannot wander about, finding new vistas, in the way that is possible at, say, Cartmel. The best thing to do, if it is fine, is to sit outside the King's Arms and admire the scene, or if wet, inside the Queen's Head and recollect it. The King's Arms has long been popular; an 1860 guidebook said of it: 'Amongst the attractions of Hawkshead, the comfort and moderate charges of the Red Lion should not be passed over.'

Hawkshead has the same problems as such other exquisite little towns as St Paul de Vence in the Alpes-Maritimes. Thousands of tourists throughout the year, and tens of thousands in the summer, want to come to see it. Short of turning it into a Disneyland, and charging admission, there is probably no alternative to the solution that has been adopted, but the results are saddening, and an example of how the tourist industry has affected Lakeland.

Wordsworth's grammar school and the church lie at one end of the town. The school is, like many locally, an Elizabethan foundation, initiated by Edwin Sandys, Archbishop of York and a Hawkshead man, born in Esthwaite Hall, until quite recently still a Sandys property. Sandys is often dismissed as an adamantine Puritan, cast in the Calvin mould, hot against 'massmongers', but in reality he was that not uncommon figure, an independent and cantankerous northerner,

255

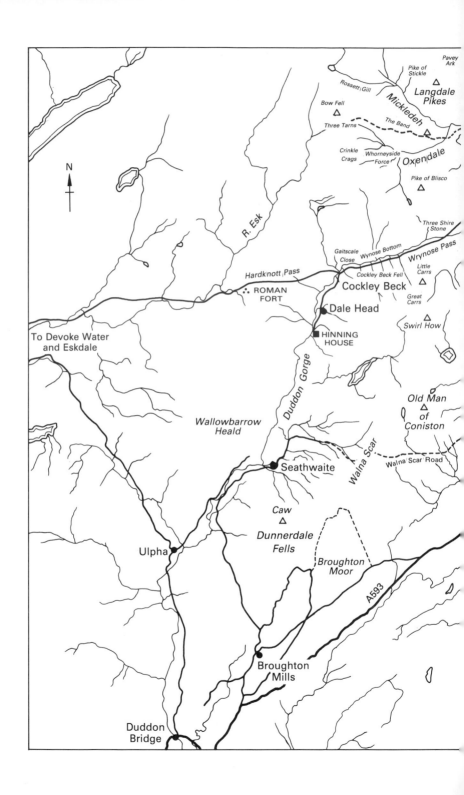

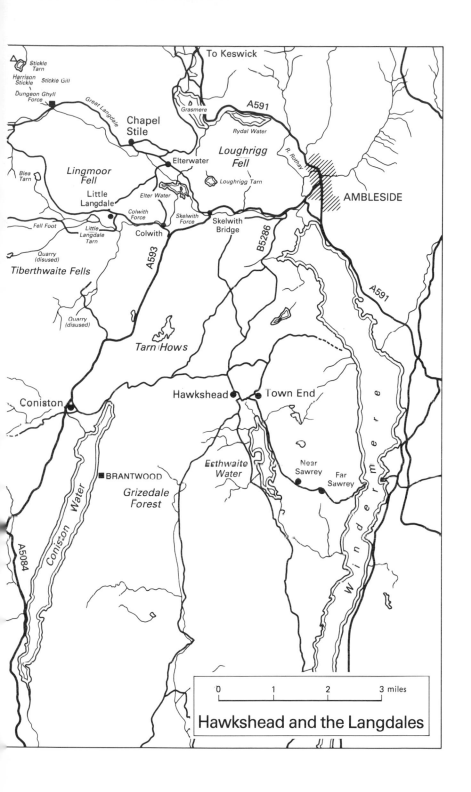

Hawkshead and the Langdales

always willing to fight his corner, and one who in this case had had his temper exacerbated by seeing his old teacher, John Bland of Furness, burned alive by Bloody Mary's orders. Few people got the better of Sandys, but one who did, at least for a time, was a Robert Stapleton, who attempted to bribe the Archbishop by means of what is now known as a 'beaver trap' – by introducing a married lady into Sandys' bedroom.

The school is a modest two-storey building, the whole ground floor occupied by a single large schoolroom. Until a few years ago this was a typical Lakeland school; I attended two such over in the Eden Valley, more than fifty years ago, where a single teacher coped with children of all ages and abilities. The guide will show you Wordsworth's initials carved in his desk, proving that graffiti are not twentieth-century phenomena.

The grammar school fees were such as to make the cost of education a serious matter: twelve guineas a year, in Wordsworth's time, including board and lodging but with firing extra, and a guinea 'cock-penny' for the master on Shrove Tuesday. He was, as the accounts show, fond of cakes, and paid as much as eighteen pence for one. Since this was the same price as a leg of mutton, it must have been a substantial confection. Hawkshead cakes today are really pastries, rather like upmarket Eccles cakes.

Hawkshead church sits dramatically on a hill above the town and school, its size indicating the past prosperity of the town. As much as Lavenham or Sudbury, Hawkshead is a wool church, but one which reflects the relative quality of Cumberland and Suffolk cloth and the period of construction. It resembles that of Grasmere: both are larger than any dales chapel, but still put together in the unhelpful medium of slate, which dictates simple, even clumsy, shapes. The arcades of Hawkshead, low with massive pillars and round arches, look as though they might be Norman, but date only from the period just before the Reformation. There had been a church on the site long before that, traces of which are to be seen in the towers and west wall; as it now stands Hawkshead is, again like Grasmere, a Tudor building. Its more conventional twin-aisled shape and clerestory make it much lighter and less odd than Grasmere, and the white-painted plaster adds to the attractive impression of spaciousness. As in other Lake District churches, the necessity to plaster over the random slate walls offered an irresistible surface for decoration, which at Hawkshead was first used in about 1680 by James Addison, who did the great work at Kendal. His are the 'Sentances of Scripture decently Florished', remaining in the north aisle, together with the borders to the arches and pillars. A local man, William Mackreth, added more a generation later; his is the one over the pulpit, where he has found himself short of space in the third line and used the local form 't'Word' instead of 'the Word'.

Two large – one enormous – florid monuments flank the tower arch, looking much out of place, as well they might, since they were brought here from a London church in 1878. They are of Daniel Rawlinson, who emigrated from Hawkshead in the seventeenth century, and his son Sir Thomas; his is the more massive of the two, ornate and verbose, highly suitable for a man who had been a wine merchant and Lord Mayor of London.

In the chancel the Sandys table-tomb must be the work of a local mason. It cannot on the evidence of the inscription be before 1580, but the figures of William in full armour with a lion at his feet and Margaret in a gown and wimple might have been carved almost exactly so a century earlier.

One historical curiosity is the framed 'Burials in Wool' affidavits. These are the results of the Restoration Acts intended to protect the woollen industry by insisting that every 'corps was not put in wrapt or wound or buryed in any shirt shift sheet or shroud made or mingled with flax hempe suke gold or silver, or other than what is made of sheeps wooll oncly'. To ensure that this was so, every burial had to be conducted in front of a magistrate or priest, and duly recorded.

Until 1875 the exterior was also plastered and lime-washed in keeping with the town. Wordsworth described it:

> I saw the snow-white Church upon its hill
> Sit like a throned Lady, sending out
> A gracious look all over its domain.

White no longer, but grey-green, the church is an impressive sight.

The other ecclesiastical buildings in Hawkshead are worth attention – the Quaker meeting-house at Colthouse and the monastic gatehouse and Baptist chapel on Hawkshead Hill. The Colthouse meeting house was built in 1688, and has some very fine ingenious panelling, especially that separating the women's meeting-house from that of the men (larger, of course, but much less cosy, and without a fireplace). Nearby Town End used to be Causey End, the termination of the raised causeway that bridged the head of Esthwaite water, passing the Priest's Pot, which may have been the fish stew kept for the benefit of monks posted to Hawkshead from Furness.

The gatehouse of Hawkshead Hall survives since it served also as a manorial courtroom known as Hawkshead court house, and is kept by the National Trust in the grounds of a private house, the key being available from the Trust's office in Hawkshead. Only the abbot's mitre above the pointed archway identifies it as a monastic building, and merely a single empty room with a medieval fireplace can be seen, but it is a good, unaltered piece of fifteenth-century domestic architecture, and therefore something of a rarity.

The Baptist chapel is a mile further on, just by the road to Coniston. It is even earlier – 1678 – than the Quakers' meeting-house, but has been more restored.

Ann Tyson's first cottage, where Wordsworth lodged in his school-days, is on the edge of the town; the Tysons moved from Green End cottage to Colthouse in 1783, taking Wordsworth with them. He was obviously fond of Mrs. Tyson and his lines on her are full of a clear affection; they might well describe so many other good northern ladies 'in monumental trim':

> This chiefly, did I view my grey-hair'd Dame,
> Saw her go forth to Church, or other work
> Of state, equipp'd in monumental trim
> Short Velvet Cloak (her Bonnet of the like)
> A mantle such as Spanish Cavaliers
> Word in old time. Her smooth domestic life,
> Affectionate without uneasiness,
> Her talk, her business pleas'd me, and no less
> Her clear though shallow stream of piety . . .

Hawkshead has just acquired a new attraction, the Beatrix Potter Gallery, housed in what was the office of William Heelis (Beatrix's husband). One ground-floor room has been retained as a country lawyer's office – hardly so much a work of restoration as a preservation, for Cumbrian solicitors have not changed their habits much in the last half-century.

Upstairs a selection from the five hundred water-colours left by Beatrix to the National Trust is on show. The originals have a decisiveness and freshness that are not apparent in the older editions of the books (but recently Frederick Warne have improved the reproduction considerably). I must admit to finding the wicked animals – Tommy Brock, Mr Tod, the Fierce Bad Rabbit and the ineffably horrid Whiskers – much more entertaining than the goodies – especially Lucie and Mrs Tiggy-Winkle. It is also borne in on one that a major attraction is Beatrix's sonorous prose: 'hopelessly volatile'; 'the cat neglected its duties, and was upon the worst terms with the cook', and of course, 'but I am persuaded that the string would have proved indigestible, whatever you may have urged to the contrary'.

Esthwaite is as small as a lake can well be without becoming a tarn, but has one great advantage: lots of fish. The Hawkshead trout farm, at Fordgate, keeps it stocked with rainbow trout which reach up to eight pounds, and can be caught all the year round by any method short of hand grenades; not the most sporting of angling, but certainly the most reliable, and on a warm day, from a row boat (powered vessels are of course banned), a pleasant pastime. You *can* hire boats from the trout farm just to row about the lake in, but they prefer you to fish, and indeed Esthwaite without fish is rather dull.

Before the Reformation tenants had started enclosing small arable fields to keep out the sheep; these became the 'grounds' one still comes across all over High Furness. Roger Ground, near Hawkshead, is the most conspicuous, and Waterson Ground, to the north. The 'Intakes' – which are all over, particularly in the woodland – are later, and larger, enclosures of originally common land, but on nothing like the scale of the later enclosures of the eighteenth and nineteenth centuries. J. C. Curwen procured an Act of Parliament in 1794 to enclose Claife Heights, and begin his programme of replanting. The Youth Hostel at Esthwaite Lodge, a handsome early nineteenth-century house, was the home of Francis Brett Young until he found Lake District rain too much for him. Young's novels are not much read, but *Marching on Tanga*, his account of Smuts' East African campaign, is a good book.

The popular walk from Hawkshead is up the hill past the church and on to **Tarn Hows**, a famous beauty spot, but I would not recommend it. On any summer day, and especially on Bank Holidays, it is likely to be crowded with motors, people and even ice-cream vans. The view over the Langdales is good, true enough, but good views are ten-a-penny, and the foreground – which is all artificial, the tarns being of nineteenth-century construction – is reminiscent of municipal gardening. But it does, at least, concentrate lots of people who might otherwise be cluttering up more desirable spots.

The Langdales and the Duddon Valley

Taking Great and Little Langdale together with the Duddon Valley it might be said that this is walker's Cumbria pure and simple. No lakes, few villages of more than hamlet size, not a tourist shop to be seen, no grand houses or churches, not even a pele, since no raider would find anything profitable. Just magnificent scenery crammed within a small compass. Wordsworth pronounced of Great Langdale that it: 'should on no account be missed by him who has a true enjoyment of grand separate Forms composing of a sublime Unity, austere but reconciled and rendered attractive to the affections by the deep serenity that is spread over everything'. Indeed, since the massive heads of the Langdale Pikes dominate so many views, it is impossible to remain unconscious of their impressive grandeur.

The attractions of Langdale should not make anyone neglect Loughrigg, the hill that separates the Rothay Valley (Rydal and Grasmere) from the Brathay (the Langdales), and has something of everything – crags, tarns, views and Wordsworthian approbation. The whole fell is so well served by paths that it is easy to take any route that suits, but the climb to the summit (not very high – 1100 feet) is worthwhile for the view of the Langdale hills and Windermere. Loughrigg Tarn was described by Wordsworth as 'Diana's Looking-glass . . . round, clear and bright as heaven'. It still is an agreeable spot, but rather too popular to see it with quite the enthusiasm it inspired in Wordsworth and in his friend Sir George Beaumont, who bought it with a view to building a house on its shores, but was discouraged by the hostility of Wordsworth's landlords, the le Flemings of Rydal Hall.

Whether they come from Loughrigg or from Skelwith Bridge, most visitors will start by going as far as the road will allow them up Great Langdale, which has the pick of the walks, and parking near the Old Dungeon Ghyll Hotel. If pressed for time, however, it is better to stop at the 'New' Hotel – more than a century old – half a mile before. This enables a quick look at Dungeon Ghyll itself, which is, whether in spate or not, something of a curiosity, before making for Pavey Ark, the most exciting of the climbs. Dungeon Ghyll Force, well sign posted, is about half a mile from the car park; the water falls precipitously through a chasm and in front of a dark hollow – the 'dungeon' – while overhead leaning rocks make a natural bridge. Wordsworth, for whom this was a favourite spot, described it much more clearly:

> Into a chasm a mighty block
> Hath fallen, and made a bridge of rock:
> The gulf is deep below;

And in a basin black and small,
Receives a lofty waterfall.

It is possible to press on up the hill, which has another good
waterfall, to the summit of Harrison Stickle. This involves getting out
of the ravine when the going gets unacceptably rough and finding the
path to the right. At about the 1900-foot contour the path passes
through a scree slope, which is the site of a Stone Age axe factory,
and where it is possible, though highly unlikely, to find a rejected
stone axe from 2000 BC and earlier. One thinks of flint as being the
perfect material for implements, but the volcanic tuffs produce a
material – porcellinite – that chips in a very similar fashion and that
can be given a sharp edge. It may seem anachronistic to refer to a
heap of stones on a stony slope 2000 feet above the sea level as a
'factory', but the description is not inapt, for this was truly the first
stage of an organized manufacturing and distribution process. The
blanks were chipped out *in situ* before being sent down to coastal
settlements for polishing, using the local sandstone, and for mounting
and shipment. Langdale axes were exported almost as widely as the
much better known flint tools produced in Grimes Graves near
Thetford. Almost incredibly, a specimen survived complete, with its
wooden handle, preserved in the bog of Ehenside Tarn (see p. 304)
and is now in the British Museum.

A return can be made down Stickle Gill, using a new pathway
built by the National Trust to prevent further erosion, for this is the
way up to Pavey Ark, a much-used route. Or perhaps, to be more
accurate, to Stickle Tarn, for most tourists content themselves with
the short – well, under an hour – walk up to the tarn, and the view
across it to Pavey Ark, a great 500-foot-high slab of rock, which is
stupendous, with Dow Crag the most striking combination of cliff
and water to be found in the region. Bolder persons have a choice of
three ways up to the top of Pavey Ark: in ascending order of difficulty, the grassy path to the north shown on the Ordnance Survey
map, Easy Gully, and Jack's Rake. As often when taking a particular
fell the 1:25,000 Ordnance Survey map is not clear enough, and
recourse should be had to Wainwright.

Easy Gully is not that easy, but Jack's Rake is downright difficult.
Wainwright says this path 'is classified as a ROCKCLIMB . . as WALK
it is both *difficult and awkward* . . . about the limit that ordinary
common or garden fell-walker reasonably may be expected to
attempt'. This was written more than thirty years ago, and things

have not got better. Walt Unsworth calls it 'the one challenge that every fell-walker feels obliged to accept sooner or later . . . fairly easy if you are experienced in climbing – but not as easy as some would have you think'. My own advice would be to avoid it, go up the easy way, and cheat by getting someone to take a picture of you silhouetted against some fearful precipice.

Omitting Pike of Stickle, where there is a better-known axe factory than that on Harrison Stickle, but hardly one worth clambering up to see, and Bow Fell, the other attractive Langdale tops are Crinkle Crags and Pike o'Blisco. Crinkle Crags is the walk to go for, and one reasonably easy to follow on the map: up The Band from Stool End to Three Tarns, then south along the ridges of crags themselves, a superb ridge walk, descending Brown How and Oxendale, calling in at Whorneyside Force, an impressive waterfall. The views of Scafell are remarkable. At Three Tarns a right-hand turn takes you up to Bow Fell, even more magnificent, down Rossett Gill and Mickelden back to the hospitable Old Dungeon Ghyll Hotel.

This welcome inn has a climbers' bar, originally a cow byre, and only slightly changed: no jukebox, fruit machines, carpet or chairs, but respectable beer, benches polished by the breeches of generations of climbers, a dartboard and fine black range from the foundry of Bowerbank and Pugmire at Penrith. Climbers record new routes in a tattered exercise book kept in the bar for the benefit of posterity, and have left other souvenirs in the shape of cartoons and a large oil painting of one Black Jack in paradise with houris and uninterrupted drink.

The hotel was left, together with 700 acres of land, to the National Trust by G. M. Trevelyan, who wrote his Garibaldi trilogy at Robin Ghyll, a mile or so off, and who is buried at Chapel Stile, and one may stay there, or in the Trust's beautiful campsite on the other side of the road.

In his long poem *The Excursion*, Wordsworth describes an expedition to Blea Tarn; his directions are sufficiently clear to enable one to follow his steps, verses in hand, and admire the precision of his descriptions, although some allowance has to be made for the passage of time; no one in Lakeland today wrests a meagre living from the soil.

> Urn-like it was in shape, deep as an urn;
> With rocks encompassed, save that to the south
> Was one small opening, where a heath-clad ridge

Supplied a boundary less abrupt and close;
A quiet treeless nook, with two green fields.
A liquid pool that glittered in the sun,
And one bare dwelling; one abode, no more!

... Full many a spot
Of hidden beauty have I chanced to espy
Among the mountains; never one like this:
So lonesome, and so perfectly secure;
Not melancholy – no, for it is green,
And bright, and fertile ...

Blea Tarn is a typical corrie tarn, held in position high over Little Langdale by a great stopper of rock. One shore is backed by a picturesque wooded mound that owes more to art than nature, for landscape artists have been at work.

It would make a theatre set for some *fête-champêtre*, with lightly or unclad maidens disposing themselves round the margin of the lake, and exposing themselves to all manner of bronchial complaints. The whole has been planted with conifers and rhododendrons in such size and profusion that the path exactly resembles those around Gulmarg in Kashmir, where I have ridden with my family; but Westmorland? It is as though a Victorian industrialist had transformed the tarn into a likeness of his shrubbery, perhaps with fond memories of Shalimar. It is, however, striking, and lightly clad maidens would at least be more fun than Wordsworth's 'Solitary'.

There is a convenient car park just off the road; you can swim subject to the usual warnings, from some pleasant spots on the shore. A walk to Blea Tarn and over Lingmoor brings you back to Great Langdale at Chapel Stile, and more Wordsworth. This is his 'sequestered and simple place of worship', in whose churchyard his epitaph to his friend Owen Lloyd is carved. It can hardly any longer be called simple, for the chapel has been rebuilt into a substantial mid-Victorian edifice; only perhaps the pretty Gothic benches are earlier. One careful modern window shows St Francis, with lifelike rabbits, and one St Damain, whom I take to be Peter Damian; it is the penalty of stained glass artists who can't spell to have their mistakes recorded for posterity. Nor is it sequestered, for between Chapel Stile and Elterwater is the Langdale Partnership time-share complex. Opinions differ as to the merits of these institutions; it is undeniable that if they are sited in already popular areas they may add intolerably to the congestion, and if developed in less frequented places may spoil what is left of the lonelier parts. But the Langdale one seems to be unexceptionable: situated among old gunpowder works, it is well hidden, tolerably easy to get at, and not in a place of absolute natural beauty. Since families tend to occupy more space there is less congestion than there would be with an hotel of comparable size, and the occupancy tends to be spread evenly throughout the year. Neither coach parties nor caravans are tempted there, and the extensive facilities of the place are made available – at a price – to local residents, which must considerably add to their amenities, especially in winter.

In summer **Elterwater** is almost taken over by customers of the popular Britannia pub, which faces onto the green with its handsome maple tree, a good place to drink. I worry about the inn sign, which shows a First Rate in full sail and fine weather about to crash on the rocks in an appalling demonstration of bad seamanship.

The car park here is the starting point of a good low-level walk, the first stage of which passes alongside Elterwater to Skelwith Bridge, where there is a famous cascade. Elterwater has the romantic derivation of Elptarvatn, or Swan Lake, but is not a very romantic lake, being small and shallow.

The Kirkstone green slate quarries have a showroom and coffee shop at Skelwith Bridge. Their pretty green slate makes handsome flooring material – especially if naturally cleft – cills and cladding, but its use in little ornaments should be discouraged, since it contrives to appear dull and artificial. The path goes on up the south bank of the River Brathay, passing Colwith Force, more secluded than that of Skelwith, as far as Slaters Bridge, a fine unaltered packhorse bridge in the shadow of the abandoned quarries, then up past the hamlet of Little Langdale back to Elterwater. Over the whole six miles or so of this route the views are spectacular and the surroundings delightful.

If you climb up Betsy Crag, to the south of Little Langdale Tarn, and poke about in the old quarries, you may come across Lanty Slee's cave. Lanty was a famous distiller of illicit whisky, who did a considerable trade in the middle of the nineteenth century, and his cave, with the remains of his apparatus, was discovered by Harry Griffin a hundred years later. It was not the only still he had, since he preferred, in the best traditions of undercover work, to vary his movements, although eventually most of the whisky found its way over Wrynose and Hardknott to Ravenglass.

The Three Shires Inn in Little Langdale gets its name from the fact that Cumberland, Westmorland and Lancashire used to join a couple of miles away at the Three Shires Stone on Wrynose Pass. It is a good pub, but has been modernized, with lots of Kirkstone slate, plush chairs and flowered wallpaper, of doubtful virtue in a dales inn.

Care needs to be taken when passing through Little Langdale by car, for the only road is narrow and twisting. It leads past Iving How, just to the right up a track. This was the scene of a bit of Wordsworthian jobbery in 1818, when, scurrying about on behalf of his patrons the Lonsdales, he organized a syndicate to buy plots of land sufficient to allow each member to vote as freeholders – for the Lonsdales, of course. Remembering Wordsworth's youthful idealism, and the drying up of his talents with success, one can see what Browning meant in 'The Lost Leader':

> Just for a handful of silver he left us,
> Just for a riband to stick in his coat –
> Found the one gift of which Fortune bereft us,
> Lost all the others she lets us devote.

At one time the terraced mound above Fell Foot Farm was thought to have been a Thing mount, a meeting place of the Thing, or Norse assembly, but there is no evidence for this. What there is no doubt about is that Wrynose was the Roman route from Ambleside to Ravenglass. Undisturbed by any cultivation in the last 1700 years, considerable sections of that route can be seen, crossing the Wrynose Beck and paralleling the modern road on the other side of Wrynose Bottom down to Cockley Beck. The summit of Wrynose is a good place for a little cheating, if you can find a place to leave your car. Pike o'Blisco lies to the north, only a longish mile away and a thousand feet up, Great and Little Carrs and Swirl Hows rather further on the other side, all very dramatic and forbidding.

From Fell Foot Farm right through the pass to Cockley Beck there is not a house to be seen, nor anything but the odd scrubby tree, stones, rocks and patches of poor grass. Cockley Beck has the air of an oasis, and marks the transition to ampler lands; providing you turn south, that is, for continuing to the west takes you over Hardknott, an even more desolate spot. It is here that Wordsworth's sonnet sequence on the River Duddon starts, and follows the river on its short course, of not more than fifteen miles, to the sea. Short it undoubtedly is, but the walk – and it is essential to walk rather than drive through the Duddon Valley if one is to get the best of it – is throughout magnificent, as it winds through an unbelievably wide range of scenery. The Duddon sonnet sequence is not the sort of verse one takes on an expedition; it uses the scenery partly in an allegorical fashion, the progress down the valley being paralleled with a human life, partly as a structure to connect a number of discrete insights. But taking the walk will improve enjoyment of the poems, and even if you never open a volume of Wordsworth it makes a wonderful outing.

From the summit of the pass down to Hardknott junction at Cockley Beck and on to Dale Head, the stream, still shallow, and crossed by stepping-stones, flows through a widening barren valley. At Gaitscale, opposite Cockley Beck, the Herdwick sheep used to (and may still) have an extra pair of ribs (making fourteen in all).

Shortly after Cockley Beck, at Hinning House, the woods and the hills close in; the valley becomes a narrow glen, the path following close by the river on the west side. The Froth Pot and Birks Bridge are the features here, the latter being a much photographed and picturesque bridge over a deepish pool. After a glimpse of more open country at Troutal the motor road veers off to the east, leaving the path and the river to fight a way through the defiles of the Duddon Gorge; all very picturesque and romantic. The river itself is a place to linger over, almost a continuous cascade, with intervening pools, running under fine crags, especially at Wallowbarrow.

Seathwaite is on the road, and demands a small detour from the path, which at this stage of the walk will almost certainly be made in order to get at the Newfield Inn, a simple but very welcome pub. Dorothy and William Wordsworth stayed there in 1804: supper, bed and breakfast, stabling and ale cost 4s 6d for the two, and they had char, a treat for their supper.

The valley widens out at Seathwaite and forms a romantic setting for the church where 'Wonderful Walker' was a minister for sixty-six years from 1735 to 1802. Robert Walker owes his immortality to Wordsworth, who produced a long note on his life as an addendum to the Duddon sonnet. On an income of £17 a year Walker contrived to bring up and educate a large family and act as generous benefactor to his parish. This was done by constant industry and frugality – but never meanness – to the extent that when he died he was able to leave a fortune of £2000. Wordsworth met Walker not long before he died, and was forcibly struck by the saintliness of the man.

There is not much of Wonderful Walker about the present church, which looks for all the world like a Primitive Methodist chapel, with benches rather than pews. Only a small brass plate, and a flat stone outside on which he sat to shear his sheep, remind us of the famous man, but all the windows and tablets are to his progeny, which must count for something.

The churchyard, well wooded and sheltered, is a favourite place for birds: a pied flycatcher is in residence in the season.

Below Seathwaite the river and road run more or less parallel through a broader valley between the still craggy and broken although lower slopes. A fell road branches off south over Dunnerdale Fells to Broughton Mills, over wild and lonely country, while the valley road continues on the other side of the river to **Ulpha**.

The church here has survived much better than that at Seathwaite, although in a nineteenth-century restoration it lost what must have been, judging from the scraps that are left, some entertaining eighteenth-century and earlier wall painting. Unusually, for this was a feature that attracted restorers with a bit of money in their pocket, the sixteenth-century east window has not been replaced, much to the benefit of the whole. Even more unusually there is a crucifix – in a dales chapel! – although admittedly in a discreet corner.

The story is told that a party of undergraduates, visiting Ulpha in the early nineteenth century, and trying to be clever, asked for their bill in Latin. The landlord said nowt, went off and came back with the account neatly written out in Greek. There is also a story told of Ulpha Old Hall ('that embattled House, whose massy keep . . . fallen and diffused into a shapeless heap') of how the lady of the house, frightened by wolves, fled down the valley and disappeared. Her ghost is, of course, frequently seen.

Two roads branch off at Ulpha, one up the fell and past Devoke Water into Eskdale, the other round the west of Penn to meet the river road at Duddon Bridge.

Below Ulpha the river has another passage, but not so dramatic, between ragged-sided hills before reaching the salt marshes at Duddon Bridge.

Moving aside from the valley, it is possible to combine the walk from Cockley Beck to Seathwaite (perhaps in two stages – there is no sense in hurrying these things) with crossing over to Coniston by Walna Scar Road, which joins the Duddon Valley not far to the north. The contrast then between the dark, damp, rocky and overgrown river and the bleak uplands, culminating in passing under Dow Crag, is striking.

The Dunnerdale Fells themselves are spiky and jagged volcanic rocks, to be seen at their best on Caw, a mile due south of Seathwaite.

269

On the other side of the fells, up the Appletreeworth beck near to the farm ruins, a bloomery site has been confirmed as pre-Roman. This is also a good spot for identifying the narrow band of Coniston limestone.

12

The West Coast:
Millom to Ravenglass

It is sometimes forgotten that Cumberland has a sea coast: lacking in fashionable resorts, with tricky sailing for small boats and given over to industry to a great extent, it is too often neglected. Yet there are good stretches of shoreline, mostly unfrequented, and a fair number of interesting places to visit. It is also the best way of approaching that most impressive of valleys, Wasdale. Norman Nicholson, a man of great sensibility, tells us that we must love **Millom,** and since he chose to remain there all his life his judgement should be respected. Otherwise, it must be said, there is not too much to attract one to a small run-down industrial town, the centre of the third Lakes peninsula.

Old Millom is quite apart from the new, and consists of the remains of the castle and the church. The Hudlestons were Lords of Millom, and happy to live in the castle, even when ruinous, since they held 'themselves content, that the old manner of strong building there, with the goodly demesnes and commodities which both land and sea afford them, and the stately parks full of huge oaks and timber woods, and fallow deer, do better witness their ancient and present greatness and worth, than the painted vanities of our times do grace our new upstarts' (1610).

The Hangstone on the Marsh near the railway records that 'on this spot stood a Gallows, the ancient Lords of Millom having exercised Jura Regalia within their seigniory'. Privileges attached to the manorial rights, although not that of the famous 'droit de seigneur'. The Hudlestons had the less dramatic but more useful concession of free access to the fish market for the first quarter of an hour, so that the best fish could be bought for the castle.

Most cases tried were not matters of life and death – verbal abuse, throwing stones at mother-in-law, windows, and slandering the schoolmaster. During the Civil Wars the castle was besieged by the Parliamentarians and since then has decayed considerably. Not much remains beyond the massive pele, which is big enough to be a real keep, and taken together with the curtain wall and entrance tower

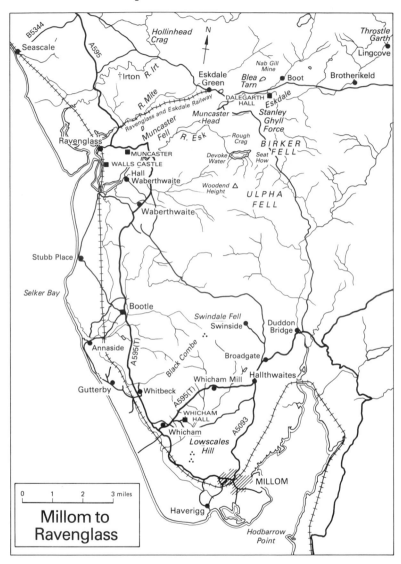

Millom to Ravenglass

must have constituted an impressive fortification. Nor is there much left of the original Norman church beyond the chancel arch – even this was rebuilt in the 1930s – and the north door, but the church is one of those that has seen changes in every period, all of which add to its interest. The thirteenth-century east window is textbook-typical, the fourteenth-century Hudleston chapel is splendid, and the Hudlestons have three tombs of the fifteenth, sixteenth and early eighteenth centuries. The seventeenth saw the church badly knocked about and the nineteenth a restoration.

Although all the original glass has gone, the windows in the Hudleston chapel are still fine; the east window contrasts with that in the chancel, and is probably later than the three south windows. The mandala of the west window is meant to resemble the bladder of a fish, hence is the Vesica; which seems a tortured explanation to me.

The best of the Hudleston tombs is that of Sir Richard, who died in 1494, with effigies on top and children arranged below around the tomb-chest. Old Sir Richard, 'Terrible Dick', who fought at Agincourt, is commemorated in a badly knocked-about wooden effigy. Two other good bits of carving are the font – it bears the arms of Furness Abbey – which is medieval and well preserved, and a sundial in the churchyard, which since it bears the arms of the Broughtons of Broughton, the last of whom – Sir Thomas, who backed Lambert Simnel – died before 1500, must also be ancient.

Before Millom town, which only took its name in the nineteenth century, there was nothing more here beyond the village of Holborn Hill, at the terminus of the route across the sands. The Ship Inn, and a plaque dated 1745 which modestly advertises sustenance and guidance –

> William and Ann Barren live Heare
> Who mostly keep Good Ale and Beer
> You that intend to Cross ye Sands
> Call Here a Gide att your command.

– are the only relics of its past.

The harbour also allowed some coasting traffic, but even after the railway reached Holborn Hill in 1851 no great industrial activity was noticeable. But in 1868 a rich seam of haematite – that blood-red iron ore – was discovered at Hodbarrow on the tip of the peninsula, and Millom was built. Fifty years of prosperity followed before extraction began to tail off, ceasing completely exactly a century after it

273

began. With the closure of the mines there seemed no reason why Millom should not, like some mining villages in West Durham, merely disappear. But Millomers liked it there, and the town has, against all the odds, survived. Communications are dreadful, but they will tell you that this keeps them pleasantly apart from all the nastiness of the rest of England. Some of the enthusiasm that can be generated by Millom is evidenced at the little museum. There is not a great deal of it, but the reconstructed miner's cottage and section of a drift mine give a vivid impression of what mining was like (if you want to see the real thing, Beamish museum has a whole row of miners' cottages as well as an actual drift). The anecdotes of friendly ladies who staff the place are even better than the exhibits.

As well as the rural parts of old Millom the site of the Hodbarrow mine is of interest. There, in order to protect the mining works, a great lagoon, protected by expensive breakwaters, was created, which now serves as a holiday village, offering sailing, water-skiing and windsurfing tuition. But the attraction of life in Millom lies more in its surroundings than in the limited intrinsic merit of the town itself: from Hodbarrow right up to Ravenglass the beaches are deserted for most of the year, and at any time offer, with a little selection, secluded spots, sheltered from the wind, having marvellous views. Haverigg dunes are some of the best outside Northumberland. Silecroft can be crowded, but only during school holidays, and never by Blackpool standards.

All this part of the world is dominated by Black Combe, a mass of Skiddaw slate, which asserts itself vigorously over the landscape. Not all that high – a shade under 2000 feet – the hill is impressive partly due to its mass but also to the fact that it is the only Lakeland fell that comes straight out of the sea. As a result the view from the summit is unique. Wordsworth quotes 'that experienced surveyor, Colonel Mudge', as saying that it commanded 'a more extensive view than any point in Britain . . .' The whole Cumbrian coastline from Walney to St Bees Head is visible, and the hills right round to Ill Bell. Snaefell on the Isle of Man is generally there and Colonel Mudge claimed to have seen Ireland more than once. The Galloway hills are clear, and people have seen Snowdon.

The best path up is from **Whicham**, a pleasant hamlet at the foot of the Whicham Valley. St Mary's church, a little chapel, has a plain Norman doorway. Just on the other side of the valley a road leads past Po House – always good for a laugh, especially since Low Bog House is at the other end – on to Lowscales hill, where there are two

Grange in Borrowdale: the twin bridge

Derwentwater and Cat Bells in early morning

Ravenglass: a smuggler's paradise

Muncaster: the Salvin library

stone circles. The stone circle of the area, however, is at Swinside, on the eastern flank of Black Combe, an impressively large and intact monument, in a natural amphitheatre between the hills. Wordsworth, who called it

> '. . . that mystic round of Druid frame
> Tardily sinking by its proper weight
> Deep into patient Earth . . .'

recorded that it was locally named the Sunkenkirk.

Swinside can be reached by continuing from the top of Black Combe, following the ridge, and then taking the path back into the valley at Hall Thwaites, but it is easier to go from the fell road, for which you turn left at Duddon Bridge or Broadgate. The church at Thwaites is modern, but has a font and some furniture from St Anne's chapel, of which now only the churchyard survives.

Only the deaf and dumb are buried in **Whitbeck** churchyard, according to Norman Nicholson's granny. St Mary's church is thirteenth-century with a later chancel and an early effigy known locally as the Lady of Annaside. She was probably a Hudleston widow who had taken vows and retired, possibly at Seaton convent near Bootle. Although weather-worn, she is a handsome figure, with well carved drapery and costume, her feet on a little dog. There is a tablet dedicated to 'those regretted relatives of whom, within half a century, four successive generations departed' by 'a grateful survivor'. Grateful additionally, one presumes, since he was also an inheritor.

Annaside, a solitary little hamlet, is on the beach past Gutterby where the Ordnance Survey claims there is a spa. The beach here is one of the less popular bits, probably because the foreshore is shingle, although the sands take over beneath the high-water mark.

Bootle is the metropolis of Black Combe, with a church, originally thirteenth-century, but almost nothing of it is to be seen after the nineteenth-century rebuilding. Getting into it demands dedication, and the only thing to be seen, apart from a sixteenth-century font, is an attractive little brass in the chancel of Sir Hugh Askew 'late of the Seller to Kynge Edward the VI, which Sir Hughe was made Knyght at Musselboroughe felde in the yere of our Lorde 1547'. Musselburgh battle is also known as Pinkie, the last great Border battle between the English and the Scots (those of the 1715 and 1745 were much smaller affairs and between Government and

anti-Government: there were Englishmen and Scots on both sides).
Pinkie was fought between 18,000 English under Protector Somerset
and 30,000 Scots, as part of the 'rough wooing' of the infant Mary. A
contemporary ballad recorded the result:

> On the twelfth day in the morne
> The made a face as the wold fight,
> But many a proud Scott there was downe borne,
> And many a ranke coward was put to flight.
>
> But when they heard our great gunnes cracke,
> Then was their harts turned into their hose;
> They cast down their weapons, and turned their backes,
> They ran soe fast that they fell on their nose.
>
> The Lord Huntley, wee had him there;
> With him hee brought ten thousand men,
> Yett, God bee thanked, wee made them such a banquett
> That none of them returned againe.

For his services at Pinkie and elsewhere Sir Hugh was granted
Seaton Hall on the Dissolution; the nunnery ruins are about a mile
north off the main road on the right. He must have been another man
of 'metle', as he proved when, having served Queen Katherine of
Aragon as cellarer, he lost his place after the divorce. The Lord
Chamberlain said that the best post he could offer Askew was that of
charcoal carrier. 'Well,' he is reputed to have replied, 'help me in
with one foote and let me gett the other in as I can.' He then made
sure that the time came when a friend of his was standing near the
King, and 'got on his velvet cassock and his gold chine, and baskett
of charcole on his back, and marched in the King's sight with it. "O,"
saith the King, "now I like yonder fellow well, that disdains not to do
his dirty office in his dainty clothes; what is he?" ' The friend then
told King Henry, who let Askew have his old job back.

There are said to be the remains of Roman vessels in Selker Bay,
which were visible into the eighteenth century, about a mile from the
present shore. Roman is unlikely, but Norse possible, and worth
investigating.

Wordsworth spent a summer holiday at Bootle in 1811 and grum-
bled fearfully about it:

> Far from our home by Grasmere's quiet lake,
> From the Vale's peace which all her fields partake,

Here on the bleakest point of Cumbria's shore
We sojourn stunned by Ocean's ceaseless roar;
While, day by day, grim neighbour! huge Black comb
Frowns deepening visibly his native gloom . . .

This Dwelling's Inmate more than three weeks space
And oft a prisoner in the cheerless place,
Whose breath would labour at the lute in vain,
In music all unversed, nor blessed with skill
A bridge to copy, or to paint a mill,
Tired of my books, a scanty company!
And tired of listening to the boisterous sea.

To make matters worse, like a Spanish hotel, the house was not even finished: 'Whole rugged walls may still for years demand The final polish of the plasterer's hand.'

Bootle is the last of the Combe coast villages; the geology changes here from slate to granite, which begins to appear in the houses, a sharper red than Shap granite, coloured by the haematite, but coastal sandstone still continues to the east of the road, right up to St Bees. A loop road leads along the sea, but this is only visible at Stubb Place, where there is a good beach, for the rest of the shoreline right up to the estuary is covered by a Ministry of Defence proving range.

Waberthwaite church is outside the village, at Hall Waberthwaite, right on the bank of the Esk estuary, surrounded by farm buildings. Norman Nicholson was struck by its sense of tenacity: 'Its antiquity is irrelevant and it goes on with its job with the persistence of a farmer who still uses the horse plough to turn a field which the tractors cannot tackle,' but the feeling is surely not uncommon in any church by the sea where the site itself suggests a permanent resistance to hostile elements. The interior of St John's is pure pre-Tractarian Anglican, with box pews and a prominent pulpit with a bench in front for malefactors. The altar, crowded in by the eighteenth-century pews, is dated 1630. You need to look for this since both the date and the motto are covered by the frontal. *Vae mihi si non verum praedico* – 'Woe betide me if I do not preach the truth' is the motto – hiding it must be something of a Freudian slip. In the churchyard is a fragment of a cross shaft, quite early, but too much eroded to be of much interest.

At anything less than high tide a pleasant path leads from the church across the estuary, and along the coast to Walls Castle and Ravenglass, at the mouth of the Rivers Irt, Mite and Esk.

277

Most people will go to **Eskdale** for a ride up 'L'aal Ratty' – the Eskdale and Ravenglass railway, the survival of which, against heavy odds, has been due to successive waves of enthusiasts. When the Nab Gill mines closed in 1912 the line should have been finished, but Bassett Lowke, the model engineer, heard of it and converted it to a more economic 15-inch gauge. After the war Sir Aubrey Brockle-bank of Grizedale started the Beckfoot granite quarry which gave the railway a new lease of commercial life, but by 1953 this had to be wound up and the railway was once more imperilled. This time it was Douglas Robinson of Muncaster who led the relief, finding enough money to buy the line as a going concern. Now supported by the Wakefield family and well-wishers, L'aal Ratty must have an assured future as one of the best things in Lakeland, for not only is it every schoolboy's dream, with real miniature steam engines, but the line passes through the most delectable scenery.

Ravenglass station adjoins the main line, so that you can travel from Euston right up to Eskdale, Ratty depositing you almost at the foot of Scafell. A small museum gift shop and café, and the Ratty Arms, a free house, make waiting for the connection pleasurable. A service is maintained all the year round, but by diesels, and rather chillily, in the winter. The spring, when the primroses are out, is a good time to take Ratty. Muncaster Mill is the first stop, a working corn mill with a shop and a collection of friendly animals. From there the track passes under Muncaster Fell up the Mite Valley, giving a view up to the Wasdale fells, Great Gable and Scafell showing clearly. Muncaster Mill is complete, with a three-quarter-mile-long race, and large kiln, a necessity in these parts to dry the grain before milling, and untouristy, the animals running about the place adding a medieval flavour.

Eskdale Green station is between the village and the pleasant King George IV Inn, which used to be the King of Prussia until sentiments changed in 1914; the terminus is at Dalegarth, 6.9 miles from Ravenglass, gained in forty minutes. Ratty does not hurry.

The Eskdale Green church is St Bega's, a light art-nouveauish building with a handsome terracotta trefoil font. William Hartley started making swills – those shallow, almost indestructible baskets – in the village in 1917, and still keeps his hand in with less demanding work. Swill-making being a conversational job, the old men used to congregate in Hartley's workshop every morning to chat, bringing their coffee and walking slowly back home for their dinners.

Starting from Eskdale Green station a tour of the valley can be made in one day, or split into parts, which taken together make one of the most agreeable possible excursions. Passing, if that is judged absolutely necessary, the King George IV, you take the path to the left on the south side of the river, through fields and woods, diverting to look at Dalegarth, Stanley Ghyll Force and St Catherine's church (see page 280), on to Doctor's Bridge and the Woolpack Inn. A path leads off the road there through Christcliff to Boot and thence north up Boot Bank to the top of Hollinhead Crag, past Blea Tarn and back to Eskdale Green. The whole is about eight miles with less than a thousand feet of climbing, lots of entertaining scenery, geology, pubs at start and finish and two more en route: what more could be asked?

Upper Eskdale became yet another possession of Furness Abbey in 1242. It formed the established sheep farm of Brotherikeld, the name of which still attaches to the farm by the river, just before Hardknott Pass, which must make it one of the oldest named farms in existence. By 1284 Brotherikeld was enclosed by a wall high enough to keep sheep in, but low enough to afford passage to deer. About four feet will do this nicely, unless the sheep are Herdwicks, but deer will clear six feet easily. There are traces to be seen of that wall, together with a sheepfold and a packhorse bridge, at Throstle Garth and Lingcove, at the junction of Ling Cove beck and the River Esk. In wet weather there are some good waterfalls both in that valley and up Scale Gill.

Eskdale was in the past something of a centre of communications. The main road, as it were, was the old Roman military road from Ambleside, which can be seen clearly enough on the ground at the dale head, taking an entirely different route to the modern road, from Cockley beck south-west, then climbing in zigzags, alongside the modern plantation, swinging round to the north of Hardknott, and down towards Brotherikeld. After that there is nothing to be seen for certain until almost at the coast.

The drove roads are easier to trace; one runs to Cockermouth via Santon Bridge and Strands. A second follows the south side of Muncaster Fell to Ravenglass, and a third south to Bootle, crossing the Esk at Stock Bridge. There are a number of packhorse trails, too, converging, like the drove roads, on Eskdale Green, and packhorse bridges at Boot, over the Whillan beck, and Doctor's Bridge over the Esk, near to Woolpack Inn; appropriately enough, Doctor's Bridge is called after Dr Edward Tyson, who had it widened in 1734.

The Nab Gill mine, now owned by the National Trust, lies just to the north of **Boot**, reached by a path that continues the village street.

There is not a great deal to be seen, beyond some fenced-off shafts and ruinous building, but the spoil heaps are there, and attractive specimens of haematite can be grubbed out. Over a pretty packhorse bridge is Boot mill which has been there since the thirteenth century, although the present buildings date from the eighteenth century. The track that leads off to the right by the mill is the old corpse road from Wasdale. A miraculous revival occurred here once when the coffin of a dead woman bumped into a rowan tree, which is well known to have miraculous powers. She revived, and was taken home, only to succumb again; on that sad second journey as they neared the same spot the widower was heard to call anxiously to his son, leading the horse: 'Tak heed o' yon rown, John.' Boot's pub, the Burnmoor, which used to be the Mason's Arms in the nineteenth century, is just over the bridge from the mill, and has bedrooms, as well as sustaining food.

The drystone walls round Boot are worth noticing. Being made from the granite boulders lying about, which were often huge, the builders have had to employ quite different techniques from those used in slate or limestone country, where the stones tend to be suitably stratified. Eskdale walls are thicker, up to five feet in width, and tall, built without benefit of mortar. In spite of their size, the profusion of stones was such as to necessitate separate heaps being made during the initial, enormous task of field clearance.

St Catherine's church was restored in 1881, when the medieval stained glass was 'lost', but it retains the features that make dales chapels attractive, the most important of which is the lovely site, isolated by the river. It has one singularity in that, being built of local granite, it has not had to be pebble-dashed like so many other churches. One bell, the treble, is medieval, with a dedication to St Catherine, and the font, also (*pace* Pevsner) medieval, has what appears to be a Catherine wheel emblem. Anything else ancient has been removed, but there is a modern piece of stained glass in the chancel with an almost photographic likeness of its subject, Theodora Taylor. Tommy Dobson, a local hero, founder of the Eskdale and Ennerdale Hounds, and its master for fifty-three years, has a stone in the churchyard with his portrait head flanked by a drooping fox and mournful hound.

Dalegarth Hall was built by the Cumberland Stanleys, a cadet branch, and used to be substantial and well ornamented, with stained glass armorial windows, fragments of which have found their way to Ponsonby church. Much has gone, but what remains still makes a handsome farmhouse in a pleasant position.

There seems to be a major disagreement as to whether the name of the waterfall coming down off Birker Fell to join the Esk just below the church should be Stanley Ghyll Force, Stanley Force or Dalegarth Force. Whatever name is chosen, it is a very lovely place, the pink granite of the ravine alternately washed clean or grown over with moss and lichen. The rhododendrons are colourful in season, but questionable in that setting; purists will prefer the ferns, and the autumn when the trees turn and water is abundant. The fall itself is a single shaft of water, crashing into a clear pool, one of the finest in the Lake District, with the added interest of making it easy to compare its granite rocks with those of the Coniston limestone at Church Beck and the Borrowdale volcanics at Lodore.

Ravenglass has the great advantage that you can get to it by sea, although it takes confidence, a rising tide, and a boat able to take the mud. Once there it is pleasantly sheltered, and secluded anchorages can be had even when the village is crowded with holidaymakers. By rights Ravenglass ought to be a town, since as long ago as 1280 it had a charter for a weekly market and an annual fair. This last offered the opportunity to send beasts over to Ireland, and farmers from as far afield as Kendal and Blencow attended. But the eighteenth century saw a decline, probably due to the rise of Whitehaven, and by 1880 Ravenglass was almost deserted and the market little more than a name. Even before that date any popularity that Ravenglass enjoyed was due to it being a convenient place to land rum without having to bother the excisemen. Today it is a lovely spot, with a sheltered micro-climate, old cottages that back right into the sands and a pub, the Pennington Arms. The street – there is but the one – runs straight down a ramp onto the sands, which makes it possible to launch trailered boats, well sheltered, but only at high water.

Walls Castle is a little way off alongside the railway, and is no castle, but the well-preserved bath-house of the Roman fort of Glannoventa. The walls stand almost to roof level, and appear to have been used after the Romans left, an unusual event, since the invaders were wary of the work of the 'old men'. A tradition existed in the sixteenth century that this was Lyons Garde, home of King Eveling, who is Evelac, and also the Lord of the Underworld. But it takes an impressionable person to find much sinister about this pleasant pink ruin, which only the railway prevents from becoming a belvedere. It is also said that the Penningtons made Walls their home after moving from Furness and before building Muncaster, but I find it difficult to credit that. The thirteenth century was messy in its

281

domestic arrangements; it liked to have animals and humans cosily together with nice convenient dunghills. There is no evidence of any such thing at Walls, nor traces of the adaptations that would have been necessary. The fort, which lay between the bath-house and the sea, has been cut up by the railway, leaving little to be seen.

There is a path right along the top of Muncaster Fell, descending to Muncaster Head at the east and returning along the drove road on the south slope, where the remains of a Roman kiln for tile-making, and probably pottery as well, have been discovered. Some of these Muncaster tiles seem to have found their way to the Norman walls of Egremont Castle.

On the opposite side of the Esk Valley, up on Birker Fell, literally hundreds of prehistoric remains have been found – 1200 within a two-mile radius of Devoke Water. Today these seem inhospitable and unwelcoming habitats; Devoke itself is a bleak spot, and at 800 feet one of the highest and largest of Lake District tarns. From the tarn there is no sign of habitation, except the Muncasters' empty fishing lodge: but climb one of the surrounding heights – Seat How, Rough Crag or Woodend Height, and the whole of the coast is seen together with the fells back to Scafell, Pillar, Pike o'Blisco and over to the Isle of Man. Devoke also has the unpleasant distinction of housing the most radioactive freshwater fish in England, showing an average reading of 1250 bequerels a kilo (*Independent,* 22 October 1987). Loweswater comes next: the fact that both are on the doorstep of Sellafield may, of course, be purely coincidental.

Going further up Eskdale means abandoning Ratty for a steep climb up **Hardknott Pass**. Hardknott is the most difficult of all Lakeland passes that can be driven over; it has 1 in 4 gradients, is single track, and has some tricky hairpins. If the road is damp it can be practically impassable. But it is a convenient way to get from the coast to Keswick, and has the very real attraction of Hardknott Roman fort. Hardknott defies adjectives. It is simply the most impressive relic of the Roman occupation in this country, not even excepting the Wall. The isolation and inaccessibility of the place has resulted in the remains being relatively undisturbed. No one in their right minds would want to build anything other than a sheepfold or fox trap anywhere near that exposed and unrewarding place, so Hardknott has escaped the usual fate of serving as a convenient quarry. And the bleakness now lends a romantic attraction.

The views are superb – down Eskdale to the sea, to Scafell Pikes on the right and Harter Fell on the left; on a fine day, I am told, you may see the Isle of Man, but I have never visited Hardknott on a fine day. In raw weather, the rain lashing the grey stones with no one else about, the fort is a magical place. It follows the standard plan of Roman forts: a square, about three acres in extent, with gates in the centre of the east wall. Within are the foundations of the granaries, the commander's house, and the *principia* – the orderly room. For a good deal of their lengths the walls are man-high, and a few yards away, towards the road, are even better preserved remains of the bath-house. This contains the usual sequence of *tepidarium*, heated by warm air, to promote perspiration after undressing, *caldarium*, where the hot bath was taken in a tub or basin, and *frigidarium*, for a final cold plunge. Hardknott, doubtless as some recompense to the troops posted to this remote place, has the less common feature of a Laconian bath, a sauna-like chamber easily recognizable by its bee-hive shape.

A couple of hundred yards to the north-east of the fort a parade ground, together with its tribunal on the northern side, was formed; the defensive ditches which guarded this, the only possible direction from which attack could come, can still be discerned.

The nearest present-day equivalents to Hardknott I have seen are the forts on the road to the Khyber Pass, near Landi Khotal. The British soldiers who kept that outpost of empire have now been replaced by smart Pakistanis, who have preserved the memorials as well as the tradition of that other vanished empire.

Hardknott was built about AD 130 by the Emperor Hadrian, as attested by an inscription discovered outside one of the gates and now in the Carlisle Museum. It was initially manned by the Fourth Cohort of Dalmatians, but seems normally to have been occupied by fewer troops; both the incomplete commander's house and the relatively small bathing facilities suggest this. Professor R. G. Collingwood has suggested that after some time the fort was left to a caretaker and the bath-house used as an inn for travellers between Ravenglass and Ambleside.

Muncaster is probably the most splendid of Lakeland houses, and is still in the hands of the connections of that Gamel de Pennington who lived in Furness and built Pennington church. Even if the house were not as fine as it is, the view from the terrace would make it unique, for there is nothing quite like it anywhere in England. Half a mile of terrace walk looks up Eskdale to Scafell, down to Black Combe, and out across the sea; it is a prospect to marvel at.

The estate was granted to the Penningtons in 1208, and a castle built there half a century later, on Roman foundations, although the oldest parts of the present house are, as so often here, a fourteenth-century pele. After early nineteenth-century alterations Salvin – here again – remodelled the house in the 1860s, and it is one of his most successful works. The south front, which incorporates the pele, is a balanced castellated range, while the north front is bold and uncompromising, looking forward to the sculptural effects of Lutyens' Castle Drogo, the whole in sparkling pink granite, dappled with lichen. As a result it has a unity of character which Holker, its nearest competitor, being essentially two separate houses, lacks.

The great hall is medieval at bottom, but has been Salvinized into a light and spacious room, full of splendid objects, the best of which are some Flemish carvings, including a magnificent dormition of the Virgin. Lying close by, typical of the relaxed approach the family has to these matters, is a huge Star of Ethiopia, given by the Emperor to Sir William Pennington-Ramsden who, as a boy, showed the Negus how to operate his lawnmower. The other rooms all lead off the hall; the dining room has Spanish leather walls setting off the seventeenth-century table and chairs which form a set with two fine settees. An extensive collection of Paul Storr silver is displayed on the sideboard and table, and a showcase by the door is full of a marvellous Derby service, perhaps the finest produced, which (typical of Muncaster) had been lying around in a cupboard until recognized quite recently for what it is.

Being a lived-in house, the lofty octagonal galleried library not only has the obligatory rows of calf-bound volumes, but also a table piled with the owner's latest enthusiasms. Again, the furniture is seventeenth century, but the room has a Salvin-designed octagonal carpet, with some splendid rugs. Textiles are a feature throughout the house; as well as oriental rugs there are Flemish and English tapestries and Bokhara hangings.

Certainly the most elegant room is the drawing room, grey and white with a coved ceiling and a superb eighteenth-century white marble chimneypiece with caryatid supports. Among the family portraits are four Reynolds, and a contemporary portrait of Protector Somerset. When the last Lord Muncaster died in 1917 the estate went to his mother's family, the Ramsdens, who joined Pennington to their name: the Ramsdens were connected to the Dukes of Somerset.

Apart from the textiles, the carvings and the seventeenth-century furniture, the best things in the house are a set of Canova marble reliefs of long-legged dancing girls and a full-length portrait of

Thomas Skelton, fool to the sixteenth-century Penningtons, who caused the word 'Tomfoolery' to be incorporated into the language. Lugubrious Tom, wearing a green, white and yellow chequered gown, is carrying a hat, staff and bowl and is holding his last will and testament, a long document explaining the significance of the portrait, e.g.:

> The dish with Lugges that I do carry here
> Shows all my living is in good strong beere . . .

He is no capering cap-and-bells figure, but Feste himself, poor Tom in Lear, and his portrait should be in every book that purports to explain Elizabethan England.

Even if you do not approve of rhododendrons, and it must be admitted that they are a showy, even vulgar shrub, the gardens of Muncaster are a magnificent splash of colour in the early summer; and there are magnolias and camellias for the more sensitive souls, as well as many noble trees.

Unduly susceptible persons should, however, avoid the owlery; owls make it their business to be inconspicuous, and the most obvious sight is a multitude of day-old chicks and bits thereof – the owls' rations for the day. But Muncaster is doing great work on behalf of these dignified and imperilled birds, taking in wounded and abandoned individuals, and returning them to the wild. The jaundiced spectator can gain considerable amusement by observing the speedy change as mums bring in their offspring, primed with ideas of Wol, friend of Pooh Bear, to be confronted with the gory reality of Wol's horrid breakfast. The guardroom on the ground floor of the pele tower houses exhibitions, including a fabulous collection of imperial Russian soldiers – Cossacks, Siberians, Astrakhan guards, Cuirassiers, and the Tsar's guards in magnificent uniforms.

Survivals of pre-Salvin work are visible outside: the gates, stables and curtain walls being in a light-hearted Gothic. Muncaster church is in the grounds, and like St Michael's, Lowther, combines the functions of family chapel and parish church. The four handsome Holiday archangels in the nave – very beautiful creatures – are in memory of some unfortunate tourists, friends of Lord Muncaster, who went with him to Greece in 1870. There they were all captured by bandits, who, while Muncaster was negotiating a ransom, killed all their hostages in a fit of nervousness. The west window is much less good, a fussy piece, but it has a full-bosomed lady who must have delighted generations of small boys.

Penningtons were Lancastrians, allied to the Percies, and in June 1464, after the Battle of Hexham, and the subsequent judicial murders by the Yorkists, are said to have succoured King Henry VI, who was found wandering on the fellside (the place, Chapels, is now marked by an eighteenth-century tower). In gratitude, the King gave Sir John a small glass bowl. This is the 'Luck of Muncaster', still kept in the family and used on special occasions.

The best known Pennington is the first Lord Muncaster, a colleague of Wilberforce in the anti-slavery movement (the Penningtons were altogether of sounder opinions than the Lowthers), who must have been an outstanding man. Colonel Pennington of the 30th Foot, before he began a political career, got the better of Dr Johnson with a good deal of spirit and ingenuity. According to Boswell, when they met at Fort St George, after silencing the doctor on the subject of civilized and natural man, he demolished Garrick's verse speaking: for instance, in Hamlet 'I will speak *daggers* to her; but *use* none'. Dr Johnson did not seem to mind: 'I shall always remember this day with gratitude,' and Boswell said it was 'brilliant . . . like enchantment'.

The Ravenglass gullery is on the west shore of the estuary. I have to confess to not liking gulls overmuch; terns, cormorants, gannets, cuddy ducks, guillemots and every sort of wader are a delight; but gulls, especially after Alfred Hitchcock's *The Birds*, are menacing creatures. Much better to eat their eggs, with brown bread, garlic salt, and some fresh shrimps, than to have them develop into those strident fowls. But if you like gulls, Ravenglass is the place to indulge yourself, although you have to get permission first.

The straight road east from the A595 just before Holmrook leads past the track signposted to **Irton** church. St Paul's is usually visited in order to see the ninth-century cross, one of the famous Cumbrian crosses. Irton is an odd man out among these, since the style is purely and unmistakably Irish. Carved from a single block of red sandstone, ten feet high, it is stylized and intricate, and partakes of the nature of jewellery in stone; and it is nearly perfect, with only a chip off the top of the cross. Surprisingly, in view of the friable nature of the stone, it is not too badly eroded, and stands in its original socket on the south side of the church.

Although the workmanship is Irish, the cross was commissioned by a Saxon since an inscription, now no longer visible, recorded a Saxon dedication. The church itself does not look enticing: undistinguished modern pebble-dash and sandstone dressing, rather the worse for wear. But the interior has some good things, especially two marvellous pre-Raphaelite windows in the north aisle. These look very much like Burne-Jones and Morris, but are ignored by both Pevsner and the church guide. There is also a series of naïf, almost comic-strip, windows which must have kept lots of children entertained during long services. There used to be a bell cast in 1715 which proclaimed the downfall of the Old Pretender: *Impostor fugatus ano George II Regis Secd'*, but that has found its way to Irton Hall.

The Lutwidges of Holmrook are commemorated by the font and a memorial in the east window to Admiral Skeffington Lutwidge, Lieutenant of HMS *Carcass* when she made her expedition to the Arctic in the course of which young midshipman Nelson got into a brawl with a polar bear. If the name Lutwidge stirs any recollection today, however, it is due to the Admiral's great-nephew, Charles Lutwidge Dodgson – Lewis Carroll.

13

The West Coast:
Wasdale to St Bees

There is no greater contrast anywhere in Lakeland than that between the grandeur of Wasdale and its fells, the unspoilt scenery of Ennerdale and Loweswater, and the jaded mining villages and ports of the coast, only a few miles off. Yet even these have their individual and sometimes remarkable merits.

Just after Santon Bridge the first, unforgettable view of **Wasdale** appears. Someone said, I think it was T. S. Eliot, that anyone who read *Paradise Lost* attentively would be permanently changed by it. Wasdale is like that. It would be very difficult for even the most insensitive to pass a reasonable amount of time in that valley without experiencing an overwhelming sense of the timelessness and vastness of the universe.

It was in Wasdale that I first understood what Wordsworth was going on about in his Ode on the 'Intimations of Immortality'.

> Not in entire forgetfulness,
> And not in utter nakedness,
> But trailing clouds of glory do we come
> From God, who is our home.

When there is no hint of any other cloud in a cerulean blue, Great Gable can fly a horizontal pennant, a mere rag of mist, from the crest; quite literally, a trailing cloud. With that came the appreciation that Wordsworth, uniquely, means what he says: it may be naive, trite, or just plain daft, or it may pierce the heart of reality; but it is exactly what that awkward genius meant.

Wasdale lies open to the west, and almost indeed to the sea; only the inconvenient mass of Latterbarrow prevents it from being a fjord. It would make a remarkably good fjord, since the fells drop precipitously into the lake. Until you get right to the head of the dale there is room for little in the valley except the lake; the road on the north side has to pick its way among the broken terrain, while on the south there is space for nothing more than a footpath hanging precariously at the bottom of the famous Wasdale screes.

These resemble, according to your fancy, either upended Gothic fan-vaulting or enormous slag heaps. Although I favour the latter, there is no denying that they constitute an impressive jumble of rock. But what catches the eye, and makes driving up the valley hazardous, is the breathtaking view of Great Gable at the head of the dale. It is almost as though the top thousand metres of the Matterhorn had been chopped off and stuck here, and this characteristic has made Wasdale almost the birthplace of British climbing. You don't have to struggle up miles of boring foothills for the rough stuff; there it is, right in front of you.

If Wastwater is really a fjord, Wasdale Head is an alp – a summer meadow, and not much of it, merely a few acres of good land, enough to support a decent farm or two when taken together with the fell grazing. One of those farmers in the first half of the nineteenth century was Will Ritson, who kept a small inn as a sideline. When this furthest-flung outpost of the Lakes became popular, Ritson became famous. There are two large photographs of Will Ritson in the coffee room, now, naturally, the residents' lounge, and in the bar; both are masterpieces. Ritson, gaunt, ironic, has that innate diffidence that characterizes the Cumbrians; a diffidence often well concealed in an open and lively delight in sport and conviviality, and not incompatible with a readiness to defend one's own rights if tampered with, but with no sign of aggression. He sits, pipe in mouth, glass by hand, a hint only of humour in the eyes, ready to chat with anyone; especially if they are buying the drinks. Edwin Waugh wrote of him:

A very fine tall, stark man, about sixty, sat on a low chair by the fire. His wiry hair was sprinkled with grey, and his long weather-worn face beamed with manly benevolence. A little, white-headed lad stood between his knees, playing with a book. Muttering to himself, he climbed the old man's limbs, unbuttoned his waistcoat, poked his fingers into his ears, like a kitten teasing a Newfoundland dog, . . . [Ritson] spoke of Wordsworth as 'a varra quiet-like aad man, who had nea pride aboot him, an varra lile to say'. But Professor Wilson 'banged 'em all for fun'. Ritson had been a famous wrestler in his youth and had won many a country belt in Cumberland. He once wrestled with Wilson, and threw him twice out of three falls. But he owned that the Professor was 'a varra bad un to lick'. Wilson beat him at jumping: he could jump twelve yards in three jumps, with a great stone in each hand, while Ritson could only manage eleven and three-quarters. 'T'first time that Professor Wilson cam' to Wastd'le Head,' said Ritson, 'he hed a tent set up in a field, an' he gat it weel stock't wi'bread, an'beef, an'cheese, an' rum, an'ale, an' sic like.

'Aa remember there was a "Murry Neet" at Wastd'le Head that varra time; an' Wilson an't t' aad parson was there amang t' rest. When they'd gotten a bit on, Wilson med a sang abbot t' parson. He med it reight off o' t' stick end. He began wi' t' parson first, then he gat to t' Pope, and then he turned it to t' divvul, an' sic like, till he hed 'em fallin' off their cheers wi' fun. T'parson was quite astonished, an' rayder vext an' all, but at last he burst oot laughin' wi' t' rest.'

The Wasdale Head Inn today has mementoes of those days: the fine portrait of Ritson by that great early photographer, George Abraham, and many other vintage mountain pictures. Some of the original farmhouse furniture has been built into the walls, and the residents' bar, which has the pick of these things, together with a good selection of draught beers and malt whiskies, is still one of the best possible places to pass an evening.

Wasdale claims to have the highest mountain and deepest lake, the smallest church and the biggest liar in England. The first two claims are incontestable. Scafell Pike is not as high as Snowdon, nor as many of the Scots peaks, but it is, by a few feet, higher than any English hill, and a great deal more frightening than most. And Wastwater, at an average of 120 feet depth and a maximum of 260 feet, is unquestionably the deepest lake, which gives it the peculiarity of rarely freezing in spite of its generally sharply-increasing depth, which makes fishing difficult, although brown trout can be had.

The smallest church is more debatable, for there are at least two other churches smaller, not counting private chapels, but Wasdale is tiny, the appropriate size for a community so small and isolated. There must have been a congregation gathered at Wasdale Head well before the Reformation, for in 1550 the Bishop of Chester came down on the parishioners for a contribution to the church at St Bees, and it is likely that the present building was in existence then. It is little more than a pious shed, a shelter against the elements, minuscule against the huge hills outside, but the atmosphere is one of great tranquillity. Until its restoration in 1892 there was an earthen floor, no window glass, a hurdle to keep out the sheep in place of a door, and no pews. The dedication has only been in place since 1977; it is to St Olaf, the martyr King of Norway, a suitable dedication for this essentially Norse settlement. Olaf is better known as Olave in

England, and even, corrupt, as Tooley, as in Tooley Street by London Bridge.

While much of the rest of the Lakes has changed under the pressure of tourism, Wasdale Head and its church remain as an example of how forcibly the simplicity of the county and its people must have struck the early visitors. All the distinctions of society and the quibbles of theology disappear into insignificance when this stark country is confronted. The philosophical traveller, however, is best served by avoiding the summer, when hundreds of bright anoraks and motor cars distract from meditation, and you can't get a bed at the inn.

Will Ritson was the biggest liar, and festivals are still held in his memory at the Santon Bridge Inn (politicians and newspapermen are excluded as being incapable of telling the difference; and one wonders about lawyers). It would be interesting to analyse these contests, if any observer could remain sober enough; they are not so much lies as ancient Scandinavian jests – about the bullock that got itself lost inside one of Will Ritson's turnips or about the broken-winged eagle he mated with a foxhound. Even in ordinary conversation, especially if there is an innocent offcomer present, Cumbrians will sometimes tell the most fantastic untruths while remaining entirely po-faced: the trick is to be as outrageous as possible without letting on.

Climbing was an offcomers' introduction; no hard-working upland shepherd is going to waste energy scrambling up rocks for the fun of it; something might be done in pursuit of a fox or to retrieve a lamb, but the mountain crags were on the whole left to themselves until the tourists came.

At first they were horrified. In 1793 a party went up Skiddaw, not the hardest of climbs. One man, 'on looking around, was so astonished with the different appearances of objects in the valley so far beneath us that he declined proceeding. We had not gone much further till the other companion was suddenly taken ill and wished to lose blood and return.' Contemporary poets were tougher. Scott, Wordsworth, Coleridge and de Quincey all climbed Helvellyn; Coleridge left an account of his scramble up Scafell (see pages 199–200).

The first local to make himself at home on the tops was the Reverend James Jackson of Sandwith, born towards the end of the eighteenth century. He only began climbing in the 1850s when he started 'to knock about amang the hills until I may almost say I knew ivery crag': this was the time when the visitors – Baumgartner. Dymond and Sir Leslie Stephen (Virginia Woolf's father) – began to climb. Pillar Rock was Jackson's favourite climb; he wrote:

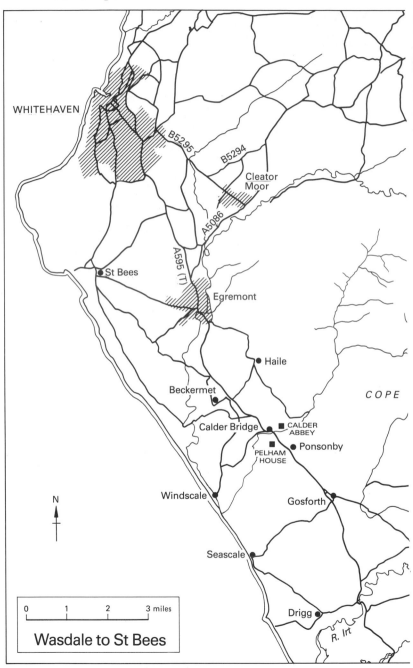

WHITEHAVEN

B5295

B5294

Cleator
Moor

A5086

A595 (T)

St Bees

Egremont

Haile

Beckermet

COPE

Calder Bridge

CALDER
ABBEY

Ponsonby

PELHAM
HOUSE

Windscale

Gosforth

N

Seascale

0   1   2   3 miles

Drigg

R. Irt

Wasdale to St Bees

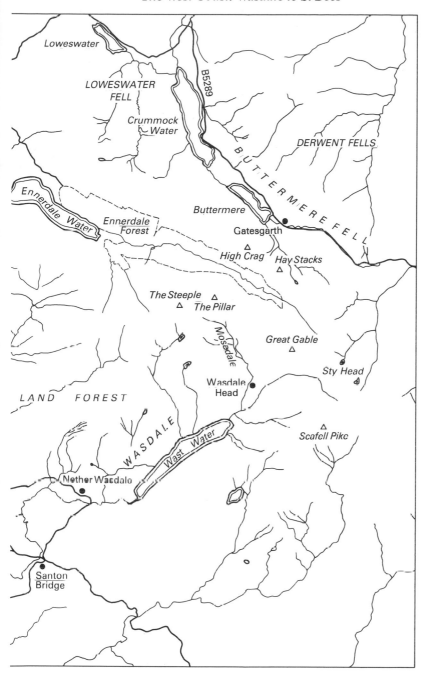

293

If this in your mind you will fix
When I make the Pillar my toy
I was born in 1796
And you'll call me a nimble old boy.

Appropriately enough he met his end in 1878, when he slipped in the snow on Pillar and fell into the Great Doup.

That is a local name but it was the Victorian climbers who gave the mountain features their more imaginative names – Fat Man's Gully, Rake's Progress, Keswick Brothers (the Abrahams – whose photographs are still the best), the Promised Land, Pisgah, Jordan, Tophet Bastion.

George Abraham described the Wasdale Head Hotel at the turn of the century:

> [in] . . . the historic entrance hall ice axes, ropes, rucksacks and other climbine implements are seen adorning every spare resting place whilst a chaos of mountaineering boots covers the floor. The love of mountains makes the whole world kin. Conventional attire is, of course, unthought of; most of the diners will be wearing tattered Norfolk jackets, others may be clothed in coarse flannel shirts or loose jerseys . . . It is the custom to place all the clothes that have been drying overnight along the upper part of the stair rail in the tower landing, and the search for one's under garments amongst such a vast collection is a trying ordeal. Fortunately lady climbers are not usually in evidence.

It would be a pity to come to Wasdale without trying at least one of the magnificent peaks that are best got at from there, but in summer I would be inclined to give it a miss, since then Scafell can look like a start of the London marathon. May is a good month if you avoid bank holidays, as the days are long, and winter is fine if you are experienced and properly prepared. For these are serious expeditions; even in the best of weather, Scafell and Scafell Pike are tough going, although there are reasonably easy routes up both of them.

If there was to be one choice, it would have to be Scafell, even although it is a little lower than Scafell Pike. If you are feeling fit both can be managed quite easily, but the map can be deceptive, since the two look close enough together on paper but are in fact separated by Mickledore, which is more or less impassable, and necessitates a fair detour. In fact most maps, even the 1:25000 Ordnance Survey, usually all that is required, are useless on Scafell. This is one place where Wainwright is essential (he is always useful and pleasurable) and where some careful preliminary work pays dividends. He is justly admonitory: "The ascent of Scafell Pike is the toughest proposition that the "collector" of summits is called upon to attempt . . . There is no bigger trap for the unwary and uninformed walker than this' (the ridge between Scafell and Scafell Pike). And, it should be added, his guide was published in 1960, well over thirty years ago. Things have got worse since then, as thousands of boots and half that number of behinds have eroded and polished the rock. Lord's Rake, in particular, a rough and steep corridor that slashes across the face of Scafell, is now considerably nastier than it was then.

But not only are the views superb, the rock features of Scafell, uncompromising in their ruggedness, are unmatched. The best description naturally is Wordsworth's:

> . . . I ought to have mentioned that round the top of Scawfell Pike not a blade of grass is to be seen. Cushions or tufts of moss, parched and brown, appear between the huge blocks and stones that lie in heaps on all sides to a great distance, like skeletons or bones of the earth not needed at the creation, and there left to be covered with never-dying lichens, which the clouds and dews nourish, and adorn with colours of vivid and exquisite beauty. Flowers, the most brilliant feathers, and even gems, scarcely surpass in colouring some of those masses of stone, which no human eye beholds, except the shepherd or traveller be led thither by curiosity; and how seldom must this happen! For the other eminence is the one visited by the adventurous stranger; and the shepherd has no inducement to ascend the Pike in quest of his sheep; no food being there to tempt them.

This is not really William's account, but Dorothy's as amended by her brother, and bears all the marks of her precise observation (what a wonderful novelist she would have made, had so frivolous a trade been admissible). Her expedition was made with a friend, Mary Barker, in 1818, when both ladies were well into their forties: it is understandable that even now they might justifiably have expressed themselves pleased by their 'uncommon performances'.

They took, of course, a guide with them; as late as 1889 travellers were still advised that it was 'always prudent to engage a guide'. Harriet Martineau, who thought Scafell Pike 'the greatest mountain excursion in England', was insistent on the point. But today we have Wainwright, who has served as guide to thousands.

Great Gable, although below the magical figure of 3000 feet, is a rewarding climb, but the obvious way up from Wasdale is also the hardest (and one can cheat easily on Great Gable by attacking it from the Honister Pass car park, which saves a good few hundred feet of climbing).

Since guidebooks are obliged to deal with easily defined areas, it sounds confusing that Honister, which is described here, quite reasonably, with Borrowdale, should be so near Great Gable, in Wasdale, a good forty miles away by road. This reflects the fact that only some of the Lakeland passes have been made suitable for motors (for which we should be grateful). Many of the most important packhorse routes exist only as footpaths. There are three of these routes paralleling each other between Buttermere/Honister and Wasdale/Eskdale: Black Sail, Moses Trod and Sty Head, all of which provide good walks, especially when the weather on the tops is uncertain; all are clearly marked on Ordnance Survey maps. Scarth Gap/Black Sail takes you from Gatesgarth, at the head of Buttermere, past some of the most impressive crags in the region; Haystacks to the east, Red Pike, Steeple, High Crag and Pillar to the west, before descending into Mosesdale and Wasdale. The view from the summit of the pass over to Scafell is unforgettable, as Baddeley remarked: 'Few things can be imagined, grander than this sudden burst of England's greatest mountain.'

If you want to see the famous Pillar this is easily done by taking the path from the top of the pass past the little tarn to the summit, either directly – quite easy – or via Robinson's cairn to Pillar Rock. This is, with Dow Crag, quite the most magnificent of Lake District crags, rising a sheer and rugged 500 feet. Either way takes you about 1000 feet up from the pass, but any temptation to try the face of Pillar Rock should be resisted by all except those who have come there equipped for that. It was the scene of the earliest attempts of Lakeland rock climbing and many routes are, I am told, still regarded as being decidedly difficult.

Sty Head, the next pass, is easier than Black Sail, which can be hard going. It is, in fact, so well graded that there were serious proposals afoot in the early years of this century to turn it into a motor road. The packhorse road follows the Lingmell beck and rises in a series of easy zigzags to the col, much pleasanter going than the higher path that later walkers have arrogated to themselves. The 1:25000 Ordnance Survey map is misleading, and you need Wainwright *(Great End 7)* to give the right way, which he calls the 'Valley Route': 'There is as much difference between the Valley Route and the direct route as there is between sweet and sour. It would be nice to keep the Valley Route a secret for the discerning few.' To my mind, at any rate. walking through such a pass as Sty Head, which has been part of the Cumbrian life for centuries, gives a much greater insight into the history of the area and its character than climbing the fells.

The old road carries on east past Sprinkling Tarn to Rosset Gill, and into Langdale, and north past Styhead Tarn to Borrowdale, another important former trade route. In between Black Sail and Sty Head comes Moses Trod, sometimes known as Moses Sledgate, on the supposition that slates were dragged across on their way from Honister to the coast. Moses is said to have been a quarryman who had a sideline in smuggled whisky; certainly smuggling through Ravenglass was a major activity well into the nineteenth century.

On a less rugged note, Wasdale is also a good centre for walking. You can follow the Burnmoor Trod, the old corpse road, past the rowan tree, if you can find it, to Boot. Burnmoor tarn is one of the largest in Lakeland; it is a dour place, suitable for the melancholic. You have to take the right-hand path at the tarn, for the left leads down into Miterdale, which had a sinister reputation at one time, but now contains nothing worse than many acres of Forestry Commission trees and an Outdoor Pursuits Centre. Miterdale is a pleasantly unfrequented valley, which brings you out at Eskdale Green.

A variation of this is to branch off straight up the fell before you get to the tarn, to Illgill Head, and walk along the edge above the screes, which shoot down to the water below in a vertiginous fashion. You then trot down to the foot of the lake and make your way back, stopping frequently to admire the views up to Great Gable. Just past the youth hostel Wasdale Hall, a stone country house, in handsome grounds – there is a seat strategically placed in quite the best position for viewing.

Nether Wasdale, or Strands, is altogether different, in gentle, wooded countryside, a world away – although only a mile distant from the stark screes. It straggles pleasantly on either side of a long green where the Screes Hotel, which serves good beer amiably, and the Strand Hotel, more residential, face each other. Next to the Screes a castellated fountain, adapted to serve as a communal wash-place such as one still sees in use in some French villages. It is a magnificent granite affair, twelve feet high, the gift in 1880 of one Eleanor Irton of Calder Abbey. The Irtons were one of the oldest families in a region notable for lineage; twenty-five generations are said to have lived at Irton Hall.

297

The church at Nether Wasdale, situated for a change in the middle of the village, has a handsome pulpit, lectern, and some panelling which was brought from York Minster after the disastrous fire there in 1829 started by the mad Jonathan Martin, brother of the not-entirely-sane but greatly-gifted painter John.

Gosforth

There are two Gosforths – the other is a suburb of Newcastle where during Race Week, still the centre of the Tyneside year, everyone lets their hair, never in that region very firmly coiffed, decidedly down. Cumberland Gosforth is more sedate, a pleasant straggly small town equipped with hotels, banks and a restaurant. Its fame stems from its collection of pre-Conquest sculpture and, in particular, the Gosforth Cross. This is the latest in the series of the three famous Cumbrian crosses – Bewcastle, Irton and Gosforth, and is very different from the others. Exaggeratedly long and slender, it lacks the precision of detailing that marks both the earlier works, and mixes both the abstract knotwork of Irton with the representational nature of Bewcastle, but the abstract designs are crude, if lively, and the figures lacking all the finesse found in Bewcastle.

It is worthwhile getting Anglo-Saxon art into perspective, and Lakeland provides a unique opportunity for doing so. While archaeological discoveries help the Dark Ages to become progressively lighter, most of us still remain profoundly ignorant of what was going on in the four centuries between the withdrawal of the legions and the reign of King Alfred, or even about the much better documented tenth and eleventh centuries. None of the Lakeland guides are much help: Wainwright, masterly on mountains, is dismissive about artefacts, and places the Gosforth Cross an impossible two hundred years before its time. Even Pevsner is bitty on the subject.

To begin at the beginning, one should really go just beyond the boundaries of what can reasonably be called Lakeland, to Bewcastle, out on the Spadeadam Waste past Carlisle. The cross there was erected some time after 670. With the Ruthwell cross (in Dumfries) Pevsner says 'there is nothing as perfect as these two crosses and of a comparable date in the whole of Europe' – not unnaturally, since at this time Northumbria was the refuge and centre of all that remained of civilization north of the Alps. Bede, that *'massif* of English scholarship . . . King of infinite space', was born about the time that the Bewcastle cross was carved, and the remaining stones of his monastery of Jarrow share the same classical elegance with those on the cross, an elegance reflected in Bede's own Latin, as in his description of heaven:

Nox ubi nulla rapit splendorum lucis amoenae
Non dolor aut gemitus veniet nec fessa senectus.

There is nothing anywhere in our area quite like these early works – which really are worth going a long way to see – but the fragment at Heversham gives some indication of the high standard of seventh- and eighth-century Anglo-Saxon sculpture.

By comparison with the earlier pieces the figures on the Gosforth cross are stilted, but the vigour and symmetry of the whole thing more than compensates; Gosforth is an object of international importance, by some way the greatest work of art in Lakeland. It is not only its intrinsic merit that makes the cross remarkable, but its extraordinary nature as a document of English history, recording the transition between Viking paganism and Christianity. The story told in the carvings is that of the Edda, the Norse downfall of the Gods, mingled with the emergence of the new religion; very much what was then taking place, in the tenth century, after the Norse incursions from Ireland had developed into a permanent settlement.

Start at the bottom of the south side: the curled-up little figure is a primeval giant (compare him with the giants in the Athens agora), Odin is on horseback, with 'Oak thorn' the tree of life, a wolf and a stag. On the west side the demon Loki bound (as he is in Kirkby Stephen church), with his wife Sigga above him emptying out a cup of venom. Odin again, and Heimdal with his horn and staff defending Valhalla from attacking dragons. On the north side Odin is fighting Surt, the fire god, and being attacked by a dragon. Only on the east side (where one might expect it) is there a sign of Christianity. At the top it is still pagan: Vidar, the only god to survive, is snapping apart the wolf-jaw of Fenris with a foot and a hand; and at the base, at last, there comes a Crucifixion, without a cross, but with the wound, the spear, and a Mary, and crowning the whole thing, comprehending the pagan myths, is the empty Christian Cross, symbol of the Risen Christ.

There are more treasures inside the church, notably a fine pair of hogback tombstones of about the same period. These have a three-dimensional architectural quality lacking in many others, such as those badly damaged specimens outside Penrith Church, which look

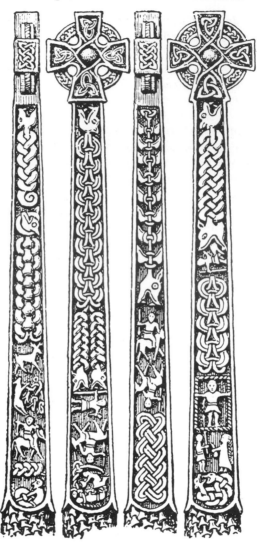

rather like slices of toast. The Gosforth Hogbacks have a substantial trapezoidal section, enabling one to exhibit Christ and the other a warrior – although he is a bit difficult to spot – on their end faces. The lighting makes it hard to see all the detail (it really ought to be possible for some department of government to provide grants to enable a poor parish to exhibit such pieces properly). The 'Fishing

Cross' fragment has a lamb trampling a serpent, Christianity defeating paganism, and, below paganism, Thor and the giant Hymir fishing for the World Serpent with an ox head for bait.

The monument to Sir Humphrey le Fleming Senhouse RN, of the Netherhall Senhouses, records that he died upon his ship, HMS *Blenheim*, at Canton in 1840, after the attack on the Chinese forts. Sir Humphrey is actually buried in the Protestant Cemetery of Macao, commemorated by a handsome obelisk. This was during the first Opium War which coincidentally was started by a Cumbrian family, the Dents of Flass, Maulds Meaburn. The two great opium houses at Canton were Jardine Matheson and Dent. who made it their business to ship opium from India to China, through their warehouses in Canton. The Emperor of China. naturally enough, attempted to suppress this nefarious trade, sending a high-ranking mandarin, Commissioner Lin, to do so. Lin arrested Lancelot Dent, whom he described as 'the greatest opium trader of them all', and destroyed all the opium he found.

The British government objected and sent an expedition to force the Chinese to make restitution and allow the import of opium. The unfortunate Sir Humphrey, who had served under Pellew at Trafalgar, was the senior naval officer in this discreditable adventure, and led the attacks on the fortresses that commanded Canton. Chinese resistance crumbled before Western technology, but Sir Humphrey perished, like so many of his men, of the fever. The Chinese had to agree to the Convention of Chuenpi, by which Hong Kong was ceded to the British; this was not enough to satisfy the Foreign Secretary of the time, Lord Palmerston ('Hong Kong will never be a mart of trade'), who insisted on renewing the war.

The British envoy who had signed the treaty, Captain Charles Elliot, was bundled off in disgrace to become chargé d'affaires in the Republic of Texas; and a bell taken from a fort stormed by Sir Humphrey's men rests in Gosforth church as a memorial of the whole disgraceful affair.

Another unlikely casualty commemorated in the church is Captain Charles Parker, of the Royal Marines, who died leading the attack on Petropaulovsky in Kamchatka, of all places, during the Crimean War. English history books keep quiet about this unlucky expedition, and you have to rely on the French (and Americans – J. S. Curtis's *Russia's Crimean War* is authoritative) to get at the truth, which is that the Anglo-French squadron was so mismanaged that Rear-Admiral David Price, commanding, shot himself before the action

301

was opened, and that the storming party was repulsed by the Russians with severe loss. Outside, in the churchyard. is a large and unlikely cork oak, said to be the furthest north recorded example.

It may be that the Red Admiral, on the road to Calder Bridge, which now sports a butterfly on its sign, originally commemorated the exploits of Sir Humphrey Senhouse, an Admiral of the Red.

Back at the coast, when the Ministry of Defence and radioactivity permit, **Drigg** is worth a visit for the sands of the Irt estuary used to be a valued pearl fishery of which Camden remarked 'the shell-fish, eagerly sucking in the dew, conceive and bring forth pearls, or (to use the Poet's word) shell-berries. These the inhabitants gather up at low water and the jewellers buy them.' A little further inland are a number of flint-knapping sites. which appear to have been worked over a very long period. Both pearls and flint tools are said still to be found.

Ponsonby church sits in the middle of the park of Pelham House (which used to be Ponsonby Hall), and is domesticated by being given a ha-ha rather than an obtrusive wall. It sits on a commanding knoll and offers a fine view of Seascale, which may not be thought much of an asset. Bits of it (*pace* Pevsner) are of the original thirteenth-century structure, but the best things are inside. The monument to Thomas Curwen, dated 1653, on the south wall of the Tabernacle, is a splendid piece of folk art: two sorrowing gentlemen in billycock hats, with neat goatee beards and enormous buttons, one holding an axe, the other resting mournfully upon a skull, support the table. They are like nothing more than fairground figures. The other memorials are all to Stanleys, who lived at Pelham, and provide an example of how far the techniques of lapidary inscription have degenerated in the last century. There are also a couple of well-preserved coffin lids with the sword and shear motif. The shears are of a type still used by conservatively-minded farmers with small flocks: I remember when I first learned how to use them my instructor Bernard Staley took one look at the hacked-about animal and said, 'Well, she'll mebbe live.'

Artistically speaking the Morris windows are worth the pilgrimage; the east one is by Morris in 1877, the west by Henry Holiday for the company some twenty years later. It is interesting to see how strongly the tradition is maintained. There is a handsome memorial inscription of 1578 to Frances Patryckson, daughter to Sir Thomas Wyatt, knight and privy councillor to King Henry VIII: 'God gave this wyfe a mynde to praye in grones and pangs of deth and to heaven elevating hands and eyes smylinglye to yeld breth.'

Hesket Hall: Sir Wilfred Lawson's Cumbrian Palladian

Mungrisedale

Whitehaven: Victorian Commercial

Whitehaven: the early eighteenth-century lighthouse

In 1889 it was reported of **Seascale** that 'there is nothing very inviting about it, unless it be its proximity to the sea, and to some of the finest scenery in the Lake District', and by Baddeley as 'an eminently safe and salubrious place for paterfamilias to deposit his wife and bairns at'. Neither would be true today; there is something very positively uninviting in the shape of the British Nuclear Fuels reprocessing plant overshadowing the whole coast. and no wise father would dream of leaving his children there for any length of time.

There is probably not much danger in the couple of hours it takes you to go round the Sellafield Visitor Centre. BNFL are very pleased to explain to you how entirely safe their operation is; the truth is they don't know. Barring Chernobyls which really are most unlikely in the UK, where nuclear generation is taken very seriously indeed, there is no indication that conventional nuclear steam plants are anything other than very safe. The problem comes in decommissioning plants and in disposing of the waste, which is what BNFL specializes in. Since no nuclear installation has been fully decommissioned there are no reliable estimates of costs, nor are the techniques of nuclear waste disposal clearly understood. (Nor, indeed, is the housekeeping at Seascale above reproach: spills occur, and they have apparently mislaid, and have never been able to trace, a couple of tons of plutonium, which must be a little worrisome for them.) Electricity generating authorities tend to justify the financial case for nuclear energy by putting in arbitrary figures for closing down plants which are almost certainly too low; and the whole business of reprocessing is largely unexplored territory. There is no doubt now that the vicinity of Seascale has dangers, especially for children, and that the risks involved are real and unquantifiable.

And there can be no question that the Sellafield plant is going to grow and become even more of a disfigurement to the landscape than it is at the moment.

The pretty village of **Beckermet** is on the other side of the works. Beckermet has three parish churches, two St Bridget's and one St John's, which is pretty good going. Old St Bridget's is very ascetic, a small barn of a place on the other side of the railway by the sea, but one of some antiquity. Its origins are Norman, but two cross shafts in the churchyard prove an earlier existence and are of considerable interest. One of these is on a circular base, like that at Gosforth, with a puzzling Runic inscription that has been variously interpreted by good authorities as:

Here enclosed Tuda, Bishop: the plague destruction before
and reward of paradise thereafter.

Here beacons 2 Set up Queen Arlec
for her son Athfeschar.

O thou loved offspring Edith, Little maid,
in slumber waned years XII.

Made for John MacCairmbre gone to rest
in the keeping of God.

and dated between 664 (which it certainly isn't) and 1103 (which is
highly unlikely). St Bridget, who is also St Bride, of Brideswell, and
St Brigit, was Irish if she really existed – and very popular.

The second Beckermet church, St John's, is by Joseph Birtley, a
Kendal architect, and also has a collection of cross fragments, corbels
and coffin lids which constitute a small gallery of pre-Conquest
work, coming from eleven different crosses. The interior of the
church itself is rather well done, using sandstone of contrasting colours with terracotta.

It is very easy to miss Cumberland's Caernarvon Castle, even if it
adjoins the A595, just north of the Beckermet roundabout, since there
is nothing much to be seen, except the remains of a motte on a natural
mound. It is Caernarvon because it is 'the castle opposite Man';
rather larger, the Welsh one is the castle opposite Mona (Anglesey).

The third Beckermet parish church, also St Bridget's, is really at
Calder Bridge, facing the Stanley Arms Hotel across the River
Calder. The church is an uncompromising 1846 red sandstone building which cannot lay claim to easy charm, but the east window has
some Holiday stained glass, the central light of which includes a
portrait of the church.

When Ehenside Tarn. between Beckermet and the sea, was
drained in 1871, vast numbers of stone tools were discovered: 'We
found *lots* of stone axes. the shoemakers came from far and near and
took them, to sharp their stones on.' Even so, a good many were
preserved in various stages of completion, together with rubbing
stones, indicating that this was a finishing site for the axes blanked
out at Langdale.

Calder Abbey lies within the policies of the eighteenth-century
house and has indeed partly been absorbed into it, the nearest the
public can get to it is by a footpath that runs a hundred yards or so
away. While this arrangement has the merit of preserving the ruins in

the eighteenth-century manner, as an addendum to a gentleman's residence, picturesquely overgrown, not surrounded by clipped English Heritage lawns, ticket booths and illustrated guides, it does leave a lot to depend on the ability and willingness of the owner to keep it up, and at the moment Calder Abbey is not being kept up. There is too much barbed wire, wire netting and an air of general dereliction about the place. The trees are untended and the fabric itself overgrown. While Calder is not the most important of monastic ruins it deserves better than this.

Calder was founded as a colony of Furness in 1138, but almost immediately thoroughly ravaged by the Galewiciae – Galwegians from across the Solway, described as '*debacantes et sanguinem Anglorum sitientes*' – 'raving and thirsting for English blood'. Rebuilding was prompt, starting the next year, but of this only the west doorway survives. The rest – parts of the church, including the north arcade of the nave, bits of the chapter house, refectory and calefactorium (which is remarkably commodious) – is of later thirteenth- and fourteenth-century work.

The monastery was suppressed on the grounds of evil living by a commission headed by Thomas Leigh, who, since he was promptly granted the property as a reward, may not have been perfectly unbiased. The Earl of Sussex admitted this when in a note to the King he asked: 'How and by what means, the monks might be ryd from the said Abbey?'

Haile's church is another of those dales chapels, built on some ancient sacred spot by a stream in a grove, removed from habitation. It keeps its character well, a numinous spot; as the Rector of Egremont pointed out, there have been some 8000 people buried in the little plot in the last millennium, so some feeling of departed shades is to be expected.

The most visible external memorial to these is against the west end, a memorial to John Ponsonby, carved after 1670 but in the style of a century before:

> Learn Reader Under This Stone
> Doth Lye
> A Rare Example Cald John Ponsonbye.
> If I Said Ylsese I am Sur I lyd
> He was a Faithful Friend And Soe
> He Dyd November 25 in the
> Year 1670 . . .

In the vestry there is a Roman altar and a piece of a Viking cross.

The Ponsonbys have been at Haile since the fourteenth century and are still there, the most prominent recent representative being the late Tom Ponsonby, the affable Labour Chief Whip in the House of Lords.

Egremont sounds grander than it actually is – Disraeli chose the name for the hero of *Sybil*, and suitably dashing it sounds – but Cumberland Egremont, although both historic and agreeable, is anything but dashing. Theoretically it has everything needed by romantic tradition: its antiquity is not in doubt, for it was a flourishing medieval town, and has well-preserved muniments, a castle and its own legend.

The Burgesses of Egremont were meant to follow the laws of the town laid down under King John, which included the following against gossip: *Si uxor burgensis dixerit aliquod convitium vicinae suae, et illa inde convicta fuerit, dabit domino pro forisfacto 4 denarius;* and fornication (but not with country girls) *si aliquis qui vixerit secundum legem villae fornicatus fuerit cum filia alicujus rustici infra burgum; non dabit merchet, nisi eam desponsaverit.*

Egremont's legend is rather good. It relates that the Lord of Egremont was captured in the Crusades; his younger brother refused to ransom him, and took his place at home: but the baron, aided by the love of a good woman, was released (she had to scalp him in order to do this) and made his way home, carrying the 'hatterell of his hair' and his horn. On his return the rightful lord sounded his horn outside the castle gate: the younger brother, recognizing the note, trembled and fled. All ended happily, however, and the brothers were reconciled. There are many variants of this story, one of which Wordsworth used in his poem 'The Horn of Egremont'.

Horns are legendary commonplaces, as are wronged brothers, but there is something about that 'hatterell of his hair' that carries a note of authenticity.

More historical, and amply authenticated, is the story of the Boy of Egremont, William Fitzwilliam, heir to William Fitz Duncan, son of the Earl of Moray. Father William earned himself a reputation for cruelty, which was quite hard to come by in the early twelfth century, by leading a ferocious Scottish army through the north of England on behalf of the Empress Matilda:

They first slew children and kindred in the sight of their relations, lords in the sight of their serfs and the opposite, and husbands in

306

the sight of their wives; then, Oh most shameful! they led away noble matrons, chaste virgins, mixed alike with other women and the booty, driving them before them naked, in troops, tied and coupled with ropes and thongs, tormenting them with their lances and pikes.

This had been done previously, but never to such an outrageous extent.

The son of this William, the Boy of Egremont, was heir to a great slice of the north of England, as well as the Earldom of Moray, and was quite likely to have become King of Scotland. He did not live at Egremont but at Skipton, in Yorkshire (well, the Boy of Skipton didn't sound nearly as well!), but Egremont was the most important of his English possessions. He went out one morning with his dog, and never returned. The forester who was looking after him was only able to tell how, when the boy jumped across a chasm in the River Wharfe, known as the Strid, the hound held back for a moment, causing the boy to slip and crash into the torrent. His body was never found.

In rose-pink local sandstone, the castle makes a good ruin, built about 1140: the remains of the curtain wall and gatehouse are of that time. A curiosity is the large number of tiles used in the herring bone courses of the curtain wall: these are almost certainly Roman, and probably came from the tile works on Muncaster fell, either directly, or via their use in some abandoned Roman work, there being no traces of Roman settlement at Egremont. As a concession to domesticity a great hall was built towards the end of the thirteenth century, providing what must have been at the time quite magnificent quarters, and cutting off the inner bailey and donjon from the outer bailey.

Unlike some other Norman town plans, which have the castle and church at some distance, those at Egremont stand close together. Not much remains of the thirteenth-century church of St Mary and St Michael apart from some of the chancel windows, the present building being late-nineteenth-century by Thomas Lewis Banks of Whitehaven. It is impressive enough, with tall monolithic sandstone pillars supporting the transept arch, but the best features are the carvings, especially that of the reredos, in wood and the pulpit in alabaster. The most striking is in the baptistery, a kneeling angel holding the font, skilfully back-lit from apsidal windows, with reflections from the polished brass dedicatory strip. It is a copy of

Thorwaldsen's work in Copenhagen Cathedral, and Pevsner, rather sweetly, describes the angel as 'life size'. Scholastics spent much effort discussing how many could dance on the head of a pin, but it is clear that our contemporary notions of angels are firmly anthropomorphic.

Egremont quarries, from which the characteristic sandstone comes, were famous, with Corfe, Folkestone, Pevensey and Reigate the best known in England; the stone was used as far afield as Windsor, on the roof of St George's Chapel. A survival from those days is the Egremont Crab Fair which has been held on the third Saturday in September since 1267. This is the most entertaining of Lake District folk festivals, the highlight of which is the World Gurning Championship, where the most hideous imaginable faces are pulled using a horse collar as a frame. If you have never been in an underground mine the opportunity to do so exists at the Florence Mine, just outside the town; but visits need to be arranged beforehand.

St Bees is by some way the grandest medieval coastal church, and of great interest. Externally it presents an odd spectacle: an obviously fine Early-English chancel fronting the road with a squat Victorian crossing tower and an odd bit of pitched roof squeezed between them. Then, arriving at the west door, one is confronted with a monstrously magnificent Norman doorway, with triple column reveals each as wide as the door itself. Facing the door is an equally fine sculptured lintel, possibly from an earlier church: its dragon, however, is pure Viking, and testifies to the continued existence of Scandinavian culture well after the Conquest.

Surprise increases when you step inside, for the chancel has disappeared, replaced by a huge Victorian iron screen and a stubby sanctuary, unmistakably the work of that brilliant, but hardly subtle Victorian, William Butterfield. Viewed in isolation, the screen is magnificent, but with the shallow sanctuary looks for all the world like a Gothic proscenium arch. The explanation is that the Early-English chancel was walled off in the seventeenth century and left to decay, being renovated in the early nineteenth to serve as lecture room for a theological college, and now as music room to St Bees school. Two centuries of neglect have not left much to see – if you can get inside – except the masonry itself, but what there is is singularly pure, untouched by later restoration.

In the rest of the church, what is not Butterfield is the original Early-English arcades, with seventeenth-century clerestory windows;

it has not been well looked after, being in part floored with terrible plastic tiles, but there are a couple of interesting monuments. That to Captain Willcox (died 1798) shows, not a romantic sword, but a workaday flintlock carbine leaning against the tomb; he must have been a rifleman. William Aingers (died 1840) is by John Lough, who did the Southey memorial at Crosthwaite.

Facing the church on the other side of the road is St Bees School, founded by Archbishop Edmund Grindal in 1583 as a grammar school, now a minor public school, but one with handsomer and older buildings than many a more famous institution. It seems an isolated place for a boarding school and must owe something to the English middle class's predilection for sending its offspring as far away as possible for their education. Grindal was a charming old gentleman, who became the first Bishop of London after the murderous Bonner, before being translated to become an ineffectual Archbishop of Canterbury – though not ineffectual enough to please Queen Elizabeth.

During some recent excavations at St Bees a well-preserved fourteenth-century corpse was discovered and subjected to a full examination, the rather horrid photographs of which are in the Whitehaven museum. The injuries, which included a smashed jaw and punctured lung (the blood in the chest cavity was still liquid), indicated a death in battle, and the expensive nature of the burial a personage of some importance.

The coast round here is popular for family holidays, although it is not always easy to get to. Nor are there many hotels or entertainments, but the shore itself holds much interest.

Fleswick bay is a rich field for the stone hunter. Agate, carnelian and jasper pebbles can be found lying around the beach with other exotics from Scotland, already rounded and polished by abrasion. St Bees beach, between the lifeboat station and the railway, is also a good spot for pebbles. In fact, the whole of this area makes for good geologizing, for the cliffs show both St Bees and Whitehaven sandstone (the latter darker in colour) and limestone strata. There is also a derelict alabaster mine in Saltom Bay.

14

Ennerdale to Caldbeck

From St Bees north the coastal plain widens and changes from sandstone to carboniferous limestone, causing a dramatic alteration on the ground from small farming villages to coalmining towns and industrial ports. The mountains both recede and change from Borrowdale volcanics to Skiddaw slate, becoming rounded and more domesticated after the crags and screes of Wasdale. The mining villages – Cleator and Cleator Moor, Frizington, and Arlecdon – are not unattractive, mainly because the colour-washed rendering of the cottages is so much livelier than the drab brick of Lancashire or Durham; and the mountains are still only a few miles away, always visible. Cleator has retained something of its village character, with two churches, St Leonard's, Norman in origin, with an elegant font from St Bees, and the Catholic church by E. W. Pugin, very much the lesser of the Pugins. It would make a magnificent wedding cake. The latest addition to Cleator Moor's attractions – and there are not too many – is a fine Miners' Memorial by Conrad Atkinson, a native of the place.

This is the place where hound trailing has become the favourite sport. Trail hounds are small, light, and more like beagles than foxhounds, bred for speed and the ability to follow a scent laid over the fells. A good hound will make considerable sums for his owner, both in prize money and bets, and promising dogs are as cherished as prize leeks and fed with as original a range of encouraging concoctions. Successful dogs become the mascots of the village, assured of a respected old age.

If you find a collection of cars on a prominent ridge during the summer months they will belong to the fanciers following the progress of the hounds on the fellside. Heavy money is put on the hounds, who have taken the place – or almost taken the place – of cock-fighting as the local gambling fancy.

It is less than four miles from Cleator Moor to **Ennerdale Water**, a schizophrenic sort of place; the lower valley smiling green rounded hills – Skiddaw slate – the upper craggy granite precipices. The context of horror is appropriate enough since the dale is famous for the monstrous Dog of Ennerdale, which terrified the whole valley in

310

1810. 'The Ennerdale Vampire, in his long debauchery of rapine, surpassed his kind in wanton devilry and fiendish epicurianism as much as he did in strength and cunning,' according to his biographer, A. G. Bradley. After killing upwards of two hundred sheep he was eventually shot by one John Steel in Eskar Woods, and his stuffed remains exhibited in Keswick Museum.

The loneliness of the upper valley is partly due to its having remained a deer forest until the eighteenth century. Its only habitation was a couple of cottages at Gillerthwaite: 'a narrow tract of cultivated land . . . whose verdure receives additional beauties from the stony desert with which it is environed, where the mountains are barren in the extreme. This little spot has 2 cottages upon it, and has no neighbouring habitations to alleviate the gloom of its situation.'

That was 1793; the gloom has been intensified in the twentieth century by the Forestry Commission's planting, carried out unimaginatively in the 1920s – great slabs of single species pegged out on the mountainside so unthinkingly as to cause great outcry. But even public bodies see the light, and recent planting policies have been much improved. The lower valley was comparatively prosperous, supporting a community able to muster 40 armed men in 1534 most equipped with bows or bills and 'Jaks Sallets'; in the next century the valley formed part of Queen Catherine of Braganza's jointure on her marriage to Charles II.

It is difficult to forgive the destruction of the Anglers Inn, described as recently as 1954 as: 'The famous old inn stands so close that there is only room to walk past and the water laps beneath the windows in a way of which one could never tire. The situation of the inn is unique. As with Venice one hardly believes until one sees it.'

This vandalism was presumably excused by the lake being used as a reservoir, but could easily have been avoided; it stood where the car park below How Hall Farm now is. Motor traffic is allowed as far as Bowness Knott, on the north side of the lake, but the best views are from the old inn site, over to Anglers Crag and up the valley towards Pillar and Steeple.

Taking the Forestry Commission for better or for worse, there are some pleasant walks to be made from Bowness Knott, where the planting starts. The Forestry Commission has provided well-marked trails, with an accompanying pamphlet, in the area around the lake head, or you can press on up the valley of the River Liza to Black Sail youth hostel, the most isolated hostel in the country, nestling between Pillar and Haystacks, an unmatched centre for young and

311

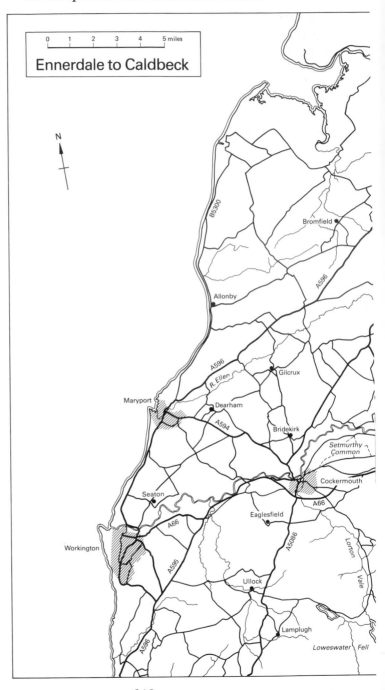

0 1 2 3 4 5 miles

Ennerdale to Caldbeck

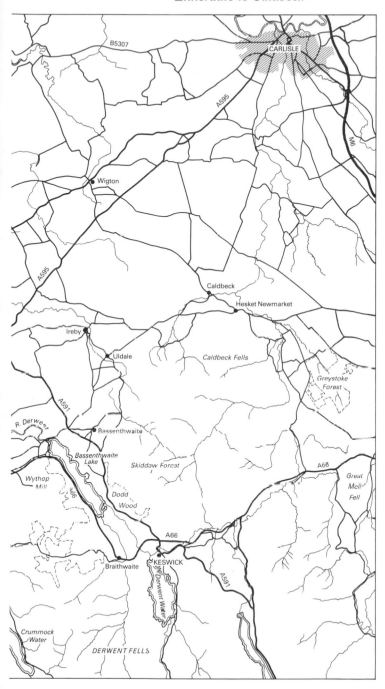

energetic climbing holidays. Pillar and Pillar Rock are seen to advantage from the head of the lake, above the serried ranks of conifers. But even if the planting is unimaginative it has the considerable advantage of stabilizing the soil and stopping erosion, so that better forestry policies will enable the look of the landscape to be improved. Meanwhile, the forests provide shelter for birds and small animals.

Ennerdale Bridge is prettily set on the River Ehen (going into the lake it is the Liza; it changes its name on leaving). The churchyard is the setting for Wordsworth's poem 'The Brothers' which has the splendid start:

> These Tourists, heaven preserve us! needs must live
> A profitable life; some glance along,
> Rapid and gay, as if the earth were air,
> And they were butterflies to wheel about
> Long as the summer lasted; some, as wise,
> Perched on the forehead of a jutting crag,
> Pencil in hand and book upon the knee,
> Will look and scribble, scribble on and look
> Until a man might travel twelve stout miles,
> Or reap an acre of his neighbour's corn.

The churchyard is still much the same, but the church was entirely rebuilt last century.

There is not much at **Lamplugh** apart from St Michael's church; the only original building by William Butterfield in Lakeland, and therefore demanding attention. In spite of his expensive work at such places as All Saints, Margaret Street (London), Butterfield was capable of building to a price – he once designed a church that could be constructed for £250. Lamplugh is plain enough, with only a few Butterfield oddities, such as the two-storey chancel arch which incorporates an earlier Perpendicular arch above a wide and shallow opening and serves no aesthetic, structural or ritual purpose at all.

The most interesting features are the three windows from the Kempe workshop, each made ten years apart from 1891 to 1910, which show an interesting progression. The first two are set in formal architectural backgrounds, while the latest, which is by Kempe and Tower (with the Tower mark being incorporated in the usual Kempe wheatsheaf 'signature'), is altogether livelier and lighter with splendid white and gold wings of angels forming the background.

There is also a handsome monument, with a bust and an urn, of 1731 to Mrs Margaret Briscoe:

Mistress of all the graces that adorn the female mind –
modest chaste and prudent,
Temperate affable and courteous . . .
She gained the esteem and admiration of all who knew her,
excepting only those whose envy made them repine
at her virtues.

Moving back to the coast, **Whitehaven** is often missed by tourists, and should not be. The town is the first example of a modern planned urban settlement in England; it can be compared with Winchelsea in the thirteenth century or with Newcastle in the nineteenth. Like so much else of Cumberland, Whitehaven is a Lowther creation. Before the Restoration there was nothing on the site of the town but a few cottages. By the end of that century the community was bigger than Penrith; a hundred years later it was twice the size of Carlisle, and the biggest town in the county.

This expansion was the result of the methodical development of the coalfield and the construction of a harbour, initiated by Sir John Lowther, and completed by his son, 'Farthing Jemmy'. As it stands, the plan is late seventeenth century, and not only the street plan, for Sir John insisted on a fifteen-foot module for frontages, and on the use of common elements in detailing. In spite of dereliction and thoughtless commercialization (chain stores have much to answer for) some fine buildings have survived, and a walk round the town is instructive.

Even at its best Whitehaven lacked the grandeur of contemporary Charleston, and its fate has been less fortunate. Two of its three Georgian churches have gone: one, St Nicholas' in Lowther Street, has doubly perished, rebuilt in 1888, and burned down in 1971: only the tower housing the tourist information office remains. Even the surviving original church, St James's, which used to have what Pevsner called 'the finest Georgian church interior in the county', has been carved up. The magnificent pulpit has been dismantled and stowed in the gallery, and the altar rails have been replaced by a fair reproduction of the lounge bar of an Essoldo cinema, designed by a colour-blind philistine. It is the visual equivalent of the new prayer-book, equally crass and insensitive.

There is enough left – the fine altarpiece by Giulio Cesare Procaccini, originally in the Escorial and bought from the French who had looted it, and the pretty ceilings – to let the visitor know what he is missing, and to madden the worshippers. It is entertaining to reflect that this elegant church was designed by Carlisle Spedding, the Lowther agent and engineer, which indicates how unnecessary architects can be.

The Lowthers' house, Whitehaven Castle, has been hospitalized almost out of recognition, but is still at least the shell of a good house, which is hardly to be wondered at since it is an early essay by Robert Adam. What it was like before the twentieth century hit it can be judged from Adam's drawings in the Soane Museum in Lincoln's Inn Fields.

The best collection of houses is near the junction of Scotch Street and Roper Street, which must form one of the most distinguished townscapes in the north of England. Union Hall, just opposite the Civic Centre, and 19–20 Irish Street, a hundred yards away, make an interesting contrast, the one unstructured and lively, the other dignified and solid, A Pall Mall club transported to Cumbria. (Sydney Smirke, who designed it, also built the Oxford and Cambridge Club with his brother Robert, and the resemblance is unmistakable.)

The theatre originally used to be in Roper Street, until civic vandalism put an end to it; at least some of the fittings of the Victorian music-hall, formerly attached to the Royal Standard, have been transferred to the Rosehill Theatre. What Roper Street retains, however, is Michael Moon's bookshop, one of the best in the north, and worth coming especially to Whitehaven to visit.

Industrial archaeologists should take a look at the Wellington pit on the hill to the south of the harbour; the chimney, lodge and walls remain, designed by Sydney Smirke in order that the colliery buildings should not spoil the look of the town.

Whitehaven's largest monument is the harbour, compact enough to understand as a whole, and the best representation of a seventeenth-century coasting harbour that I know of. Old Quay, the earliest part, is 1687, with eighteenth-century additions, the whole being finished by John Rennie in the 1820s. The masonry and fittings are largely original; even the lighthouses, one eighteenth century on Old Quay and one nineteenth on West Pier, have been preserved. There is not much traffic now, but when the sealock is built, and yachtsmen begin to use the planned marina, the seafront will be livelier.

One of the ships that traded from Whitehaven was Mr. John Younger's brig *Friendship*, 179 tons, Robert Benson master. Sometime in the spring of 1761 she sailed for the port of Fredricksburg, Virginia, with a thirteen-year-old Scottish apprentice by the name of John Paul on his first voyage.

John Paul continued to serve with Mr Younger until 1764, when

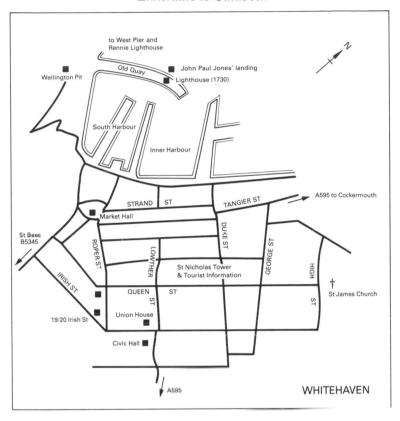

Friendship was sold, and John Paul was released from his apprentice-ship. He then shipped as third mate on *King George*, a Whitehaven slaver; Whitehaven was not directly involved in the slave trade, as Whitehaveners are anxious to point out, but this is doubtful pleading. Like the merchants of Liverpool and Bristol, those of Whitehaven provided the capital and the ships that made the round voyage to Africa and the West Indies, returning with a cargo of rum, tobacco, or whatever might be obtained.

The young man became disgusted with what he called that 'abominable trade', and left it as soon as he could, transferring into the brig *John* of Liverpool. He became very quickly a successful master and part-owner of a full rigged ship *Betsy* of London, until he was caught up in the American Revolution. Choosing the rebel side,

317

John Paul added 'Jones' to his name, and went on to be an even more successful naval commander.

In April 1778 Captain John Paul Jones, in command of the USS *Ranger*, set off on a commerce-destroying cruise. As part of this design Jones planned a raid on his old home port, not with any special animosity in mind, but simply because, knowing it so well, he could easily find his way around in the dark. In the early morning of 22 April with two boats' crews he descended on the port. One contingent landed at the Old Quay slip, promptly made for the nearest hostelry and started drinking. The captain and a single midshipman had to spike the guns on both the north and south batteries. Since his crew were either drunk or near-mutinous Jones was able to do little damage. He estimated that there were over two hundred ships in the harbour, but only managed to destroy one, the collier *Thompson*. Any danger of a fire spreading was averted by the alarmed and angry townspeople assisted by the almost inevitable Cumbrian rain which Jones should not have forgotten.

The effect on morale was, however, great; not since the Dutch had burned Sheerness a century before had anything of such temerity been attempted and Whitehaven became headline news as a result of what one townsman called 'the late insolent attack of the provincial privateer's men'.

Baffled at Whitehaven, Captain Jones, again using his local knowledge, slipped across the Solway to Kirkcudbright in an attempt to kidnap the Earl of Selkirk. But the earl was away, and Jones's men made do with taking the Countess's silver. Captain Jones, a romantic soul, was annoyed at this, and very decently restored the silver intact at the end of the war.

You can see something of this in the sparkling new 'Visitor Attraction'; the Beacon. Opinions divide sharply on the merits of this difficult-to-define institution. Some exhibits from the old museum survive – and the Beilby glass goblet commemorating the launch in 1762 of the Whitehaven slaver *King George* is superb – but many are un- or badly-labelled. Information is meant to be provided by two children chatting about the exhibits on a soundtrack assisted by recordings supposedly emanating from waxwork groups. Small children will probably love it; those in search of real information should make arrangements to see the reserve collection. At £9 for a family, it is an expensive 30 or 40 minutes' worth of entertainment, but the meteorological display on the top floor is fascinating.

If Whitehaven had more in the way of hotels it would have a good centre for exploring the coast and western fells, but it does offer a good swimming pool on the Cleator Moor road, a useful resource on wet days.

To the north, **Moresby** is a remarkable little spot, with a church, Roman camp and one of the most striking houses in the region all cheek by jowl. There is nothing to be seen of the camp except the emplacement itself, but that is dramatic enough, a flat rectangular parade ground on the top of a cliff, the sea below and the church behind. It is the southernmost of the chain that carried the Wall defences round the coast, with the Workington and Maryport forts immediately to the north. The fact that these were built at the same time as the Wall itself gives some idea of the massive investment made by Hadrian in defending the Empire's northern frontier.

St Bridget's as it stands is a chaste nineteenth-century church, but its ancient history is proved by the fourteenth-century chancel arch standing in the churchyard. The fabric dates from 1822, but a good deal of work was done in the 1880s, happily entirely in keeping with the earlier structure.

The church's only monument, a small brass plaque, has had a chequered history recorded by Ian Kyle, the Whitehaven barber. It disappeared at the time of the rebuilding, and when it turned up again the authorities frowned on its sentiments, since the 1703 inscription included the clearly papistically flavoured petitions: *'Requiem aeternam dona eis Domine et lux perpetua luceat eis. Requiescat in pace.'* It was, however, restored, and placed inconspicuously in the gallery; but today you will look in vain for it. Whether through evangelical disapproval or sheer carelessness, the plaque has recently been heavily painted over, and is quite unrecognizable. John Wordsworth, William's son, who married Isabella Curwen, was rector here for some years.

Moresby Hall aroused Professor Pevsner's enthusiasm: 'An eminently interesting building with a splendid façade of 1690–1700. It is all rusticated, as if it were in Bohemia.' The façade, which is certainly strikingly attractive and un-Cumbrian, is backed by a much earlier pele and hall, just visible in the rear.

The Rosehill Theatre, in the grounds of an eighteenth-century mansion, has acquired the proscenium arch of the Royal Standard Music Hall, now set in an Oliver Messel interior. Performances and recitals are varied, but even if what is on offer lacks appeal it is worthwhile going just to admire the theatre and the house, now an old people's home. The restaurant is open all the year round, and is famous for its Sunday lunches.

In spite of a natural desire to write off **Workington** as a nest of barbarians who allowed the fine house, Workington Hall, one of the area's best and most historic buildings, to fall into irreparable ruin, the town should be visited. At any rate St John's church was magnificently restored by Sir Ninian Comper, and can serve to show Whitehaven St James what should be done. It is a dramatic, heavily porticoed George IV building, which, if the later tower was removed, would much resemble the handsomest barn in Christendom, Inigo Jones's St Paul's, Covent Garden.

The parish church, St Michael's, is some way off, overlooking the River Derwent as it nears the sea. Largely rebuilt after a fire in 1881, it remains Georgian in plan, with some details remaining from earlier buildings, notably the Norman archway from the baptistery, and even earlier in the form of ninth-century carved stones, one of which features a strange serpent-like creature. The best monument is that of Sir Christopher Curwen and his wife. Sir Christopher, in full fifteenth-century armour, has his head resting on that of his favourite horse; his lady's spaniels are biting at her inattentive stone skirts; it is oddly direct and touching, much more so than finer works of funerary art.

Workington is as much a Curwen town as Whitehaven is Lowther, and the two families form an interesting contrast. Both are ancient – the Curwens were originally Colwens, and go back to Ethelred the Unready – but the most famous Curwen was born John Christian of Unerigg, a much less distinguished family, best known for producing Fletcher Christian, the *Bounty* mutineer. John Christian became John Christian Curwen when he married his cousin Isabella. He became one of the most distinguished practical reformers of his day, a friend of Grey, and a tenacious Whig opponent of the Tory Lowthers. Some of his comments have not lost their relevance: 'To suffer so large a part of our population to remain unemployed must be ruin to us. The first object of every state must be to find full employment for its population.'

Workington Hall – what is left of it – makes a romantic ruin, a splendid setting for the plays performed there in the summer. Derek Woodruff, who looks after it, is a local historian, who has written a good short account of the Curwens and their house. John Christian's great experimental Schoose Farm, where he put into practice some of the methods of farming that have become standard, especially in dairy farming, is also ruinous. The tall windmill and arcaded store-houses remain, and make picturesque ruins, the importance of which is now altogether ignored.

On the other hand the Helena Thomson Museum, just on the left as you approach from the Cockermouth road, reflects every credit on local endeavour. It is the home of the Curwens' stewards, and contains a well-preserved historical collection, staffed by enthusiasts, which includes some entirely beautiful nineteenth-century dresses. None of the exhibits are of first-class importance, but the whole is thoroughly enjoyable; children especially like the nineteenth-century musical box which operates on a small payment, making a loud and tuneful noise.

Workington harbour has facilities for launching small boats, at the Vanguard sailing club, and a good swimming pool, but, like Whitehaven, is short on hotels and restaurants.

It has to be admitted that Cumbria's coastal plain, from Cockermouth northwards, once the mountains swing off to the east, although pleasant enough farming country, is not scenically of the greatest attraction. However it is scattered with villages many of which have something to offer. **Eaglesfield** has a secluded Quaker burial ground and meeting-house, used only for funerals. John Dalton, one of the great theoretical scientists of modern times, who formulated the atomic theory, was born and brought up in an Eaglesfield Quaker family, and he is recorded as making, in answer to an enquiry, a response every writer must have wanted to give at one time or another: 'I have written a book on that subject, and if thou wantest to know more thou canst buy a copy for 3/6d.'

Four Norman churches close together make Cross Canonby, Dearham, Bridekirk and Gilcrux worth visiting, and **Bridekirk** alone merits a journey for its magnificent font. It is casket-shaped and richly ornamented with beasts and birds, a baptism of Christ, and a portrait of the sculptor chipping away with his hammer and chisel. The inscription indicates that he is one Richard, probably the famous Master Richard of Durham, who always carried with him a fragment of St Cuthbert's chasuble; it is – and this is a century after the Conquest – still in runes, but in English, unlike the Norse of Furness: 'Rikarth he me wrokt, and to this merthe gernr me brokte' (to this beauty eagerly me brought). Apart from the ruinous chancel with its east window, romantically desolate, not much remains of the original fabric at Bridekirk, but there is more at **Cross Canonby**, and indeed even earlier work, for part of the chancel arch, with its niches, is Roman, from the Maryport camp. The sculpture here consists of a fine tenth-century cross fragment, with curiously Chinese dragons, a hogback tombstone and an odd coffin lid with an inexplicable little figure.

321

Dearham's sculptures are even better: The 'Kenneth Cross' is supposed to represent St Kenneth; not the Irish St Canice, but the Welsh 'Kyned', who was dropped in a stream, or according to other sources rescued from a coracle, by a bird: the cross certainly has a bird holding a baby, but that is the only apparent connection. The 'Adam' stone is more promising, and easier to understand if it is seen, not as interpreted by Pevsner, but as lying on the ground rather than upright as it stands, where the bottom half, with the word ADAM, seems to be upside down. When the well-preserved Norse cross, complete with wheel head, the Norman font, with its dragons, and the numerous coffin lids are added, Dearham is almost an early medieval museum; taken with Cross Canonby and Bridekirk the whole is unparalleled.

Gilcrux has not as much to show in the way of sculpture, but is a delightful small church, with its fabric well preserved, about 1100, the south aisle a little later. The reredos is interesting, a copy of Leonardo's *Last Supper* by the Chance Brothers of Birmingham, using their then newly invented 'antique' glass, which was the first of modern times that reproduced medieval glass at all successfully. Another medieval church, that of Camerton, is hard to find and even harder to get into, but has a good 16th century effigy of 'Black Tom' Curwen, pirate and convicted murderer; his great sword is worth noting.

On the coast **Maryport**, like Whitehaven, is the creation of a single family, this time the Senhouses, who lived at Netherhall, now derelict.

The little town is fairly shabby, but not without interest. Any harbour has something to offer, and Maryport has a little marina, due to be supplemented by an aquarium. The Maritime Museum is well worth a visit, having been founded by the admirable Miss Annie Robinson MBE. JP, who has collected and arranged for the presentation of an instructive display of the town's maritime past glories. Maryport was a considerable shipbuilding centre right up until the present century, launching not just coasters either, but splendid full-rigged ocean-going ships, such as the *Kinkora*, 1999 tons, and *Peter Iredale*, 2075 tons, and the beautiful barque *Midas*, lost only two years after her building. The bigger ships had to be launched sideways into the narrow river in what must have been a nerve-racking operation. Although some of the fascinating story of the men who built and sailed these ships has been collated (by Hugh Falkus in his book *Master of Cape Horn)*, much remains to be told of Maryport's great history.

On no account should the Senhouse Roman Museum be missed. Housed in a rare example of a Victorian coastal artillery battery it contains a unique collection of Roman military altars, fifteen from the same unit, the First Cohort of Spaniards. Those of the Baetasians – also from Spain – are particularly fine. There are some interesting Celtic carvings, including an enormous phallic serpent. Behind the battery the earthworks of the fort in which the legionaries lived are still clearly marked. Few of them were native Romans; one commander, Lucius Varianus, was an African who must have found Maryport disagreeably chilly.

Allonby may be somewhat beyond our boundaries, but it is worth going there if only for the sake of the splendid view across the Solway Firth to Galloway. Although one is conscious of the hills across the sea all the way from Whitehaven north, the view is at its best at Allonby, the first of those great west of Scotland sea-and-mountain-scapes that make that region so unforgettable. The village stretches along the coast for a good mile. It set out in the early eighteenth century to become a sea-bathing resort, and by 1799 was able to muster a 'numerous and genteel congregation' in the church, among whom were 'several of the principal gentry of the county'. Half a century later Charles Dickens paid a visit with Wilkie Collins. They stayed at the Ship Inn, Collins having a sprained ankle. The doctor's assistant so impressed Collins that he makes two appearances in the novels – Ozias Midwinter in *Armadale* and Ezra Jennings in *The Moonstone*.

And there it seems to have stopped. The only relics of its fashionable days are at the former sea-water baths, now a house, and an elegant terrace at the north of the village, rather well preserved as holiday accommodation. Allonby survives as a pleasant and unpretentious place, with cobbled street, some pubs, and a green populated by a drove of relaxed ponies.

A little further south the remains of a salt-works can be seen. The most prominent is a round filter, or kinch, from which the brine trickled into a lagoon before being slowly boiled using locally dug coal for the firing. It is said that the remains of the pump scaffold are visible just offshore at low tide.

Allonby being as far as our geographical limits allow, we go back up the valley of the River Ellen to what are now the foothills of Skiddaw. **Aspatria** sounds better than it looks – it used to be Aspatrick, less euphonious, but clearing up the dedication – although it has an interesting church with some Norman work and a number of cross fragments. 'The queerest thing that ever was seen', they tell you in West Cumbria, 'is **Plumbland** church on Parsonby Green,' the joke being that it is in the wrong village. Parts of the original church, built about 1130, survive; it was famous, and clearly big, as the size of the chancel arch indicates. These have been incorporated into a majestic 1879 construction by Cory and Ferguson of Carlisle. Bishop Nicolson complained that there were no monuments in the church, and admitted that his duty to 'my own deceased parents (who both ly bury'd in the Quire of this church)' would oblige him 'to erect something of that kind; were my Abilities answerable to my Will'. There is now a handsome monument to Sara Farish, *'ex familia Cracherodiana apud Trinobantes'* in learned Latin and with a spot of Greek, that would please the bishop.

Torpenhow church is dark and magnificent, one of the other fine Norman churches in the neighbourhood. Again, parts of the church are even older since the Roman station at Old Carlisle was looted for masonry; there are two carved stones inside the chancel, and some long ashlar pieces outside.

The chancel arch is heavily dog-toothed, and supported by two corbels said to represent the forces of good and evil; that on the north, the bad side, from which all misfortunes came, is in dark stone, with intertwined struggling figures, crudely like those at Souillac in France; on the south, in light sandstone, a series of curious – in both senses of the word – creatures are looking on: they appear again in the old respond of the arcade.

Also Norman, and massively impressive, is the south door, now protected by a porch, which also conceals and therefore renders useless a sundial.

Thomas Addison, who was one of the Crosby Ravensworth Addisons, and an uncle of the essayist, lived at Low Wood, in the parish: 'Wanting a seat answerable to his present quality offered to cover the Middle Isle with a fair painted canopy of Firr, on condition of having leave to erect such a seat at his own Charge.' Addison's seat has disappeared, but his canopy remains, and very odd it looks. All the nave is covered with an Inigo-Jonesy ceiling, painted with cherubs and garlands, now quite difficult to see. Apparently Addison, with an eye to a bargain, bought it from a defunct livery company in 1689 and had it altered to fit.

Incised grave slabs, some of which are very fine, stand against the west wall, and one of them serves as a lintel to the west window.

Whitehall lies off the road, but can be seen by appointment with the owner. Any casual passer-by, however, should take a short walk up to the ruinous Old All Hallows church, a desolate almost overgrown Norman chapel, what is left of the interior boarded up. Through the cracks it is just possible to see the white marble statue to George Moore, who gave generously to his native county, now shamefully neglected, surrounded by dead leaves and feathers. The French have more decency, since the new Mealsgate church, a thoughtfully built turn-of-the-century edifice, has a plaque dated 1962, from the French government expressing their gratitude for Moore's work in helping Paris during the 1871 siege and commune. Moore is worth remembering; he brought to philanthropy all the attention to detail and organizational powers that had made him rich; although he gave away huge sums he was capable of raising Cain at any sloppiness, as when someone lost the receipt for an omnibus ticket. Moore came from the humblest of backgrounds, and went to London to seek his fortune at the age of nineteen; his first triumph was scored the very next day after his arrival when he won a wrestling match at Chelsea.

Some of the original nineteenth-century farm gates survive, forming, with their elegant cast iron gates and latches designed to be operated from the saddle, a humiliating contrast to the modern galvanized tubing contraptions.

At **Harby Brow** an inscription dated 1550 proves that inflation is not new!

> Thys house was bui
> lded in the fourth yere of
> the ryne of King Edwar
> de the sex whan a bousc
> hel of wete was at viis
> a bouschel of bere a
> nowbel mault
> 1111s St more

That is, being interpreted:

> wheat 7
> barley 6/8
> malt 10/8

Pevsner described **Boltongate** church as 'one of the architectural sensations of Cumberland'. From the outside this is not apparent, but you see what he means when you open the door and find yourself in a steeply arched pointed tunnel vault, like nothing else in England, a fashion that came from Languedoc via Scotland. A Scottish influence is also discernable in the east window, which is certainly unusual and said to be like those at Linlithgow. The simple explanation for all this Scotticism south of the Border is that Boltongate church was built in a single night by the Oxford wizard Michael Scott, but commonsense tells us that since Scott died in 1291 he would doubtless have arranged the church in a contemporary style rather than that of a century or more later; but you can never tell with wizards. Daniel Hechstetter, a descendant of the Keswick Germans, was rector here between 1666 and 1686, but in 1703 Bishop Nicolson found that: 'The old Curate (poor Mr Keddy) looks as tatter'd as ever but will, hereafter, I hope, have his salary rais'd.'

Ireby is the metropolis of this part of the Ellen Valley, and still looks something of the market town it once was, with a prominent moot hall in the centre of the village, a butter cross, and a sufficiency of pubs. The old church is some way off; Bishop Nicolson was scathing:

> The Quire has been lately a little brush'd up, in expectation of my comeing to see it; But 'tis still very Tawdry, and unbecoming the wealthy Abilities and pretended Zeal of (my good Cousin) Mr. John Relf, . . . Here are no Rails; and the Floor is not half levell'd. There are in it three clumsie Seats, for the Impropriator and the Tenants of Prior Hall . . .
>
> They want a Flaggon for the wine at Sacraments; and a Platter for the Bread. No book of Homilies. One Bell they have good; the other being broken and lost. Mr. Ballantine petitions for a Gallery: but will be slow in erecting it.

The new, 1847, church, was built with stones from the nave of the old, and is not disagreeable, fitting in to the village well enough. Rabbits are now very much at home in Ireby Old Churchyard. Only the chancel of the old church remains, locked and inaccessible. Some crude incised slabs are visible in the east exterior wall, showing Celtic crosses and swords: by contrast two inexplicable pillars, substantial and elegant, stand outside the west door.

Although Ireby is well outside the Wordsworth country at least one of England's great poets visited Ireby: John Keats stayed the night at the Sun Inn – which is still there, selling Jennings beer – on 30 June 1818, while on his walking tour of the Lakes. As might be expected, his descriptions summarized the appeal of the region more succinctly and aptly than any other: '. . . The two views we have had of [Windermere] are of the most noble tenderness – they can never fade away – they make one forget the divisions of life; age, youth, poverty and riches; and refine one's sensual vision into a sort of north star which can never cease to be openlidded and stedfast over the wonders of the great Power . . .'

At Ireby he came across the other great attraction of the Lakes – the people:

> After Skiddaw, we walked to Ireby the oldest market town in Cumberland – where we were greatly amused by a country danc- ing school, holden at the Tun [a copyist's error for the Sun], it was indeed 'no new cotillon fresh from France'. No they kickit & jumpit with mettle extraordinary, & whiskit & fleckit, & toe'd it, & go'd it, & twirld it, & wheel'd it, & stampt it, & sweated it, tattooing the floor like mad: The difference between our country dances and these scotch figures, is about the same as leisurely stirring a cup o'Tea and beating up a batter pudding. I was ex- tremely gratified to think, that if I had pleasures they knew nothing of they had also some into which I could not possibly enter. I hope I shall not return without having got the Highland fling, there was as fine a row of boys and girls as you ever saw, some beautiful faces, and one exquisite mouth. I never felt so near the glory of Patriotism, the glory of making by any means a country happier. This is what I like better than scenery.

His confusion between Cumberland and Scotland (let alone the High- lands) has to be pardoned; it was after all an Englishman who invented the kilt.

It is possible that the oldest road in the region is visible on Aughertree Fell. Nothing remains of the settlement there except the earthworks, but it seems that a Bronze-Age farm was also used in medieval times. The clearly marked road, however, leads into a cir- cular and therefore Bronze-Age enclosure, and is a sample of a pre-Roman farm road.

Uldale is 'wolf's dale', and the church is some way out of the village on a cliff overlooking the mill, a pleasant situation. Thomas Thomlinson taught here at what was the Uldale grammar school, one of the many tiny academies that served their villages well, 'with so much credit to himself and satisfaction to his employers', before leaving to make his fortune in America. This he did, in the beautiful town of New Berne, North Carolina (Neubern according to his

327

memorial, but in fact founded by Swiss emigrants, and still possessing some fine eighteenth-century houses). It is a beautifully secluded and peaceful valley, with a pretty tarn, Over Water, and an impressive seventeenth century house, Orthwaite Hall.

There are not many buildings at **Bromfield** perhaps, but it has everything a village needs – a pub, a church, and a post office. Ye Olde Greyhound Inn, a Youngers house, has a carved dog, which betrays an admixture of collie blood, as a sign. It conveniently adjoins St Mungo's church, the fifth to be built on the site, which is said to have been in use since the second century. Certainly the south door and parts of the nave are Norman, but the chancel arch is a little later. Its two corbels are entertaining: that on the north is a jovial tonsured monk, with buttoned sleeves, on the south a gloomy moustachioed head. They are said to represent the Latin and Celtic churches respectively.

In 1673 the Reverend Richard Garth's memorial was carved, but the lettering might have been a century earlier, although the sentiments are entirely typical of the Restoration: 'Rebellious Spirits he always did hate; Obedient to the church, true to the State.'

Two possible connections with Kentigern himself, who almost certainly did visit here, are the steps of a cross in the churchyard, which now support a monstrous sandstone tomb, and a covered well in the neighbouring field.

The demarcation between the Lake District and the Borders is easier to spot on the ground than to formulate, and in deciding it for the purposes of this book I have to some extent indulged myself. It would have been pleasant to go even further: the churches at Newton Arlosh and Abbeytown are both of great interest, and the shores of the Solway Estuary a fascinating country. Red brick is a touchstone: Carlisle and the surrounding villages have much, and the Lake District none. Tarns turn to loughs somewhere along a line between Wigton and Carlisle: Moorhouse has a tarn, but Thurstonfield Lough is only four miles to the north.

Wigton is sandstone, like Penrith, and the market town for the region known as Back o'Skiddaw, which is John Peel territory, and since Peel is at the very heart of Lakeland tradition, Wigton indisputably qualifies. To see Wigton at its liveliest you go there in October, when the horse sale is on, and the place is crammed with some dubious but all entertaining characters in various stages of insobriety. The trouble with buying horses in England is that we don't eat them. In any sensible country a badly formed or neurotic animal goes straight into the butcher's, with the result that poor specimens are weeded out. But in England we sentimentalize over wilful caricatures of beasts which end up at such places as Wigton. Fortunately today it is worthwhile shipping off these creatures to become hamburgers in Brussels, and the standard of the remaining animals is greatly improving. (To see what serious horse-breeding management can do you should go to Hungary, where any farmer's work horses would win prizes at the best English shows.) Good horses can be had in Wigton and it is the centre of the Fell pony market, although you are more likely to buy a Fell privately, for first-class Fells are not easy to come by, since good breeders let them go only to homes where they will be well looked after and properly worked. Although they love it, like all horses, pampering does not suit Fells; they are not children's ponies, but working horses.

Wigton church closes its doors during horse fairs, a sad but just commentary. It is the marra of St Cuthbert's, Carlisle, and very like St Andrew's, Penrith, a dignified Georgian church designed and built by local masons and joiners. It was lucky to have John Ford (father of a talented daughter) as incumbent in the 1950s, since he had it redecorated in a splendid range of colours and added a side chapel with a fine reredos. John Betjeman called it 'a triumph in paint, a study in grey and gold and strawberry-pink', and justly called attention to the 'excellent taste in ornaments and flowers'. The church is lovingly cared for, and the lectern in particular is a magnificent piece of eighteenth-century carving. The parish records are kept in an ancient chest, just opposite the tomb chest of Thomas Warcop, vicar from 1612 to 1649, who carved his own epitaph:

> Thomas Warcop prepar'd this stone
> To mind him oft of his best home.
> Little but sin and misery here,
> Till we be cam'p'd on our beere . . .

'Bold Barwies', a contemporary, has a brass describing him as:

> Stout, Wise, yet humble, fitted in each part
> For more command, of comely body, pious heart,
> Who liveing was Life's lively purtrature;
> &, dyeing, Colonel, lives crowned sure.

Architectural splendour in the remainder of Wigton, which is a pleasant enough town, but lacking the charm of Penrith, is confined to the quite magnificent fountain erected in memory of George

Moore of Whitehall. A very splendid affair, in gilded granite with panels depicting acts of mercy, 'very good indeed, still with classical discipline, but also with genuine feeling', as Pevsner rightly says. Any town could be proud of it, as also, in a rather different way, of the monstrous contemporary tower, 130 feet high, that crowns High-moor, a house just to the south.

Old Carlisle, the Roman fort, lies on the A595, a little further again to the south. The earthworks are well marked, but all the stones have long since found other uses.

Norman Nicolson calls **Back o'Skiddaw** 'the barest country in the Lakes . . . as un-homely as the tundra', and it is true that apart from the uncompromising backside of the Skiddaw massif, a very dull piece of landscape, there is not much in the way of physical features. But there are charms, even if they take some looking for. One of these is due to the fact that Skiddaw slate gives way to carboniferous limestone, which makes for such attractive karst features as Caldbeck Howk as well as for many abandoned quarries between Caldbeck and Uldale, which constitute a rich source of fossils (if approached with due care, and keeping well away from rock faces).

One well-hidden spot is the **Castle Sowerby** church of St Mungo/Kentigern, approached from the minor road that skirts the west edge of Greystoke forest. It is miles away from any village, down a lane, across a ford over the Gilcambon beck, almost in Sowerby Hall farmyard. Its isolation must mean that this was really one of the places at which Mungo preached on his missionary journey: there is no other explanation that makes sense. Bishop Nicolson was entertained at Sowerby by the vicar, Mr Waterson, then aged seventy-nine, with 'oaten bread and butter, pretty good beer, and English spirits at 18s a quart'.

Caldbeck became notorious when some anti-blood sports fanatics attempted to dig up John Peel's bones from Caldbeck churchyard. Predictably ineffective, they failed to do so, but were apprehended and sent down for a good stretch by Judge Tony Edmondson, whose name is therefore perpetually revered by good Cumbrians. It is some-what surprising that more than a century after Peel's death his name has such power to arouse, but it is quite right to accept him as an archetype of foxhunting.

Not of course the smart man of the shires, neatly kitted out on an elegant hunter; Peel's coat was 'grey' not 'gay', and his horse – when mounted, for he often hunted the pack on foot – was the practical 14.3 'Dunny', built for endurance, as Peel's son confirmed: he would 'stand for a week for owder me fadder or me'. Peel when not hunting, according to his old kennelman and nephew, Willie, 'was aye drinking'.

Caldbeck church is yet another dedicated to Kentigern/Mungo, and one of the largest. Its core is thirteenth-century, but there are remains of earlier work in the chancel masonry and in the beakhead ornament over the south door, and much later rebuilding, mostly of the early sixteenth century. It is true that the tower looks medieval, and Pevsner refuses to believe that it is not, but the evidence is solidly there: 'This steple was builded in the year 1727: Jeff Wyberg Rect: Thomas Backhouse esq. Richard Addison, Richard Bewley, William Scott, churchwardens 1727.' The warden's spelling was a bit shaky; as well as 'steple' Messrs. Addison and Backhouse describe themselves as 'wardings' on a slightly earlier bell.

One of the other bells was given by that remarkable character Philip, Duke of Wharton, and – according to the Old Pretender – of Northumberland as well (see page 16).

Caldbeck was once a prosperous mining and milling town with eight mills on the beck. One of these, Priest's Mill, next to the church, has been handsomely restored, and houses galleries, a bookshop and a tea shop. It is the 'priest's mill' because it was built in 1702 by the same Rev. J. Wybergh who was responsible for the 'steple' and in this slow-changing countryside parsons stayed priests until the nineteenth century sharpened distinctions. Between the church and the pretty vicarage and the village cricket pitch, Priest's Mill is a picturesque spot.

It was the mines, however, that made Caldbeck famous in Elizabethan times, and paid for the renovation of the church·

> Caldbeck and Carrock Fells,
> Are worth all England else . . .

An exaggeration, but there were extensive lead and copper mines stretching up to Carrock Fell, that still carry on intermittent production, helped by the demand for barytes. Geologists will find a trip on to Carrock rewarding, taking the road – motorable – from Mosedale west up the valley of the Caldew to Swineside, and proceeding on foot up Grainsgill Beck, where they will find a potentially rich assortment of specimens.

Caldbeck's best walk is up the river to the Howk, where it is obvious that even if the heights above are slate we are in limestone

331

country again as the beck passes through a deep gorge, with a series of cascades, pools and a fairy cavern. On a sunny day the dappled light reflecting from the moving water and shining stone is a scene waiting for Monet.

Hesket Newmarket should be seen if only to inspect the extraordinary Hesket Hall, built by the Sir Wilfred Lawson of the time in 1630. It is square, almost cubical. Projecting gabled wings with mullioned bays form each face, crowned with swagged urns, and finials; all not quite right, but trying hard; Palladio in hodden grey. It is said that the wings are arranged so that the angles serve as a sundial, but this sounds fanciful.

There is no church, but a pub, looking onto the big central green, and a well-mannered eighteenth-century market cross.

Sebergham is beautifully situated in the Caldew Valley; the church has a fine relief by Musgrave Lewthwaite Watson, the young sculptor who might have been an English Rodin had he lived.

It is certainly an indulgence to end with **Rose Castle**, the palace of the Bishops of Carlisle, for this is a part of Carlisle and the Borders rather than the Lake District, however generously interpreted. But so much of Cumberland and Westmorland – the coastal plain, Furness and the Eden valley: all the area dealt with here, in fact, except the central Lake mountains – has been stamped with the effects of centuries of border warfare, that this reminder of those stormy times deserves inclusion. Quite apart from the fact that Wordsworth and Coleridge, who inspected the house in 1803, were delighted and found 'all, all perfect – Cottage Comfort and ancestral Dignity!' Rose Castle is not generally open to the public, but you can get a good view of it from the public footpath running from Rosebank to Raughton Head. Although it now looks a typically romantic Victorian house, it is a skilful confection of many centuries, put together by Thomas Rickman. The oldest part is the Strickland tower of 1300, the original pele; Bell's tower is late fifteenth-century; Kitels tower early-sixteenth. As the number of towers suggests, Rose was a real castle; it needed to be. Since the Bishops of Carlisle took up residence there in 1230, William Wallace dined in the hall in 1290, and Edward Bruce made himself at home there in 1314, but burned it down the following year. King Robert did so again in 1322, in 1337, and probably in 1345; Parliamentary General Lambert stormed it in 1648, leaving a Major Cholmley to look after it, who contrived to set fire to what seems to have been a remarkably combustible residence.

It is little wonder that not a great deal of medieval work survived.

By the eighteenth century conflicts were conducted more civilly, as that which took place when Bishop Lyttelton, in 1762, took over from Bishop Osbaldeston, who had been translated to London. Bishop Lyttelton had paid a sum for fixtures and fittings which he found were not all they had been said to be. His steward reported: 'Ye rats are so very plenty that will most likely Eate ye Hangings at ye first putting up.' The Bishop himself complained: 'some of the Wines also that I paid for as sound and good, prove as sour as verjuice.' The Bishop of London argued, and the correspondence grew increasingly cross, but was eventually settled by a payment of £250.

The nineteenth-century work was paid for by Bishop Percy, brother of the Duke of Northumberland, who employed Paxton to design the gardens. He showed the fighting spirit of the Percies when, at a time when a Chartist attack was – quite erroneously – feared, he had crates of muskets brought to the castle, labelled as hardware, an early use of a now common term.

Having got as far as Rose Castle anyone would certainly go on to visit the stark castle of Carlisle, with Berwick, the grimmest evidence of Border wars, its battered but splendid cathedral and the excellent Tullie House Museum, but that is another story for a different time.

333

Bibliography

A tolerable bibliography of Lake District literature would be a substantial volume in itself, but of the great mass of books some stand out, and of these Norman Nicholson's works are pre-eminent. *The Lakes, Greater Lakeland, Cumberland and Westmorland* and *Portrait of the Lake*, are nothing less than masterpieces. More prosaic, but immensely learned, are W. G. Collingwood's *Lake District History* and *The Lake Counties*.

Alfred Wainwright's series of 'Pictorial Guides' is essential for the serious walker, and the volume on *Outlying Fells*, 'written primarily for old age pensioners and others', is particularly useful. A good introduction to the sterner stuff is Walt Unsworth's *The High Fells of Lakeland*.

The literary sleuth will find Grevel Lindop's *Literary Guide* – from which I have drawn several extracts – invaluable.

The area is covered by two volumes in Sir Nikolaus Pevsner's *Buildings of England*; unfortunately neither is entirely satisfactory, and one must hope for a revised edition.

The collections of essays by Molly Lefebure and Harry Griffin are richly entertaining.

In addition to the books mentioned above and in the text I have found the following to be especially helpful:

Barrow and District, F. Barnes, Barrow 1968
Cumbrian Villages, Kenneth Smith, London 1973
Hell-Fire Duke, Mark Blackett-Ord, Windsor 1982
The Lake District, Millward & Robinson, London 1970
The Lake District, Cumberland Geological Society, London 1982
The Lake District, Chris Barringer, London 1984
National Tourist Board publications
North Country Life in the 18th Century, Edward Hughes, London 1965, and of course the Transactions of the Cumberland and Westmorland Antiquarian & Archaeological Society
Portrait of Windermere, C. D. Taylor, London
Roads & Trackways of the Lake District, B. P. Hindle, Ashbourne 1981

Bibliography

Scottish and Border Battles and Ballads, Michael Brander, London 1975
Vernacular Architecture of the Lake District, R. W. Brunskill, London 1974
Wordsworth and the Lake District, David McCracken, Oxford 1984

Index

Index

Index

Index

Index

Index

Index

Index

353

Index